DATE DUE			
NOV 1 8			

TECHNIQUES FOR PRODUCING **VISUAL INSTRUCTIONAL** 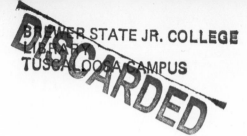 **MEDIA**

TECHNIQUES FOR PRODUCING VISUAL INSTRUCTIONAL MEDIA

SECOND EDITION

Ed Minor

Professor of Communications
Communication Studies Department
California State University, Sacramento

Harvey R. Frye

Associate Professor of Education
and Supervisor of Graphic Arts
Audio-Visual Center
Indiana University

McGraw-Hill Book Company

New York   St. Louis   San Francisco
Auckland   Bogotá   Düsseldorf   Johannesburg
London   Madrid   Mexico   Montreal
New Delhi   Panama   Paris   São Paulo
Singapore   Sydney   Tokyo   Toronto

TECHNIQUES FOR PRODUCING
VISUAL INSTRUCTIONAL MEDIA

1234567890 VHVH 783210987

This book was set in Helvetica by University Graphics, Inc.
The editors were Jean Smith, Helen Greenberg, and James R. Belser;
the designer was Jo Jones;
the production supervisor was Robert C. Pedersen.
The cover was designed by John Hite.
Von Hoffmann Press, Inc., was printer and binder.

Library of Congress Cataloging in Publication Data

Minor, Ed.
    Techniques for producing visual instructional media.

    Published in 1962 under title: Simplified techniques for preparing visual
instructional materials.
    Bibliography: p.
    Includes index.
    1. Visual aids. I. Frye, Harvey R., joint author. II. Title.
LB1043.5.M44 1977   371.33   76-28288
ISBN 0-07-042406-3

CONTENTS

PREFACE

Ever since its debut in 1962 as *Simplified Techniques for Preparing Visual Instructional Materials,* this book has served as a basic resource for thousands of professional and nonprofessional producers of visual instructional media. We believe that visual media, such as slides, overhead projection transparencies, charts, graphs, and individualized instructional materials, can be designed and produced with a basic knowledge of simple graphic production techniques. To serve this purpose, we have developed a step-by-step approach adaptable both for the person without skills in art, graphic art, or photography and for the professional seeking new solutions to visual media production problems. Since we feel that excellence does not imply complexity, we have avoided complicated instructions and terminology, relying instead on more than 800 clear, simple illustrations to clarify the techniques described.

The second edition is divided into nine sections. Section 1, "Planning for Visual Media Production," is new to this revision. It presents a systems approach for the production of visual media and should be read carefully before beginning production activities. Section 2, "Media Design: Ideas and Techniques," another new addition, presents our approach to design and production, as well as size standards and specifications for visual media. Section 3, "Basic Production Materials, Tools, and Aids," covers the basic materials involved in the production process. Section 4, "Illustrating Techniques and Aids," deals with techniques and aids for producing professional-looking visuals. Section 5, "Coloring Techniques," treats the problem of adding color to visual media. Section 6, "Lettering Techniques and Aids," provides a variety of solutions to the lettering and printing problems of visual media. Section 7, "Mounting and Laminating Techniques," covers the most modern and practical techniques for mounting and preserving visual media. Section 8, "Photographic Techniques," deals mainly with producing transparent visual media, such as slides and overhead projection transparencies. High-contrast photography has also been included because of the demand of users of the first edition. It is a remarkable technique, and we are happy to include it here. Section 9, "References," includes what we trust is the most comprehensive collection of resource information available today. Included are more than 300 annotated publications and audiovisual sources on the design and production of visual media, more than 600 entries in the "Index/Sources," and a complete "Address Directory" of suppliers of the materials listed in the "Index/Sources."

This text has given us an opportunity to share our graphic production knowledge, experience, and enthusiasm with our readers. We owe much to our many students from all over the world who have motivated us to put into print what we have shared with them over the years. In addition, we are most indebted to several persons without whose support and inspiration this book would not have been possible. They are Martha Dixon, Mary Frye, Bertha Minor, Helen Greenberg, and Steve Walters.

Ed Minor
Harvey R. Frye

1 PLANNING FOR VISUAL MEDIA PRODUCTION

Physical Characteristics of Visual Media
Identifying and Selecting Production Techniques
Developing a System of Production

When creating a work of art, whether it be a musical composition or a fine painting, the artist through training and experience creatively structures an approach which unites materials and techniques to produce the most effective end product. The production of effective visual media is a creative process demanding a similar approach—planned procedure and knowledge of materials and techniques creatively blended to form an effective visual communication product.

The following analysis of the production process as well as the structuring of a model program is presented in the hope that it will serve to develop a consciousness of the importance of a planned program structure and knowledge of materials and techniques. Although there is strong emphasis on structure, in the final analysis this approach permits greater creative freedom and flexibility than is possible without structure.

In the process of creating a visual, what are the areas of production one must know? To answer this question an analysis was made of over 300 journal articles written by teachers, training personnel, and instructors describing their procedures for producing their own instructional materials. These articles covered a wide range of visual media from simple chalkboard drawings to complex overhead transparencies.

PHYSICAL CHARACTERISTICS OF VISUAL MEDIA

The first observation made was that the physical characteristics of the media discussed fell into one or more of three categories—opaque, translucent, and transparent—and that successful creation of materials requires a thorough understanding of these three terms.

Most common are those materials in opaque or transparent form. Translucent materials are not often considered important, but they do make an important contribution to the effectiveness of visual materials.

Opaque refers to visual materials which are impervious to light; they are not transparent but are visible when light is reflected off their surface (1). Many instructional media may be classified as opaque: still pictures, charts, maps, exhibits, displays, felt boards, chalkboards, signs, etc. Visual media in this form can be used only with opaque projection when light is reflected off the original through a lens to the screen. A large percentage of all transparent visual media originates from opaque copy in the form of original drawings, paintings, graphic designs, newspapers, etc. Through methods such as photography or Xerography the image is converted to a projectable transparency. Combinations of opaque, translucent, and transparent art materials may be used to create an opaque original; as long as the final artwork is entirely impervious to light, it is classified as opaque. Since such materials as paints, inks, glues, acetates, shading sheets, and tapes often come in opaque, translucent, and transparent forms, it is important to know each material's characteristics and proper use.

Translucent materials are those which permit a partial passage of diffused light. They include frosted or etched glass or acetate, vellum, tracing cloth, and drawing and tracing paper. Artwork executed on these surfaces forms masters which may be reproduced

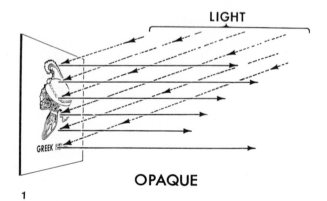

LIGHT

GREEK H

OPAQUE

1

as blueprints, whiteprints, diazo copies, photographic negatives, etc. Drawings made with ink or colored pencils on frosted acetate or glass, when transparentized, make good transparent projection materials, and inversely certain areas of transparencies can be subdued when masked with translucent materials (2).

Transparent refers to visual materials which are pervious to light; they are not opaque (3). This is the classification which includes projected materials such as slides, filmstrips, films, and overhead transparencies. Many transparencies are created directly by using opaque, translucent, and transparent acetates, inks, paints, paper, shading sheets, etc., on a transparent base. Because of the great demand for transparent visual media, many methods of converting translucent and opaque originals have been developed through the use of photographic, diazo, thermal, electrostatic, and gelatin processes.

As shown in the illustration (4), there may be some discrepancy in identifying materials in these three areas, for it is sometimes difficult to make a clear-cut classification due to overlap of characteristics.

This book contains many references to these three classifications of materials. Understanding how to classify and use audiovisual materials will give you greater flexibility in creating effective visual media.

IDENTIFYING AND SELECTING PRODUCTION TECHNIQUES

The second observation made in analyzing the above-mentioned survey of literature revealed that the basic materials, techniques, and equipment used by the writers of the articles, when classified into related categories, fell within six basic areas. Due to the large sampling of articles analyzed, these core areas might well serve as the nucleus of a comprehensive system of visual production. The

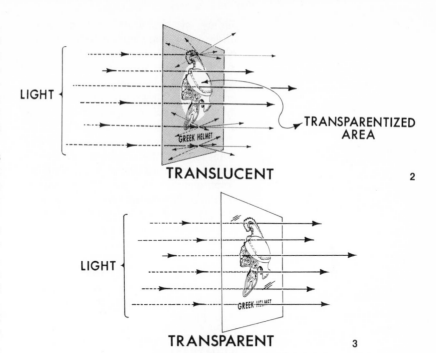

TRANSLUCENT   2

TRANSPARENT   3

4

variety of situations and conditions under which the visual media were produced indicate that this system of production might apply to an individual working alone in a very simple situation or to a large supervised program where more complex equipment, materials, and techniques are available.

The areas basic to a production program fell into the categories of illustration, mounting or preservation, lettering, color, simple photography, and conversion and duplication. When these areas are organized in a logical sequence (5), they constitute a model production program. As one's working knowledge grows in each of these areas, greater flexibility and creativity will result. The balance of the chapter describes how an audiovisual production program might be organized.

ILLUSTRATION

Creating the image is usually of first concern when producing visual media. If one can draw on or has access to professional help, the problem is simplified. In many situations, however, the producer will have to resort to the use of a picture "morgue," clip-art files, stock photographs, or the many other sources of existing imagery. Integrating these image materials into the final visualization will require a knowledge of such methods as tracing, enlarging, reducing, and distorting so that the image can be converted into usable form for the preparation of opaque, translucent, or transparent visual media.

MOUNTING OR PRESERVATION

Since flat, opaque visual materials are commonly used in almost every instructional situation, knowing how to mount and preserve them is extremely important. Besides making a visual more attractive and usable, such knowledge may help in preserving or restoring *older, damaged* illustrative materials.

LETTERING

The importance of lettering cannot be overemphasized, for often it will constitute the entire content of the visual. Because the great variety of styles and sizes of lettering available places great demands on the producer's knowledge of the subject, a large variety of lettering methods has been developed. Lettering serves to identify, label, emphasize, explain, clarify, and reinforce, and often to add supplementary information.

COLOR

Color is logically the fourth area for the production of simple, opaque visual materials, although not necessarily for the production of certain more complex, nonopaque materials. The vast number of coloring materials available today may be found in opaque, translucent, and transparent forms. Therefore, it is important to know how, when, and where to use the various coloring methods. Sometimes color is inherent in some reproduction methods, such as the diazo and hectograph systems; they too, then, belong in this fourth area.

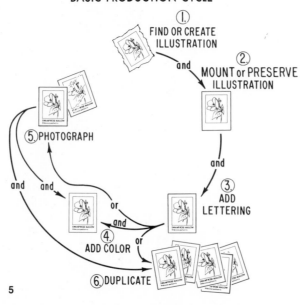

SIMPLE USE OF THE
BASIC PRODUCTION CYCLE

① FIND OR CREATE ILLUSTRATION

and

② MOUNT or PRESERVE ILLUSTRATION

and

③ ADD LETTERING

④ ADD COLOR

⑤ PHOTOGRAPH

⑥ DUPLICATE

and   and

or   and   or

5

PHOTOGRAPHY

From the vast field of photography, certain areas are most useful to the producer of audiovisual materials. The first is line photography, a basic form demanding only a limited amount of experience as well as equipment. It is invaluable to the development of graphic materials, whether developed for projected or non-projected use. High-contrast photography is one of the methods of converting materials into the opaque, translucent, and transparent forms. Furthermore, so doing permits the enlargement or reduction of the image to the size needed for visual presentation.

CONVERSION AND DUPLICATION

The last area affords the producer processes and techniques such as thermocopy, spirit duplication, and diazo by which original materials may be converted from one form to another or duplicated in quantity.

DEVELOPING A SYSTEM OF PRODUCTION

The sequence described above not only suggests a system of production but offers other benefits to the novice who wants a well-rounded media production experience.

NEED FOR GROWTH

Although most teachers and instructors recognize the value of visual media, constant stimulation is necessary to encourage them to devote time and energy to the design, development, and use of new and varied visual approaches to instruction. Professional growth through participation in a program that encourages and aids one in seeing greater possibilities in the use of media will encourage variations and change in teaching methods. Change, which is often referred to as a vital need for people, will serve as an important stimulant to encourage one to become involved in visual production processes. The above production sequence, if properly understood and followed, will serve this purpose.

BEGINNING SLOWLY

Initiation into the visual production processes should be slow and basic, so that each process systematically builds firmly on the previous one. Too fast an introduction to the many, varied facets of media production can be overwhelming and demoralizing to the point where all effort in this direction is abandoned.

ORDERLY DEVELOPMENT

As shown in the diagram (6), the sequence begins with area 1. Through the collection of visual imagery a picture file or picture "morgue" is created. Experience in assembling visual imagery gives one insight into the problems of visualization and teaches one to "see" rather than merely "look." With a gradual sequential introduction to the other areas an ever-expanding pattern of growth takes place, leading to a proficiency in *developing the most sophisticated forms* of visual media.

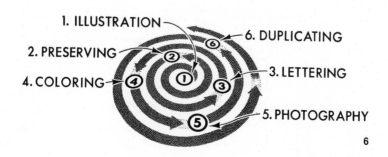

1. ILLUSTRATION
2. PRESERVING
4. COLORING
6. DUPLICATING
3. LETTERING
5. PHOTOGRAPHY

6

DANGER IN EARLY SPECIALIZATION

As shown in the diagram (7), any one of the six areas may become an area of specialization. The spiral in area 3 indicates emphasis has been placed on an almost endless growth in the area of lettering. It is most important, however, for the beginner to first develop an overall knowledge of the total program before specializing too deeply in one area. Through an understanding of the *interaction* of the six basic areas the creative potentials of the total program can be more greatly appreciated. Ignoring the value of any one area's contribution to the total program will greatly limit its flexibility and potential.

SAMPLE STRUCTURE

In diagram (8), lines drawn to four basic media products illustrate how choices in the production process might be made. The number of possible choices (and there are more!) shows the freedom a producer has in the way a particular visual might be created. The choice of *which* type of illustration, preservation method, etc., to use to produce flat pictures, overhead transparencies, etc., depends on forces such as cost, experience and training, and space, as well as desired quality and quantity of the product.

DEVELOPING YOUR OWN STRUCTURE

In the following sections of this book a broad variety of materials, techniques, and equipment is illustrated and discussed, all of which might be included in one or more of the basic areas. It is the hope of the authors that through careful study of the instructional and descriptive information given, you might structure your own comprehensive program of visual media production.

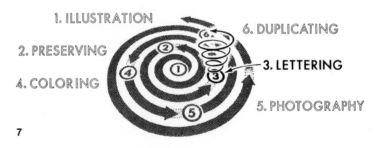

1. ILLUSTRATION

2. PRESERVING

4. COLORING

6. DUPLICATING

3. LETTERING

5. PHOTOGRAPHY

7

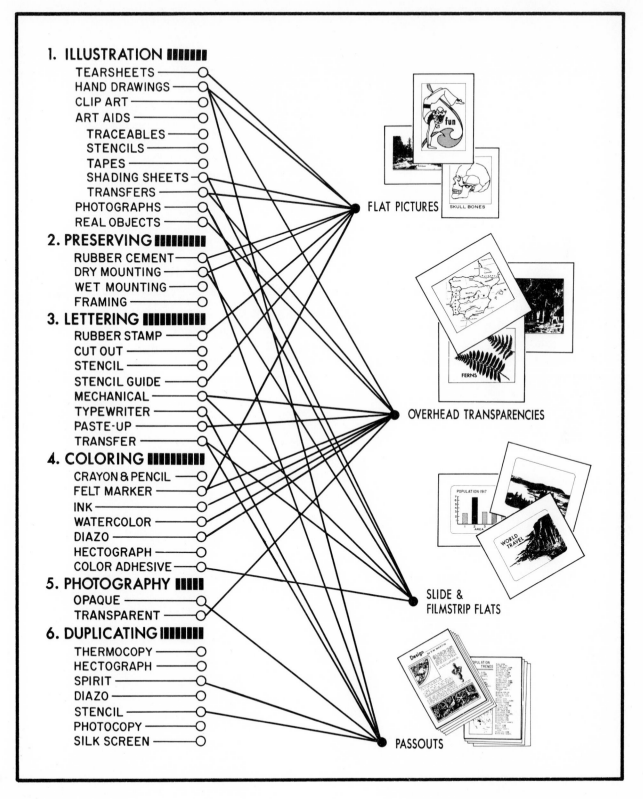

1. ILLUSTRATION ▮▮▮▮▮▮
- TEARSHEETS
- HAND DRAWINGS
- CLIP ART
- ART AIDS
  - TRACEABLES
  - STENCILS
  - TAPES
  - SHADING SHEETS
  - TRANSFERS
- PHOTOGRAPHS
- REAL OBJECTS

2. PRESERVING ▮▮▮▮▮▮▮▮
- RUBBER CEMENT
- DRY MOUNTING
- WET MOUNTING
- FRAMING

3. LETTERING ▮▮▮▮▮▮▮▮▮
- RUBBER STAMP
- CUT OUT
- STENCIL
- STENCIL GUIDE
- MECHANICAL
- TYPEWRITER
- PASTE-UP
- TRANSFER

4. COLORING ▮▮▮▮▮▮▮▮▮
- CRAYON & PENCIL
- FELT MARKER
- INK
- WATERCOLOR
- DIAZO
- HECTOGRAPH
- COLOR ADHESIVE

5. PHOTOGRAPHY ▮▮▮▮
- OPAQUE
- TRANSPARENT

6. DUPLICATING ▮▮▮▮▮▮
- THERMOCOPY
- HECTOGRAPH
- SPIRIT
- DIAZO
- STENCIL
- PHOTOCOPY
- SILK SCREEN

FLAT PICTURES

OVERHEAD TRANSPARENCIES

SLIDE & FILMSTRIP FLATS

PASSOUTS

2 MEDIA DESIGN: IDEAS AND TECHNIQUES

Design Ideas: Sources and Techniques
Basic Form
Size Standards and Specifications
Methods of Developing Media
Readability of Visual Media

9

Probably the most difficult time in the production process is when one begins to create the image in tangible, viewable form. The moment of "breaking the ice" is often so frustrating that the intended visual or visual sequence never becomes a reality (9), especially if it is relatively complex.

Preliminary thought and planning do not always resolve all the problems. How much art ability does the producer have? Will the drawing of the image be extremely difficult? What are the unique problems of creating visual images for projection? What about colors used? What about sizes and styles of type? How large and in what proportion should the artwork be made? Have all the details in the visual and verbal content been carefully defined? (This is especially important if the visual is being designed and executed for someone else.) These are only a few of the many questions one might face in producing visual media.

DESIGN IDEAS: SOURCES AND TECHNIQUES

10

You may be interested in visual production but have little or no art training. This does not mean that your task is hopeless. It *does* mean that you must try to become familiar with the many available aids, such as stencils, clip art, shading sheets, and tapes. When viewing these materials, try to think of alternative methods that might have been used in designing various media (10). Was the best method of presentation used? Read current magazines and books pertaining to techniques, methods, and processes of media production. Study illustrations and picture stories in books and magazines, and look at sequential visuals that are found in "do-it-yourself" model kits.

Studying a well-illustrated general art supply catalog will be extremely valuable in alerting you to the many art aids available. You should also establish a comprehensive, well-organized collection of tear sheets. This collection, often called a "picture morgue," will supply both visual ideas and basic imagery (11). It is also important to learn methods of tracing and transferring drawings, including the process of photosketching. Learning how to enlarge or reduce imagery through the use of a photo enlarger or a pantograph or by grid drawing methods will be very beneficial.

Many other helpful techniques in the areas of illustration, mounting, lettering, coloring, photography, and reproduction are included in the following sections of this book.

BASIC FORM

The process of creating visual media must start with some form of initial imagery. If this visual image does not exist in the form of a photographic transparency or print, it must be found in the form of original artwork, such as a painting, drawing, diagram, graph, or even lettering alone. Imagery may be used in its original form or (depending on its use) converted to another of the three forms—opaque, translucent, or transparent—from which evolve filmstrips, slides, transparencies, motion-picture animation and titles, opaque projection flats, TV slides and flats, turnover charts, flannel board materials, or any other of the many forms of visual media. In making your decision, keep in mind how the various methods of presentation limit the physical form of original artwork (12).

SIZE STANDARDS AND SPECIFICATIONS

A number of important points must be taken into consideration when developing artwork for use as opaque flats, filmstrips, slides, or transparencies. Although almost any size or format of artwork may be copied onto a slide, carefully planned, proportioned, and executed artwork designed for particular projection media will lead to better-quality results. Standardization of the format

11

12

on which artwork is executed will save time and ensure good reproductive quality and legibility.

All original artwork for a particular type of projection, whether for motion-picture animation, filmstrip, 35mm, or 3¼- by 4-inch slides, must be designed in a format proportionate to the projectable area of that particular slide, if the maximum projectable area is to be used (13). In the case of 35mm slides, the size of this area can be affected by two factors. The *film aperture* of the camera determines the area of the artwork to be recorded on film. When the film is bound into a slide, the *aperture of the slide mask* will again slightly affect the size of the viewable area. In the case of the filmstrip and the 16mm motion-picture film, the image area is first determined by the film aperture of the camera and then will be slightly reduced by the mask aperture of the projector. When projected materials are transmitted through standard television systems, the final cropping of the slide is determined by the TV receiver. However, if the presenter wants to obtain special effects, an endless variety of cropping proportions may be used. The choice is limited only by the maximum proportions of the slide. In the case of the double-frame 35mm slide (2 inches by 2 inches), the image may be presented in either a vertical or a horizontal position. This is not true of the 3¼- by 4-inch slide. Due to the

small format, few if any changes are made in the format by masking the 35mm slide, filmstrip, and motion-picture image. This, however, is not true with the 3¼- by 4-inch and larger overhead transparencies. Although both have the limitations of the aperture of the projector, presenters tend to adapt the masking formats of these transparencies—which can lead to dynamic and interesting effects. Although the trend has been away from the 3¼- by 4-inch slides, their use in the past reflects some very interesting masking techniques. A study of old supply catalogs reveals that at one time more than twenty-five different masking formats were available commercially. These masks included a variety of sizes in circular, oval, horizontal, and vertical shapes. By choosing the proper mask, one could build variety, change, and dramatic emphasis into a slide presentation. Although the projection mask aperture of the overhead projector is commonly found in a square format of 10 by 10 inches, some projectors may have smaller or larger apertures. However, in practice transparencies are usually made in a format that works with traditional photographic film size, e.g., 8 by 10 inches for the 10- by 10-inch projector.

To make a 10- by 10-inch transparency photographically, it is usually necessary to use an 11- by 14-inch piece of film. Because of this inevitable waste,

IMAGE AREAS

15.9mm. by 22.9mm.   22.9mm. by 34.2mm. $2\frac{3}{16}$ inches by $2\frac{3}{16}$ inches $2\frac{3}{4}$ inches by 3 inches

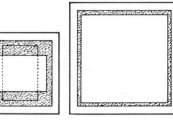
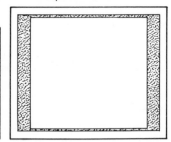

2 BY 2 INCH SLIDE   2 BY 2 INCH SLIDE $2\frac{3}{4}$ BY $2\frac{3}{4}$ INCH SLIDE $3\frac{1}{4}$ BY 4 INCH SLIDE
13   SINGLE FRAME   DOUBLE FRAME

the photographer usually uses 8- by 10-inch film, which necessitates cropping 2 inches off the maximum aperture of the projector. Due to the square aperture of the projector, the 8 by 10 film may be projected in either a horizontal or a vertical position, depending on the subject matter being shown. With the maximum 10- by 10-inch aperture of the overhead, a great variety of possible cropping formats may be used to emphasize and strengthen the visual presentation (14).

It is important, as indicated above, to develop a systematic, planned approach to the layout and execution of artwork designed for use as slides, transparencies, etc. As artists work in a standardized format, they develop the ability to judge which visual element will be legible and which will not. They will know how to effect emphasis and subdue unimportant detail. Consistency in emphasis of color, lettering, and visual imagery between slides or transparencies will be more predictable and lead to a more unified presentation. The following factors are important when developing the art format:

1 The size of the base material upon which all the artwork is to be developed is the first consideration (15).

14

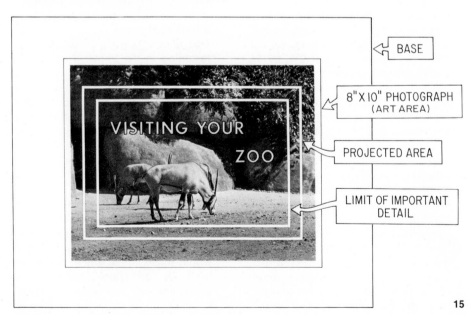

BASE

8" X 10" PHOTOGRAPH (ART AREA)

PROJECTED AREA

LIMIT OF IMPORTANT DETAIL

VISITING YOUR ZOO

15

Although this is usually cardboard, it may be transparent or translucent material of various kinds. The proper size of this material is important for several reasons. It furnishes margins for the artwork and protects the visual imagery from handling, dropping, tearing, etc. It furnishes excess margin areas for register marks or register pinholes, for added instructions, for sequence numbers, etc. If it is a standard format, it will simplify the handline, copying, and filing processes. Since this base material will usually be cardboard, it may be wise to use a size which is cut from standard cardboard sizes. If registration pins are used, space must be allowed at the top edge for this purpose. Since a combination of direct artwork and photographic material will probably be used when making the originals for slide presentations, it is wise to design the basic art format around standard photographic print sizes. Although an 11- by 14-inch photographic print size may be used, the most common size will probably be 8 by 10 inches. Thus a larger base material is required upon which to mount the photograph. An often suggested size for this is 10 by 12 inches. However, standard 22- by 28-inch cardboard will cut 11 by 14 inches, giving extra-large margins on all sides. It may also be cut $9\frac{5}{16}$ by 11 inches, but this greatly limits the margin areas. Many artists feel that working in the smaller format makes it easier to judge readability factors of the visuals they are creating.

2   The artwork itself is the next area of concern (15). It is important that the artwork or photographic image area be proportionately larger than the area to be recorded through the film aperture of the copy camera. Finished imagery must extend slightly beyond this area so that if any slight deviation occurs as the camera records the image, it will still record acceptable imagery. Remember, however, that no important visual materials should be included in this fringe area.

3   The third area of concern is the area determined by the aperture of the projection mask (15). As planned, this is smaller than the area discussed in item 2. Remember, there is a difference in proportion between the projected area of a single-frame filmstrip slide (17.5 by 23mm) or motion picture or TV (7.21 by 9.65mm) and the projected area of a 35mm masked slide (23 by 34mm). The former are in more or less a 3:4 ratio, and the latter about 2:3. These dimensions represent the limits of the area viewable on the screen. When using a total art format of 8 by 10 inches for filmstrip and motion picture, the actual projected artwork will be in an area approximately 6.47 by 8.5 inches centered in the total 8- by 10-inch art area. If the 11- by 14-inch format is used, the projected artwork would be in an area 8.18 by 10.75 inches. With the 35mm slide, the projected visual would be in an area about 5.75 by 8.5 inches centered in the total art area of 8 by 10 inches. In the case of the large 11- by 14-inch format, the area would be about 7.28 by 10.75 inches. With the 10- by 10-inch overhead, standard 8- by 10-inch film will permit a format of about $7\frac{1}{2}$ by $9\frac{1}{2}$ inches. This allows $\frac{1}{4}$ inch on all sides for fastening in the frame. If larger film sizes are used, the full 10- by 10-inch area may be utilized with the exception of the corner cutoffs of the projector's aperture. With the same considerations mentioned above, artwork for the $3\frac{1}{4}$- by 4-inch slide should be designed for a total masked aperture area of $2\frac{3}{4}$ by 3 inches.

4   Although the above dimensions include the total projected area of the image, the visual should be designed so that important details fall well within these limits. It is important to have an "air space" between the frame line and any important visual imagery (15) for two reasons. First, in

cases where the aperture of the projector frames the visual (motion picture), it cannot be assumed that all projectors will frame exactly the same. Second, a very undesirable effect results when elements of the visual, as in the case of lettering, touch or merge with the frame line. When working with an 8- by 10-inch art format, keeping lettering and other important visual details ½ to ¾ inch in from the frame line will improve the appearance of the projected visual (16).

5 If the above projected material is to be used for standard television transmission, greater allowance must be made for cutoff by the receiver. In the case of the total 8- by 10-inch format, the important visual imagery should be designed in a centered area approximately 4½ by 6 inches (17). This will keep important visual information from being cut off by the receiver—a common situation when standard motion pictures are transmitted on television.

16

17

15

When you are designing artwork for a specific slide size, the use of a proportion scale will quickly give a variety of sizes you can choose from. Another method is to scale the desired artwork area by drawing a diagonal line from the lower left to the upper right corner of the slide, extending the diagonal line well beyond the upper right corner of the slide (18). Any vertical and horizontal lines intersecting this line can determine a proportional area of the original slide. Projecting a slide mask on an overhead projector or in a photographic enlarger will also give proportional sizes that can be the basis for artwork sizes. Remember that if the visual artwork is to "bleed" beyond the projected area of the slide, it must extend some distance beyond this projected area.

METHODS OF DEVELOPING MEDIA

Creating visual materials begins with some form of original artwork. It may be a photograph, painting, drawing, or dia-gram, and in some rare cases actual objects. Some form of visual image must exist which may be used directly or converted to some different proportional size or physical form to create the visual, whether it be for filmstrips, slides, transparencies, motion-picture titles or animation, opaque projection flats, TV slides or flats, turnover charts, flannel board materials, or any of the many other forms of visual imagery. You may decide to create the original artwork in opaque form, or you may choose to use combinations of opaque, translucent, and transparent materials.

Opaque materials consist of two forms of artwork. The *first* includes visual materials as original artwork or existing reproductions of paintings, illustrations, photographs, etc., which are ready to use in their original forms or which may be converted directly into continuous-tone or high-contrast transparencies. Original artwork in this form may be copied in a variety of ways, including thermographic, photographic, diffusion transfer, electrostatic, and many others. Remember, however, that some of these

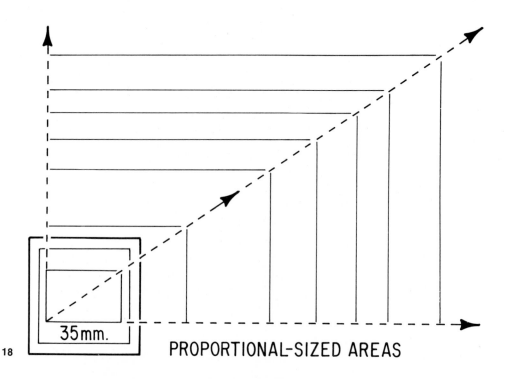

35mm.

18

PROPORTIONAL-SIZED AREAS

methods give good results only when high-contrast images are copied, while other methods will reproduce continuous-tone and high-contrast images with equally high quality. The copying and reproduction of colored artwork are usually limited to photography. However, by careful planning, limited amounts of color may be obtained by using the color potentials of some of the reproduction and conversion methods. Remember that in almost all cases color may be added to the final transparency by using a variety of hand methods. This applies most generally to the larger-size transparencies such as used in the 3¼ by 4 projector or on the overhead. With careful planning of the original artwork very colorful and effective 35mm slides can be produced by hand tinting. The *second* form of opaque originals is that artwork executed by the paste-up method. Although in one sense paste-up has some limitations, because it depends on existing visual imagery, in another sense it can be a great aid for the novice or producer with little art experience. In paste-up the elements of the visual have been created by collecting and assembling visual images from various sources, one common source being professional clip-art services. By maneuvering the separate paste-up elements of the visual into various positions, you can find the most effective visual design. Practice in paste-up techniques can make the less experienced person a very effective producer of visual media. In paste-up the elements of the visual are cut out, assembled, and mounted on a common background. This is usually the procedure followed when creating images having high-contrast characteristics, as when high-contrast line drawings are combined with type, music, etc., to form a single visual. When the paste-up is completed, the cut edges of each element are usually visible to the eye. Although great care may be taken to hide these distracting lines by painting over them with white poster paint, they may reproduce unless special care is taken to choose and use carefully the right copy method. If an intermediate negative is made, as with high-contrast photography, the undesirable lines may be opaqued out before the final visual product is made. With other methods they may be removed by bleaching or erasure. Although paste-up artwork is often the easiest to render, extra care must be taken when converting it to the desired form, whether opaque or transparent.

To shorten the process of converting original artwork into opaque or transparent forms, it is often best to create the original visual in translucent form. Frosted glass, tracing tissue, and vellum are good examples of translucent material. Frosted acetate, similar to frosted glass, has an excellent surface on which to draw. Because the surface is "frosted" and has a "fine-tooth" finish, it is easy to work on with ink and pencil as well as brush and airbrush. The surface permits the development of either clean, sharp, high-contrast images or soft, continuous-tone shading of airbrush or pencil. Because the frosted surface is partially transparent, it serves as a good master for reproduction on materials such as diazo foils and papers.

For special effects translucent originals may be overlayed on opaque artwork and copied by one of the conventional photographic methods. It is also possible to use the translucent original (especially if drawn on frosted acetate) as a transparency by converting the frosted finish to a completely transparent surface.

At times it may be desirable to have some areas frosted and others transparent as a means of subduing some parts of the visual and highlighting others. The original artwork may be done on the frosted materials using transparent colored pencils, crayons, ink, watercolor, etc., as well as opaque pencils and ink. After the artwork is completed, the frosted surface is sprayed with a thin coating of gelatin or acrylic spray. This fills in and neutralizes the frosted surface, converting the translucency to a transparency ready to use on the projector.

The above discussion is based on the assumption that you are using a frosted-surface material such as etched glass or acetate. If the visual has been executed on translucent tracing tissue or a similar material composed of paper fiber, complete transparency cannot be attained due to the fiber structure of the material. However, by coating the reverse surface of this material with a transparentizer, such as a thin solution of wax or oil, you can attain a greater degree of transparency to permit ease of reproduction by methods requiring transmission of light through the original. Paper materials treated in this way seldom reach a degree of transparency that will permit their direct use for projection purposes.

Often artwork designed for projection is executed directly on a transparent base material. Handmade slides date from the beginning of slide projection. If the slides were not hand-drawn, they were often hand-tinted glass photographic slides. Filmstrips and 35mm slides have also been made by drawing directly on clear film in projectable image size. In fact, some very exciting full-length motion pictures have been made in this manner. Only artists having extremely fine drawing and coloring ability can develop these types of materials. It is more practical to create the original artwork for these sizes of projection in larger forms and reduce them to the more appropriate size through photography. However, for larger-size overhead transparencies and overlays, it is often more expedient to create the artwork directly as a transparency, especially when only one copy is needed. When creating transparent originals, you must work very cleanly to avoid abrasions and smudges. It is wise to protect the finished transparency with a protective sheet of acetate to prevent scuffing or scratching of the image when using the transparency. Care must be taken to use the appropriate transparent pencils, felt markers, toning sheets, inks, tapes, dyes, etc., to ensure a clean, crisp projected image. When opaque imagery is desired, true opaque inks, pencils, tapes,

etc., must be used. Often it is difficult to draw directly on the surface of clear standard acetate or glass. Artists in the past coated these surfaces with a thin layer of gelatin, which, when dried and hardened, would accept various liquid transparent inks and dyes. Today specially coated acetate may be purchased which accepts any liquid drawing medium. It is generally referred to as prepared acetate. Transparent colored pencils and felt markers have been developed which can be used directly on standard acetate surfaces. Some of these materials may be removed using water, while others require other types of solvent. Colored acetate inks adhere well to an acetate surface and are almost impossible to remove.

Etched lines on the transparent surface will project as fine, dark lines and are permanent. Silhouettes made of opaque paper, colored film, etc., may be adhered to a transparent sheet to create a projectable image. In the same manner many real objects having opaque qualities may be used in conjunction with transparent base material as projected silhouettes. Forms cut out of translucent film may be combined with a transparency when light-gray areas are desired in the projected image.

Transparent visuals may also be placed on an opaque background and copied by an appropriate copy method. For the creative producer intermixing the varied forms of opaque, translucent, and transparent materials, the possibilities for developing visual imagery for all forms of presentation are endless.

READABILITY OF VISUAL MEDIA

As the producer designs forms of visual media by combining the above-mentioned types of materials, he is faced with another important responsibility, that of readability. The term in this case refers not only to the verbal elements of the visual, but also to all other important elements of the imagery being created—

the lines of a drawing, the structure of a graph, the scale of grays in a continuous-tone photograph, a painting converted to a continuous-tone black and white photograph, the high-contrast posterization of a continuous-tone picture, and color relationships—as well as readability of lettering from the standpoint of style, size, color, and placement.

LETTERING

There are many suggested standards on the proper lettering sizes for good readability of both projected and nonprojected visual media. Discrepancies often appear in these standards due to the many variables that can exist in the conditions of the presentation, such as light conditions of the room, etc., and, in the case of projected materials, the light output of the projector.

Below are some basic methods you can use to increase readability.

1 Space lettering slightly wider apart than normal on turnover charts and other nonprojected visual media.

2 Minimize the amount of lettering on each visual, and use commonly known abbreviations.

3 Present complex information in simplified form with detailed explanations, data, etc., distributed to the audience as a printed passout.

4 Use a simple, bold style that is easy to read; authorities believe that sans serif type tends to be more easily read than a style with serifs.

5 Use a simple contrasting color on the background; ornate and textured backgrounds should be avoided, especially if the lettering is relatively small. This also applies to background photographs that may have complex or fine details (19). If this type of background must be used, shadow lettering will help readability, the shadow tending to separate the basic letter form from the background images and textures (20). If the lettering is on a cel overlay, often the airbrush is used to

19

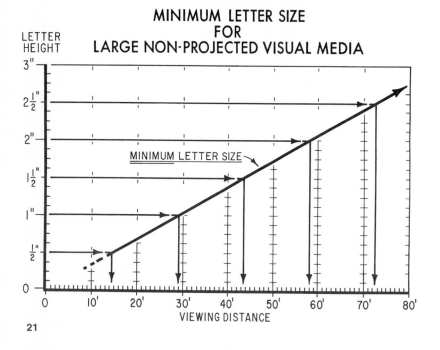

MINIMUM LETTER SIZE
FOR
LARGE NON-PROJECTED VISUAL MEDIA

LETTER HEIGHT

MINIMUM LETTER SIZE

VIEWING DISTANCE

21

1913	ALBANIA	900,000
1910	AUSTRIA-HUNGARY	49,458,421
1913	BELGIUM	7,516,730
1913	BULGARIA	4,800,000
1911	DENMARK	2,775,076
1911	ENGLAND	34,045,290
1911	FRANCE	39,601,509
1910	GERMANY	64,925,993

22

spray a light tint of opaque color on the reverse side of the cel—which tends to subdue the background, making the lettering more readable.

6   Typed captions can be used but should be properly sized in order to be satisfactory for the average situation. A great many producers of visual materials have developed their own simple formulas for sizing lettering for good readability. For projected materials one good suggestion is that lettering on a horizontally designed format should be one-twenty-fourth the height of the artwork. Typed material prepared on a 3- by 4-inch format will satisfy the above size specifications and will be satisfactory for projection providing that a new ribbon is used and that the typewriter type has been thoroughly cleaned.

7   It is important to keep the screen size proportional to the size of the audience. The above specifications for letter size are very satisfactory if they are based on the principle that the length of the screen image be about one-sixth the distance from the screen to the back row of the audience.

8   When nonprojected visual media such as turnover charts, maps, graphs, etc., are designed, the lettering should be at least 1 inch high if it is to be viewed from a distance of from 28 to 30 feet (21). It is assumed that the lettering is of a simple, bold, easy-to-read style.

9   Some producers prefer to use negative lettering with white or lightly tinted letters on a black or deep-colored background (22). The effectiveness of negative lettering will depend upon the degree to which the room has been darkened. Too great a contrast may not be desirable under some room conditions. Projected dark-colored or black lettering on a white background if projected for a long period of time may tire and strain the eyes (23). In this case it is often wise to use a soft,

pastel color as a background, yellow or light amber being the often-preferred colors (24).

10 Readability of a visual may be affected by a great many other elements in its design, including too much or extraneous detail, too small or too large images, too much irrelevant ornamentation, misuse of color, and failure to use such things as methods of emphasis, methods of directing eye movements, tricks of attracting attention, and ways of subduing secondary information.

11 The producer cannot always predict the readability of a visual by simply viewing the original artwork. He or she must understand how the materials will copy on black and white or color film. It adds to the difficulty if the visual is to be reproduced in both black and white *and* color, as when colored artwork is to be projected on television with both color and black and white receivers in use. To ensure good readability you can redesign colored visuals using reproducible tones of gray for black and white projection.

12 In copying color on color photographic film, it is important to understand how the hue, value, and chroma of each color will record. The medium used will also greatly affect the resulting transparency or slide. You can best understand how color photographic film reproduces various forms of color media by running some simple test exposures. From these tests some predictable standards can be developed.

13 When making handmade transparencies or when hand-tinting photographic transparencies, be certain to use colors with sufficient light transmission properties to project clear images on the screen. Of course, the environmental conditions under which the slide or transparency will be projected are important to take into consideration (although they may not always be known).

1913	ALBANIA	900,000
1910	AUSTRIA-HUNGARY	49,458,421
1913	BELGIUM	7,516,730
1913	BULGARIA	4,800,000
1911	DENMARK	2,775,076
1911	ENGLAND	34,045,290
1911	FRANCE	39,601,509
1910	GERMANY	64,925,993

23

1913	ALBANIA	900,000
1910	AUSTRIA-HUNGARY	49,458,421
1913	BELGIUM	7,516,730
1913	BULGARIA	4,800,000
1911	DENMARK	2,775,076
1911	ENGLAND	34,045,290
1911	FRANCE	39,601,509
1910	GERMANY	64,925,993

24

PHOTOGRAPHY

When original continuous-tone photographs are used as the basic visual, whether black and white or color, their readability will be greatly determined by the manner in which the photographer approaches the subject matter. The photographer's use of camera angle, lighting, swings and tilts (in the case of the view camera), and other factors greatly contributes to the value of the visual. Readability of the photograph can often be greatly enhanced through the use of the many existing retouching techniques. Areas of the picture can be emphasized or de-emphasized, extraneous detail can be removed with an airbrush, and small details can be made more visible by using enlarged inserts. Attention can be called to specific details through the use of arrows, encircling techniques, etc.

GRAPHICS

Charts, diagrams, maps, graphs, and other similar graphic materials often require simplification for good readability. The clever use of keys, stylized symbols, and abbreviations will all contribute to presenting the most essential information in the clearest way. It is important to avoid overloading a visual with too much information. If necessary, supplementary and/or detailed data may be handed out before the presentation. Complex information may be broken down into sections and designed into visual sequences. This not only will aid readability but may also contribute to a better pacing of information during the final presentation.

COMBINATION ELEMENTS

Combining graphic and photographic images will often help to create more readable visuals. Graphic images drawn on transparent overlay sheets placed over continuous-tone photographs often make very effective visual masters—this is a common technique when making title slides.

It is always important to keep in mind relationships of figures to background. What is to be emphasized? What is to be subdued? Keep the message-carrying elements dominant, and subdue those of secondary importance. Be sure that color and tone values are compatible with each other, as well as with the style of art or photography being used. Decide whether the information is best presented in pictorial or symbolic form or in some combination. If a photographic print is to be modified, it may require some form of graphic treatment to give maximum readability.

It is often easy to settle for "safe" methods guaranteeing readability—using over and over the same sizes and styles of type, the same color combinations, the same design techniques. This can lead to the development of stereotyped, monotonous materials. To avoid this, think of yourself as a "researcher" trying new ideas based on information gained from past experience.

3 BASIC PRODUCTION MATERIALS, TOOLS, AND AIDS

Surface and Base Materials
Cutting Tools and Techniques
Pens, Pencils, and Inks
Drawing Aids

SURFACE AND BASE MATERIALS

Surface and base materials are, for most visual media, the foundation—the stage on which the elements of the media designer/producer's images are played. Excellence in the final production can be, in part, achieved by selecting the surface or base material whose physical and aesthetic qualities complement the design elements.

Visual media demand, because of their physical characteristics and use, specific types of surface and base materials. Presented here are descriptions of the most commonly used surface and base materials and their application to the production of visual media. Purchase sources for each can be located in Section 9.

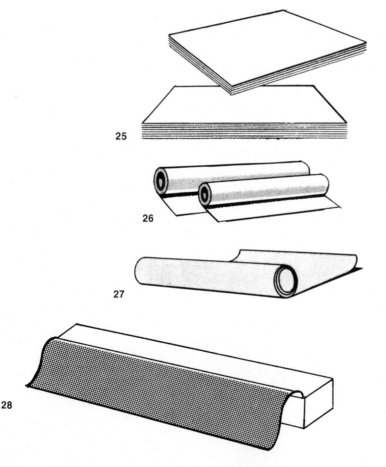

25

26

27

28

PAPERS

Drawing Paper (25)

A great variety of papers ranging from coarse pulpy sheets to 100 percent selected rag papers, with almost as many different surface finishes. Each visual producer should experiment with different media on different qualities of paper to determine the best combinations for his or her individual purposes.

Mounted Drawing Paper (26)

White drawing paper mounted on muslin for added strength and durability. Used for all permanent flat visual media where a quality mounted drawing surface is desired. Double mounted sheets have muslin sandwiched between two sheets of drawing paper. Single mounted sheets have a sheet of paper backed with muslin. Available in sheets and rolls.

Tracing Paper (27)

Papers that run from high transparency through various translucencies to opaque. The clear type is used for general purpose tracing and for overlays and even for transparent drawing paper.

Transfer Carbon Paper (28)

A special-colored carbon-coated paper used to transfer-trace visuals, letters, etc., to any kind of paper, wood, glass, metal, or cloth. Carbon paper produces a sharp, grease-free colored line that can easily be erased. Available in five colors.

Adhesive-backed Paper

High-quality paper with a pressure-sensitive adhesive back. Uses include nameplates, paste-up art, labels, signs, displays. Available in a variety of colors and surfaces.

Construction Paper (29)

A wood-pulp paper of sufficient body to accept crayon, chalk, paint, charcoal, or pencil. Its many uses include visual and letter cutouts and chart making. Available in assorted colors.

Sign and Poster Paper

A 16-pound, smooth, white, multipurpose roll paper designed mainly for signs and posters. Available in 36- and 42-inch-wide rolls.

Gummed-back Paper

Lightweight paper with a watergum adhesive on one side. Moisten the adhesive to adhere. Ideal for visual media requiring a colored-paper medium. Available in assorted bright colors.

Newsprint Paper

An inexpensive wood-pulp paper for making quick drawings and work not demanding permanence. Available in sheets, pads, and rolls.

Kraft Paper

A heavyweight brown paper for murals, posters, and projects which require a strong, heavy paper.

Butcher Paper

A strong, bleached white kraft paper. Usually comes in 36-inch-wide rolls. Uses include murals, posters, banners, signs, and projects which require a strong, heavy white paper.

Background Paper (30)

A heavyweight wide paper that will accept most markers, chalk, tempera, etc. Ideal for productions requiring extremely wide paper; comes in 80- and 107-inch widths and in assorted colors.

Flannel Board Paper

Special paper with a black-flocked back that adheres to flannel (for flannel board). The front of each sheet has a pressure-sensitive adhesive. By adhering this paper to the back of visuals, they can be applied to and removed from flannel boards. Available in 8- by 10-inch sheets.

Velour Paper (31)

Medium-weight colored paper with a velvety surface that imparts great depth to visuals, giving them a three-dimensional quality. Ideal for preparing display materials, cutouts, and letters, and for use on the felt board. Available in colors.

Stencil Paper

A semitransparent, oiled paper which retains sharp lines and is easy to cut out. Used as a letter or visual stencil on all surfaces.

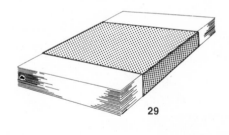

29

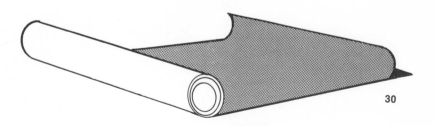

30

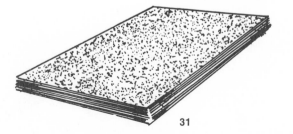

31

BOARDS

Poster Board

A smooth-surfaced board especially suited for use with showcard colors to make posters, signs, and other visual media. Not intended for general drawing because its surface will not withstand repeated rubbing or erasing. Regular poster board is 14-ply (a little less than 1/16 inch thick). Lighter-weight boards, often called railroad boards, may be 4-, 6-, or 8-ply.

Mat Board (32)

Heavyweight cardboard with or without textured (pebbled) surfaces. Used for mat cutting, mounting, posters, displays, and visual media requiring a special-surfaced board. Ranges in thickness from 1/16 to 3/16 inch. Available in assorted colors and surfaces.

Chipboard (Newsboard)

A gray, uncoated heavy cardboard used for mounting, easels, construction models, etc. Usually comes in 30- by 40-inch width, with thicknesses from 1/16 to 3/16 inch.

Illustration Board

Made of fine drawing paper mounted on still backing boards. Surfaces range from very smooth to very rough. The surface will accept most drawing mediums: inks, airbrush, crayon, pencil, watercolors, etc.

Single and Double Shading Screen Boards (33)

Bristol board on which are processed one or two invisible shading screens: one a light tone, the other a darker. Application of the appropriate liquid developers with a brush or pen makes each screen visible where desired. Available in a variety of patterns.

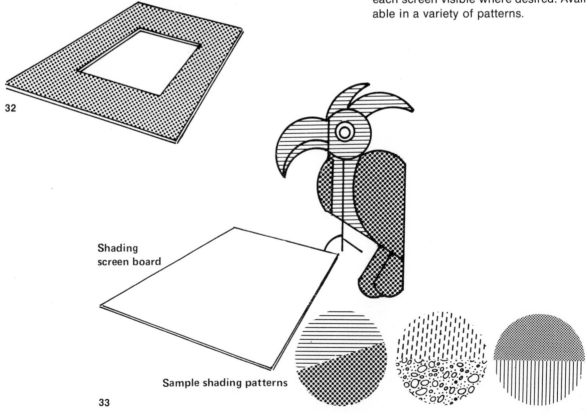

32

Shading screen board

Sample shading patterns

33

Scratchboard (34)

A high-quality, white-coated paper board for scratchboard visual technique work. After coating the surface with India ink or some other black medium, part or all of the visual is made by scratching the surface with a scratchboard tool. The result is a brilliant contrasting black and white visual. A precoated black scratchboard is also available.

Corrugated Board (35)

An exciting material which has found a place in the production of visual media such as displays, bulletin boards, and visual and letter cutouts. This board is made up of two layers of thin, strong paper welded together. The base layer, as shown in the accompanying visual, is flat; the second layer consists of a series of corrugations glued to the surface of the base layer. Available in assorted colors and sizes.

Foam-cored Board (Foam-Core) (36)

Foam-cored board with a smooth white surface (two sides). Combines strength with much lighter weight than an ordinary board. Resists moisture and remains rigid and strong during use because of its styrene foam-core center. Uses include displays, signs, wall art, models, and mounting. The surface accepts markers, poster colors, inks, etc. Cuts easily with a razor blade. Available in $\frac{3}{16}$- and $\frac{1}{2}$-inch thickness.

ACETATES

Clear Acetate (37)

Transparent plastic used as a protective cover, as a base to which films are adhered for color separation overlays, and in see-through maps, charts, etc. An excellent transparent drawing surface that will accept certain nylon-point pens and markers. Available in a variety of thicknesses and sizes—in rolls and sheets.

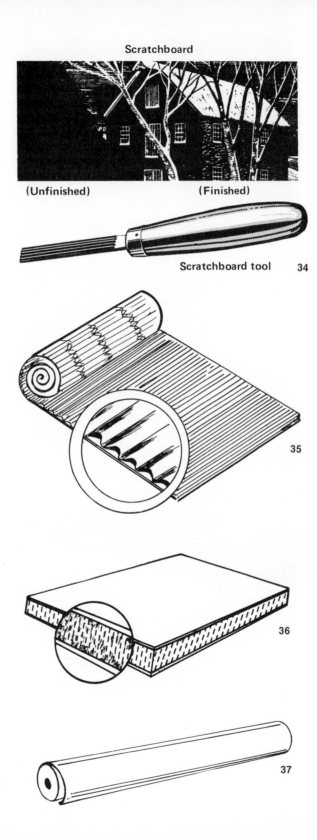

Scratchboard

(Unfinished)   (Finished)

Scratchboard tool   34

35

36

37

Prepared Acetate

Clear plastic treated to take inks, paints, and dyes without the necessity of adding anything to the medium. Use like paper. Both sides coated to accept the medium used. Corrections are made by washing off areas; does not affect working qualities of the surface. Usually available in one thickness (0.005). Available in sheets, pads, and rolls.

Colored Acetate (38)

Acetate sheets and rolls in vivid transparent colors. Can be used to add color background for overhead projection transparencies and other visual media requiring transparent color background.

Matte (Frosted) Acetate

A noninflammable cellulose acetate with a frosted (matte) surface on one side. The frosted side permits the use of lead and colored pencils, inks, etc. The smooth (base) side permits the use of marking pens. Available in sheets, pads, and rolls.

SPECIAL-SURFACED MATERIALS

Dry Backing Cloth

A high-quality cotton fabric with a thermoplastic adhesive on one side. Ideal for mounting maps, charts, and other flat materials where a cloth backing is desired. Requires a dry mounting press or hand electric iron for mounting. Available in sheets and rolls.

Sign Cloth (39)

A white, durable coated or treated cloth especially designed for outdoor signs and banners. Also an excellent surface material for charts, maps, and other visual media requiring a strong cloth-surfaced material. Available in widths of 50 and 54 inches.

Vinyl Plastic by Con-Tact (40)

Vivid, solid-colored vinyl plastic by Con-Tact with a pressure-sensitive adhesive back. Comes in 18-inch-wide sheets. An excellent color medium for visual media requiring a strong paintlike color application. Ideal for cutout visuals and letters, wall and window supergraphics, etc. Vinyl plastic should only be applied on smooth, clean, flat, firm surfaces that are completely sealed, such as enameled or oil-painted plaster, wood, glass, tile, metal, Formica.

38

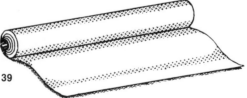

39

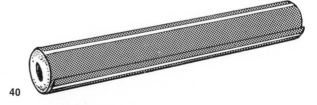

40

CUTTING TOOLS AND TECHNIQUES

CUTTING TOOLS

The common single-edge razor blade, because of its availability, is one of the most common cutting devices. Special inexpensive razor blades are available in quantity lots from art supply houses. The extensive use of the razor blade for scraping and cutting has led to the development of a great number of handles and holders to facilitate use.

Some holders have been developed for single-edge blades (41, 42), while others are to be used with double-edge blades (43). Although these holders are available, often the blade is used in its original form. When the single-edge blade is used without a holder, the index finger usually furnishes the necessary pressure for cutting. After a while, the pressure on the narrow top edge of the blade causes the finger to become quite sore. Several windings of drafting tape around the finger will help alleviate this irritation (44).

A great variety of special cutting knives is available, from the stencil knife with a very delicately pointed blade (45) to the heavy-duty mat cutter (46). When it is necessary to make a straight cut through heavy materials, the heavy-duty mat cutter works well. For greater maneuverability in cutting out delicate designs from lightweight paper, film, or tissue, a finely pointed knife is essential. Some specially designed cutting devices are available that satisfy the needs of specific cutting problems. The swivel knife is designed to cut lightweight materials (47). Because of the swivel head in the blade holder, it is possible to cut irregular curves with ease. A compass with attached cutting blade facilitates the cutting of circles of various sizes (48). When cutting odd shapes from lightweight color or texture adhesive sheets, you will find that the cutting needle works well (49). A number of special cutting devices are designed to cut beveled edges (50). After the blade has been adjusted, they may also be used for

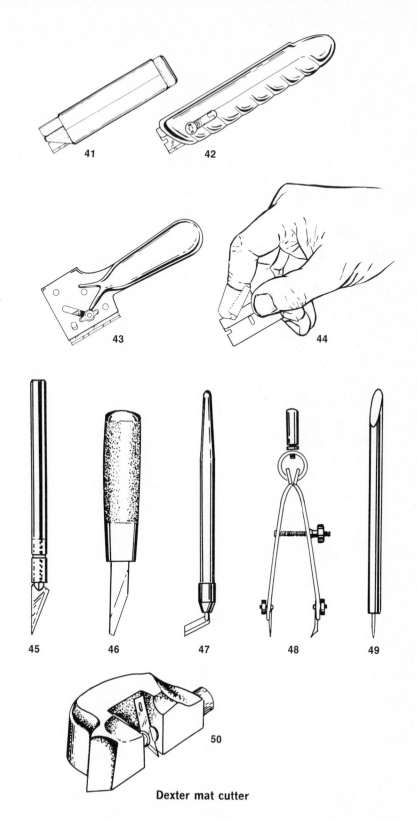

Dexter mat cutter

scoring and straight cutting. No one cutting instrument will satisfy all needs.

No matter what type of cutting device is being used, it is essential to have the blades sharp at all times. The blades for some cutting knives are inexpensive and should be replaced as soon as they become dull. In other cases, the blade should be sharpened to keep it in good cutting condition. A dull blade will tend to tear the paper. To protect the blade of the knife as well as ensure a clean, finished cut, one must always work on a smooth, firm surface that will not damage the blade as it passes through the material being cut. Scrap cardboard works well for this purpose.

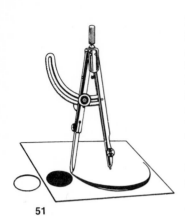

51

"Graphic Arts" Compass and Circle Cutter (51)

A 6-inch compass combination (available from Alvin) equipped with interchangeable pencil, pen, divider needles, and a cutting blade that permits cutting circles.

Micro Circle Cutter (52)

A metal compass device for cutting perfect circles out of such materials as paper, acetate, and thin cardboard. It is used much like an ink or pencil compass. The model illustrated can be adjusted to cut circles from $\frac{1}{16}$ to $3\frac{3}{4}$ inches in diameter.

Bow Divider (53)

A drafting instrument that can substitute as a circle cutter. Used the same as a regular circle cutter.

X-Acto Beam Compass and Circle Cutter (54)

A metal compass device for drawing and cutting circles from $1\frac{1}{2}$ to $15\frac{1}{2}$ inches.

Yardstick Compass Circle Cutter (55)

A yardstick beam compass consisting of two metal parts that fit a standard-size yardstick. Adjust to make and cut circles up to 66 inches in diameter. For cutting circles, the pencil holder should be replaced with a 24E blade or a #11 X-Actoknife blade.

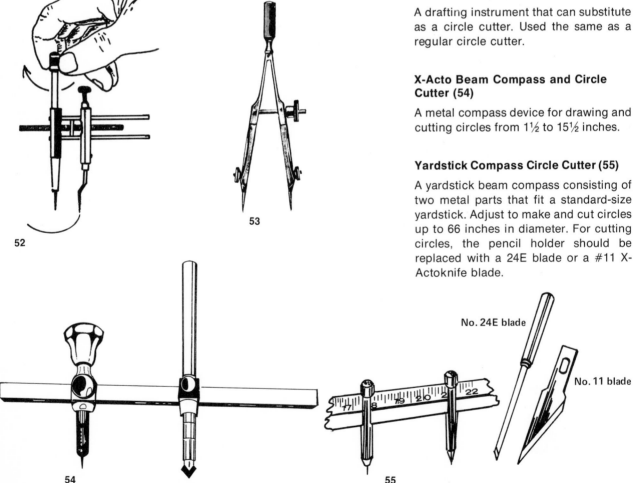

52

53

No. 24E blade

No. 11 blade

54

55

Corner Rounder (56)

A metal cutting device for rounding corners of paper, cardboard, leather, acetate, etc. Cutting blades are interchangeable. The Lassco Model 20 illustrated is capable of cutting the corners shown in the diagram (57). The machine will cut fifty or more sheets of paper at a time.

BASIC CUTTING TECHNIQUES

Single-Blade Tools

When the cutting blade is properly used, the heavier cardboard materials can be cut with relative ease. Use a series of repeated cutting strokes, and hold the blade at about a 30° angle for greatest efficiency (58). At this angle the blade tends to have a "sawing" effect and cuts the more resistant paper fiber quite easily. Holding the blade in too vertical a position tends to cause a buildup of paper fibers in front of the cutting edge (59). The blade, instead of cutting the more resistant material, tears it, causing a roughly cut edge. This is especially true if the cutting edge of the blade is slightly dull. If the blade is held at a low angle, the cut will be quite satisfactory, but because of the extensive amount of cutting edge imbedded into the paper surface, maneuverability of the blade is impaired (60). Thus, it may be difficult to follow a prescribed line, especially if it is other than straight. Although the razor

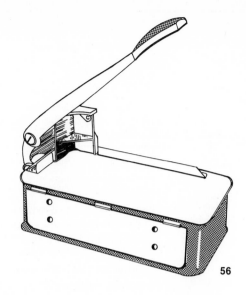

56

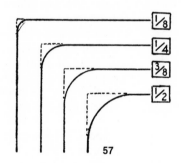

1/8
1/4
3/8
1/2

57

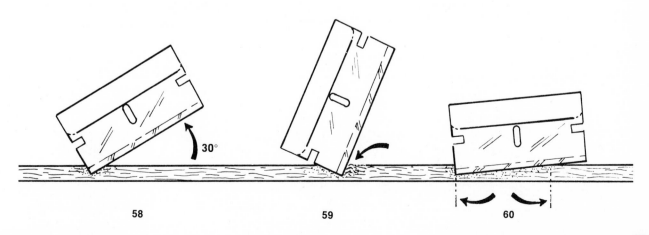

30°

58   59   60

First stroke

61

blade has been used to demonstrate these principles of cutting, they will apply to almost any single-edge cutting device.

After proper positioning of the blade, a second consideration is the application of even pressure on the blade as it is drawn along the paper or cardboard surface. With the heavier paper materials, the first cut should be made with a light, even pressure to create an accurate initial cut which will serve as a guide for repeated strokes of the blade in completing the cut. Each following draw of the blade should be made with a firm, even pressure so that each cut is of a uniform, even depth (61). The thickness of cardboard has been exaggerated in the diagram.

Often the applying of excessive pressure on the blade tends to lead to a variation in depth of cut. After repeated strokes of the cutting blade, the irregularities in cutting depth are amplified, causing irregular areas of paper fiber to accumulate (62). Then as the blade is

forced through these heavy areas, tearing takes place; a roughly finished cut results. Where it is necessary to cut around extremely complicated forms, a sharply pointed blade, other than a razor blade, is recommended because of the greater maneuverability of a small blade in a depth of cardboard.

Obtaining a clean, flowing cut through cardboard or paper with a sharp blade is to a great extent dependent upon the position and movement of the arm in the cutting process. One of the most natural movements for the arm is moving in a straight diagonal line across the front of the body (63). Working with a cutting blade in this position helps ensure greater ease and accuracy in the cutting process (64). By rotating the artwork during the cutting process, it is possible to take advantage of this natural arm movement (65).

The process of cutting out irregularly shaped images will be greatly simplified if a few moments are taken to plan the cutting sequence. First, it is important to

62

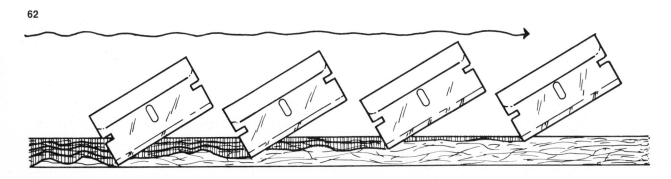

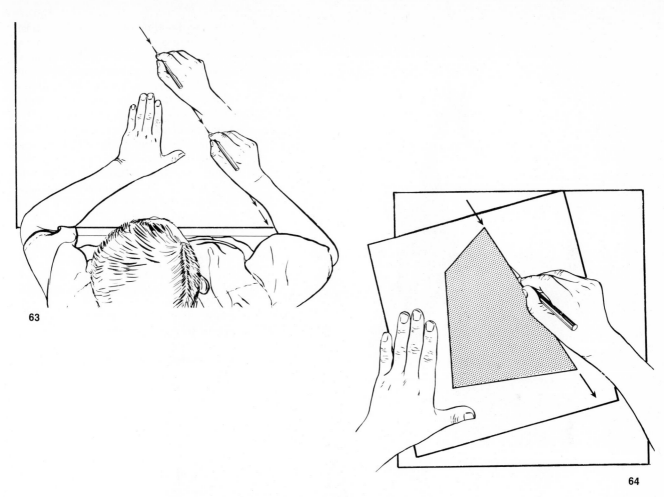

63

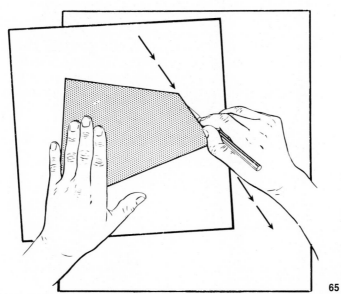

64

65

66

plan the direction of each cut. It is best when cutting irregular shapes to move the blade in an outward direction away from the center of the image. This will help prevent a possible slip of the cutting blade into the image area. The dotted lines on the diagram (66) suggest the direction of some of the basic cuts. Second, it is important to place the line to be cut in such a position that it approximates the natural movement of the cutting arm (67). This requires a new positioning of the image before each cut is made. In order to avoid rough or torn edges, it is important to use a sharp blade, especially when the image is printed on lightweight paper. If the cutout figure is to be mounted by the dry mounting process, the mounting tissue should be tacked to the back of the image before the cutting process is begun. In this way, the mounting tissue and the image will be cut simultaneously, guaranteeing perfect register of form (68).

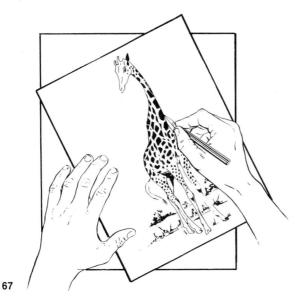

67

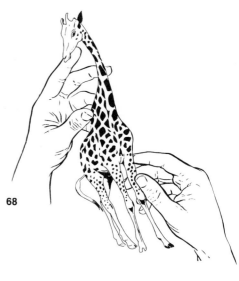

68

Paper Cutter

To most people the paper cutter is a simple cutting device, but it also is possibly the most misused and neglected. A carefully maintained cutter will ensure a clean, accurate cut through the weight and thickness of material for which it has been designed. Excessive thickness of paper or cardboard will tend to throw the cutting blade out of line. Cutting cheap cardboard and paper containing impurities should be avoided. Metal staples, often overlooked, can cause serious damage to a sharp blade. Excessive inward pressure on the blade handle will cause great wear on the board blade, gradually developing a slight curve in the blade; this makes cutting a straight edge almost impossible. When both the handle and board blades are sharp and in proper adjustment, the cut should be made with ease as the handle blade is lowered in a straight, downward movement. Spring adjustment in the handle should be carefully set to avoid too strong an upward force. On large paper cutters excessive spring tension can cause the handle to spring back and cause injury to the operator. When cutting very lightweight tissue paper or similar material, it is often advantageous to place the material between two other lightweight sheets of scrap paper. This tends to prevent the tearing and shifting of the material being cut.

Generally, it is desirable to trim pictures, photographs, and magazine pages in a square or rectangular format. The paper cutter has been designed to do this with ease. When a known straight edge of the material being cut is placed against the ruler, the cutting blade should make a clean, right-angle cut (69). However, if you are working on an unfamiliar cutter, you cannot assume that the ruler is at a right angle to the cutting blade. A quick check can be made by placing a large triangle on the cutting board to determine if the ruler *is* at a right angle to the cutting edge (70). On most cutters the ruler can be adjusted by loosening the screws which hold it in place. Make the necessary adjustment, and tighten the screws in place.

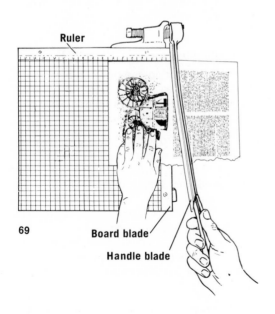

69

Ruler

Board blade

Handle blade

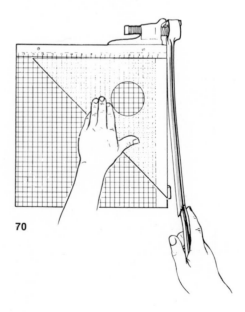

70

Where it is not feasible or possible to make adjustments on the ruler, the grid lines on the surface of the board will help in squaring the paper to the cutting blade (71).

Make sure that a known straight edge of the material being cut lines up with the grid lines on the cutting board for each cut. When the picture is rotated each time a cut is made to make certain the edge coincides with grid lines, a true square or rectangular picture format results. (72).

When difficult paper or cardboard is being cut or when the blade is dull, there is a tendency for the material to shift as the blade is lowered. This can be prevented by pressing down firmly on a strip of stiff cardboard or a straightedge that has been placed over the material close to the cutting edge.

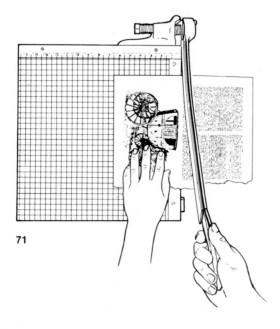

71

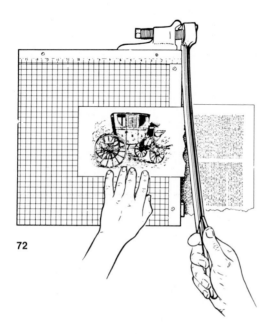

72

PENS, PENCILS, AND INKS

PENS

There are various types of pens on the market today, each particularly suited to specific effects. Several new pens have emerged to provide an added dimension to the world of pens. In the following pages the various pens, and their applications, are described and illustrated. Additional information on each pen can be obtained from the sources given in Section 9.

Speedball Lettering Pens (73)

Metal lettering and drawing pens that fit into a wood, plastic, metal, or fountain-type (Auto-feed) pen holder. Four point styles available follow:

A For producing square poster-type letters with a single stroke
B For making single-stroke round Gothic letters and for drawing and sketching
C For duplicating strokes of the flexible hand-cut reed pen
D With oval marking tip, for producing bold poster Roman alphabet with "thick" and "thicker" elements

Speedball Pens for Left-Handers (74)

Special pens available for left-handed users (any style).

Speedball Auto-Feed Pen (75)

A fountain-type pen which feeds ink into regular Speedball lettering and drawing pens. Fill like a fountain pen, and simply press the button on the side for more ink in the reservoir of the pen. The holder will accept all standard Speedball pens.

Metal Brush Pens (76)

A unique concept in lettering pens. The pens are made of flexible layers of steel and produce lines with a single stroke from $\frac{1}{16}$ to 1 inch wide. Pens are ideal for making large posters and signs. Speedball steel brushes (pens) are available in four sizes. Coits pens are available in nine sizes.

Crow Quill Pen (77)

A fine-line pen that has a flexible point with a tubular shaft that fits a special holder. Ideal for fine-line pen and ink drawing on opaque and transparent surfaces that will accept India ink lines.

Hunt Bowl Pointed Pen (Model 512) (78)

A bowl-pointed extra-fine pen recommended for lettering and drawing on prepared and matte (frosted) acetate.

White Opaque Ink Pen (79)

A pen (Unigraph) designed and engineered specifically for white opaque ink. It uses any free-flowing white ink and will lay down a strong white opaque line. It is recommended for drawing and lettering and for correcting and marking negatives, photostats, blueprints, etc. Available in three point sizes.

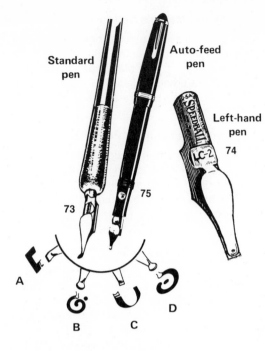

Standard pen

Auto-feed pen

Left-hand pen 74

73

75

A

B

C

D

78

77

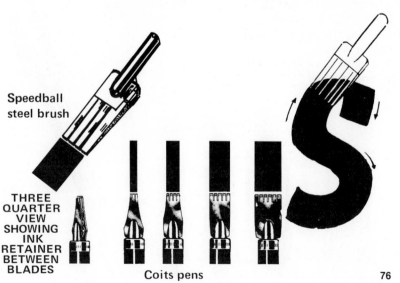

Speedball steel brush

THREE QUARTER VIEW SHOWING INK RETAINER BETWEEN BLADES

Coits pens

76

79

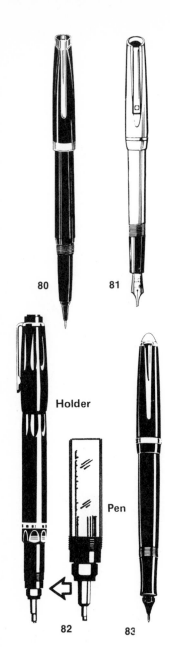

Dr. Ph. Martin's Color Pen (80)

A replaceable cartridge-type pen designed to use Dr. Martin's standard watercolors. The plastic pen tip will produce a broad variation of lines, depending on the pressure applied.

India Ink Fountain Pen (81)

A fountain pen designed for use with India ink. The pen is equipped with a flexible nib that allows the user to change line width with fingertip pressure control.

Reservoir Pen (82)

A fountain-type pen designed for those doing a considerable amount of lettering or ink drawing. These pens have a translucent plastic reservoir that holds sufficient ink for many hours of lettering. Keuffel & Esser (Leroy) and Letterguide pens will fit into mechanical lettering scribers also. Pen line widths range from 0.008 to 0.250 inch (pen size from 0000 to 14).

Technical Fountain Pen (India or Drawing Ink) (83)

A nonclogging fountain-type pen which uses India or regular drawing inks. Some models will accept acetate inks. Pen line widths range from 0.008 to 0.067 (pen size from 0000 to 6). This type of pen is ideal for drawing directly on clear or matte acetate and for use with transparent irregular and ellipse guides (see page 46).

Pelican (Pelikan) Graphos Pens (84)

Fountain-type pens, with sixty interchangeable nibs (points), which are suitable for technical drawing, freehand drawing, sketching, lettering, or ruling. The pen illustrated is the T ruling pen, which is designed for broad lines and for poster work. The line widths for this pen are also illustrated.

Art Brown Freehand Lettering Pen (85)

For all types of freehand lettering and showcard work. Makes the same width of line no matter which direction the pen is moving. Available in eight point sizes.

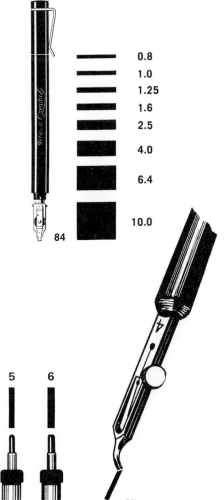

▬	0.8
▬	1.0
▬	1.25
▬	1.6
▬	2.5
▬	4.0
▬	6.4
▬	10.0

84

Pen size: 0000 000 00 0 1 2 2½ 3 3½ 4 5 6

Higgins Boldstroke India Ink Pen (86)

A ball-point cartridge-type pen/marker that produces broad-stroke India ink lines that are reproducible with all duplicating processes. Uses Higgins India ink cartridges.

Wrico Brush Pen (87)

A metal brush pen designed for use with the Wrico Sign-Maker lettering system (see page 133). Ideal also for producing ink lines from 1/16 to 1/4 inch wide. Recommended for use with India ink only.

Ruling Pen (88)

A drafting instrument designed for drawing precision ink lines on opaque and transparent surfaces (see page 49). Drawing inks of various colors can be used in this pen.

Contour (Curve) Ruling Pen (89)

A special ruling pen for drawing curves with the aid of irregular (French) curves and other similar drawing aids. The drawing blade turns easily and follows the smallest curve. The pen can also be converted into a regular ruling pen.

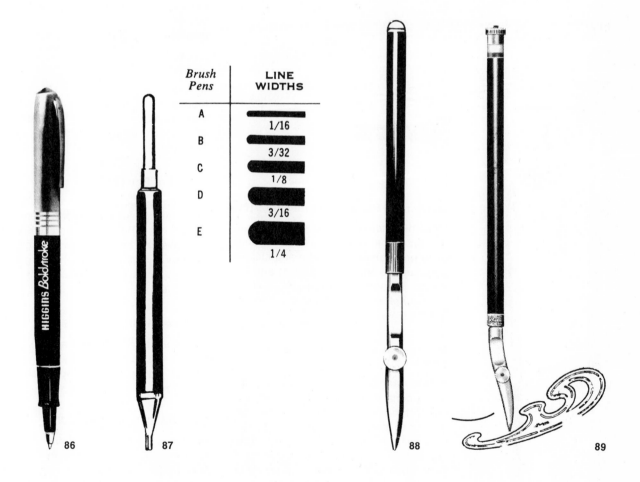

Brush Pens	LINE WIDTHS
A	1/16
B	3/32
C	1/8
D	3/16
E	1/4

86

87

88

89

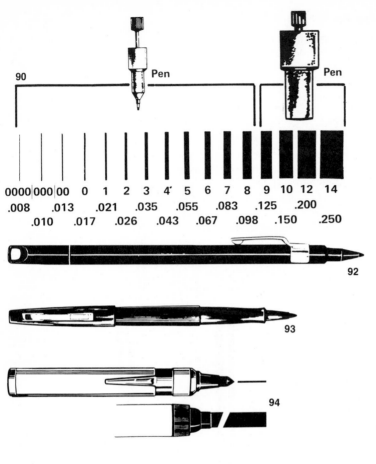

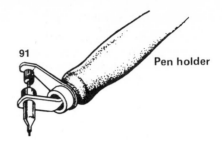

0000	000	00	0	1	2	3	4´	5	6	7	8	9	10 12	14
.008		.013		.021		.035		.055		.083		.125	.200	
	.010		.017		.026		.043		.067		.098		.150	.250

Mechanical Scriber Lettering Pens (90)

India ink lettering pens designed for use in mechanical lettering scribers. A complete unit consists of a pen and cleaner pen. See the chart for pen sizes and line widths. These pens can also be used in a special holder for freehand lettering and drawing.

Mechanical Scriber Lettering Pen Holder (91)

Accepts standard mechanical scriber lettering pens. Designed so that when held comfortably in hand, the pen is perpendicular to the drawing or lettering surface. Ideal for freehand lettering, drawing, and ink line ruling. Leroy (Keuffel & Esser) also manufactures a holder which accepts the larger pens (sizes 9 to 14).

Overhead Transparency Projection Pen (92)

A nylon-point pen especially designed to produce vivid transparent color lines on overhead projection transparencies and other acetates. These pens are available in both permanent and removable colors. The removable (nonpermanent) pen lines can be removed with a dampened chamois cloth or soft paper tissue.

Nylon-Point Pen (93)

A fountain-type pen with a specially tapered point made of nylon or synthetic fiber which produces vivid colored lines on most surfaces. Assorted colors available.

Felt-Point Pen (94)

A fountain-type pen with a special felt point designed for assorted-size and -shape lines. Permanent and removable ink lines can be made with these pens. Ideal for layouts, drawing, coloring, overlays, and fine arts too. Assorted colors available.

Taubman India Ink Pen (95)

A ball-point pen that uses a black indelible ink that dries instantly and will not run or smear. Uses a replaceable ink cartridge.

India Ink Ball-Point Pen (96)

Produces clean, sharp "India" ink lines for reproduction. Available in three different points: medium, fine, and superfine.

Nonreproducing (Light-blue) Ball-Point Pen (97)

For nonreproducing guidelines on mechanicals, layouts, charts, graphs, and general artwork.

PEN ACCESSORIES

Pen Humidifier (98)

A revolving humidifier pen container (manufactured by Koh-I-Noor) for storing reservoir pens. The humidified interior of the container prevents ink points from drying out. The base section contains an integral sponge ring to maintain a humid interior atmosphere. Humectant (Koh-I-Noor product) is used to activate the sponge ring, or it can be moistened with water.

Ultrasonic Pen Cleaner (99)

An electrically powered unit designed specifically for cleaning all types of artist inking pens. Just immerse the tip of the pen into the cleaner to start the ink flow. Will also clean pens that have not been used for some time—the 80,000-cycle-per-second action will free the point so that the pen can be disassembled without damage. Only Ultrasonic cleaning concentrate is recommended for the cleaning unit.

Liquid Pen Cleaner (100)

A liquid cleaner solution for removing dried ink from pens, brushes, and drawing instruments. Some units contain a retrieval tray for cleaning small articles.

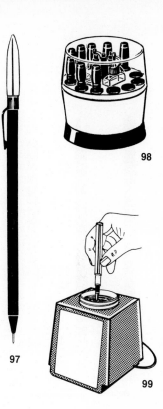

98

97

99

PENCILS

Pencils are not ordinarily thought of as a medium for finished artwork. However, they play an important part in the production of a number of visual media in one form or another. The pencils presented here relate in some degree to a number of techniques treated in this book. Pencil sources are listed in Section 9.

#2 Lead Pencil (101)

The lead pencil recommended for drawing, writing, and lettering on white paper for preparation of thermocopy transparencies (see page 235 for use).

Thermocopy Reproducing Pencil (102)

Contains a special lead that can be reproduced in a thermocopy machine. Pencil lines give strong, clear copies. A soft lead pencil can also be used as a reproducing pencil.

100

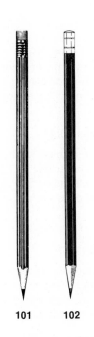

101   102

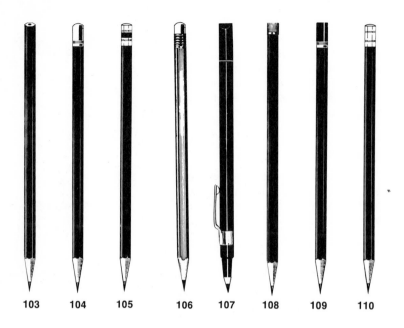

103   104   105   106   107   108   109   110

Offset Master (Direct-Image) Reproducing Pencil (103)

A high-quality medium lead pencil which produces a reproducible image on direct-image offset masters. Used for handwriting, ruling, drawing, or underscoring. Printed copy has the same pencillike appearance as the original copy.

Nonreproducing Pencil (104)

Produces a light shade of blue which is nonreproducing in line artwork. This special color pencil is also used to block in and mark key lines on sketches and line mechanicals.

Color Drawing Pencil (105)

Special colored lead pencils used where a pencillike line in color is desired. Some pencils have leads that can easily be erased if desired; others have leads that will not smear or run under moisture. All pencils are available in many assorted colors.

Transparent Color Marking Pencil (106)

A pencil that has been especially created for use with overhead projection equipment. Leads are smooth and strong and appear in deep transparent color when projected. Markings can be removed with a damp chamois or soft cloth.

Opaque Color Marking Pencil (107)

Opaque color all-purpose marking pencil with a lead that writes in dense color on glass, plastic, acetate, cellophane, metal, etc. Marking pencils are also known as *grease* or China marking pencils. A damp cloth can be used to remove unwanted pencil marks from nonporous surfaces. Available in assorted colors.

Watercolor Pencil (108)

Contains a water-soluble or special lead that has exceptional strength and brilliance. When colors are washed over with brush and water, the soluble colors blend into a watercolor wash.

Spirit Duplicator Pencil (109)

An indelible copy pencil for use on spirit and hectographic duplicator masters. Writing, drawing, and lettering can be done directly on the master with this pencil.

Spirit Duplicator Correction Pencil (110)

A special pencil for making corrections on spirit and hectographic masters. Simply rub the pencil over the error. The pencil contains a substance similar to the coating on the master. This substance combines with the carbon deposit on the master. For best results, remove the raised carbon deposit with a razor blade.

INKS

Many pages could be written just on the variety of inks available for drawing and lettering—inks for opaque surfaces such as paper, cardboard, and chalkboards and inks for transparent surfaces such as clear or matte acetate and glass. In selecting the best type of ink to use, one should take into consideration the type of surface on which the inking is to be done, whether the ink line is to be projected or not, whether permanent or water-base (nonpermanent) ink is desired, and so forth. The inks most widely used are briefly described here. Section 9 lists sources from which additional information can be obtained.

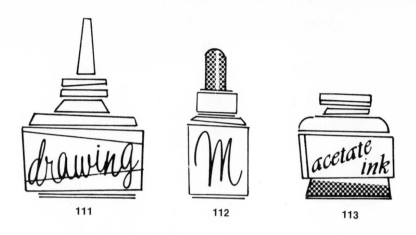

111   112   113

Drawing Inks (111)

Transparent, free-flowing color drawing inks. White is the only color that is not transparent. All colors are intermixable and work well in brushes, pens, and airbrushes.

Dr. Ph. Martin's (Aniline Dye) Watercolors (112)

High-quality aniline dye watercolors available in two forms: synchromatic-transparent and radiant-concentrate. The synchromatic-transparent is recommended for photographic surfaces and for flat washes on illustration boards and papers. Radiant-concentrate colors are extremely concentrated to achieve the greatest possible brilliance and radiant tones in design and illustration on paper surfaces. Over thirty-five colors available. Colors can be used in Dr. Ph. Martin's color pen (see page 38).

Acetate Inks (113)

Opaque or transparent inks designed for use on acetate or plastic surfaces. Some inks are permanent; others are removable. Inks can be applied with brush, pen, or airbrush. Transparent inks project in brilliant color. Special fountain-type pens are available for use with acetate inks.

114   115

116

Lantern Slide Inks (114)

Special transparent inks for use on etched lantern slide glass and matte acetate. Assorted colors available.

India Ink (115)

Black drawing ink used in drawing and lettering and whenever a dense black image is required. Waterproof ink is ideal for use as a drawing or lettering ink for paper, cloth, and film.

India Ink Cartridge (116)

A special dropper-cartridge designed specifically for filling lettering and ruling pens direct from the fine-nozzle cartridge.

Masking Ink (117)

A special ink for producing color separation masks from line artwork. Takes on all plastic surfaces. Thins with water. Can be ruled, pen-drawn, airbrushed, and scribed. Available in black and red; black is dense enough to be used as a film negative; red is transparent and photographs black.

White Ink (118)

For dense white marking on practically all surfaces. Will work on x-ray films, photographic negatives, plastics, leather, cellophane, glass, and wood. Can be thinned for use in lettering pens (see page 37 for special pen). Ordinary food coloring added to the ink can produce beautiful pastel shades.

Gold and Silver Inks (119)

Ready-to-use gold or silver ink for use with pen or brush.

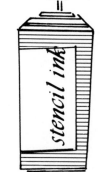

Hectograph (Gelatin) Ink (120)

A specially formulated ink for use in the preparation of hectograph masters. Inked masters will produce up to sixty good copies in assorted colors.

Offset Master (Direct-Image) Ink (121)

A writing, drawing, and lettering ink for use on direct-image offset masters. Can be used in a ruling pen for precision lines. A knife blade or razor blade and special eraser are used to make corrections.

Felt-Point Pen Inks (122)

Special inks for felt-point pens that can be refilled. Two types of inks are available: water-base, which can be removed with a damp cloth, and permanent-base. Assorted colors available.

Stamp Pad Ink (123)

Special ink for stamp pads. Assorted colors available. Sanford Ink Company manufactures a stamp pad ink in a roll-on bottle. Bottle inks often come with a handy brush-cap applicator. Stamp pad ink for direct offset is also available.

Stencil Ink (124)

Opaque ink in an aerosol spray can or bottle for use with metal interlocking and oil board stencil letters. A fast-drying, pigmented ink for all kinds of surfaces: wood, cardboard, and metal. Bottle inks can be applied with a stencil brush or airbrush. See page 131 for use.

Chalkboard Ink (125)

A white ink designed especially for the chalkboard. Will resist erasing or sponge washing with water. Color chalk marks are easily erased from ink lines. Ink is easily removed from the chalkboard with a cloth dampened with solvent furnished with ink and pen set or with most dry-cleaning solvents or cleaning powders.

DRAWING AIDS

A number of drawing aids are available to the professional and nonprofessional producer of visual media. Illustrated here are the more widely used drawing aids.

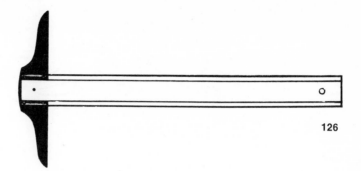

126

T SQUARE (126)

A T-shape metal, plastic, or wood ruler for drawing parallel lines. Also used as a support for lettering and symbol templates, triangles, and other flat drawing aids. To use, hold the T square head against the left side of the drawing board, for the top and bottom of the board may not be square (127). Line up the drawing surface with the top edge of the blade. While holding the T square firmly against the board, hold the pen or pencil vertically and draw horizontal lines. Move the T square downward for additional lines.

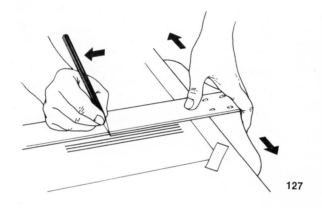

127

PLASTIC TRIANGLE (128)

A transparent plastic triangular drawing device for drawing vertical and angle lines. To use, hold the pen or pencil vertically and draw against the left edge as illustrated (129). Use the left hand to hold the triangle in place against the top edge of the T square. To raise the triangle off the working surface to prevent ink from smearing, tape small thin coins to the reverse side.

Small coins

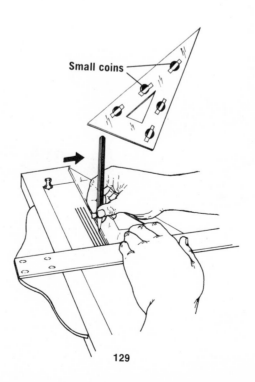

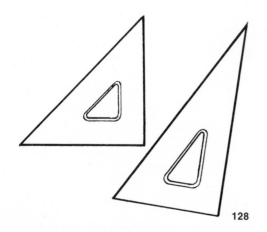

128

129

130

IRREGULAR (FRENCH) CURVES (130)

Curves that cannot be made with a compass can be made with these assorted-shape drawing aids. First, sketch the curve line in pencil, positioning the curve to get the desired line; then finish the line in the desired medium (ink, pencil, etc.). Ball-point, contour, reservoir, and technical fountain pens are recommended for use with irregular curves (131).

131

ADJUSTABLE (FLEXIBLE) CURVE (132)

A plastic or metal device that easily can be bent into any desired curve or shape. Once bent, the curve holds its shape without being held. The smooth edge of the curve permits drawing with a pen or pencil. This device is also useful for the preparation of visual layouts.

SYMBOL TEMPLATES (133)

Transparent plastic outline guides (circles, squares, ellipses, etc.) for use on opaque and transparent surfaces. Ideal for use on stencil and spirit masters. Tracing the symbol outline can be done with a ball-point pen, stencil stylus, or technical fountain pen (134). To raise the template off the working surface while inking, the use of an ink riser template is recommended; small coins can also be taped to the reverse side of the template.

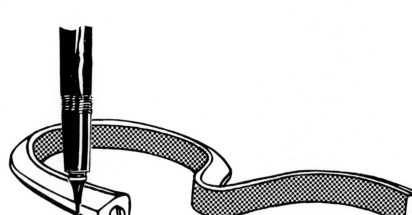

132

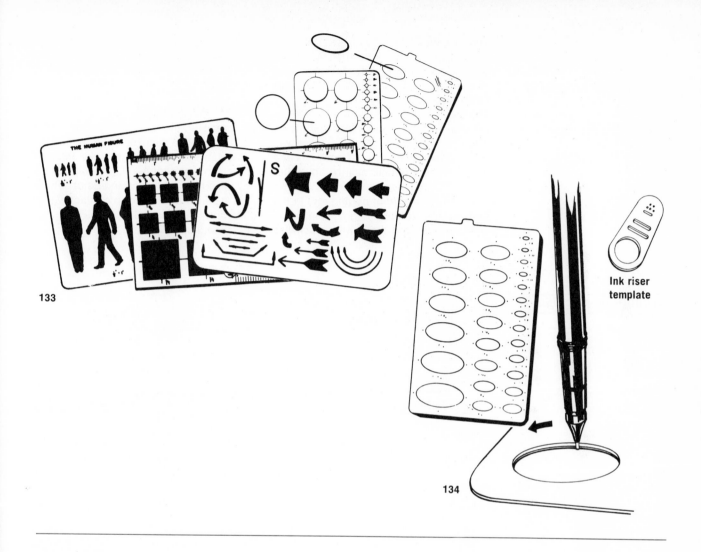

133

Ink riser
template

134

COMPASSES

Compasses are available for practically every illustrating requirement.

The chalkboard compass (135), made of wood or metal, holds chalk, pencil, or crayon in an adjustable holder on one leg. Useful for making large circles on the chalkboard, on cardboard, and on wood.

The ink compass (136) is designed for making circles in ink on transparent and opaque surfaces (acetate, paper, cardboard, etc.).

The pencil compass (137) is for making circles in pencil.

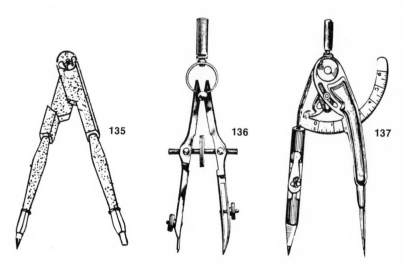

135   136   137

The yardstick beam compass (138) consists of two metal parts that fit a standard-size yardstick. Adjusts easily and makes accurate circles up to 66 inches in diameter.

The handmade beam compass (139) is made out of cardboard, plastic, or metal. A wood or metal standard yardstick will make a good compass. To draw or cut a circle, place a pencil, nail, or any other similar pointed instrument in the left-end hole and a drawing or cutting tool in the hole desired (determined by the circle size desired), and move in a clockwise direction to complete the circle. To make a compass, simply drill or punch ¼-inch holes about 1 inch apart as illustrated.

PANTOGRAPH (140)

A precision-made drawing instrument consisting of a metal or wood frame with adjustable joints. Used to make enlargements or reductions of original visuals by movement of the tracing point actuating a pencil point held in contact with a drawing surface. See page 77 for detailed instructions.

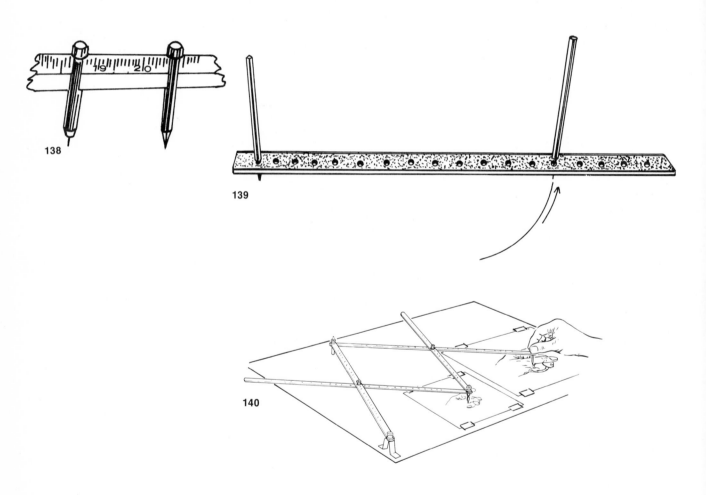

138

139

140

RULING PEN

A drafting tool used for drawing accurate ruled lines on paper, cardboard, or acetate. The adjustable screw can be set for different-width lines. To use, hold the pen in a vertical position against the drawing instrument (T square, triangle, etc.) as illustrated. The height of the ink supply should be about 3/16 inch (141). To fill both the ruling pen and ink compass, use a dropper-stopper or a black India ink cartridge (142).

INK COMPASS

Designed for making circles in ink. The compass is filled the same way a ruling pen is filled. To use, set the needle point of the compass at the center point of where the circle is to be drawn. Hold the pen vertically, and turn it clockwise by twisting thumb and index fingers as illustrated (143).

To clean pens, use a small piece of tissue, cloth, or chamois skin (144). If the ink has dried, use a solution of household ammonia and water. An ultrasonic pen cleaner and liquid pen cleaners are also available.

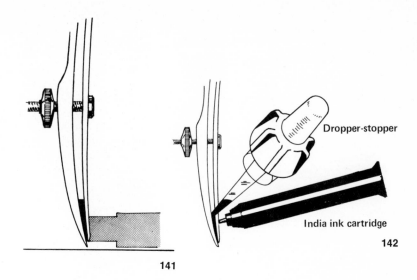

Dropper-stopper

India ink cartridge

141

142

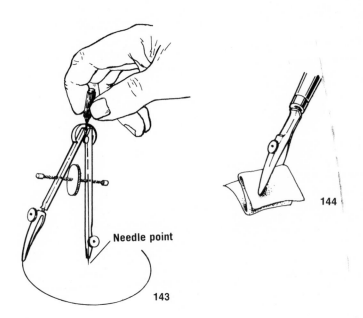

Needle point

143

144

4 ILLUSTRATING TECHNIQUES AND AIDS

Visual Transfer Techniques
Art Aids for Stencil and Spirit Duplication
Hectographic Transfer to Acetate
Direct Image on Acetate Transparencies
Enlarging Visuals by Projection
Reducing Visuals by Reverse Projection
Grid Drawing
Enlarging and Reducing Visuals with a Pantograph
Enlarging Visuals with the Rubber Band Technique
Photosketching Techniques
Printed Art Aids
Art Paste-up Techniques
Polarized Transparencies

With an ever-increasing awareness of the many valuable visual materials now available in magazines, newspapers, and other printed sources, creative individuals using the visual approach to instruction will want to turn to the production of materials based on some of their own visual ideas. When the decision has been made to visualize an idea, and the purposes, content, and method of presentation have been decided upon, the problem of the basic illustration arises. The difficulty in physically forming the image on paper or acetate becomes so frustrating to some people that they give up the idea, and all the potentials of visual communication are lost. The inability to see form, the lack of knowledge of materials and equipment, a nervous hand, a dripping pen often force the individual into an avenue of escape. Except for the few who have the advantage of training in drawing, or have access to art services, creating the visual image will be one of the most serious problems in developing materials. In recent years great advancement has been made in developing equipment and materials to help those who are not adept at creating their own graphs, diagrams, maps, and illustrations. Not only do these new materials help the inexperienced person, but they also speed production for the professional artist.

A knowledge of some of the older techniques combined with a knowledge of the newly developed materials and equipment will expand tremendously the potential of the nonartist in developing visual imagery. It is, therefore, very important for the instructor to keep informed concerning the many production aids available for the process of visualization.

Hundreds of drawing templates are being produced to facilitate the drawing of symbols of various kinds. Drafting tapes in a wide variety of sizes and patterns help to simplify the visualizer's problems. A large assortment of shading sheets is available to shortcut the monotonous drawing of repetitive patterns and textures. Symbols of various objects printed on sheets enable the individual to obtain repetitive silhouette images for use on graphs and charts. Large assortments of prepared art to be used for paste-up are appearing in the form of sheets and booklets and may be subscribed to as one would a magazine to ensure a continuous, incoming flow of new and varied drawings and illustrations. It is the knowledge and use of these art aids that is vitally important to those interested in developing their own presentation materials. The greater the knowledge one has of these visual means of expression, the more flexibility one will have in expressing an idea.

Because of the variety of visual means of expression, size of the image becomes important. The size of the image may vary from a large drawing on the blackboard to a small drawing on papers to be passed out. Methods of enlarging and reducing image size must be understood. Methods of transferring an image from one surface to another are important to know. As one's knowledge of these areas grows, the creation of meaningful visualizations becomes increasingly easy.

VISUAL TRANSFER TECHNIQUES

It is often necessary to trace a visual on tracing paper and transfer it to another surface. One technique for doing this is pounce pattern. However, this may not always be the most convenient or desirable way because of the lack of facilities or certain characteristics of the visual being transferred. There are three other techniques quite closely related to pounce pattern, any of which have certain advantages over it. With any of these techniques it is important to start with a carefully drawn original visual on lightweight drawing or tracing paper (145). It is possible, however, to use the original visual if little damage takes place. Making an original tracing does allow for clarification and simplification of the image, which may be desired.

PENCIL CARBON TECHNIQUE

A common technique for making a visual transfer is the use of pencil carbon. With the visual's drawing face down on a clean, smooth working surface, apply a heavy layer of soft pencil lead to the image lines of the visual (146). Be sure all lines are completely covered with lead. Turn the visual over, and tape to the surface on which the transfer is to be made (147). Using a stylus, pencil, or ball-point pen, carefully trace over the lines of the visual. Be careful not to use too much pressure, because this will leave an indentation on the transfer.

As the drawing instrument traces over the drawing, the pencil carbon on the back of the drawing will be transferred. When all lines have been traced, carefully lift one corner of the drawing to check the quality of the transfer (148). To ensure reregistration, if required (repeating lines not transferred as desired), simply lower the drawing back down on the surface. If the transfer is satisfactory, remove the original and complete the transferred drawing in whatever medium desired. Although this technique works quite well, there is a tendency for extraneous carbon to rub off, causing smudges on the final drawing.

145

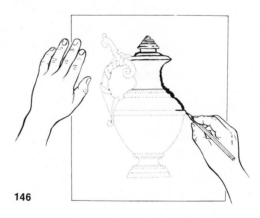

146

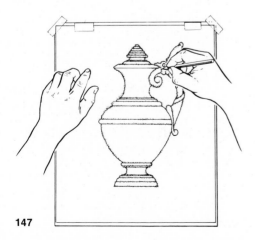

147

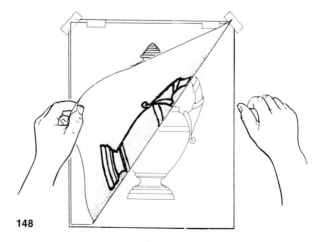

148

CHALK TECHNIQUE

Closely related to the pencil carbon technique is one using pastel crayon or chalk. These materials adapt better to large materials and are somewhat cleaner when making the transfer. If light-color chalk is used, the transfer can be made on dark surfaces. Coat the reverse side of the image with a generous layer of chalk (149). After the image is com-pletely coated, take a ball of cotton moistened with rubber cement thinner and gently pat it over the chalk surface (150). This moistening sets the chalk so that smudges will not form on the surface on which the image is to be transferred.

Tape the original to the surface selected. Trace over the outline with a pencil, stylus, or ball-point pen (151). Check the quality of the transfer (152). If

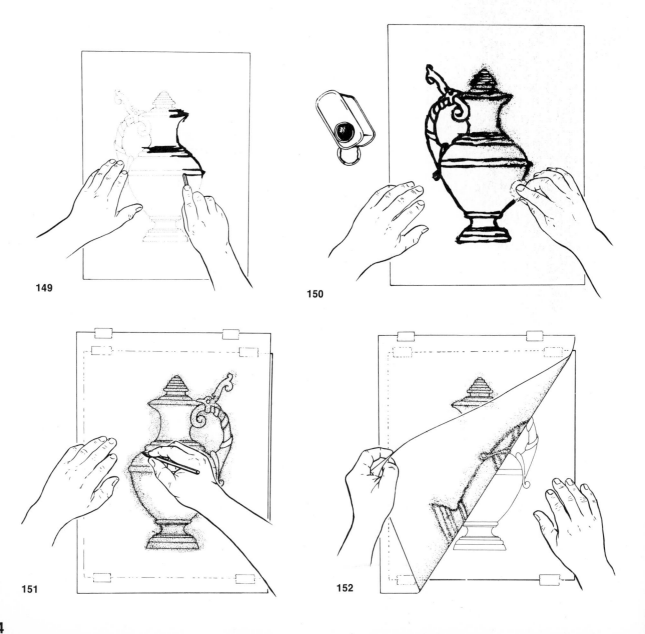

149

150

151

152

54

it is satisfactory, remove the original and complete the transfer as desired. Avoid using chalk with wax or oil content. Under some conditions oil and wax repel other forms of art media and cause difficulty when completing the final artwork.

TRANSFER CARBON PAPER

Another technique for producing sharp, clear transfer visuals is the use of transfer carbon paper. The paper, coated with a special type of carbon, come in assorted colors. To use, insert a sheet of carbon (carbon side down) under the original and tape both sheets to the surface of the material selected (153). Next, trace over the original with a pencil, stylus, or ball-point pen. Make certain no lines are missed (154). When the tracing is completed, check the quality of the transfer (155). If all detail is satisfactory, remove the carbon sheet and original; then complete the transferred visual as desired. It is important to draw carefully when making transfers; small inaccuracies multiply in each generation of the technique, so it is important to minimize defects in tracing.

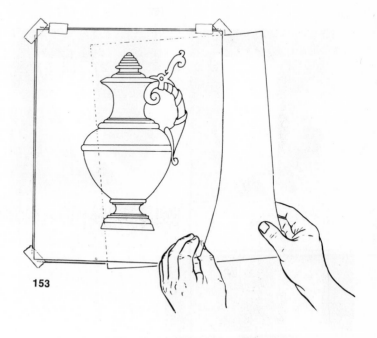

153

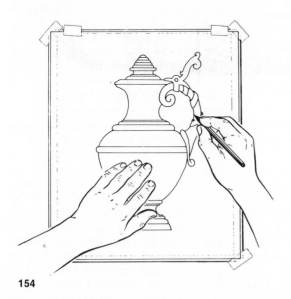

154

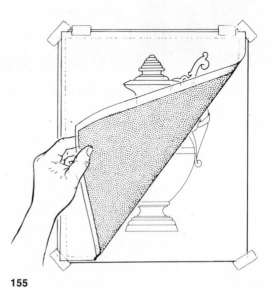

155

156

157

158

159

160

161

When all the lines on the original have been perforated, the pattern is ready for use. This perforated drawing may be transferred to any other surface by patting over the lines with powder or chalk dust. A powder puff or blackboard eraser works well for this process (158). When transferring the image to a light surface, a dark-colored chalk dust must be used. After all lines have been carefully covered with dust, check to see that a complete dot pattern has been transferred (159). Then complete the visual image by drawing along the dotted lines (160). A pounce pattern made on good-quality heavyweight paper coated with shellac or plastic spray will give years of use.

Creating Transparencies with the Pounce Pattern

An application of the pounce pattern can be made in the production of transparencies for the overhead projector. The use of this technique permits the instructor actively to develop a visual image as a lecture progresses. The original visual may be chosen from any source available, as long as it is of the appropriate size to fit on the stage of the overhead projector. For sake of explanation, assume that a tear sheet in a magazine (161) contains the visual that is desired. Remove the page from the magazine, and trim the visual to the desired size. Place the visual on a piece of tagboard or similar strong, lightweight material (162) which has been cut to a dimension slightly larger than the projection area of the projector. This may be approximately 11 by 11 inches. Carefully center the visual on the tagboard (163) and tape it in place. With a sharp cutting needle perforate the lines of the drawing. Be sure to work on a soft surface that will not be damaged by the point of the needle. Scrap cardboard or sheet cork will work well for this purpose. When all lines are perforated, remove the original. Take the perforated tagboard and hinge it with tape to the overhead transparency mount. Now place a sheet of transparent glass or heavy acetate previously coated

POUNCE PATTERN FOR IMAGE TRANSFER

An extremely old technique of transferring an image from one surface to another is through the use of a pounce pattern. This is especially effective when producing large images, such as for chalkboard drawings, signs, and murals.

Perforations are made along the lines of the original drawing using a sharp, pointed tool such as a cutting needle (156) or pounce wheel (157). A sewing machine from which the thread has been removed also serves well for this purpose. The finer the detail, the closer together the perforations are made.

162

to produce a special black opaque surface under the perforated image (164). The coated side must be up. When this coated material is used on the overhead projector and is scribed on with a pencil (or other stylus-type instrument), a luminous line will appear on a black background. For ease of use this coated acetate should be taped to the mount. With the perforated visual image over the carbon surface pat the image with a chalk eraser. The white chalk dust will record the perforated image on the black acetate. Flip the original pounce pattern back out of the way (165). Now, as the instructor lectures, he or she can draw along the dotted lines. As the drawing instrument scrapes away the black coating, an animated white line will appear on the projection screen. By careful planning transparent color acetate or tape may be adhered to the back side of the coated acetate. Then, as the drawing is revealed, different colored lines will appear on the projection screen. The perforated master pattern may be used innumerable times, but the coated acetate must be changed each time this projected visual is used.

Other Applications

The pounce pattern technique can also be used to transfer drawings, diagrams, etc., onto duplicator masters and stencils, wood surfaces, and wall surfaces, and to reproduce patterns on cloth (166).

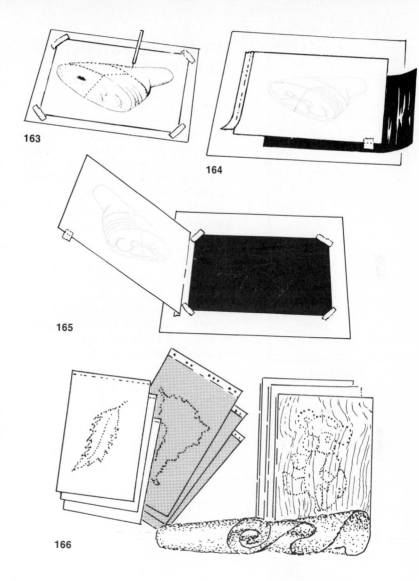

163

164

165

166

OPAQUE BLACK COATING

Mix the following ingredients together thoroughly:

6 ounces of black dry powdered poster color

7 ounces of water

½ ounce of glycerine

(The above mixture may vary slightly depending on the ingredients used and the consistency desired. With experimentation other formulas may be developed.)

Apply a thick coating of this mixture to a sheet of clean, clear glass or heavy acetate using a wide, soft-bristle brush. Be sure to get good, even coverage over the transparent material. Several may be prepared at one time for future as well as present use. The coating liquid may be stored in a closed container. After use the glass or acetate may be washed off and reused over and over.

167   Stencil unit

ART AIDS FOR STENCIL AND SPIRIT DUPLICATION (167)

For the person lacking the necessary skill for producing art (visuals, symbols, etc.) for stencil or spirit duplication, there exists a variety of art aids. The information that follows is intended to suggest aids and techniques that should make the task of producing quality visuals for duplication much easier.

ART AIDS

Stencil/Spirit Duplicator Art (168)

Easy-to-draw drawings created by professional artists for stencil and spirit duplication. Drawings are usually printed on one side of a white sheet that will permit enough light to pass through it for tracing on a viewing light box (tracing unit). Stencil art books are also available for the production of visuals. These books contain stencils of animals, space art, flowers, and numerous other visuals.

Clip Art (169)

Can be traced for use on stencil and spirit masters. Usually a tracing will first have to be made on tracing paper, then retraced on the duplicator master unit. In any event, clip art provides an excellent source of professional-quality art and art ideas. Available in book or sheet form (see page 86).

Symbol Templates (170)

Transparent plastic outline symbol templates (guides) for use on stencils and masters. Symbol templates are available in an endless variety of subject areas.

Spirit master

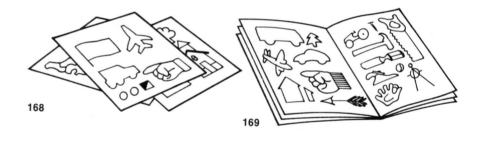

168

169

170

Plastic Shading Plates (171)

For adding shading or texture to visuals or lettering. Stencil duplicator shading wheels can also be used to create the same effects on stencil and spirit units. Shading plates and wheels are available in many attractive patterns. Shading plates require the use of special styluses.

Tracing Unit (172)

A special tracing unit designed especially for drawing, tracing, and lettering on stencil and spirit master units. The unit is usually made up of a metal frame supporting a sheet of translucent glass. Some units have electric lights to assist in the tracing operation.

Writing Plate (173)

A transparent plastic sheet designed to provide a hard, smooth surface under the top stencil sheet for drawing, lettering, and typing.

Drawing and Shading Tools (174)

A variety of drawing and shading tools is available for producing art directly on stencil and spirit master units. Each will be discussed here in regard to its use.

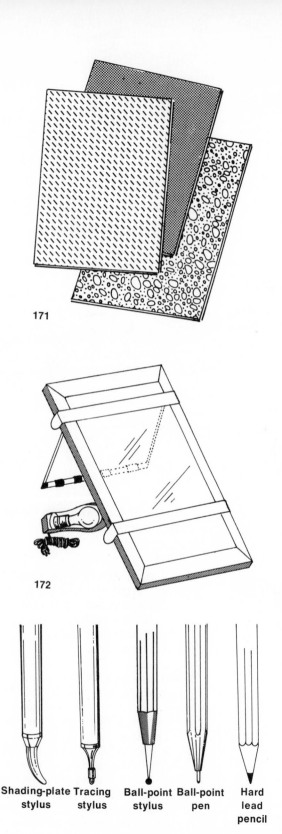

171

172

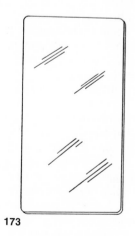

173

174   Shading-plate stylus   Tracing stylus   Ball-point stylus   Ball-point pen   Hard lead pencil

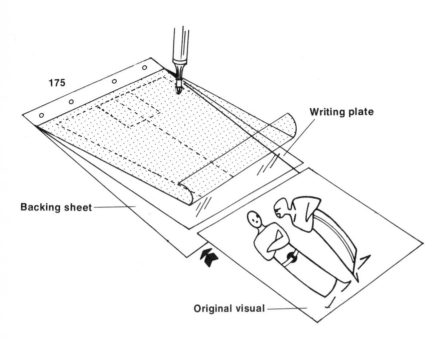

175

Writing plate

Backing sheet

Original visual

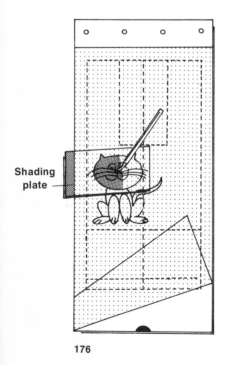

Shading plate

176

Instructions for drawing on stencil and spirit masters

STENCIL

1 *To draw,* when stencil or clip art is used, insert the art under the writing plate and trace visual outlines with a tracing stylus (175). If a tracing unit is used, push the backing sheet of the stencil back out of the way for this operation.

2 *To use symbol templates,* simply place the template in the desired location on *top* of the stencil and trace the symbol outlines with a ball-point stylus.

3 *To add shading,* place the shading plate directly under the visual area to be shaded, holding the plate firmly in place. Rub over the desired area with a shading stylus in a circular fashion to produce the plate pattern (176).

SPIRIT MASTER

1 *To draw,* trace on a sheet of paper the desired visual (from stencil or clip art, magazine, newspaper, etc.).

2 Turn the traced visual over and pencil-carbon the back (177) (see page 53 for the pencil carbon transfer technique).

3 Fold the carbon sheet away from the master sheet. Place a slip sheet under the carbon to protect it from damage. Attach, with tape, the visual to the master sheet and retrace with a hard lead pencil; #3 or #4 may be used (178). This will transfer the visual to the master sheet.

4 Remove the original visual, and return the carbon sheet to the master sheet (slip sheet removed). Retrace the transferred visual with a hard lead pencil or ball-point pen, using firm, even pressure (179). Variations in pressure will result in uneven copy. Make certain you place the master on a firm, smooth surface while drawing.

5 *To use symbol templates,* simply place the template in the desired location on the master and trace the symbol outlines with a ball-point pen or hard lead pencil.

6 *To add color,* remove the original carbon (first color) sheet, insert the second carbon sheet, and follow the instructions in item 4 for the second color; repeat for additional colors.

7 *To add shading,* place the desired shading plate directly under the area of the visual to be shaded (carbon and master sheets on top of the shading plate); hold the plate firmly in place, and rub the area in a circular motion with a shading plate stylus (180). Carefully check to see if the pattern is transferring to the underside of the master sheet.

8 *To make corrections,* use a razor blade to "lift" the image deposit which forms the error. Avoid damaging the finish of the master. Then rub gently, but firmly, over the entire error with an eraser or correction pencil. An eraser shield may be used to isolate the error.

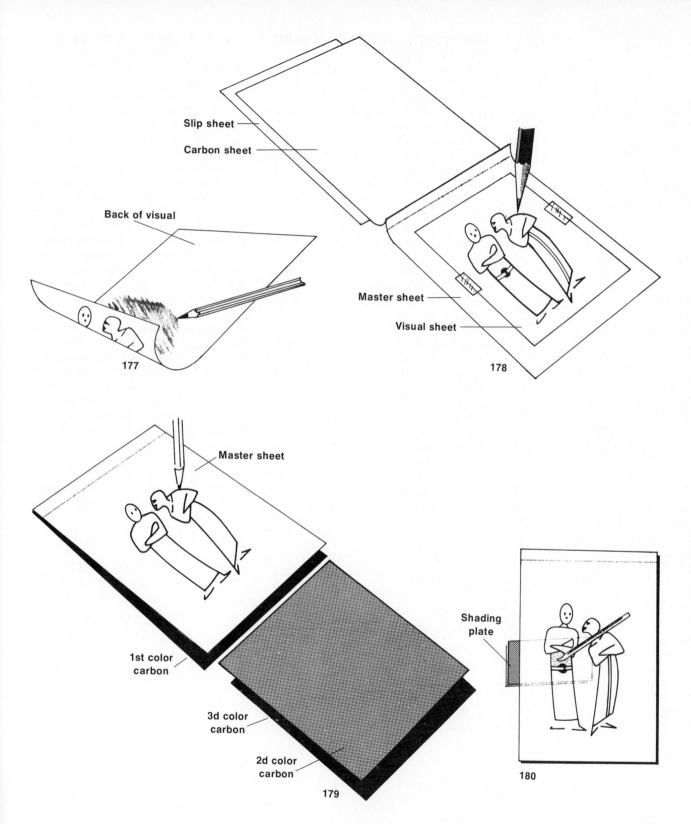

Slip sheet

Carbon sheet

Back of visual

177

Master sheet

Visual sheet

178

Master sheet

1st color carbon

3d color carbon

2d color carbon

179

Shading plate

180

61

HECTOGRAPHIC TRANSFER TO ACETATE

TRANSFER PROCESS

The hectograph process is an old duplicating method used in the reproduction of small quantities of paper prints. It is now also used to make multicolor transparencies. Not only can the instructor make a transparency, but he may also make a limited number of additional paper prints to pass out to the students. The process is simple, fast, and inexpensive. The equipment and supplies are readily available and can be purchased from stationery stores and business supply and mail-order houses. If desirable, the gelatin printing surface may be made at home with a little expenditure of time and money.

The master paper copy for this process may be produced in a number of ways. Specially prepared hectograph pencils, ink, carbon paper, and typewriter ribbons may be used alone or in combination to form the carbon image on the master paper copy (on which the success of the whole process depends). These various materials come in a limited number of colors. When copies are being reproduced on paper, the number of prints obtainable by this system of reproduction is limited by the method by

which the master is made and by the colors used. Masters made with hectograph pencils tend to give fewer copies than those made by using the special carbon paper. The color purple will be found to be the strongest of the colors and will give the greatest number of copies. When making transparencies by this method, only three or four copies—at the most—can be made. However, it may be assumed in most cases that one transparency will be all that is required for a particular teaching situation. Of course, after one transparency is made, a number of paper prints may be made.

One method, and probably the most common in preparing the artwork, is to make a drawing with ink or pencil on very lightweight paper or tracing tissue (181). A carefully done line drawing will ensure a better end product. This visual may be made by tracing from tear sheets, clip art, or original drawings, or it may be a compilation of these various sources of imagery. Next, tape down a sheet of good-quality hard-surfaced paper, which will be known as the master, onto a surface of glass, Formica, plastic, or any other smooth, hard surface (182).

Over this fasten the drawing to be reproduced. Tape it down along the top edge so that it can be lifted without

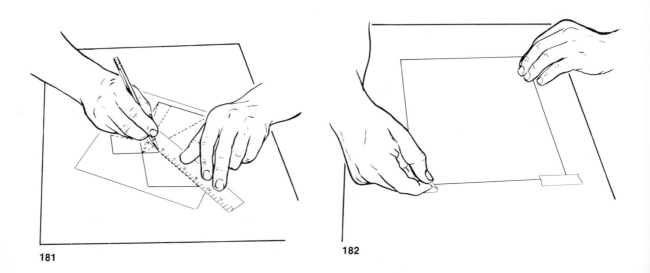

181

182

changing its relationship to the master sheet (183). Choose the color of hectograph carbon paper desired, and insert it with the carbon side down between the drawing tissue and the master sheet (184). To prevent movement, use small bits of tape.

Now trace along those lines to be in the color of the carbon now in use (185). Any smooth-tipped instrument can be used to do the tracing, such as a ball-point pen, a stylus, or a pencil. Ball-point pens have proved to be the best. Care must be taken to apply smooth, even pressure to ensure good transfer of the

carbon onto the master sheet. When all lines of this color are completed, a second color carbon is inserted (186) in the same manner, and the drawing process is continued until all lines are drawn with their respective color carbons.

Any area of a carbon that has been used once cannot be used the second time because that area will lack sufficient carbon for a second transfer. If hectograph pencil or ink is used, the drawing is made directly on the master sheet using the colors of pencils or ink appropriate to the desired end result. Special shading and texture effects can

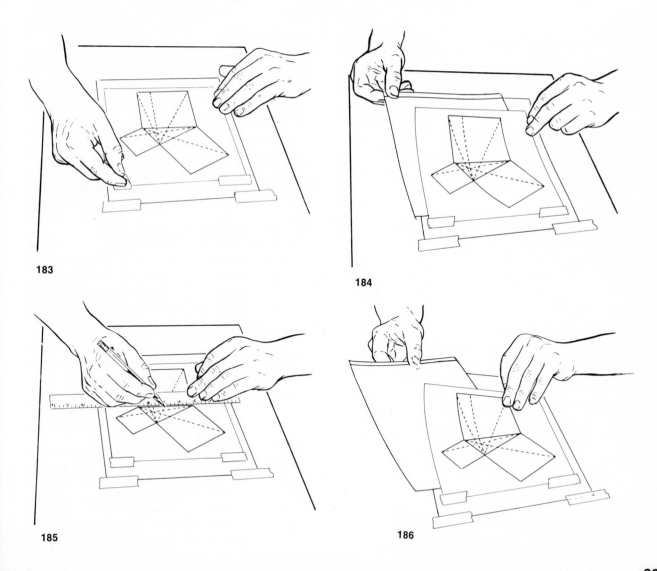

183

184

185

186

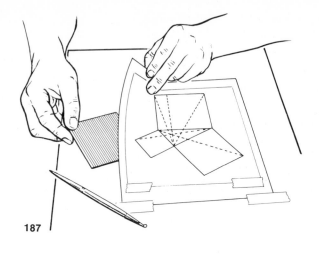

187

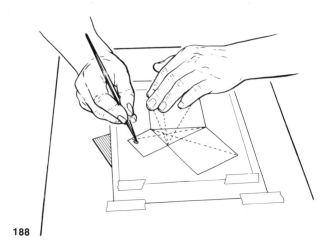

188

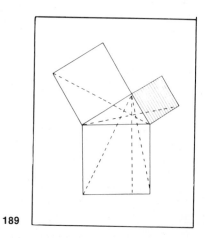

189

be obtained by inserting a shading plate beneath the master sheet (187) and rubbing over the area to be shaded with a blunt stylus (188). The rough-patterned surface of the shading plate causes a like pattern to transfer from the carbon to the master sheet. Other effects of stippling and crosshatch drawing can be very effective when appropriately used. The carbon image on the master sheet should now be checked (189). If any errors are found, the carbon may be scraped off with a razor blade, or cellophane tape may be used to cover the carbon image so that reproduction will be prevented.

Now prepare the gelatin surface of the hectograph by sponging it with cool water (190). When the gelatin is well saturated, blot off the excess moisture using absorbent paper (191).

Next, place the carbon image of the master sheet in contact with the hectograph's gelatin surface (192). Be sure that the entire image is in contact with the gelatin by rubbing over the back of the master sheet with even, firm pressure. After a period of from thirty to sixty seconds remove the master sheet (193). The gelatin surface of the duplicator has now absorbed a large amount of the carbon from the master sheet.

To make a transparency, a sheet of gelatin-coated film is now placed in contact with this image (194). The gelatin surface of photographic film which has had its image removed by bleaching and also the gelatin surface of diffusion transfer film work well in making this type of transparency. Slight moistening of the photographic film will ensure a stronger, brighter image transfer. Care must be taken to be sure that no air blisters form under the film, preventing complete contact with the duplicator image. After thirty to sixty seconds, pull the film off (195). If a little gelatin from the duplicator should stick to the film surface, sponge the surface with water and blot quickly with absorbent paper. Allow time to dry.

Place a protective sheet of acetate over the printed surface, and bind in the appropriate type of mask for projection

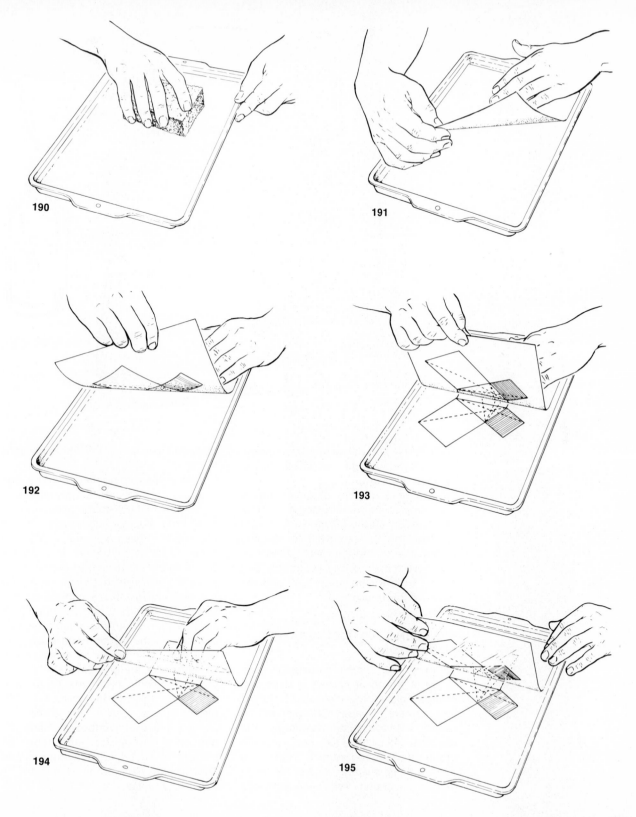

190

191

192

193

194

195

65

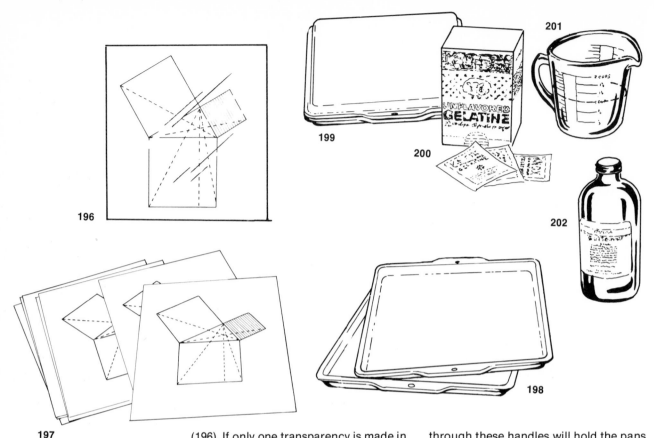

196

197

198

199

200

201

202

(196). If only one transparency is made in this manner, enough carbon will remain in the gelatin surface to permit the reproduction of a number of paper copies (197). Immediately after using the hectograph, wash off the gelatin surface with cool water to help remove the remaining carbon image and any paper fiber that may have remained on the surface. Blot off the excess moisture, cover, and put away for future use.

PREPARING THE HECTOGRAPH DUPLICATOR

To make this simple duplicator, purchase at the local hardware store two shallow baking pans (198) slightly larger than a sheet of paper. One pan will be used to hold the gelatin compound, and the other will be used as a cover (199) to protect the printing surface. Try to find pans with lip-shaped handles on each end as illustrated. Two wing-nut bolts

through these handles will hold the pans tightly in place.

The gelatin compound may be purchased from duplicator supply houses or made from materials purchased from the local drug store or supermarket. Mix 8 teaspoons of plain dry gelatin (200) into 1 cup (201) of cold water in a double boiler. Allow the gelatin to soften. Next, place the pan over hot water on a slow fire until the gelatin is completely dissolved. Warm a pint of glycerin (202) in another pan. When the gelatin has dissolved, add the glycerin and allow it to cook over boiling water for at least twenty minutes. Carefully pour the gelatin mixture into one of the pans. Try to avoid causing bubbles on the surface. If bubbles do appear, scrape them to one side, using a piece of cardboard. Place the pan on a level surface and allow the mixture to cool for twenty-four hours. The gelatin hectograph duplicator is now ready to use.

DIRECT IMAGE ON ACETATE TRANSPARENCIES

Several types of acetate can be used to produce transparent visual media such as overhead projection transparencies, slides, and visual overlays. Visual images, lettering, writing, and so forth can be done directly on the surface of acetates. A number of the illustrating, coloring, and lettering techniques included in this book can be combined with various acetates to produce a variety of direct-image transparencies.

Two different types of acetate have been selected for inclusion in this section because their surfaces are ideal for quick, easy-to-make transparencies. They include clear or prepared and matte (frosted) acetates. Each will be treated separately in the pages to follow.

CLEAR OR PREPARED ACETATE TRANSPARENCY

When visuals cannot be removed from their original source (book, magazine, newspaper, etc.) and when copying equipment is not available, tracings of visuals can be made directly on clear or prepared acetate. If the original to be traced is the approximate size, then the instructions that follow will be sufficient. If the original is too small, see pages 70 to 78 for instructions on enlarging visuals. If the original is too large, see pages 72 to 76 for instructions on reducing visuals.

Images in black or color line can be projected on the screen by drawing directly on most clear or prepared acetate with a variety of pens, pencils, and markers. The accompanying chart (203) suggests specific drawing tools for direct images on acetates. The instructions that follow are for the preparation of transparencies on clear or prepared acetate:

Instructions

Clear acetate is one of several types of transparent plastics or acetates (reprocessed x-ray film and color acetate are other examples). Prepared acetate is recommended when ink is used, because it has a special coating on both sides that will accpt inks, watercolors, poster paints, and dyes without crawling.

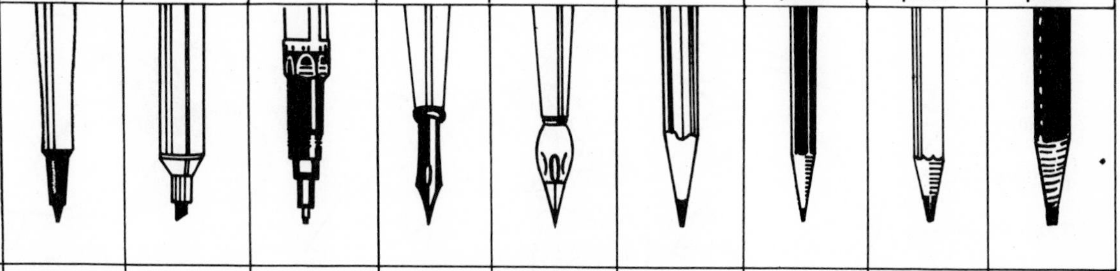

	Nylon-point pen	Felt-point pen	Reservoir pen	Crowquill pen	Hunt #512 pen	Lead pencil	Color drawing pencil	Transparent color pencil	Opaque color marking pencil
Clear acetate	O	O	O	O	O			O	O
Matte acetate	O	O	O	O	O	O	O	O	

203

1 Attach, where possible, a sheet of acetate to the surface of the visual to be traced (204). Place a sheet of protective paper (any clean sheet of paper will do) over the portion of the acetate where the hands or fingers might come in contact with the acetate. Oil residue from hands and fingers may be deposited on the surface of the acetate; this may prevent the surface from accepting the ink. In that not all clear acetates will accept ink, talcum powder or pumice can be rubbed over the surface. This will provide the "tooth" necessary to accept and hold the ink line.

2 If a quick, temporary image is desired, draw on the acetate with an opaque or transparent color marking pencil (transparent color pencil will project in color) or with a nylon- or felt-point pen containing a nonpermanent (water-base) ink. If a more permanent image is desired, draw on the acetate with India or acetate ink and pen; technical fountain, reservoir, crow quill, and Hunt Bowl Pointed pens are recommended for drawing on clear or prepared acetate.

3 To add color (205), use nylon-point pens for fine-line color and felt-point pens for broad-line color. See pages 94 to 105 for other coloring techniques.

4 Mount, if desired, for projection. See pages 212 to 214 for tips on mounting techniques.

5 To remove unwanted marking pencil or water-base image lines, use a damp piece of cloth.

6 If lettering is desired, consult the chart on page 108 for recommended lettering techniques on acetates.

MATTE (FROSTED) ACETATE TRANSPARENCY

When visuals cannot be removed from their original source (book, magazine, newspaper, etc.) and when copying equipment is not available, tracings of visuals can be made directly on matte (frosted) acetate. If the original to be traced is the approximate size, then the instructions that follow will be sufficient. If the original is too small, see pages 70 to 78 for instructions on enlarging visuals. If the original is too large, see pages 72 to 76 for instructions on reducing visuals.

Instructions

Matte acetate has a finely etched surface (dull side) which is ideal for accepting India ink, color drawing, and lead pencil lines.

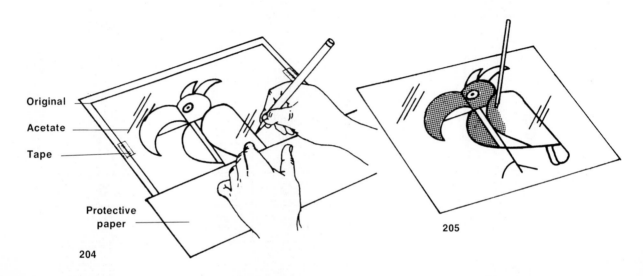

Original

Acetate

Tape

Protective paper

204

205

1   Attach, where possible, a sheet of acetate to the surface of the visual to be traced (206). Place a sheet of protective paper (any clean sheet of paper will do) over the portion of the acetate where the hands and fingers might come in contact with the acetate. Oil residue from hands and fingers may be deposited on the surface of the acetate; this may prevent the surface from accepting the ink or pencil line.

2   If an ink line is desired, draw directly on the acetate with India ink and pen. Technical fountain, reservoir, crow quill, and Hunt Bowl Pointed pens are recommended. If a pencil line (black or color) is desired, use a transparent color marking pencil.

3   To remove unwanted ink or pencil lines, use a water- or isopropyl alcohol-dampened cloth to gently remove the lines.

4   Spray the matte (dull) side of the film with clear plastic spray (207). Hold the spray can about 10 inches above the acetate, and spray back and forth to apply an even coat of plastic. The use of a larger piece of protective paper placed under the acetate while spraying is recommended. Another method is to pass the acetate through a heat laminating machine; this will seal in the image while making it more transparent. See page 184 for use of the heat laminator.

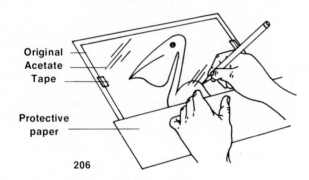

Original
Acetate
Tape

Protective
paper

206

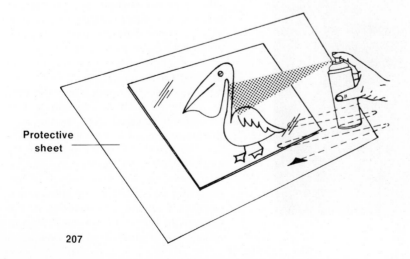

Protective
sheet

207

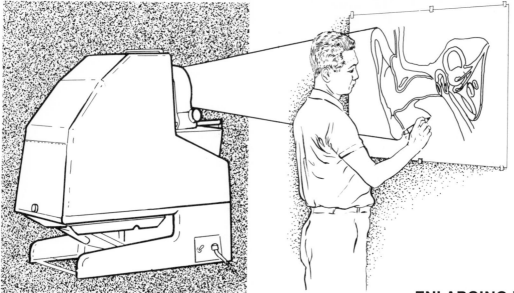

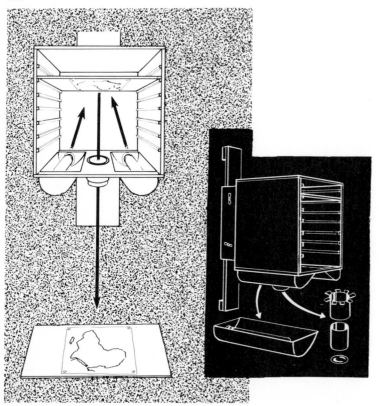

ENLARGING VISUALS BY PROJECTION

The opaque projector is often used as a means of enlarging drawings (208). Not only can tear sheets and drawings be projected, but real objects having a certain limited third dimension can serve as subject matter for tracings. Interesting drawings for wall murals can be made by manipulating visual images taken from tear sheets, mounting them into a meaningful visual, and then enlarging the composite picture onto a large panel or chalkboard. Color may then be added by using chalk, crayon, watercolor, or any other medium desired. Special opaque projectors, simple in design, may be purchased specifically for use in making enlargements for signs and murals.

In situations where there is constant demand for the enlargement of opaque material, a simple opaque enlarger may be made (209). It is basically a box mounted to a wood track on the wall. Brackets clamped to the wood track support the main body of the projector. By loosening the bolts, the projector may be raised or lowered. The main box has small strips fastened to two sides which permit the raising and lowering of the lightweight board, to the lower side of which the original drawing has been tacked. This helps in adjusting focus. To furnish the necessary illumination, two shiny tin reflectors containing lights are mounted in the bottom of the box on either side of the lens opening. The lens is a 2-inch magnifying glass mounted in a tin or aluminum sleeve, which in turn is telescoped into a similar metal cylinder that has been fastened to the main body of the projector. By adjusting the lens, the drawing board, and the projector on its track, images of various sizes can be focused on the drawing board below. The tracing can then be made easily.

Almost any type of slide projector can be used as a device for producing enlarged drawings for such visuals as charts, posters, graphs, murals, and chalkboard exhibits. Practically any subject matter in slide form can be projected on a desired surface and traced.

There is a limited number of slides or transparencies produced commercially for this technique of producing large visuals. However, it is relatively easy to copy drawings, photographs, etc., for the 2- by 2-inch slide projector (210) by using a 35mm still camera. In a like manner, special half-frame 35mm cameras can be used to produce filmstrips that can be used in a film-strip projector to produce large illustrations (211). Standard 2- by 2-inch slides can be converted into filmstrips by a number of companies offering this service. Slides for the 3¼- by 4-inch slide projector can be made photographically or by hand (212).

The image area of the 10- by 10-inch overhead transparency is ideal for preparing hand-drawn materials to be enlarged with the overhead projector (213).

The photographic enlarger (214) can also be used as a projection device for preparing large visuals from a transparent or translucent original. The material to be enlarged is placed in the enlarger the way one inserts a regular photographic negative. Avoid leaving the lamp of the enlarger on for extended periods of time; this will cause extensive damage to the optical system of the enlarger. The enlarger can be adjusted to focus an image of the desired size down on the base of the enlarger.

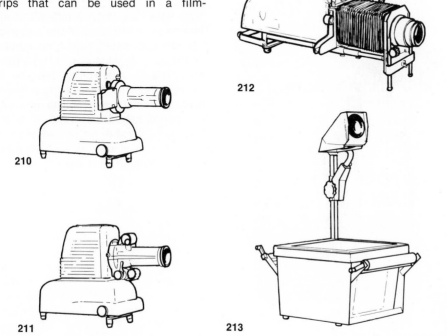

210

211

212

213

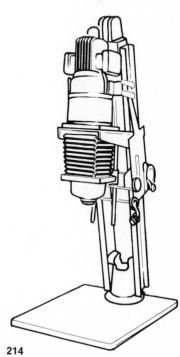

214

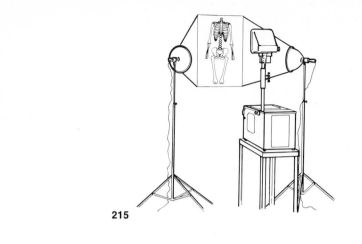

215

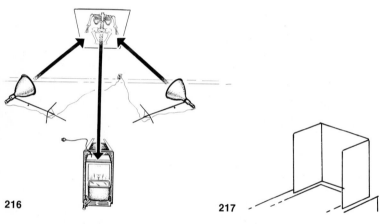

216

217

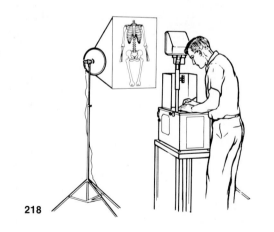

218

REDUCING VISUALS BY REVERSE PROJECTION

There are times when a large illustration, diagram, chart, or map might be more usable if it were reduced to the form of an opaque projection flat, a slide, or an overhead projection transparency. There are several ways this can be accomplished. However, if the image is such that it can be drawn readily, the reverse projection method may be the simplest approach.

In a slightly darkened room, place an overhead projector on a table or projection stand with the lens facing the visual to be reproduced. Illuminate the visual with a light source such as photofloods, lamps, reflector floods, or even floor lamps (215). Tape any opaque or translucent drawing material on the stage of the projector. The light reflection on the visual will reflect back through the projector's lens system onto the stage of the projector (216). Moving the projector away from the visual will reduce the size of the image on the projector stage; moving it closer will increase the size. The focusing device on the projector is used to sharpen the image as it is reflected onto the drawing surface. Extraneous room light may make it difficult to see the image on the stage of the projector. A simple light shield may be made out of cardboard, as illustrated (217). When everything is satisfactory, proceed by tracing along the lines of the reflected image (218). If it is desirable to draw on a transparent material, proceed as before, but place a piece of opaque white paper under the transparent surface on which the drawing is to be made.

GRID DRAWING

An easy way to reduce and enlarge existing drawings, symbols, letters, and so forth is by the squaring method. In effect, the original image is subdivided through a grid pattern into smaller, less complex areas. This enables a person with little or no drawing experience to reproduce the small squared sections of the drawing one at a time and, upon its completion, have effectively reproduced a rather complex image in any size desired from a direct reproduction to one either smaller or larger than the original.

The first step in the squaring process is to lay out a square grid pattern (219) over the image to be reproduced. The size of the squares will be determined by the complexity of the original, as well as the experience of the artist. Light pencil lines for the grid will make it easier to follow the lines of the image. A grid (220) of the desired proportion is next drawn

on the surface on which the drawing is to be made. If the grid lines are erased after the drawing is completed, this may serve as the final product. However, if it is desirable to trace the finished drawing onto some other surface, tracing paper will serve as a good intermediate material upon which to place the drawing. If squared graph paper of the desired size can be obtained, the drawing of an original grid will be eliminated. After the grid is completed (221), transpose lines from the original drawing square by square. Lettering the border squares may help in maintaining the orientation. Trace the image (222) onto the desired surface. Clean up the basic lines of the drawing, and render them in the desired medium, filling in the shading and details as desired.

Often it is impossible or undesirable to draw the grid lines directly on the original. A simple time-saving aid can be made by scratching grid lines on a clear

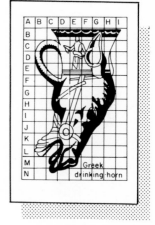

219

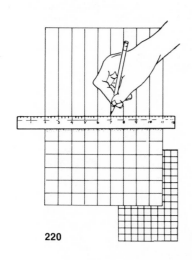

220

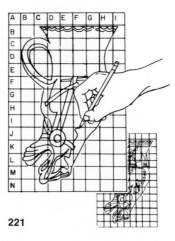

221

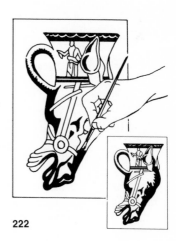

222

piece of acetate with a sharp stylus (223). It may be desirable to make several sheets having various-sized grids. By rubbing crayon or wax pencil into these etched lines, they become more visible. These acetate sheets may then serve as a grid over any printed visual without damaging the original material (224). At this point, proceed as before with the drawing process.

In order to make drawings from three-dimensional objects, a simple grid frame can be constructed. Small brads or tacks are inserted at a desired uniform distance around the opening of a frame (225). The head of each brad is allowed to protrude at least 1/8 inch (226). Elastic string or rubber bands are stretched between protruding nail heads to form a square grid (227). It is often desirable to use smaller grids when working with complex subject matter. Therefore, when making the frame, make sure that the intervals between the nails are rather small to allow for stretching the string to form various-sized grids.

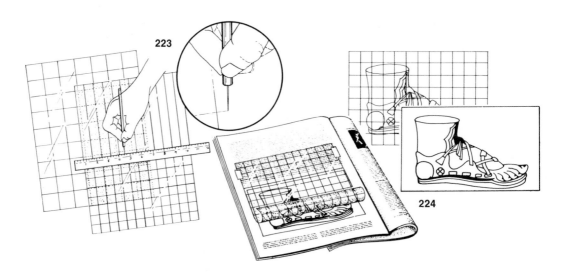

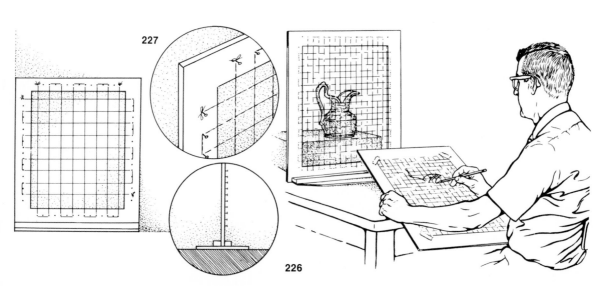

PROCEDURES FOR GRID DRAWING

In the process of drawing from an original squared picture, it is important to analyze the basic form of the object and determine which lines will be of greatest value when reproducing this imagery. An actual photograph (228) has been used here to demonstrate how this problem might be approached. First, it is important to choose only those lines in the object that will give the most meaning. Often, the inexperienced person will attempt to reproduce the lines of an image without really understanding their function. One of the valuable by-products of drawing is the fact that, as the drawing is evolving, the artist must constantly analyze and understand the relative value of each line in contributing to the image formation. This is especially important when the final drawing is to be used for instructional purposes. The drawer must continually ask himself: Where does this line come from, where does it go, and what purpose does it serve? Even though the continuity of a line is obstructed by objects in the foreground, it is important to understand the continuity or flow of the line as it forms the image. An example of this is the line forming the folds of skin that pass behind the ear in the illustration. In reproducing the head of this rhinoceros, it is important to develop a feeling of solidity in the massive head. The ears

must be cylindrical, with a cone-shaped opening. Lines showing the heavy folds of flesh are an important element in translating this photograph into a drawing. The thick folds of flesh around the nostril opening also add valuable information. In (229) black lines have been used to indicate some of the important lines in the photograph. Note in (230) how a few carefully chosen lines without shading give a feeling of the dimensionality of the ear. The grid (231) illustrates one method of locating the exact position of each line. As the arrows indicate, the draftsman first locates, by use of the grid, points of orientation. These usually fall on the grid lines. After this is accomplished, a smooth, flowing line is then used to connect the dots. After the drawing is inked in, the dots are erased. Note that even the invisible lines are drawn in (behind the ear) to help keep a smooth flow in the form being drawn. Of course, those which do not make a contribution to the final drawing are removed.

230

231

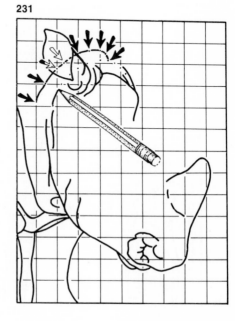

228

229

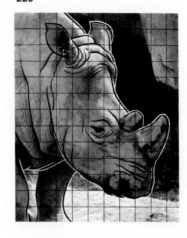

VARIATIONS OF THE PROCEDURES

Other uses, beyond simple enlarging or reducing of a drawing, may be made of the squaring process. By using grids drawn in perspective, flat pictorial images may be drawn in perspective (232). Perspective grid paper may either be developed by the user or be purchased from drafting supply stores. Grids drawn on irregular surfaces may be a great help when attempting to draw images that must appear to lie on the irregular contour of the surface. The fish design illustrated is shown on three different surfaces (233).

Distortion may be valuable in visualization. Several examples are shown. Horizontal grid distortion gives this cartoon character (234) a rugged, husky appearance by broadening the chest (235). The character takes on a thin, wiry appearance (236) when variations on the vertical grid are used. Note that the grids in areas A, B, C, D, and E all vary in size. Distortion, if carefully planned, can lead to very effective visualization.

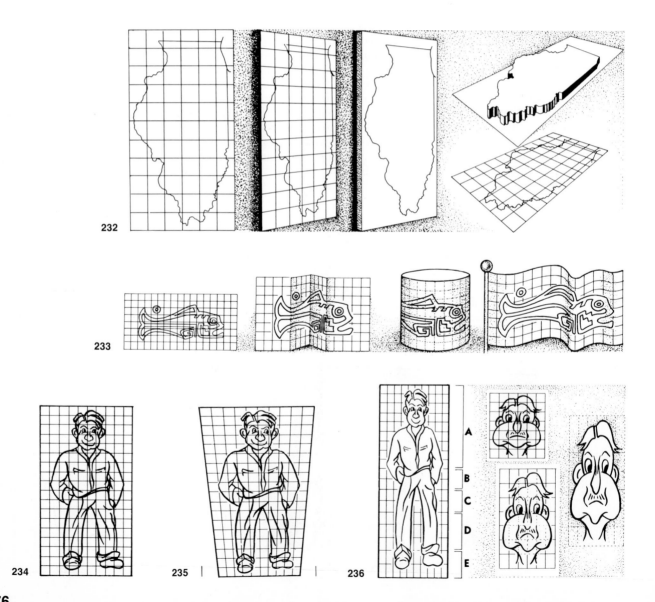

232

233

234

235

236

ENLARGING AND REDUCING VISUALS WITH A PANTOGRAPH

A pantograph is a simple drawing device used to make enlarged or reduced reproductions of drawings. It is made of four wood, metal, or plastic bars containing a series of holes so calibrated that by hinging these bars together at certain predetermined points, about twenty to forty different ratios in enlargement or reduction may be realized, depending on the particular model pantograph being used.

When working with the pantograph, a sufficiently large, smooth working surface is essential. If a drawing board is being used (237), the pivot point of the device (a) should be mounted firmly at the lower left-hand corner. Some pantographs have a simple clamping device which clamps to the edge of the board, and others are fastened by thumbtacks or more premanently mounted with nails.

To enlarge a drawing, the tracer point is attached at (b). At position (c) is located the pencil holder. How the device is operated depends upon the operator. Some people prefer to use the left hand to guide the tracing pin over the original drawing while the right hand guides the pencil. As illustrated, the tracing pin is guided by the right hand and the pencil is left free to make the enlarged drawing. In this case it is always wise to use a soft pencil lead to ensure a clean tracing. With some practice, a good reproduction can be made. It is important to guide the tracing pin smoothly to avoid exaggerated irregularities in the enlarged pencil drawing.

To reduce a drawing (238), the position of the pencil and the tracing pin is reversed. The pencil will be at (b), and the tracing pin will be at point (c). If an exact-size reproduction is desired, locate the pivot point at (b) and the tracing pin at (a) with the pencil at position (c). When it is necessary to change the pantograph to different size ratios, the connecting points at (d) and (e) are moved to the desired ratio points.

ENLARGING VISUALS WITH THE RUBBER BAND TECHNIQUE

A simple and effective enlarging device can be made from [see (239)] a pushpin (a) or suction cup (b), a long piece of good-quality rubber band (c), a small wedge-shaped pointer (d), and a pencil (e) or ball-point pen. The rubber band

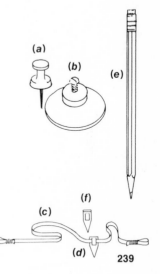

239

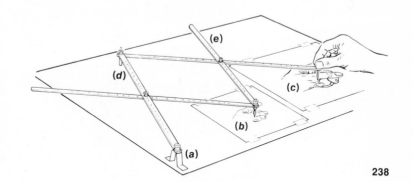

238

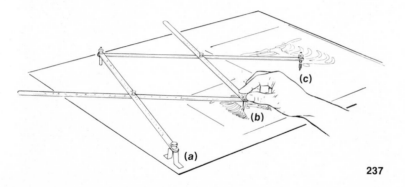

237

should be of good quality and very elastic. The length of the band needed is dependent on its elasticity and the size of enlargements desired. On both ends of the rubber band, form a small loop by folding the ends back and fastening them with narrow strips of tape or string. The loops should be small enough so that they will fit tightly around the pencil and the pivot post, whether it be a suction cup or pushpin. Cut a small wedge-shaped pointer as shown in the illustration (f) from stiff paper or lighweight aluminum. A U-shaped cut in the upper portion will serve as a small clip to hold it onto the rubber band.

The sizes of enlargements can be figured quite accurately with this device (240). If the guide pointer (b) is placed midway between (a) and (c), the enlargement will be approximately two times. If the distance between (a) and (b) is one-fourth the distance between (a) and (c), the enlargement will be four times. Thus it is easy to set up a simple scale to help determine the setting for the guide

pointer on the rubber band. Set up the original copy and the surface on which the enlargement is to be made, as shown in (241). The tip of the pointer should be just a little short of touching the paper surface when the pencil is in drawing position. Being sure that the pencil is absolutely vertical at all times, trace the original sketch with the pointer. Do not watch the drawing hand, but keep your eye on the pointer at all times. With a little practice, you will be able to execute excellent drawings by this method. After the drawing is completed and any small irregularities are corrected, the drawing is ready to use.

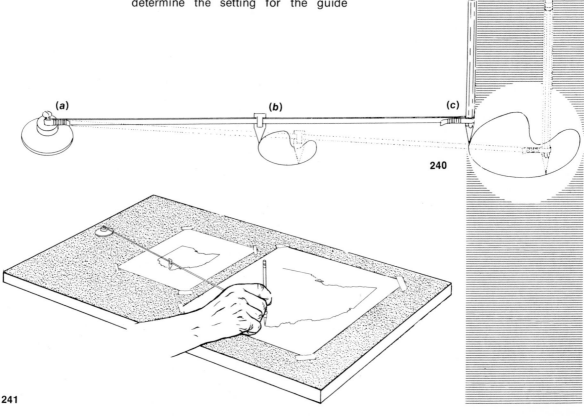

(a)   (b)   (c)

240

241

PHOTOSKETCHING TECHNIQUES

Often it is more desirable, or even necessary, to have a line or high-contrast drawing rather than an actual photograph for a visual presentation (242). This is often the case when developing masters or paste-up copy for various types of reproduction, such as used in the diazo, thermocopy, photographic silk-screen, offset, letterpress, electronic stencil, spirit, and other duplicating processes used as printed or projected visuals. For the person with minimal art training who desires to make his or her own illustrations, the photosketching process may be a great aid. Even the professional artist may find this a useful way to expedite routine assignments or effect exact reproduction in size and detail.

By this method of drawing, the beginner can obtain very acceptable results. With some training and practice, he will find the drawing possibilities almost limitless, ranging from a simple outline drawing to one complete with shading. It is important to remember that with this method of illustration it is possible to omit or add detail; to clarify images that were indistinct or too dark or light to be seen on the original photograph; to emphasize or de-emphasize parts of the imagery; to lose identity, as in the case of people appearing in the illustration; and to use an illustration which may in its original form not have been usable because of its poor photographic quality. By using any of a wide range of pens and brushes, almost any effect in line drawing can be obtained, from the simple line to stipple and crosshatched shading effects. The picture of the white

242

243

244

rhinoceros (243) has been photo-sketched (244 to 246) using different drawing techniques with treatment ranging from a simple outline drawing to one complete in all detail.

The photosketches in (247) show a variety of subject matter treated in different ways. These illustrations were drawn by pen and brush or by a combination of both.

INSTRUCTIONS

1   Using waterproof India ink, sketch directly on the surface of the photograph. Although photographs with a glossy surface may be used, the ink will adhere better to one having a matte surface. If possible, it is recommended that a light photographic print be used. Detail in dark areas of a photograph will be easier to see if placed on a light box. Generally, the light passing through the back of the print will reveal detail hard to see by reflected light. If the glossy surface of the print tends to resist ink, or if it has oily fingerprints on its surface, rub the surface thoroughly with baking soda. If a mistake is made in the drawing, the ink may be removed immediately by wiping it off with damp cotton, or it may be dried and painted out later with white opaque.

2   Allow the ink to dry thoroughly. This may require at least thirty minutes. Often ink that appears to be dry may

need more time. This is important since the image will be placed in liquid during the bleaching process (248).

3   Bleaching is the next step in the process. Regular iodine, procured from the local drugstore, may be used for the bleach solution. This iodine, as purchased, may be diluted with 2 to 3 parts of water. Place the photosketch into a pan of iodine solution (a) with the image side up. *Avoid touching the ink image during the entire bleaching process.* Be sure that the entire surface of the print is covered with iodine solution. Slight agitation helps speed up the process. The time the print remains in the bleach depends upon the characteristics of the photograph as well as the strength of the bleach solution.

4   When all traces of the dark photographic image have been replaced by one that is a dark brownish orange, remove the photosketch from the iodine solution and rinse the excess iodine off in cool water (b).

5   Place the print into a pan containing photographic fixing bath (hypo) (c). This chemical can be obtained at any photographic supply store. The solution will bleach out the remaining iodine image, leaving a clean black and white drawing. Be sure that all traces of the yellow stain are removed before removing the print from the solution.

245

246

247

6 Place the photosketch in cool running water for about five minutes to remove the remaining chemicals (d).

7 Although this print can be dried on a regular photographic dryer, it may also be air-dried by simply laying it out on a clean piece of paper for a period of time (e). If care is taken, excess water may be blotted off the sketch by using newsprint or some other absorbent material. Some curling of the sketch during drying can be discouraged by placing a heavy porous cloth on top to straighten and hold it in a flat position.

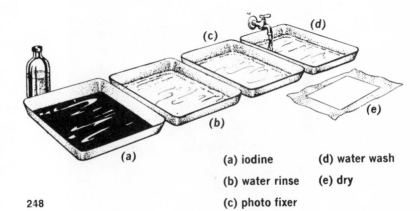

248

(a) iodine
(b) water rinse
(c) photo fixer
(d) water wash
(e) dry

The example in (249) shows a pencil drawing made from a continuous-tone photograph by the photosketching technique. It is possible to draw over a continuous-tone photograph with lead pencil and through the bleaching process convert the photograph to a pencil drawing. This may be necessary when changes or corrections are to be made on the original photograph, but it is not desirable to convert the illustration to a line drawing. By using various grades of pencils, a good range of gray tones may be obtained, giving all the characteristics of a continuous-tone picture. When using the pencil technique for photosketching, you will find it desirable to use a matte-surfaced photograph, because the rough surface will pick up the pencil carbon; it is almost impossible to draw on a glossy-surfaced photograph. The process of bleaching the photograph is the same when using pencil as it is when using ink.

There are times when it is desirable to photosketch only selected sections of a photograph to emphasize or clarify detail in a given area: because of poor lighting, distracting elements, or imperfections on the image being photographed, details may be difficult to see. Bleaching of these areas of the photograph is possible through the use of rubber cement, often used for mounting flat pictures. Any area of the photograph

coated with this cement will not be affected by the bleaching solution. Thin the rubber cement so that it will flow freely from the brush. Good-quality cement will be made of genuine rubber and be very clear. This makes it rather difficult to see when it is being applied. To assure complete coverage of the area to be masked, a small amount of mimeograph ink or dark oil stain added to the rubber cement will make it easier to see. Apply two coats of rubber cement to assure complete coverage. In (250), (A) indicates the areas to be masked with rubber cement and (B), the area that will be photosketched. In (251) we see the final results after bleaching.

PRINTED ART AIDS

CHARTING (DRAFTING) TAPES

Charting tapes include a wide variety of special tapes designed mainly for drafting and chart making. The use of these tapes has opened up a fresh new approach to a drafting task that in the past required many hours to perform. And the wide choice of tapes, many having different basic characteristics, enables one to produce visual materials of high quality without professional training. Charting tapes include color, shading, and symbol tapes in color and black and white. The printed surface of the

249

251

tapes is either transparent or opaque, either glossy or dull. The dull surface is preferred when the finished product is to be photographed. Tapes with a heat-resistant adhesive are designed for the preparation of art that is to be reproduced in a heat-type copying machine.

Charting tapes range in width from $\frac{1}{64}$ inch to 2 inches. The wide-width tapes (252) are ideal for making bar graphs; the narrow-width tapes (253) are excellent for producing lines of various patterns.

Special tape dispensers are designed to produce tape lines with the aid of a straightedge (254). Flexible tapes in narrow widths can be used to make curved tape lines with the aid of an irregular (French) curve or an adjustable curve (255). When circles are to be "drawn," the flexible tapes can be attached to a special tape compass to produce tape circles of varied diameters.

Special tapes have been designed for use in the preparation of plant and office layouts, printed circuit designs, and many other special tasks. A wide variety of border-design tapes is available for artwork requiring professional-looking borders.

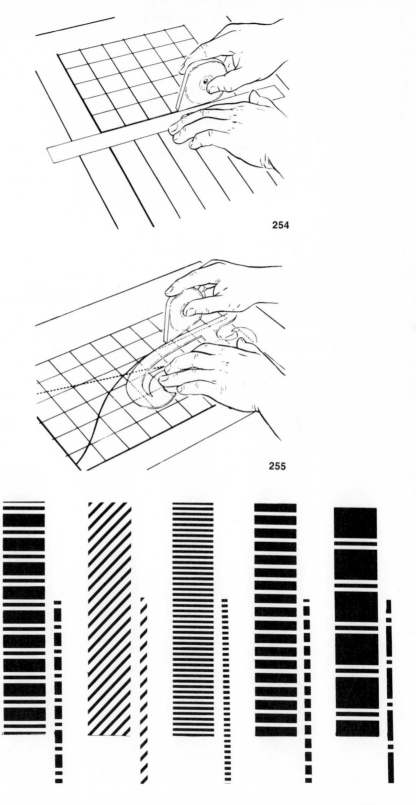

254

255

252

253

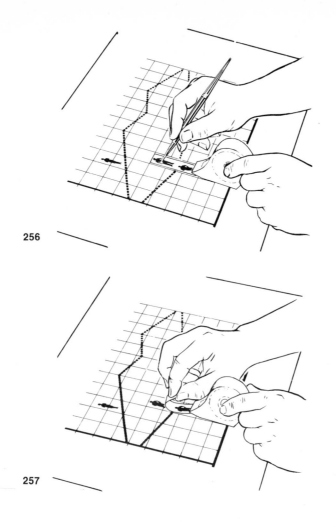

256

257

Symbol tapes, both adhesive-back and dry transfer, cover a variety of subject areas such as transportation, buildings, and human figures. Several manufacturers offer custom-made symbol tapes as a special service.

Dry transfer symbol tapes are unique in that the symbols transfer from the tape to the drawing surface when a pencil or ball-point pen is rubbed over the symbol (256), and as the tape is lifted (257), the symbol remains on the drawing surface.

SHADING (TEXTURE) SHEETS

To help the user bypass extensive amounts of monotonous, repetitive drawing, adhesive-backed acetate sheets have been developed on which are printed repetitive opaque patterns (258). These sheets may be backed with a wax-type or pressure-sensitive, heat-resistant adhesive. Shading sheets used in heat copying machines must be of the heat-resistant variety. Shading sheets may be purchased with a glossy or matte finish. If the material is to be photographed, nonreflective matte finish is preferred. In some cases it is desirable to use these materials directly on transparencies. Should this be a requirement, the clear, transparent, heat-resistant material is recommended. It is important to

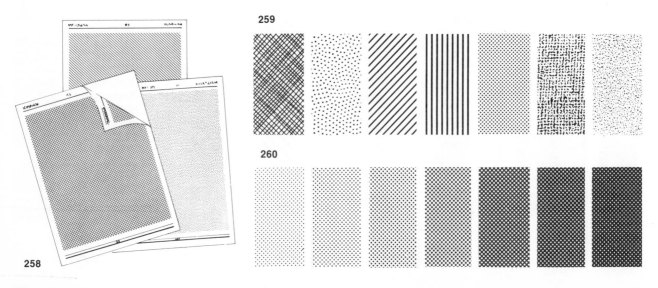

258

259

260

place any unused material back on the support sheet for storage in a cool place.

The great variety of patterns (259) that can be obtained includes crosshatch, stipple, diagonal lines, vertical lines, dot patterns, weaves, textures, and many others. Special patterns have been developed for draftsmen working in such areas as geography, geology, and architecture. Standard and graduated dot-screen patterns (260) may be obtained in a variety of line and density relationships. If shading sheets are to be used, it is very important to choose a pattern appropriate for the visual being constructed.

With the shading sheet still on its backing, lay it in position over the area of the illustration to be shaded, and, being careful not to cut into the backing paper, cut an area of the shading material slightly larger than the area to be shaded (261). Peel the material from its backing. Place it over the drawing, lowering it onto the surface of the illustration (adhesive side down) so that air pockets and wrinkles do not form (262). Be sure to have a sharp cutting instrument. Carefully cut around the image, and peel off the excess material (263). Press the shading material down for good adhesion. Other areas may be shaded in a similar manner.

Two variations should be mentioned. First, some shading materials are available which have the image printed on the top surface of the shading sheet. This permits the user to remove small areas of the pattern by etching off the surface with a sharp instrument. In this way, fine detail can be added that would be extremely difficult to add if the material had to be removed by cutting. The second variation involves shading and texture sheet material of the dry transfer variety. When using this material, you must remove the printed sheet from its backing and place it over the area of the visual that is to be shaded. When the surface of the sheet is burnished, the printed pattern is transferred to the visual image (264). As the sheet is lifted from the visual, the printed pattern remains (265).

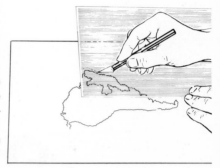

261

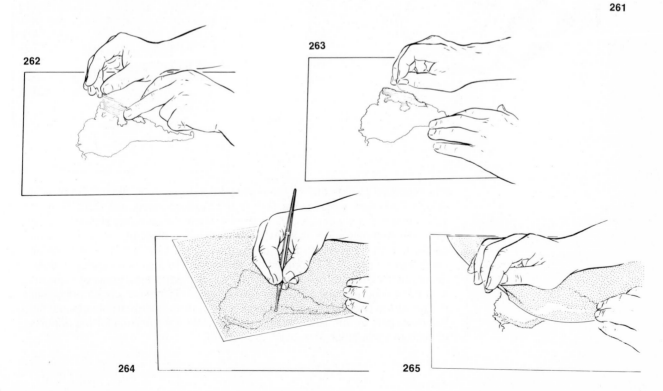

262

263

264

265

85

Wherever shading and texture patterns are needed, these adhesive-backed printed sheets can save time as well as furnish sharp, clean copy for a visual illustration.

CLIP ART

When the person producing visual materials does not possess special drawing skill, or when time is a factor in the preparation of art, clip art may be the answer. Clip art is line and tone ready-to-use illustrations covering every practical subject classification from A to Z. Many clip-art books (266) and sheets (267) contain symbols, decorative borders, and so forth. Several companies offer a subscription service through which subscribers receive updated and newly designed clip art periodically.

Some clip art is available in the form of sheets. These have a variety of drawings in various sizes and positions which can be manipulated with drawings or lettering from other sources to produce an original for electronic stencils, thermocopy, photographic, or other forms of reproduction. In addition, old drawings, covering a wide range of subject matter, have been collected and reprinted in book form to serve as a source of ideas for the person having need for this type of art.

266

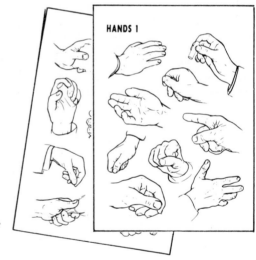

267

It is important to note that all the printed art aids, such as clip art, are closely related. Too often printed tapes, texture and shading sheets, and clip art are set off in separate, distinct categories, when actually they are very similar. First of all, these materials serve as some form of art aid in paste-up art. They may all be printed on transparent, translucent, or opaque base material. With some exceptions, most of these printed art aids adhere to a working surface (drawing paper, illustration board) with similar types of adhesives. Some of these art aids adhere by the dry transfer method: the art is printed on a translucent plastic carrier sheet and transfers to a working surface with the aid of a pencil, ball-point pen, or burnisher. Several companies offer a service for the printing of custom art in color or in black and white.

Printed sheets of repetitive silhouette visuals (268) are available in a variety of subject areas. These sheets usually contain a choice of four or five sizes of visuals. They are ideal for use where repetitive symbols are required. Clip art also includes squares, circles, arrows, asterisks, stars, and so forth (269).

The paste-up of a simple poster might include a variety of art aids and techniques. In (270), the frame is printed tape, the map is hand-traced on lightweight paper, the shaded area is from a shading sheet, the zebra is clip art, and the spears of grass are hand-drawn. All these aids and techniques have been combined to create an original which can be reproduced by a variety of methods (271).

ART PASTE-UP TECHNIQUES

The term *paste-up* refers to art prepared in paste-up form specifically for any number of reproduction techniques (thermocopy, photocopy, electronic stencil copy, etc.). The true art of paste-up requires some professional know-how. However, an attempt has been made here to simplify the technique.

As a preliminary to the paste-up, it is a good idea to prepare a rough draft of what is intended to be the finished paste-up. This will help you visualize how the finished art will look and will serve as a guide in fitting all the art, lettering, shading, and so forth together on the finished paste-up. The "rough" should be done on paper the size of the finished art.

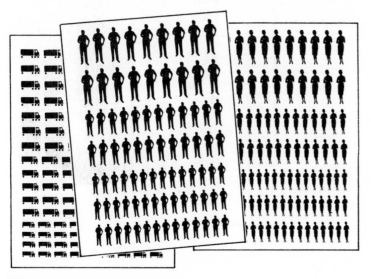

268

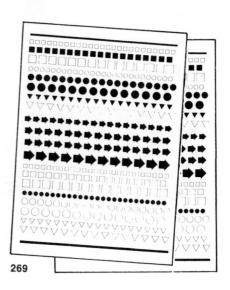

269

270

271

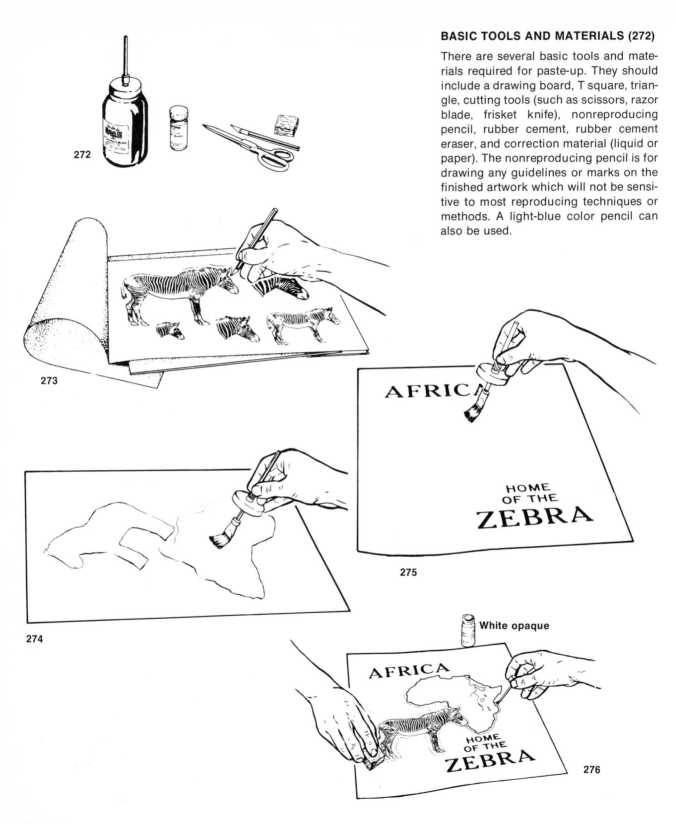

BASIC TOOLS AND MATERIALS (272)

There are several basic tools and materials required for paste-up. They should include a drawing board, T square, triangle, cutting tools (such as scissors, razor blade, frisket knife), nonreproducing pencil, rubber cement, rubber cement eraser, and correction material (liquid or paper). The nonreproducing pencil is for drawing any guidelines or marks on the finished artwork which will not be sensitive to most reproducing techniques or methods. A light-blue color pencil can also be used.

272

273

274

AFRICA

HOME OF THE ZEBRA

275

White opaque

AFRICA

HOME OF THE ZEBRA

276

Instructions

Cut out the art (273) (clip art is illustrated here) with one of the cutting tools. Note that protective cardboard is being used to prevent cutting the next sheet in the clip-art book.

2 Apply rubber cement to the reverse side of all paste-up art requiring adhesive (274). Next, apply cement to the areas on the working surface (paper, cardboard) where the art is to go (275). Allow both cemented surfaces to dry. The rubber cement should be thinned, 4 parts rubber cement to 1 part rubber cement thinner (solvent). This will allow the cement to flow freely from the brush.

3 Attach the art to the working surface (276). Remove excessive cement from around the visual with a rubber cement eraser, or rub off with a clean finger. Opaque out the cut line around the visual with white correction liquid. See pages 84 to 86 for instructions on adding shading.

4 The paste-up is ready for reproduction (277). Instructions for paste-up, related to a specific reproduction technique or method, should be followed very closely. What is presented here is intended only to be general instructions.

POLARIZED TRANSPARENCIES

A new dimension can be added to overhead projection transparencies with the use of polarizing (Polarmotion) materials (278). Almost any existing or new original overhead transparency can be made into an exciting instructional medium. Polarizing is an invaluable technique in conveying concepts of sequence, flow, and cause and effect. Even subject matter that is considered static in content can be made more interesting and exciting with the application of polarized materials. In addition to polarized material applied directly to the surface of the transparency, all that is needed is a manual- or motor-driven polarized spinner; the result is a projected transparency with "motion."

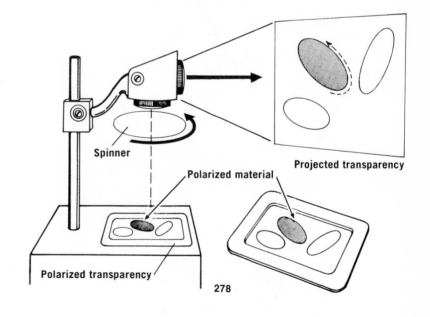

Spinner

Projected transparency

Polarized material

Polarized transparency

278

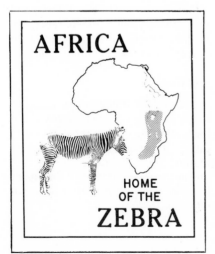

AFRICA

HOME OF THE ZEBRA

277

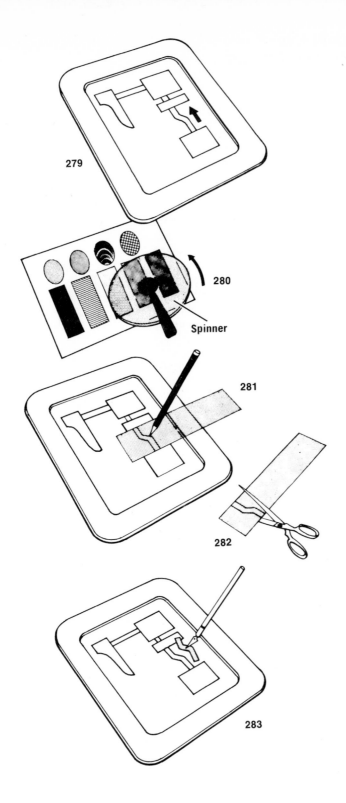

279

280

Spinner

281

282

283

Instructions

1 Place the finished transparency, less the polarizing material, on a viewing light box (light table or tracing board) or on the stage of the overhead projector. This will provide a light source for analyzing the transparency for polarizing and for the actual placement of the material (279).

2 Select the desired polarizing (Polarmotion) material with the aid of a manual spinner. This can be done by placing the sample sheet (Polarmotion demonstration plate) on the stage of the projector or by holding it up to a light source and rotating spinner (280).

3 Place the desired motion material over the area to which motion is to be added; and while holding it firmly in place, take a pencil and trace an outline in the desired shape. Use a straightedge where straight cuts are desired. Press hard enough with the pencil to make a clear outline for final cutting (281).

4 Cut out the motion material with a pair of sharp scissors. Before removing the backing sheet, place the material on the transparency area to be animated to check the fit (282).

5 Remove the backing sheet, and with the point of the cutting knife wrapped with a piece of pressure-sensitive tape (sticky side out), pick up the motion material (knife tip on top) and position on the transparency as desired. Press material firmly in place; it will bond on contact (283).

Helpful Hints

1 Reversal film (Kodalith or negative transparencies) usually makes the best polarized transparencies.

2 Design transparencies with "motion" in mind.

3 The larger the motion area, the easier it is to work with and it is more effective.

4 Keep the design as simple as possible.
5 Use sharp cutting instruments. If possible, work under a magnifying glass. It will make cutting much easier.
6 Use bold, vivid colors that have brilliance. Diluted colors tend to wash out, and dark colors tend to mask out the motion action.

7 Use a polarizing spinner or sunglasses when working. It will help to see the motion design while laying out and cutting the motion material.

Detailed instructions and information on this technique can be obtained from manufacturers and distributors of polarizing equipment and materials.

5 COLORING TECHNIQUES

Pens, Pencils, and Markers
Watercolors
Aerosol-Can Colors
Airbrush Techniques
Transparent Color Adhesive-backed Sheets and Tapes

The application of coloring or shading, in one form or another, adds an exciting dimension to visual instructional media. Although no attempt will be made in this section to relate the psychological effect of certain colors upon the learning process, the tested coloring and shading techniques which make possible the application of coloring or shading to practically all types of instructional media will be discussed and illustrated. Visual instructional media which may require color or shading, or whose visual effectiveness may be enhanced by these techniques, include charts; graphs; maps; diagrams; posters; illustrations; photographs; television, motion-picture, filmstrip, and slide titles; overhead projection transparencies; and duplication materials.

Each of the coloring and shading techniques included in this section has certain characteristics which may limit its application to specific types of instructional media. These characteristics will be brought out in the treatment of each technique. It cannot be overemphasized that color or shading should not be used mainly for the sake of adding color or shading to an instructional material. Moreover, color or shading can be overused and, therefore, can lower the quality of the instructional material.

For the novice lacking the know-how of applying colors, color and shading ideas taken from magazines, newspapers, brochures, posters, commercial transparencies, and other printed materials can provide answers to coloring and shading problems.

PENS, PENCILS, AND MARKERS

Many methods can be used to add color to a visual. *It is extremely important to study the characteristics of the color ingredient used* since the terms pastel, chalk, crayon, and pencil are all interrelated and rather difficult to define (284). Through experimentation one must find which color characteristics work best for a particular situation. The wax crayon commonly used by grade school children differs greatly from crayons which can be dipped in turpentine so as to look like an oil when applied, and they both differ from the crayon that, after application, can be blended with water on a brush to give the effect of watercolor. All types of crayons may generally be classified *opaque,* and yet when creating handmade 3¼- by 4-inch slides was a popular practice, slide crayons were available that projected a *transparent*

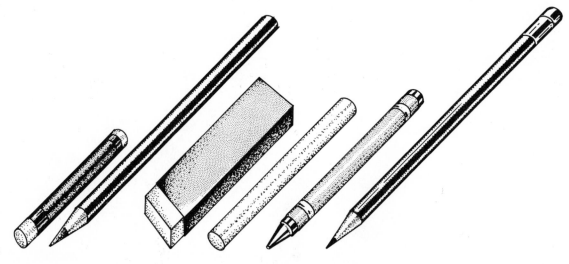

284

color image on the screen when used on frosted glass.

These color pastels, chalks, crayons, and pencils vary from soft to very firm, permitting the artist to execute a range of effects from broad, flat surfaces to sharp, detailed drawing (285). Remember that when soft pastels, chalks, or pencils are used on posters, charts, etc., the danger of the image smearing is inevitable; consequently a method of protection must be devised by either covering it with an acetate sheet, laminating it, or spraying it with some form of acrylic spray or fixative. The latter two methods may, in the case of a chalk or pastel surface, affect the coloration. The number of colors available will vary greatly from one variety of pastel, crayon, pencil, or chalk to the next.

With the rise in popularity of the overhead projector a great number of pencils were developed containing a waxy drawing substance; they are still widely used. A frequent source of confusion is the fact that their leads come in red, yellow, white, and other colors in addition to black and yet produce an opaque, black image on the screen due to the opaque, waxy base. The same thing is true of "China" marking pencils and all-purpose marking pencils. Pencils *are* available, however, that will write on acetate and project *in color* on the screen.

Watercolor pencils available in a large range of colors may be used on frosted acetate. When the drawing is completed, the surface must be sprayed with acrylic lacquer or a similar material to transparentize it (286). This will make the image projectable in color. Not all colors project equally well, and so it is advisable to choose, by sampling, those colors that work best.

Fine- and medium-tipped markers may be purchased for use on transparencies in a variety of brilliant dyes and inks. Some are waterproof, and some may be removed with water. Some may simply be wiped off, while others require special solvent for removal. The felt-tipped pen or marker is very similar and is commonly used for making both opaque materials and transparencies. Some contain transparent watercolor and are valuable for tinting photographic transparencies such as are produced by the high-contrast method. Some felt markers may be refilled, and they have a choice of interchangeable tips, including sharp, chisel, broad, and square (287).

The variety and possible use of pencils, pastels, chalks, felt markers, etc., are so great that only by experimenting will a person be able to choose the most desirable tool for the particular need. Beware

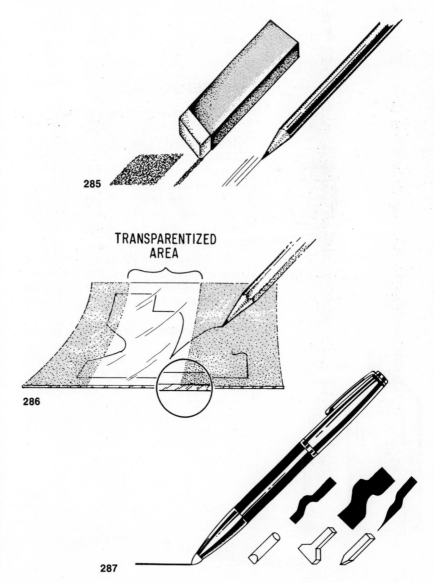

285

TRANSPARENTIZED AREA

286

287

of undesirable characteristics such as fading, smearing, and bleeding, and be very conscious that some coloring methods permit ease of removal, while some are impossible to remove or change after they have been applied. This is especially true of acetate ink, which binds very tightly with the base acetate. Also remember that the number of colors which will project well in any one system is often limited and that the choice of these colors will vary to some degree from one manufacturer to another. Pastels, chalks, and pencils may be obtained in graduations of gray, permitting execution of work for black and white reproduction.

WATERCOLORS

Transparent watercolors in their many brilliant hues have a variety of uses in the production of visual media. They may be purchased in both liquid and dry states. Liquid watercolors may be obtained in concentrated and diluted form in a number of sizes (288). Felt-point markers containing transparent watercolor are available (289). The colors are brilliant but somewhat limited in shade selection. The feature of the felt point is its ease in use and storage. Food colors available at the local supermarket, although very limited in range of color, are also excellent transparent colors.

Dry transparent watercolors may be obtained in booklet form (290). A high concentration of dry color is adhered to paper pages. When the paper is placed in water, a clear, brilliant liquid color is produced. The depth of this color is determined by the amount of water used. Transparent watercolors are also availa-

ble in dry cake form to be dissolved in water. They work well on paper surfaces; however, in many cases they are not desirable for use on transparent projected material.

The fine art of watercoloring demands extensive instruction and practice. However, by following a few simple instructions, the novice can make excellent use of transparent watercolors in the preparation of materials. This is especially true when one is working on treated surfaces such as the emulsion found on photographic films and papers. The color may be applied with either a regular watercolor brush (291) or a cotton applicator (292). If large areas on transparent or opaque surfaces have to be tinted in solid or graduated color, the use of the airbrush or transparent color in aerosol cans will greatly facilitate the process.

TINTING PHOTOGRAPHIC MATERIALS

Although the hand-tinting of photographic paper prints and slides with transparent watercolor is an extremely old technique, it is still very popular. Color may be added to continuous-tone and high-contrast photographic images on both film and paper. It will be easier, however, for the novice to tint high-contrast images where solid areas of color are desired, because tinting continuous-tone materials demands more knowledge of the application of transparent watercolor. The tinting technique is based on the principle that the photographic emulsion surface will absorb liquid watercolor. The resulting colors are brilliant, transparent, and quite permanent.

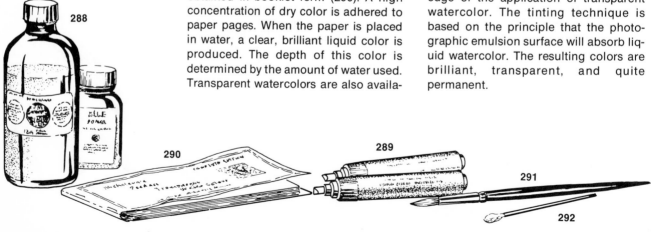

288

290

289

291

292

When tinting a photographic print or transparency, you must sometimes do masking to prevent the color from spreading beyond the desired area. A number of different kinds of liquid masking materials can be used. However, rubber cement can be adapted easily for this use. In a clean container (293) place a small amount of pure, clear rubber cement (294). To this add sufficient rubber cement thinner (295) so that the cement will run freely from the stirring stick. Because the cement is quite transparent and consequently difficult to see when applying, some color must be added. A small amount of oil wood stain or mimeograph ink (296) will furnish the necessary tinting. Be sure to mix well before using. This mixture may be stored in an airtight brown bottle for future use. Thinning may be necessary at a later date.

This masking material may be used on either transparent or opaque photographic materials. The photographic-paper print or the transparency may be tinted in either the positive (297) or negative form (298). Although there are exceptions, the positive image tends to be a bit more difficult to tint because of the problem of masking, which is often required. Many negative materials can be tinted with little or no use of masking.

It must be remembered in this regard that transparent watercolor placed on the black areas of a negative will not project on the screen because the black areas are opaque. Consequently only the color placed on the clear areas of the film will project or be visible to the eye.

The tinting of a positive transparent photographic film will be used as an example of this transparent watercolor tinting technique. Be sure to work on the emulsion (dull) side of the film. The emulsion surface must be free of all foreign matter such as wax or oil. Abrasions will also be detrimental to the tinting process, preventing proper absorption of the watercolor.

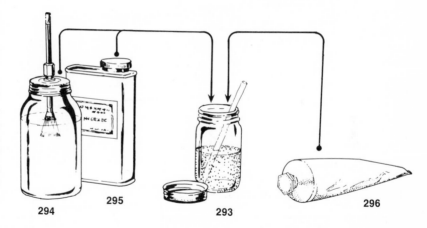

294   295   293   296

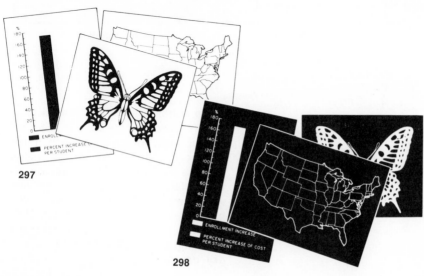

297

298

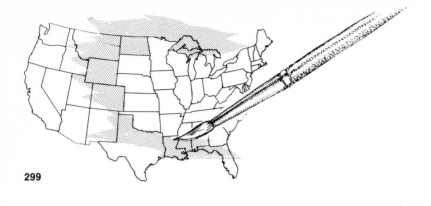

299

Instructions

First, mask the areas around the section of the film to be tinted with the rubber cement mixture (299). Allow the masking liquid to dry thoroughly. With a cotton applicator or brush, flood the unmasked area with generous amounts of liquid watercolor (300).

It is important to permit plenty of time for the watercolor to completely penetrate the emulsion. The color must be kept constantly moving to prevent dry spots from forming (301). When drying takes place, absorption is stopped and irregular tinting results. Complete saturation of the emulsion ensures an even tint over the entire area (302).

After three or four minutes, blot the film with a clean blotter to absorb any excess color that may be on the surface (303). This excess color if allowed to dry will appear opaque when projected. Wiping over the color area with a piece of

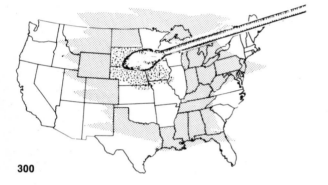

300

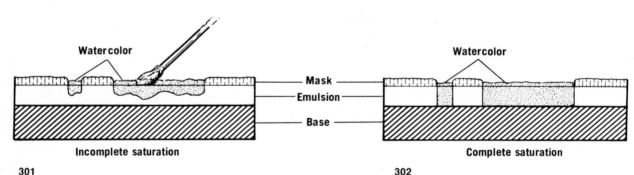

Watercolor

Mask
Emulsion
Base

Incomplete saturation

301

Watercolor

Complete saturation

302

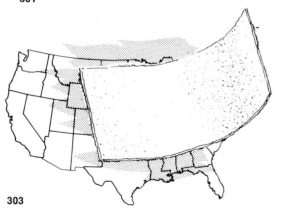

303

damp cotton will ensure removal of all excess liquid and dry color. If the color area appears uneven at this time, it may be because there was foreign matter such as oily fingerprints or wax on the film surface. This foreign matter will prevent complete absorption of the color, but the problem can often be solved by rewashing the photographic film and repeating the process. After the color is dry on the film, rub off the rubber cement mask (304). As many additional colors may be added as desired by using the same procedure. When this transparency is used for projection, it may be desirable to place a clear piece of acetate over the color surface for protection. Plastic spray may also be used to seal in the colors. Another common practice is to wipe the surface of the film with a very weak (3 percent) solution of acetic acid (vinegar). This will help set the colors in the emulsion surface, and the transparency will be ready for use (305).

AEROSOL-CAN COLORS

Along with the development of the aerosol spray can has come a new technique of applying coloring of all descriptions. Brilliant fluorescent colors, enamels, plastics, metallic finishes, dyes, and many other types of color are now available for application to a variety of surfaces. Even synthetic snowflakes in white and colors are available for special effects.

The aerosol can, with its fine spray, approximates the effects one can obtain with an airbrush. There are special handles that fit on any aerosol can that can be used to assist in the control of the spray. Replaceable aerosol cans fitted with a special control lever, spray tip, and bottle may be used to spray any paint that can be thinned enough for spraying. By combining these techniques of color application with the careful use of frisket and masking techniques, professional-looking effects can be obtained in the creation of attractive visuals in opaque or transparent form.

TRANSPARENT LIQUID COLOR (AEROSOL CAN)

For general or special use, the aerosol cans containing vivid transparent colors can be used to apply high-quality color to a variety of surfaces including acetate, paper, wood, glass, and metal. The color, when sprayed on a transparency, leaves little to be desired in the way of quality. Preparation for applying color to transparent or opaque materials is quite similar to the preparation for using an airbrush. Frisket paper may be used to protect those areas not to be colored. It is very important to be sure that the edges of the frisket are down extremely well since this rather thin dye may tend to run under small creases and folds in the frisket. As an alternative, a tinted rubber cement mask may be applied around

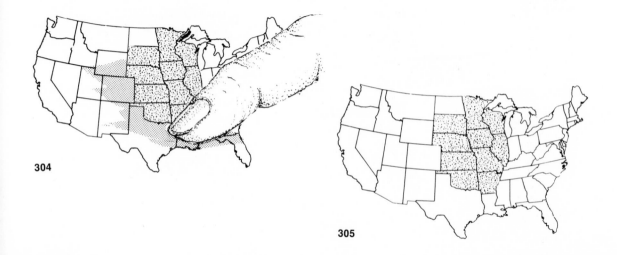

304

305

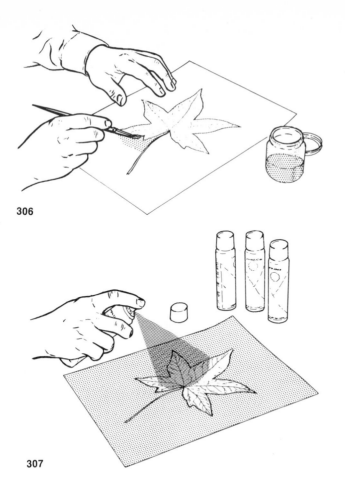

306

307

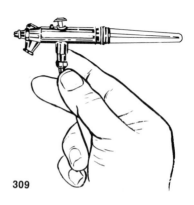

308

the image to be colored (306) and over all other areas to be protected from the spray. Rubber cement thinned to flow easily from a brush and tinted with a small amount of mimeograph ink or oil stain can be used as the masking material. When the rubber cement has thoroughly dried, spray on an even coating of the desired dye (307). If a smooth, solid area of color is desired, be sure to flood the area slightly with color. Be sure no wax or oil spots are on the area being tinted. Place the sprayed image on a dry, clean, level surface. In a short time the color will have dried. Remove the rubber cement by gently rolling it off with the tip of the finger. The dye may be removed with water, or it may be made permanent by spraying over it with plastic spray to complete the process (308). It is removable from hard, slick surfaces but not from porous surfaces.

AIRBRUSH TECHNIQUES

The airbrush is one of the most valuable tools for the commercial artist; it is equally valuable to those interested in the local production of visual instructional media. We might define the airbrush as a precision, penlike spraying device about the size of a fountain pen (309) connected by a hose to a controlla-

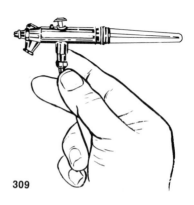

309

ble air supply which forces lightbodied ink, liquid colors, and paint from a small reservoir cup or bottle. A variety of models is available, covering a broad range of prices. The more expensive brushes are more precise, having very fine color and air-pressure control. These are designed to be used where fine, delicate detail is important. The less expensive airbrushes are good for the more general application of color. They have less complicated controls and tend to be easier to operate. Airbrushes are a valuable part of the producer's equipment. Airbrushing is simply another way of applying color to almost any surface whether opaque or transparent in nature. Often it is difficult to apply a smooth, even layer of color when using the more common methods of brush, swab, or felt marker. One of the advantages of the airbrush over these other methods of color application is that it *can* apply a smooth, even color over a broad area. Shading and blending of various colors can be done with ease. It may be used in combination with other drawing media for special effects. When internal and/or external stencils are used, complicated forms can be precisely tinted with color. Both opaque and transparent colors can be used in many forms such as inks, watercolors, alcohol colors, oil, and lacquer paints. Colors having impurities or abrasive qualities should not be used. The passing of fine grit or other abrasive material through the delicate tip of the airbrush will cause serious damage. Always check to see that the color is recommended for use in the airbrush. Colors that tend to coagulate or become lumpy will block the passage of paint through the tip of the brush, causing great difficulty. This problem can sometimes be overcome by carefully straining the paint through a fine cloth or filter before use.

The air supply needed to operate the airbrush may originate from any of a number of sources. The sources chosen will depend to a great extent upon cost, amount of use, and availability. One of the most common sources of air pressure is the air compressor (310). This is often a relatively small, portable electric unit so designed that it will give a steady, dependable flow of air to the brush. The flow of air must remain at a constant pressure with no fluctuations. Variations in air pressure will produce an uneven flow of color from the brush, causing difficulty for the operator. Special controls and gauges set the desired pressure from the air compressor. The air compressor costs more to purchase; however, it will operate for extended periods of time with little or no upkeep. A second source of air is the carbonic tank (311). It may be purchased in small sizes or in some cases rented from companies that service soda fountains. In many locations these tanks, if owned by the operator, will be refilled by the same companies at a nominal fee. They furnish an excellent source of pressure, and in cases where the airbrush is not used extensively, they are, economically speaking, a very practical source of pressure. A special gauge is attached to control the amount of pressure at all times. A third source of pressure is a small aerosol pressure tank (312). It is a 16-ounce aerosol can of propellant gas with a pressure-regulating valve. It contains enough pressure to operate an airbrush for one to three hours, depending on the size of the airbrush and the type of work to be done.

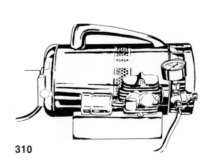

310

311

312

313

315

314

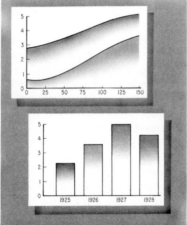

316

As with any technique of drawing or painting, learning to use the airbrush demands practice. It is, however, a technique which will permit the novice to create some simple, interesting effects (313, 314, 315). The use of stencils enables the operator to control the spread of the fine spray from the airbrush and permits the formation of intricate forms. A thin frisket paper or film with a special rubber-base adhesive on the back will serve to block out areas while the airbrush is in use. Simply peel the frisket from its backing sheet (316) and place it carefully over the image to be shaded or tinted (317). Be sure to leave plenty of protection around the area to be airbrushed so that any fine color mist will not tint the area of the drawing beyond the frisket. With a sharp tool cut along the outline of the area of the drawing that is to be tinted (318).

After the cutting is completed, remove the frisket from this area (319). Wipe the area free of any foreign matter. The area is now ready to be sprayed with the airbrush (320). When the desired effect is achieved, the piece of frisket can be replaced and another section removed, following the same procedure. This process can continue until all sections of the drawing are completed. Remove all frisket material and the shading or tinting process is completed (321).

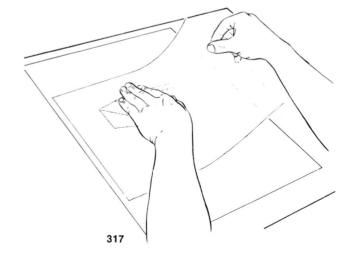

317

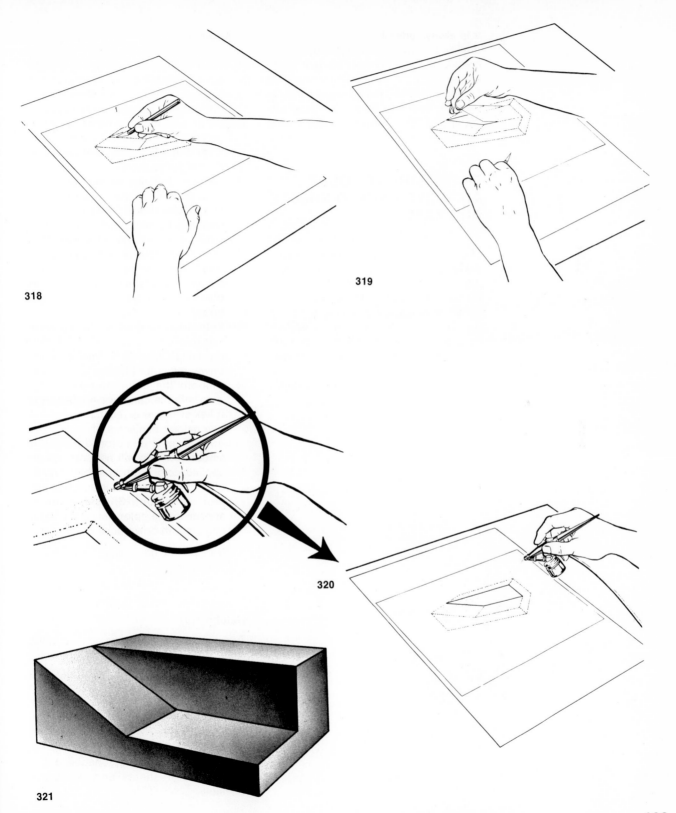

318

319

320

321

103

It is always advisable to work on good-quality cardboard during this process to ensure the least possible damage to the surface from the frisket adhesive and the cutting process. This procedure may be used for tinting or coloring photographic-paper prints as well as transparencies.

TRANSPARENT COLOR ADHESIVE-BACKED SHEETS AND TAPES

Vivid colors can be added to either side of positive- or negative-image transparencies and to the surface of opaque paper-surfaced materials by applying transparent color adhesive-backed sheets and tapes. These coloring materials are made up of vivid transparent color printed on the underside of a thin film with a pressure-sensitive adhesive back. They come in assorted colors, and some sheets and tapes even contain a texture pattern to add still another effect to color.

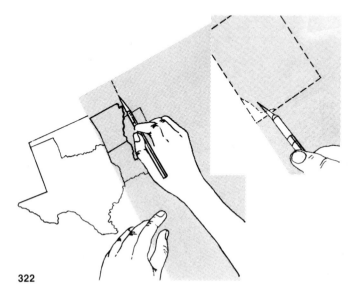

322

Instructions

1   With a cutting instrument (frisket knife, razor blade, etc.) score (cutting just through the color sheet) a section slightly larger than required for the area or image on which color is to go (322). Gently slide the point of the knife under the color sheet and peel off the cut section.

2   Position the cut section (adhesive side down) on the area or image (323). Care should be taken to position the color right the first time, since the adhesive of some color sheets will leave an adhesive residue when lifted and repositioned. It may be necessary to slightly burnish the color sheet in place to hold for cutting (324).

3   With the cutting knife, trace (cutting just through the color sheet) around the image area (325). Peel away the unwanted color (326).

4   Smooth the color over the image area with the hand or a finger so that it lies evenly. It is recommended that you use a clean sheet of white paper on top of the color during the smoothing; this will help protect the applied color from possible scratches and will also assist in assuring perfect adhesion. Should bubbles appear in the color, make a pinhole and smooth down once more.

Transparent color tapes work much like the sheets.

Helpful Tips

Two or more colors can be applied to the same area or image for different color effects.

If writing or marking is to be done on a transparency during projection, place the color on the reverse side of the film. This will prevent the writing or marking from damaging the color.

For materials requiring opaque color, opaque color sheets and tapes are available.

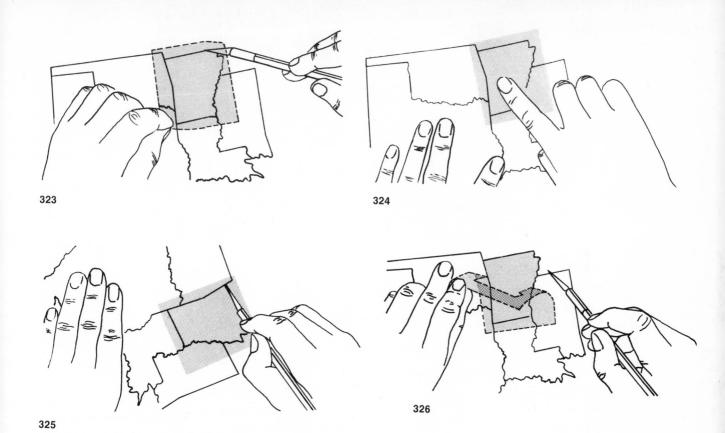

323

324

325

326

6 LETTERING TECHNIQUES AND AIDS

LETTERING AND PRINTING SELECTION CHART

This chart is designed to assist in the selection of lettering and printing techniques best suited for an item being produced. In some emergency situations, lettering techniques not recommended for a particular item can be substituted for use. *First*, locate the item requiring lettering or printing in the column below. The **X**'s to the right of each item indicate the techniques which are recommended for use. The **X**'s with superior numbers should be referred to in the KEY at the bottom of the chart. *Next*, refer to the pages indicated for instructions on the technique.

LETTERING AND PRINTING TECHNIQUES

ITEMS REQUIRING LETTERING OR PRINTING	Bulletin (Primary) Typewriter	Cardboard and Metal Stencil Lettering Guides	Composition Adhesive Type	Composition Paper Type	Dry Transfer Lettering	Dymo-Form Plastic Forming System	Econasign Lettering System	Embosograf Sign-making System	Flatbed Printing Machine	Hallmark Vinyl Plastic Letters	Hot-Press Printing	Kinder Composition Plastic Type	LeRoy Lettering System	Letterguide Lettering System	Lettering Guides for Stencil and Spirit Duplication	Letters by Projection	Panto-Varigraph Lettering System	Photype Composing Machine	Planotype Letters	Precut Letters	Reynolds Printasign Printing Machine	Rubber Stamp Printing	Scott Letter Engraving Machine	Spray-on Lettering	Tape Embossing Machine	Varigraph Lettering System	Wrico Sign-Maker System
PAGE	120	102	136	138	142	123	108	122	118	112	120	140	124	128	107	134	132	141	113	110	119	116	124	114	122	130	105
Bulletin Boards	X	X	X[1]	X[1]	X[1]	X	X	X	X	X	X	X[1]	X	X	X	X[19]	X[19]	X[2]	X[20]	X	X	X		X		X	X
Captions (for Photographs, Illustrations)	X	X	X[1]	X[1]	X	X	X	X	X		X	X[1,2]	X	X	X	X[19]	X[19]	X[2]	X[2]		X	X				X	X
Certificates and Awards	X	X	X[2]	X[2]	X	X	X	X	X		X	X[1,2]	X	X	X	X[19]	X[19]	X[2]			X	X			X	X	X
Chalkboards																X				X[7]							
Charts, Graphs, Diagrams, and Maps	X	X	X[2]	X[2]	X[2]	X	X	X		X	X	X[1,2]	X	X	X	X[19]	X[19]	X[2]	X[2]	X[20]	X	X				X	X
Clear Acetate Overlays (for Charts, Transparencies)	X[4]				X			X[3]	X[3]		X		X[3]	X[3]	X[3]	X[3,19]	X[3,19]		X[20]		X[3]	X				X[3]	
Diazo Masters	X[6]				X[9]			X[5,17]	X[5]				X[5]	X[5]	X[5]	X[10,19]	X[3,19]	X[22]			X[5]			X[5]		X[5]	X[5]
Electronic Stencil Artwork	X[6]		X[1,2]	X[1,2]	X[1,2]						X[1,2]	X[1,2]				X										X	X
Filmstrip Artwork (for Captions, Titles)	X		X[2]	X[2]	X				X		X	X[1,2]				X[2]	X[2]	X[2]								X	X
Flannel (Felt) Boards		X[8]			X[8]	X[8]	X[8]	X[8]	X[8]	X	X	X[8]	X[8]	X[8]	X[8]	X[8,19]	X[8,19]	X[8]	X[8]	X[8]	X[8]	X[8]		X[8]	X[8]	X[8]	X[8]
High-contrast Photographic Artwork	X[6]	X	X	X	X[9]	X[5]	X[5]	X[5]	X[5]	X	X	X[1]	X[5]	X[5]	X[5]	X[10]	X[5]	X	X[9]		X[8]	X		X[5]	X[5]	X[5]	X
Labels (for Files, Containers)	X	X	X[1]	X[1]	X	X	X	X	X	X	X	X[1]	X	X	X	X	X	X	X	X	X	X	X	X	X	X	X
Letters, Large Display						X										X							X	X			
Magnetic Boards		X[10]			X[10]	X[10]	X[10]	X[10]	X[10]				X[10]	X[10]	X[10]	X[10,19]	X[10,19]	X[10]	X[10]	X[10]	X[10]	X[10]		X[10]		X[10]	X[10]
Mimeograph Stencils	X[16]	X[12]												X[13]	X[13]			X[12]	X[12]				X				
Motion-picture Artwork (for Titles, Captions)			X[2]	X[2]	X	X	X	X	X	X	X	X[1,2]	X	X	X	X[19]	X[19]	X[2]	X[2]	X	X	X		X	X	X	X
Nameplates	X	X	X[1]	X[1]	X	X	X	X	X	X	X	X	X	X	X	X[19]	X[19]	X	X[20]	X	X	X	X	X	X	X	X

The following table lists lettering/artwork techniques (columns) against application types (rows). Superscript numbers refer to the KEY below.

Application														
Offset Duplication Artwork (for Photographic Processing)	X[6]	X	X	X	X				X		X		X	X
Offset Duplication Master (Direct Image)	X[15]	X[9]				X[14]	X[14]	X[14]	X[19]	X[7,14]		X[14]	X[14]
Overhead Projection Transparencies	X[16]				X[13]	X[13]			X[12]		
Acetate Spirit Master Transparency	X[16]			X[13]	X[13]			X[12]		
Carbon-coated Projection Acetate	X[4]	X	X	X[3]	X[3]	X		X[3]	X[3]	
Clear Acetate (Base and Overlays)	X[6]	X[9,17]	X[5]	X[5]	X[5]	X[5]	X[5]	X[5,7]	X[5]	X[5]
Diazo (Master)	X[6]	X[9]	X[5]	X[5]	X[5]	X[5]	X[9]	X[5]	X[5]
High-contrast Photographic (Artwork Only)	X[4,11]	X[11]	X[3,11]	X[1]	X[11]	X[11]	X[11]	X[11]	X[11]	X[5,11]
Matte (Frosted) Acetate	X[6]	X[9,17]	X[5]	X[5]	X[5]	X[5]	X[5,7]	X[5]	X[5]
Thermocopy (Artwork Only)	X[4]	X	X	X[3]	X[3]	X	X[3]	X[3]
Thermocopy Transparency Film (Processed)	X	X[1]	X[1]	X	X	X[20]	X	X
Place Cards	X	X[1,2]	X[1,2]	X	X[1,2]	X	X[19]	X[20]	X	X
Posters	X	X[1]	X[1]	X	X[1]	X[19]	X[2]	X[20]	X	X
Signs	X	X[1]	X[1]	X	X[1]	X[19]	X	X[20]	X	X
Silk-screen Artwork (Stencil Cutting)			X[18]	X[18]	X[19,21]	X	
Slide Artwork (for Captions, Titles)	X	X[2]	X[2]	X	X[1,2]	X[2]	X[2]	X	X
Spirit (Hectographic) Duplication Masters	X[16]	X[12]	X[13]	X[13]	X	X[12]	X	X
Television Artwork (for Captions, Titles)	X[2]	X[2]	X	X	X[1,2]	X	X[19]	X[20]	X	X

KEY

1 Requires photographic processing
2 For paste-up artwork only
3 Requires acetate (plastic) ink
4 Requires overhead transparency typewriter ribbon or carbon sheet
5 Requires black ink
6 Typed character must be dense, opaque
7 Must be traced
8 Finished letter(s) must be backed with flannel, felt, sandpaper, etc.
9 Black letters only
10 Finished letter(s) must be backed with metal or rubber magnet
11 For projection, dull side of acetate must be sprayed with clear plastic spray
12 Must be traced with metal stylus or ball-point pen
13 Mechanical scriber ball-point pen-stylus must be used in scriber
14 Requires offset master (direct image) ink
15 Requires offset master typewriter ribbon
16 Set typewriter on "stencil"
17 Heat-resistant black type only
18 Mechanical scriber silk-screen or swivel knife must be used in scriber
19 When extra large letters are required
20 Opaque letters only
21 Panto-Varigraph silk-screen knife required
22 Positive character (letter) on film

109

With few exceptions, practically every kind of visual medium (charts, graphs, transparencies, etc.) requires lettering or printing of one type or another. In view of the importance of lettering to the production of visual media, this section of the book illustrates and discusses what is believed to be a rather comprehensive assortment of lettering and printing techniques.

Available on the market today is an unlimited variety of letters, lettering guides, mechanical tracing lettering systems, printing machines, tape and plastic embossers, phototype composing machines, paste-up types, and so forth. Such a multitude of techniques and aids might frustrate the novice producer of visual media. However, a quick glance at the "Lettering Selection Chart" (327) on pages 108 and 109 is a suggested starting point for the selection of lettering techniques and aids designed for a particular lettering problem. To assist with creating attractive lettering layouts and designs, one can refer to page 113. With problems of letter and word spacing and alignment, a look at pages 111 to 113 should be helpful.

This section, while written mainly for the nonprofessional producer of visual media, should also be helpful to the professional visual media producer seeking solutions to media involving lettering.

Finally, it should be kept in mind that there are no hard-and-fast rules governing the selection of lettering or printing techniques. The selection should be made only after an analysis of lettering requirements of the visual media being produced. The choice may depend upon what is available or the ability of one to use a particular technique. In any event, it is hoped that from among the techniques included in this section an answer can be found for the lettering problem at hand.

LETTERING IDEAS: SOURCES AND EXAMPLES

Professional and nonprofessional producers of visual media can collect excellent lettering ideas from commercial magazines, newspapers, brochures, posters, etc. (328). For example, one can go through most any edition of the telephone *Yellow Pages* and discover many good lettering ideas.

Start a "Lettering Ideas" file, and in it place ideas taken from sources mentioned above. Some ideas may only suggest effective and interesting letter arrangement (design); others may suggest ideas for color treatment of letters.

Some lettering ideas taken from a few of the sources just mentioned are given in (329).

328

LETTER AND WORD SPACING, ALIGNMENT, AND SPECIAL EFFECTS

One of the more difficult aspects of lettering is that of letter and word spacing. Letters are not equidistant from each other, due to differences in width and shape.

LETTER SPACING (330)

Good letter spacing is the arrangement of letters in a line so that they will appear to have equal or uniform distances between them. To achieve this effect, it is often necessary to position the letters at varying distances from one another, depending on the style, size, and combination of letters involved. One way of assuring correct letter spacing is to envisage the areas between letters as being irregular containers of liquid, the objective being to space the letters so that no matter how irregular the shape of these "liquid containers," they will each hold the same amount of liquid. This technique of spacing is also known as optical spacing. Note that although the letters in (a) are equally spaced, the "containers" between them are unequal. Part (b) illustrates the results of spacing letters so that the "containers" are nearly equal.

329

330a

330b

Another good rule to follow for letter spacing is to space round letters (B, C, D, G, O, P, Q, R, and S) a bit closer to each other and to any straight letter (E, H, I, M, N, and U) next to their rounded side. Irregular formed letters (A, F, J, K, L, T, V, W, X, Y, and Z) also fit closer together according to their shape. Three letters, I, M, and W, are generally considered as problem letters. For the I, do not position too close to adjoining letters; for the M and W, do not squeeze as these are actually wider than other letters.

WORD SPACING (331)

In arranging captions, a good rule to follow is to keep the space between words about the same, even though spaces between individual letters may vary. Should one word end and another begin with narrow letters (I or T), position them a bit closer than words which end and begin with round or open letters.

LETTER ALIGNMENT

The arrangement and form given to letters contribute a great deal to the preparation of visual media where lettering is involved. Basic to lettering is alignment. Here are two suggested approaches to the alignment of letters and words.

For Precut, Preformed, Rubber Stamp, Stencil, Dry Transfer, and Composition-Type Letters

1 Write down the words intended for one line of lettering (332).
2 Count up the letters and spaces between the words. Mark the center letter.
3 Assuming that the line of lettering is to be centered on the working surface, make a light pencil mark at the center point as illustrated (333).
4 Make a light pencil guideline on the working surface for letters that require such a line.
5 Position the middle letter at the center point on the working surface. First, work to the left of the middle letter, and then work to the right of the middle letter until all letters are in place.

For Mechanical Tracing and Stencil Tracing Letters

1 Letter the intended line of letters, with the lettering device selected for the job, on a scrap sheet of paper. Make a mark at the center letter. Make certain to count all letters and spaces when picking out the center letter (334).
2 If the lettering is to be centered on the working surface, make a light

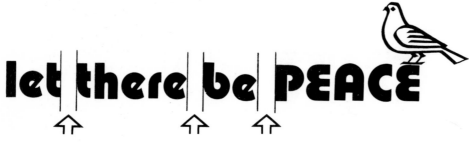

331

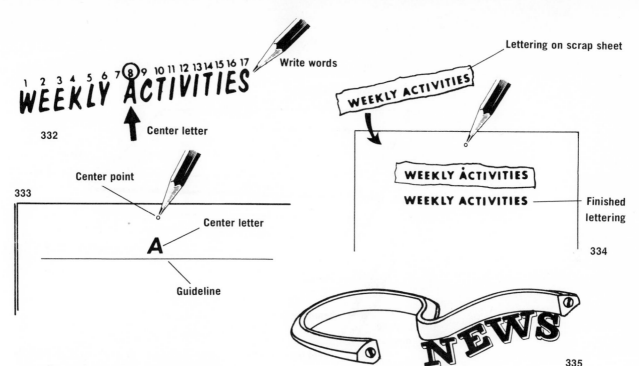

1 2 3 4 5 6 7 8 9 10 11 12 13 14 15 16 17

WEEKLY ACTIVITIES

Write words

332

Center letter

Lettering on scrap sheet

WEEKLY ACTIVITIES

333

Center point

Center letter

A

Guideline

WEEKLY ACTIVITIES

WEEKLY ACTIVITIES

Finished lettering

334

Adjustable curve

335

Irregular (French) curve

336

Record

337

pencil mark at the center point. Match up the center mark on the scrap sheet of paper with the mark on the working surface. Repeat the lettering on the working surface, using the scrap sheet as a guide for letter and word spacing. If the line of lettering is not to be centered, position the scrap sheet containing the first lettering where desired and repeat the lettering on the working surface.

SPECIAL EFFECTS

A variety of art aids and assorted-shape objects can be used to create special effects in lettering; the adjustable curve (335) can be bent into any desired curve or shape to act as a guide for alignment of letters and words. Irregular (French) curves (336) are useful for arranging small letters into special effects. Audio records are excellent for arranging letters in a circular design (337). Other round objects, such as dishes and container tops, provide adequate guides for letter arrangement. See page 111 for special effects ideas.

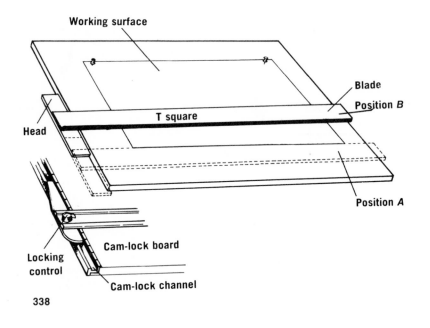

Working surface

Blade

Position *B*

T square

Head

Position *A*

Locking
control

Cam-lock board

Cam-lock channel

338

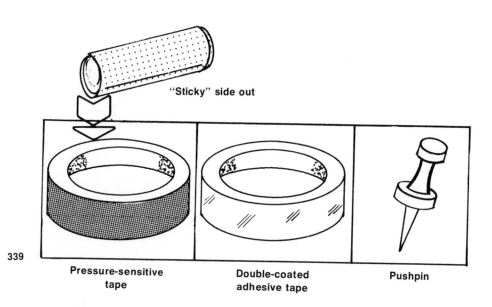

"Sticky" side out

339

Pressure-sensitive
tape

Double-coated
adhesive tape

Pushpin

114

PREPARATION OF WORKING SURFACE FOR LETTERING

Whatever technique of lettering or illustrating is to be used, the preparation of the working surface is most important and should be given careful attention. Here are a few tips for preparing the working surface for use.

A good drawing board and T square are the basic tools required for preparing the working surface. A Cam-lock drawing board or a board to which a Cam-lock channel is attached and a Cam-lock T square are highly recommended in that the T square can be locked into working position.

ALIGNING AND SECURING THE WORKING SURFACE (338)

1 Place the T square head against the left side of the drawing board and move to position (A) as illustrated.
2 Line up the working surface (paper, cardboard, acetate, etc.) with the top edge of the T square blade. Secure the surface to the board with plastic pressure-sensitive discs, double-coated adhesive tape, pressure-sensitive tape, or pushpins.
3 Move the T square to a working position (B). The desired instrument or device (such as a lettering guide or triangle) can be placed on the top edge of the T square blade.

AIDS FOR SECURING THE LETTERING SURFACE TO THE BOARD (339)

There are several good aids for securing the lettering surface to the drawing board or working surface; here are three:

Pressure-sensitive Tape

Any pressure-sensitive tape can be used to attach the working surface to secure it to the drawing board. Roll 1-inch pieces of tape, "sticky" side out, the thickness of a small pencil, and stick one to each corner contact point under the material.

Double-coated Adhesive Tape

Attach strips or small pieces of this tape to the drawing board surface at points where contact is desired. Attach the working surface to the board as instructed in steps 1, 2, and 3. If the working surface is paper or cardboard, spray where tape contact points are to be with clear plastic spray; this will prevent damage to the back of the working surface when it is removed from the drawing board.

Pushpins

Metal or glass pushpins can be inserted at corner contact points of the surface material.

PRECUT AND PREFORMED LETTERS

See pages 118 to 119 for mounting aids. See pages 111 to 113 for "Letter and Word Spacing, Alignment, and Special Effects."

Precut and preformed letters add an exciting dimension to visual media. Perhaps the greatest advantage of these letters is that they are in ready-to-use form and need only be mounted or attached to the desired surface.

Precut and preformed letters come in a large assortment of styles, sizes, and materials. Included here are several tested and approved precut and preformed letters.

CONSTRUCTION PAPER LETTERS (340)

Die-cut from colorful construction paper. Ideal for posters, charts, signs, displays, bulletin boards, etc. They can be pinned, pasted, stapled, or suspended with string.

GUMMED PAPER LETTERS (341)

Die-cut paper letters with a gummed-back adhesive. A pair of tweezers, a straightedge (ruler), a moist sponge, and a blotter are the only tools necessary to produce professional-looking lettering. See page 119 for mounting gummed paper letters.

CARDBOARD LETTERS (PLAIN BACK) (342)

Die-cut from heavy cardboard. Available in colored or uncolored stock and in a wide range of sizes and styles. Ideal for displays, signs, etc. Letters can be used for tracing and spray-on lettering (see page 123).

CARDBOARD LETTERS (GUMMED BACK) (343)

Cardboard letters with a gummed back, easily applied like a postage stamp to special guide strips and then attached to the desired mounting surface. Letters range in height from ¾ to 2 inches.

CARDBOARD LETTERS (ADHESIVE BACK) (344)

Pressure-sensitive adhesive-backed cardboard letters. Ideal for displays, signs, posters, etc. Letters range in size from ¾ to 2 inches.

TRACING LETTERS (345)

Cardboard letters designed for tracing (see page 120 for instructions). Ideal for visual media requiring large, attractive letters. Letters range in height from 1 to 6 inches.

VINYL LETTERS (346)

Die-cut vinyl plastic letters with a pressure-sensitive adhesive back that will stick to most surfaces. Height of letters ranges from ½ to 6 inches.

MOLDED PLASTIC MAGNETIC LETTERS (347)

A semiflexible molded plastic letter with permanent magnetism built in. Letters will stick to any steel or magnetic-treated surface. Letters range in height from ½ to 2 inches and come in several colors.

MAGNETIC-BACKED LETTERS (348)

Molded plastic letters with small metal or rubber magnets attached to the back. For use on magnetic boards or steel surfaces.

VELCRO-BACKED LETTERS (349)

Dimensional plastic letters backed with Velcro ("hook") tape. Designed for use on Velcro (Hook-n-Loop) surfaces and boards.

PLEXIGLAS LETTERS (350)

Translucent color letters made of Plexiglas. Designed for display and outdoor use. Range in height is from 5 to 24 inches.

STYROFOAM LETTERS (351)

Molded styrofoam letters that have the appearance of expensive metal letters. At this printing, only 12-inch-high letters are available.

WOOD OR METAL LETTERS (352)

Precision-cut wood or metal letters available in heights up to 30 inches. Designed mainly for sign and display use.

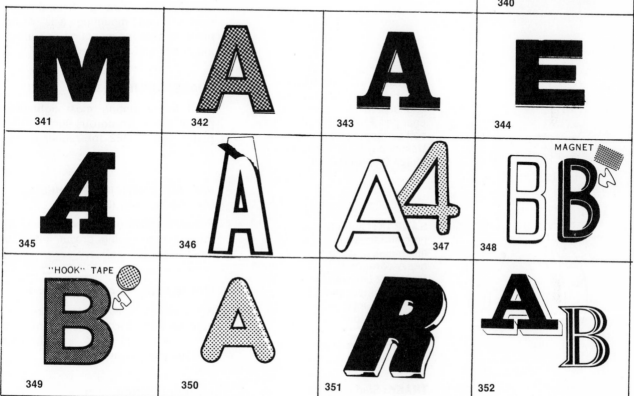

MITTEN DISPLAY LETTERS (353)

Made of precision-molded plastic ceramic or tile composition. Available in over 130 sizes and styles. Illustrated are four types of Mitten display letters.

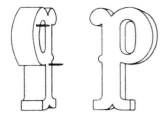

PINBAK: Pin-on letters are thumbtack-simple to apply and ideal for quick lettering changes. Pins easily into all soft surfaces: cork, Upsonboard, Homasote or Mitten Display Panels.

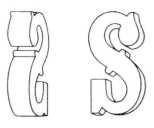

SANBAK: Glue-on letters for hard surfaces such as wood, tile, metal, glass, plastic or heavy cardboard. Recommended for indoor use with Mitten-Stay Indoor Cement or Mitten Mighty Mount pressure sensitive tape. For outdoors use Mitten Greenwood Cement or other strong waterproof adhesive.

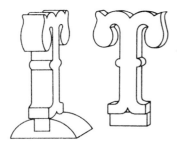

TRAKK: Standing letters which can be used either in an upright position or at an angle. The permanent lug-base on each letter is custom-fitted for easy insertion into Mitten's ready-made wooden tracks.

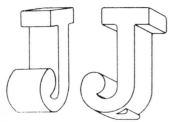

STANDEES: Extra depth letters that stand upright completely unaided. Reusable and rearrangeable in just seconds.

353

AIDS FOR MOUNTING AND ATTACHING PRECUT AND PREFORMED LETTERS

Most manufacturers of precut and preformed letters recommend certain mounting aids for mounting or attaching their letters. While not specifically designed for mounting letters, there are several good mounting aids recommended here for mounting and attaching precut and preformed letters.

RUBBER CEMENT (354)

Ideal for mounting most lightweight precut letters on porous surfaces. See pages 160 to 162 for rubber cement mounting.

PRESSURE-SENSITIVE ADHESIVE (AEROSOL CAN) (355)

Pressure-sensitive adhesive in spray-can form. For mounting precut letters on most surfaces.

LIQUID PLASTIC ADHESIVE (356)

A fast-setting white or transparent all-purpose adhesive that holds on wood, paper, cardboard, glass, and all porous and semiporous letters.

ADHESIVE STICK (357)

One of the newer forms of mounting adhesive. Comes in lipsticklike form, and can be used for mounting precut paper and lightweight cardboard letters on most surfaces.

WAX ADHESIVE STICK (358)

A colorless, odorless wax adhesive in stick form. For mounting and attaching most of the lightweight precut letters.

EPOXY CEMENT (359)

An extra-strong, clear, waterproof cement for metal, glass, plastic, and other nonporous precut and preformed letters. Consists of two tubes (one resin and one hardener) which are mixed together in the quantity required just before use.

DOUBLE-COATED ADHESIVE TAPE (360)

A double-coated pressure-sensitive tape for attaching paper and lightweight cardboard letters to most surfaces. Some tapes have a carrier strip that must be peeled away from the adhesive tape to permit mounting.

ADHESIVE-BACKED PAPER TAB (361)

A special mounting paper tab for mounting paper and cardboard letters on most surfaces. The tab has pressure-sensitive adhesive on both sides.

FOAM TAPE (362)

Double-coated foam tape. Has pressure-sensitive adhesive on both sides. For mounting most precut and preformed letters on most surfaces. 3M brand tape is packaged as "Mounting Squares."

DISPLAY PINS (363)

Steel straight pins designed for mounting and attaching display materials. Ideal for mounting paper and cardboard letters. Regular straight pins can also be used.

MOUNTING GUMMED PAPER LETTERS

See pages 111 to 113 for "Letter and Word Spacing, Alignment, and Special Effects."

Gummed paper letters require no special skill for making attractive visual media requiring precision-cut paste-up letters. Here are five easy steps for mounting gummed paper letters:

1   Use a guideline—either draw a light pencil line or use the edge of a blotter, heavy paper, or card.

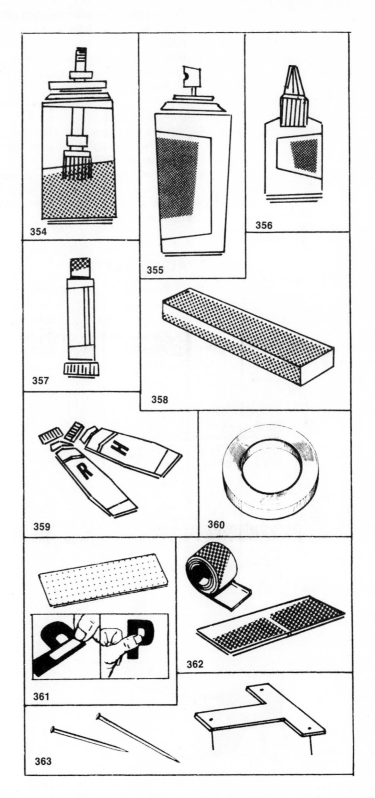

354

355

356

357

358

359

360

361

362

363

2 Pick up the letter with tweezers (364), or between the finger and a knife blade.

3 Moisten the letter slightly, keeping it firmly attached to the tweezers, and at the same time move the letter slightly so that it will not stick to the lifting tool (365).

4 Use the forefinger of the left hand to press the letter lightly while removing the tweezers (366).

5 When the line of lettering is complete, use a blotter or a sheet of paper; press over all, and the lettering is finished.

TRACING LETTERS

Trend Enterprises (write Beckly-Cardy) has manufactured a die-cut letter designed just for tracing. Letters (decorative borders too!) come in assorted styles and range in height from 2 to 6 inches (367).

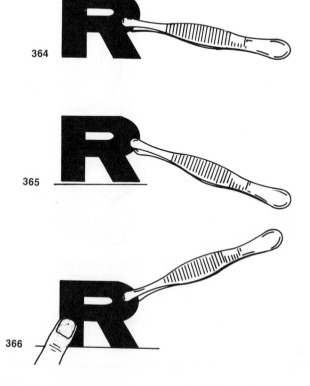

364

365

366

Kenworthy Educational Services manufactures "Trace or Paste" letters that range in size from 1 to 6 inches.

Here are two suggested uses for tracing letters:

FOR TRACING ONLY

1 Use a pencil; ball-, nylon-, felt-point pen; crayon; or chalk to trace the tracing letter (368).

2 Refine the traced line if necessary (369).

3 Color with felt-point pen or any other coloring technique desired (see Section 5 for coloring techniques) (370).

FOR TRACING AND CUTOUT

4 Select material for cutout letters (construction paper, cardboard, etc.), and trace letters with pencil or ball-point pen (371). A ball-point pen line provides a grooved guideline for cutting.

5 Cut out letters (372) (see page 31 for cutting instructions).

6 Mount letters (373) (see page 118 for mounting aids).

367

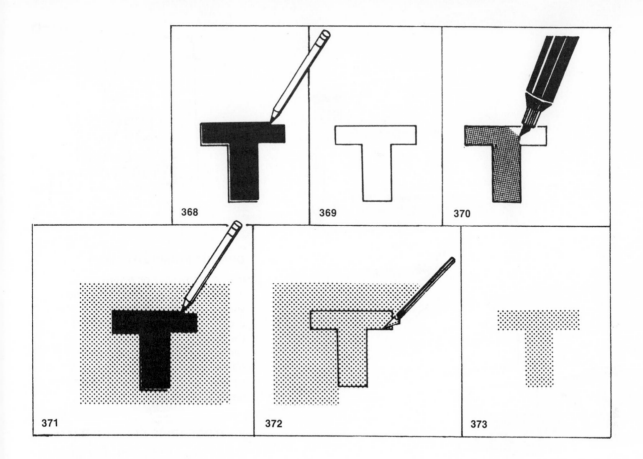

368   369   370

371   372   373

LETTERS BY PROJECTION

Where large display-type letters are desired, one of a variety of projection devices can be used very effectively. With any one of these devices, it is possible to produce large letters of any size on a variety of materials. The letter to be reproduced is inserted in the device used and projected onto the drawing surface. Precut letters are ideal for this technique. However, any printed letter that can be inserted in the projection device can be used.

Here are general instructions for producing letters by projections. For each of the projection devices, additional instructions may be given.

Instructions

1   Insert the letter in the projection device. It may be necessary to anchor the letter to a sheet of paper or clear acetate to prevent movement while reproducing larger letters.
2   Fasten the surface on which the letter is to be reproduced to the wall or floor or to wherever a projected image would normally appear.
3   Position or adjust the projection device to give the letter size desired.
4   Trace the outline of the projected letter with a pencil. For straight lines of the letters, use a ruler or yardstick as a tracing guide. Remove the finished work, and ink or complete as desired.

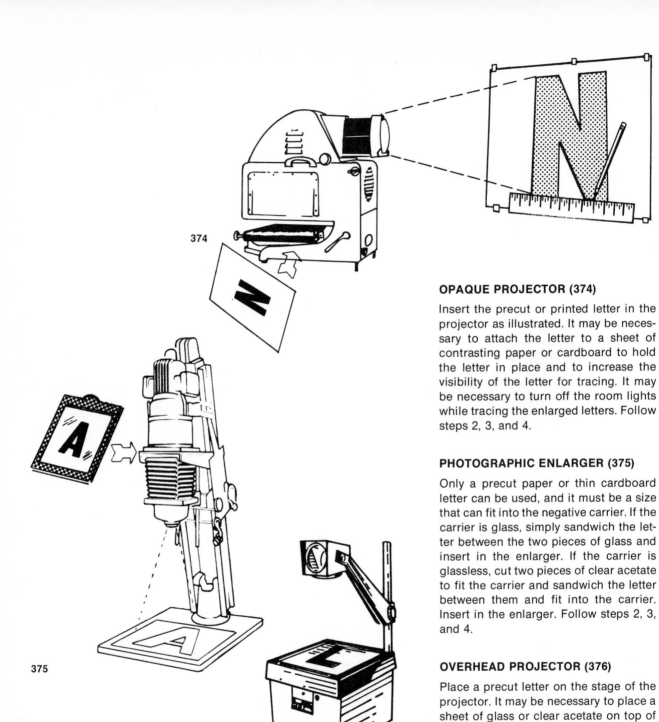

374

375

376

OPAQUE PROJECTOR (374)

Insert the precut or printed letter in the projector as illustrated. It may be necessary to attach the letter to a sheet of contrasting paper or cardboard to hold the letter in place and to increase the visibility of the letter for tracing. It may be necessary to turn off the room lights while tracing the enlarged letters. Follow steps 2, 3, and 4.

PHOTOGRAPHIC ENLARGER (375)

Only a precut paper or thin cardboard letter can be used, and it must be a size that can fit into the negative carrier. If the carrier is glass, simply sandwich the letter between the two pieces of glass and insert in the enlarger. If the carrier is glassless, cut two pieces of clear acetate to fit the carrier and sandwich the letter between them and fit into the carrier. Insert in the enlarger. Follow steps 2, 3, and 4.

OVERHEAD PROJECTOR (376)

Place a precut letter on the stage of the projector. It may be necessary to place a sheet of glass or clear acetate on top of the letter to hold it in place. Follow steps 2, 3, and 4.

SLIDE PROJECTOR (377)

Insert the precut letter between two pieces of slide cover glass or two pieces of clear acetate and insert in a reusable mount (see page 221 for mount description). Insert the mounted letter in the projector. Follow steps 3 and 4.

ART AID PROJECTOR (378)

The projector illustrated is a miniature opaque projector designed for use as an art aid (for enlarging visuals). Insert the lettering to be enlarged under the projector or in the position indicated. Follow steps 2, 3, and 4.

377

SPRAY-ON LETTERING

Attractive signs and posters can be made quickly with precut and special spray-on letters (379). Commercial spray-on letters are the best type for this technique in that they are usually made of die-cut thick sponge rubber and will not shift or move when sprayed. American Jet Spray Industries and W. W. Holes Manufacturing Company sell spray sign kits. Letters range in height from ¾ to 12 inches. A variety of aerosol spray-can paints provide excellent colors for this technique.

378

Commercial
spray-on letters

Precut
letters

Spray
paints

379

Instructions for a Two-color Sign or Poster

1 Place the surface upon which the lettering is to be done on a flat protected surface. Use a piece of cardboard or thick paper to cover one section of the lettering surface (380).

2 Select the letters and numbers desired, and arrange them on the lettering surface. A T square or straight-edge can be used to align the letters (381).

3 Select the color or colors, and spray lightly over and around the letters, holding the spray can about 12 inches away at right angles (382). The resulting letter will be sharp and clearly defined. If a three-dimensional effect is desired, hold the spray can at about a 45° angle and spray as instructed. Various angles at which spraying is done will result in a variety of effects. Allow the paint to dry; this usually takes about ten minutes, depending on the type of paint used. Carefully remove the letters from the surface.

4 Cover the sprayed section of the surface with a piece of cardboard or thick paper, and position the cutout forms, letters, symbols as desired and repeat step 3 (383).

5 To avoid possible clogging of the spray can, turn it upside down and spray short jets of air to clear the air passage (384).

Protective cardboard

380

Protected surface

381

382

Three-dimensional effect

383

384   Finished poster

James M. Thomas
PRESIDENT

386

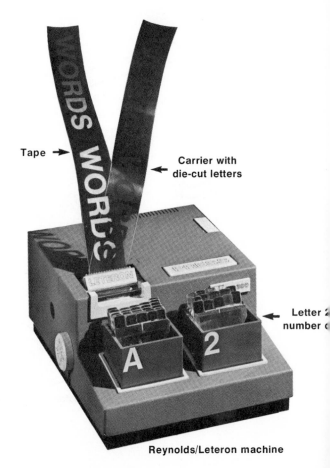

LETERON AUTOMATIC LETTERING SYSTEM (385, 386)

Here is a new and exciting lettering system from Reynolds/Leteron Company that produces pressure-sensitive-backed letters, words, and sentences *in sequence* for both indoor and outdoor lettering. The system includes a manual or electric die-cutting machine, cutting dies, and Letertape (0.003-inch acrylic material).

At present letters are available in a wide choice of styles and sizes (387). Letters range in height from $\frac{5}{16}$ to $1\frac{1}{2}$ inches (22 to 108 points). The tapes from which letters are cut come in eight colors.

Here is how Leteron works:

1. Drop the Letertype die in the slot. Press the actuator for each letter or character (388).
2. Remove the tape from the machine (389).
3. Separate the transparent carrier (letters attached) from the tape (390).
4. Positon the letters on the surface intended (391).
5. Remove the carrier from the mounted letters (392).
6. Remove the "centers" with tweezers or the tip of a cutting knife (393).
7. Roll the letters down for complete adhesion (394).

385

Tape ➡

Carrier with ⬅ die-cut letters

Letter 2 ⬅ number

387   **Sample styles 2d sizes**

Reynolds/Leteron machine

388

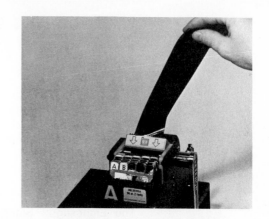

389

390

391

392

393

394

EMBOSOGRAF SIGNMAKER (395, 396)

The Embosograf Signmaker will produce embossed and die-cut letters for signs and other visual media on plastic, aluminum, and cardboard. Signs and other visual media can range in height from 4 to 12 inches and lengths up to 8 feet long (397).

EMBOSSED-TYPE LETTERING

The Embosograf Signmaker will produce embossed-type letters on plastic, aluminum, and cardboard. Here is how the Signmaker works:

1 Select and set the metal type on the setup plate of the machine (398).
2 Place the color "top paper" over the type with the color side down. This is a special paper for producing letters in color (399).
3 Lay the sign cardboard face down over the type and top paper, and push the setup plate under the pressure area. Pull down the side lever causing the type to emboss the top paper into the cardboard (400).
4 Pull the setup plate out, and pick up the cardboard. Remove any excess top paper. Repeat steps 2, 3, and 4 for duplicate signs (401).

DIE-CUT LETTERS (402)

The Signmaker will produce die-cut letters from Embosograf magnetic sheeting material (15 to 20 mils thick) and from Embosograf polyethylene foam material. The magnetic material may be painted any color and is for use on magnetic boards or other suitable surfaces. The foam material comes in color with a pressure-sensitive adhesive backing for easy application to most surfaces.

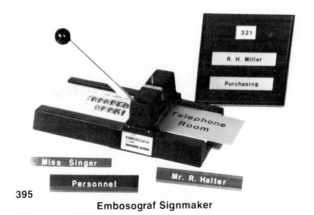

395

Embosograf Signmaker

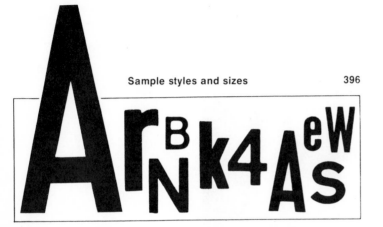

Sample styles and sizes   396

397

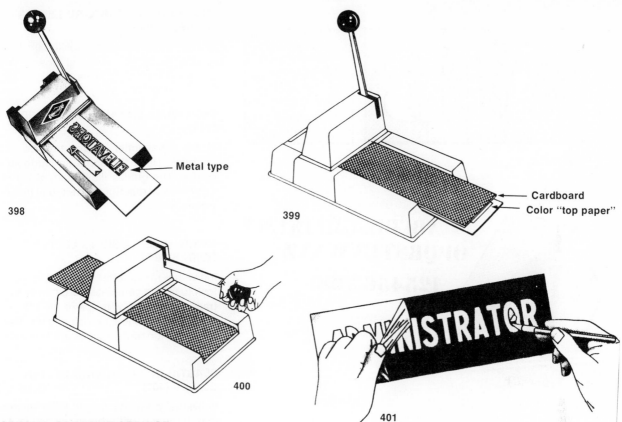

398

399

Metal type

Cardboard
Color "top paper"

400

401

SPECIAL CREATIVE SERVICE

Embosograf will help you create your own effective signs and other similar media—there is no charge unless extensive artwork is required—just write them.

STENCIL LETTERING GUIDES (403)

Cardboard, metal, and plastic stencil lettering guides provide a fast, economical way for lettering on opaque and transparent surfaces. Some guides even have features for assuring perfect spacing. Stencil lettering guides come in three basic forms: individual letter, card-type, and plastic tracing guides, with the latter two having a number of letters on a single card or plastic sheet. Today, a number of exciting letter styles and sizes are available, ranging in height from ½ to 8 inches.

402

403

404

INDIVIDUAL CARDBOARD LETTER GUIDES (404)

Sharp, clean die-cut individual letter guides made of yellow oil board. See page 131 for instructions.

INDIVIDUAL METAL LETTER GUIDES (405)

Heavy metal letter guides that do not interlock. Used the same as cardboard guides. The guides illustrated, available from Lewis Artist Supply, range in height from 5 to 40 mm.

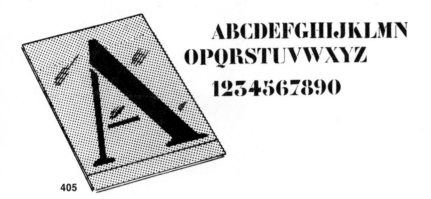

ABCDEFGHIJKLMN
OPQRSTUVWXYZ
1234567890

405

METAL INTERLOCKING LETTER GUIDES (406)

Individual metal letter guides that interlock to form a complete word that can be traced, sprayed with paint or ink, or printed with a stencil brush and ink. Vertical and horizontal guides are available.

PLASTIC INTERLOCKING LETTER GUIDES (407)

Individual polyester plastic letter guides that interlock with brass fasteners to form a complete word that can be traced, sprayed with paint or ink, or printed with a stencil brush or brayer and ink. Guides come in sets of full Gothic capitals and numbers fonts, and heights range from ½ to 6 inches.

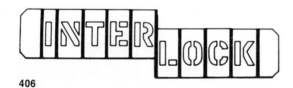

406

407

Instructions for Use of Individual Letter Guides

Individual stencil letter guides are unique in that they can be arranged to form complete words for tracing, spraying, brush, or brayer and ink application.

1 To align letters, use a straightedge (408). For best results, overlap the stencils slightly. Spacing may be varied by changing the amount of overlap.

2 Fasten letters together with pressure-sensitive tape along the top and bottom edges of the stencils.

3 Tape assembled letters to the area to be stenciled (409). If required, use protective paper to mask the area around the stencils. Spray with ink or paint, or apply ink with a stencil brush (410) or a brayer (411).

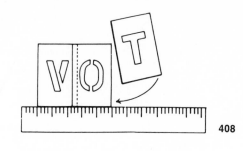

408

Tape

Finished sign

409

410

Stencil brush

411

Brayer

STENCIL LETTER CUTTING MACHINE (412)

A hand-operated stencil-cutting machine for cutting stencil letters out of stencil oil board. Models available for cutting letters range from ¼ to 1 inch in height.

Stencil letter cutting machine

412

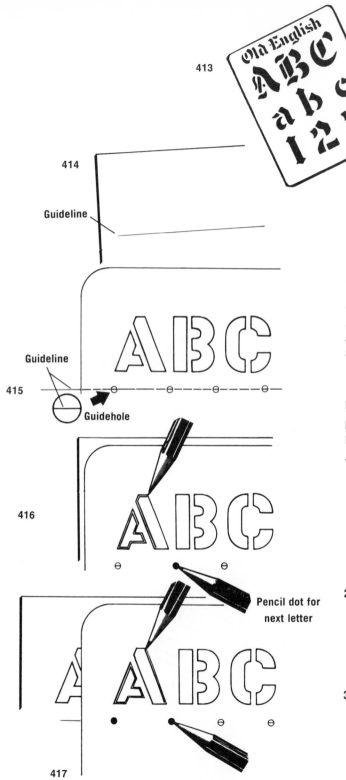

413

414

Guideline

Guideline

415

Guidehole

416

Pencil dot for
next letter

417

CARD-TYPE STENCIL LETTERING GUIDES (413)

Stencil board or plastic card-type stencil lettering guides with outlines of capitals and numbers that can be traced or filled in with any marking medium from pencil to paint. Gothic- and Roman-style letters are the more widely used; Old English and Hoot-Nany are two other styles available. Letters range in height from ½ to 12 inches.

Instructions

If using new guides, push out all the letters, figures, and guide holes.

1   Draw a light pencil guideline on the lettering surface above which letters are to be traced (414). If guide holes are at the bottom of the stencil letter, draw the guideline below where the letters are to be traced, position the guide so that the guideline appears through the guide holes below each letter (415).

2   Position the first letter, and trace the outline with a pencil or ball-point pen. The letter can be filled in with crayon. Before moving the guide to the next letter, make a pencil dot in the guide hole at the lower right of the letter just completed (416).

3   Position the next letter so that the dot just made shows through the guide hole at the lower left of the letter to be traced. Trace the letter, and repeat the foregoing steps until the word has been completed (417).

4 Erase the pencil guideline. The finished letters can be filled in with any of the marking media such as color crayons and felt markers (418).

WRICO SIGN-MAKER SYSTEM

The Wrico Sign-Maker system (419) consists of transparent plastic lettering guides, a metal guide holder, and a brush or felt-point pen. Letters range in height from $\frac{3}{8}$ to 4 inches. There are a number of letter styles to choose from, including modern mathematics symbols. The Sign-Maker is an ideal lettering system for preparing posters; signs; charts; graphs; maps; television, filmstrip, motion-picture, and slide titles; and flash cards.

Instructions

1 To fill the pen (420), press the plunger down and insert only the brush portion of the pen in ink, and, without raising the pen, release the plunger slowly. The pen is now ready for use. To adjust the pen properly for use, twist the adjustment nut until the end of the brush is even with the end of the tip of the pen. If the brush is not out far enough, turn the nut to the right. If the brush is out too far, turn the nut to the left. Finally, turn the adjustment nut a quarter of the way to the left so that the brush is recessed slightly; this will permit the ink to flow freely under the brush and allow for well-inked lines (421).

2 Place the metal guide holder on the surface to be lettered so that the rubber strips on the bottom of the holder set firmly upon the surface (422). Then rest the lettering guide in the channel of the guide holder. This permits the guide to be moved smoothly to the right or left without touching the surface to be lettered, thus preventing ink smudges. The guide holder stays securely in position wherever it is placed. This eliminates the necessity for straightedges, weights, thumbtacks, or tape.

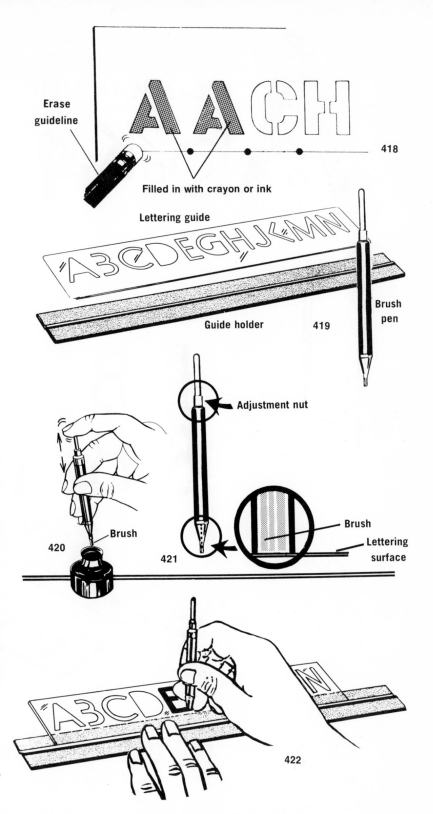

Erase guideline

Filled in with crayon or ink

418

Lettering guide

Guide holder   419

Brush pen

Adjustment nut

Brush

420   Brush

421   Brush

Lettering surface

422

133

Modern mathematics symbols

Sample letter styles

423

3 Move the lettering guide so as to position the first letter where desired on the lettering surface. Insert the pen in the first letter. Hold the pen vertically, and glide it through the letter form. Best results are obtained with very light pressure on the point. Many of the characters, both letters and numbers, are made complete with a single opening. Some require two openings. For example, when making the letter B (423), use any vertical line and then move the guide until the curved portion of the B is in position to complete the letter.

4 Slide the guide to the next letter and repeat the process (424). The lowercase letters c, f, i, j, l, m, n, o, r, s, t, u, v, x, y, and z are made by simply following the proper openings (425). The other letters require two openings. Part of the letter is made with one opening and completed with the other. The openings used for these letters are also indicated.

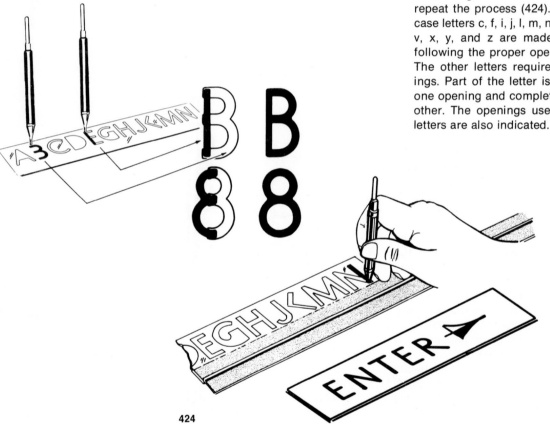

424

425

LETTERING GUIDES FOR STENCIL AND SPIRIT DUPLICATION (426)

Lettering guides for stencil and spirit duplication are made of plastic and have openings in the shape of letters and numerals. There are usually two guides for each letter set, one for capital letters and one for lowercase letters.

Stencil lettering guides work equally well for both stencils (mimeograph) and spirit masters. The use of a plastic writing plate (sheet) is recommended when using lettering guides.

Instructions—Stencils (427)

1   Where possible, a glass surface with a light source behind it should be used when lettering on a stencil (Mimeoscope and Tracing Scope are two brand-name units for use with stencils). Place the plastic sheet directly behind the stencil as illustrated. Position and secure the T square in place.

2   Choose the lettering guide and the correct stylus. The proper stylus to use is usually indicated on the lettering guide. First make a very light line in the letter selected. Then go back and forth over the line just drawn several times until sufficient stencil coating is pushed aside from the base tissue to make a clear white line (see insert).

3   Always draw toward a point formed by the junction of two lines. For example, when drawing the letter F, draw the long line first; then start at the outer points of the two short lines and draw toward the long line—never away from it.

Spacing is achieved by estimating the proper distance between each letter with the eye (see pages 111 to 112 for helpful instructions on letter and word spacing).

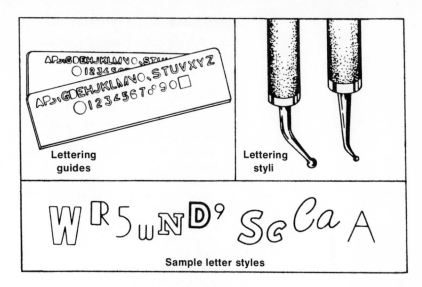

Lettering guides

Lettering styli

Sample letter styles

426

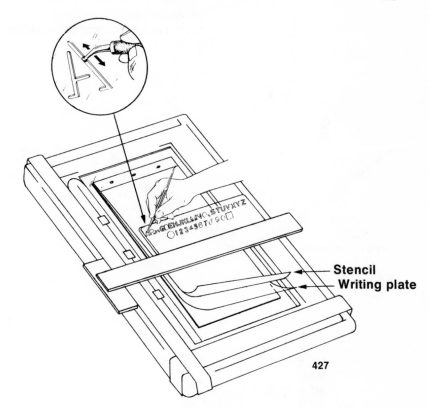

Stencil
Writing plate

427

Instructions—Spirit Masters (428)

Lettering on spirit masters with stencil lettering guides is much the same as lettering on stencils.

1   Place a plastic writing plate under the spirit master as illustrated, or, if a writing plate is not available, place the master on a hard, smooth surface. Remove the interleaf sheet so that the carbon sheet is next to the master.

2   Choose the lettering guide and correct stylus. Some ball-point pens with a fine point will sometimes work just as well as a stylus. Trace the letter with a firm, steady pressure. Check the master to make certain the carbon is transfering a solid-line letter.

3   To change the color of the letter, change the carbon sheet for another color carbon. Corrections can be made by carefully scraping carbon

transfer off the master and erasing with a correction pencil. Tear off a small section of the carbon sheet, position it under the correction, and retrace the letter.

MECHANICAL TRACING LETTERING SYSTEMS

See "Lettering Selection Chart" on pages 108 to 109 for uses.

Mechanical tracing lettering is considered one of the more versatile lettering techniques. A typical lettering system consists of a template, made up of engraved letters, and a scriber which can be equipped with a regular scriber pen, reservoir pen, pencil attachment, stylus, or special cutting knife. The system works like this—the built-in stylus of the scriber traces around the engraved letter on the template and reproduces the letter on the desired surface (429).

Some of the more complex systems have adjustable settings or controls to make enlargements, reductions, italics, and various special effects from a single template. A variety of type faces and sizes are available, each equally versatile.

Mechanical tracing lettering systems can be used to produce letters on almost any flat surface that will accept ink, pencil, or a cutting knife. Three lettering systems, LeRoy, Letterguide, and Varigraph, have been chosen for inclusion in this section, each having features distinctive enough to receive special attention.

LEROY LETTERING SYSTEM

The LeRoy lettering system is one of the more widely used mechanical tracing lettering systems today. The basic equipment includes a template, scriber (lettering instrument), and pen. Complete sets (430) are available with standard templates. Several of the large variety of letter and symbol templates styles are illustrated here (431). Special templates can be custom-made upon request. Accessories for the LeRoy system include:

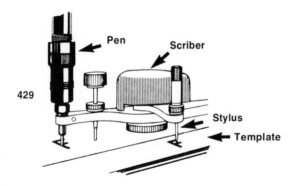

Master paper
Carbon sheet
Writing plate

Spirit duplicator master

428

Pen   Scriber

429

Stylus

Template

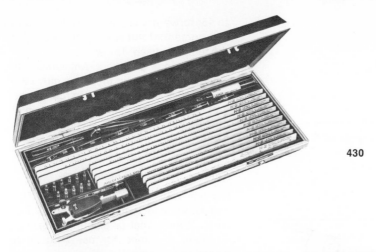

430

431

Fixed Scriber (432)

For use with all LeRoy pens up to size 8 and pencils and with all LeRoy templates up to size 650 and 60 point. Vertical lettering only. Furnished with double-ended tracer pin.

Adjustable Scriber (433)

For use with all LeRoy pens up to size 8 and pencils and with all LeRoy templates up to size 650 and 60 point (vertical or slanting letter). Furnished with double-ended tracer pin. Example letter variations are shown.

Height and Slant Control Scriber (434)

An adjustable scriber to form characters either vertical or slanting at any angle up

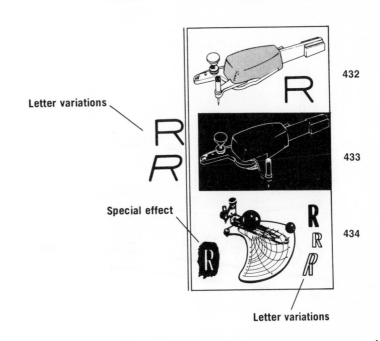

Letter variations

432

433

Special effect

434

Letter variations

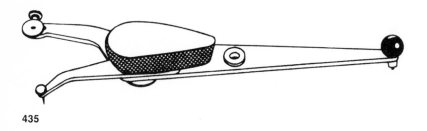

435

to 45° forward and any height from 60 to 150 percent of the size of characters on the template used. The width of the characters is not changed. Adjustment is simple: By loosening the knob, move the arm so that the small red circle of the arm lies directly under the intersection of the "degree slope" and "% height" lines desired. The knob is then retightened.

Adjustable Scriber (435)

For use with LeRoy templates size 700 and larger and templates 72 point and larger, for vertical or slanting lettering. Adapters furnished for use with pens 0000 to 14.

Letter Size Adapter (436)

For extending or condensing LeRoy lettering. With the adapter, used with the first two scribers described, the height of letters or numerals drawn with any LeRoy template can be increased or decreased by amounts up to one-third of their normal height. The width of letters and numerals is not changed.

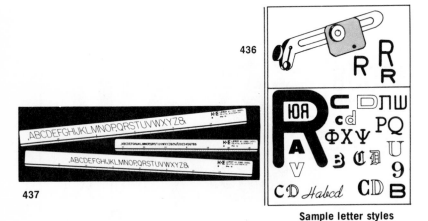

436

Sample letter styles

437

Lettering Templates (437)

Ranging in letter size from $\frac{1}{16}$ to 2 inches and available in many foreign languages such as Russian and Greek. Many letter styles are available. A few letter styles are shown on page 137.

LeRoy Pencil (438)

A precise mechanical pencil with a 0.020-inch lead. Ideal for pencil lettering work. Insert in any of the LeRoy scribers.

Reservoir Pen (439)

A fountain-type pen holding a large supply of ink which will last for several weeks. Pens 000 to 5 are designed to be used in the small fixed and adjustable scribers, and in the large adjustable scriber with a pen adapter. Pens 6, 8, 10, 12, and 14 are designed for use in the large adjustable scriber.

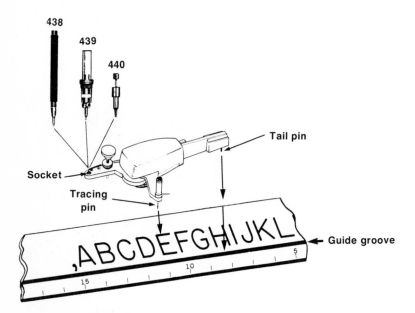

438

439

440

Socket

Tracing pin

Tail pin

Guide groove

Standard Pen (440)

Sizes 0000 to 8 are for use in small fixed and adjustable scribers, and in the large adjustable scriber with a pen adapter. Sizes 9 to 14 are for use in the large adjustable scriber.

Instructions

See page 115 for "Preparation of Working Surface for Lettering." See pages 111 to 113 for "Letter and Word Spacing, Alignment, and Special Effects."

1 Position the template on the lettering surface and next to the T square or straightedge (441).
2 Insert a pen, or desired accessory, in the socket at the upper arm of the scriber. Fill a standard pen as illustrated (442). To start the ink flowing, gently work the cleaning pen up and down.
3 Set the tail pin of the scriber in the straight guide groove of the template. With the tracer pen of the scriber simply trace the engraved letters on the template. The pen reproduces the letter or symbol in full view, above the template.

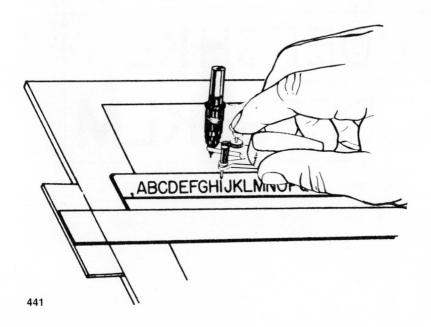

441

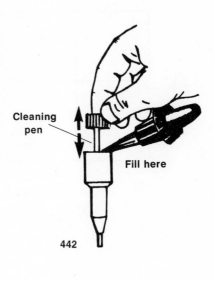

Cleaning pen

Fill here

442

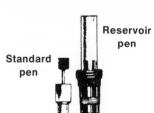

Standard pen

Reservoir pen

TEMPLATE SIZE	PEN SIZE											
	0000	000	00	0	1	2	3	4	5	6	7	8
50	A*											
60	A*	A	B	C								
80	A	A*	B	C								
100		A	A*	B	C	D						
120		A	B	C*	D	E						
140		A	B	C	D*	E	F					
175		A	B	C	D	E*	F	G				
200		A	B	C	D	E	F*	G	H			
240		A	B	C	D	E	F*	G	H			
290			B	C	D	E	F	G*	H	K		
350			B	C	D	E	F	G*	H	K		
425			B	C	D	E	F	G	H*	K	L	
500			B	C	D	E	F	G	H	K*	L	M

443   **LeRoy lettering chart (actual size)**

LeRoy Lettering Chart (Actual Size) (443)

This chart shows the wide range of LeRoy lettering effects that can be produced by combining various LeRoy templates and pens. The asterisks indicate the combination of template and pen recommended for a good proportion between the thickness of stroke and the size of letter.

LETTERGUIDE LETTERING SYSTEM

The Letterguide system (444) consists of a precision-engineered mechanical lettering scriber, lettering templates with typographical faces and alphabets engraved in plastic, and a variety of lettering accessories. Over 400 different templates are available in a variety of type faces. Sizes range from $\frac{3}{16}$ up to $\frac{3}{4}$ inch in most styles and up to 2 full inches in several styles. Accessories such as ball-point pen-stylus and silk-screen knife add to the versatility of this system. The scriber is calibrated so that with a single adjustment letters can be enlarged (height), reduced, and slanted from just one template. The templates are designed to align horizontally with a T square or straightedge.

Instructions

See pages 111 to 113 for "Letter and Word Spacing, Alignment, and Special Effects." See page 115 for "Preparation of Working Surface for Lettering."

1 Position the template on the artwork and next to a straightedge or T square. A Cam-lock T square is illustrated (445).
2 Insert the desired point in the scriber, and adjust the scriber for letter size and slant (446). If a pen is used, fill with ink as illustrated. Position the scriber on the template by placing the tail pin in the center slot of the

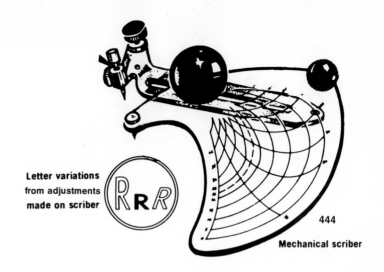

Letter variations from adjustments made on scriber

444

Mechanical scriber

445

446

447

template. Place the tracing pin in the first letter to be traced, and move both the template and scriber along the T square to position the letter on the artwork.

3 To letter, hold the template in place with the left hand and trace the letter with the right hand (447). For the next and remaining letters, slightly raise the scriber (leaving the tail pin in the center slot), slide the template to position the next letter, and repeat the instructions for the first letter.

VARIGRAPH LETTERING SYSTEM

The Varigraph lettering system was developed primarily for the production of display typography for photographic reproduction processes such as offset printing and letterpress. However, because of its versatility and increased popularity, it is now used for many additional applications such as silk-screen printing; chart, graph, map, and diagram work; posters; overhead projection transparencies; television, motion-picture, filmstrip, and slide titles; certificates; diploma and related engrossing work; displays; and exhibits.

The Varigraph system is made up of a compact, precision-built, mechanical typesetting instrument (7 by 7 by 1½ inches) (448), a metal matrix (lettering template) (449), and a pen (standard or reservoir) (450, 451) or pencil attachment (452).

Two models of instruments are available, one which produces vertical letters and another which produces back-slant or italic letters (italic model) from a standard Varigraph matrix (453). There are over 200 matrixes which make possible hundreds of sizes and shapes of type from 14 to 72 points. Here are a few of the many letter styles (454).

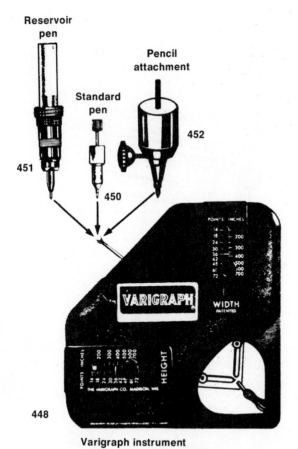

Reservoir pen

Pencil attachment

Standard pen

451

450

452

448

Varigraph instrument

449

Matrix

142

Instructions

A good T square or straightedge is most essential in that the Varigraph instrument has to move from letter to letter; it is also used for achieving parallel lines of lettering. The Boardlock T square has been designed especially for the Varigraph instrument and similar lettering systems.

1   For right-hand operation (tracing stylus in lower right corner), slide the matrix under the instrument from the left side, being certain that it goes between the supporting feet which receive the matrix, and retain it with the instrument. For left-hand operation (tracing stylus in lower left corner), slide the matrix in the instrument the same as for right-hand operation (455).

While holding the instrument stationary with the left hand, slide the matrix with the right hand to position

453

Letter variations and special effects

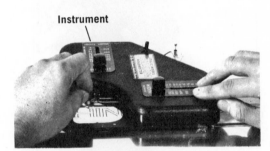

Instrument

455

Left-hand operation

454

CBADCBAEFBC

Sample letter styles

143

the desired letter in front of the pointer on the base of the instrument. With the right hand, position the tracing stylus in the groove at a point in the extreme left side of the letter. Apply only a very slight pressure on the tracing stylus, but do not allow it to come out of the letter groove before completing all the remaining instructions.

2 Observe the position of the pen, and slide the instrument with the left hand until the pen hovers over the point at which the left side of the letter is to begin. The tracing stylus must be held lightly in the groove so that the matrix will move along with the instrument and the desired letter will remain in the proper tracing position.

3 With the index finger of the left hand, push the pen lift fully forward to lower the pen. Begin tracing immediately after the pen touches the paper. Trace around the letter just once. If the pen did not write, retract the pen and raise the cleaning pin slightly up and down once or twice to start the ink flowing. Retrace the letter according to the foregoing instructions. Repeat these steps for each of the remaining letters (456).

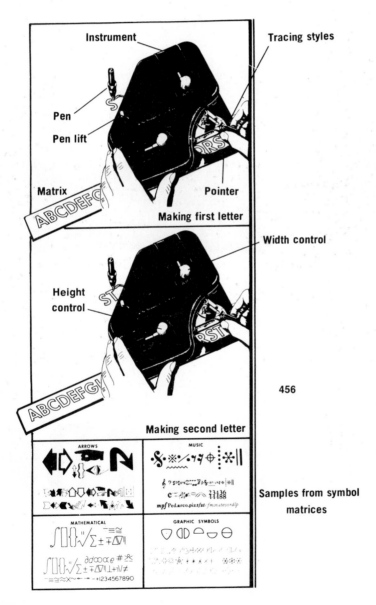

Making first letter

Making second letter

456

Samples from symbol matrices

DRY TRANSFER LETTERING

Dry transfer lettering (457), known also as *press-on, rub-on,* and *transfer type,* is considered to be one of the most modern lettering techniques available today. The letters, made up of carbon and wax, are printed on a plastic, acetate, or polyethylene carrier sheet. Letters transfer to virtually any dry surface such as paper, wood, metal, or glass by rubbing over the letter with a dull-point pencil or ball-point pen. Dry transfer letters are available in black, white, and a variety of colors (458). They are also available in transparent colors.

Dry transfer letters, while similar to composition adhesive type, are somewhat more exacting to apply in that once the letters have been burnished into position, they cannot be relocated. They can be removed with pressure-sensitive adhesive tape, razor blade, dry transfer letter eraser, or rubber cement eraser.

Since only the letter comes off the carrier sheet, there are no edges to create unwanted lines on the surface to which the letter is applied.

Backing sheet

Carrier sheet

457

Sample letter styles

458

Dry transfer letters are ideal for charts, graphs, maps, diagrams, posters, exhibits, displays, signs, bulletin boards, captions for photographs, television title cards, filmstrips, slide and motion-picture titles, overhead projection transparencies, diazo masters, logos, silk-screen artwork, and publications.

For artwork intended to be used in heat-producing reproduction equip-ment, heat-resistant dry transfer letters are recommended.

Instructions

1   Draw a light pencil line on the surface to which the lettering is to be trans-ferred. *If the lettering is to be done on clear or matte acetate,* draw the line on a sheet of white paper and

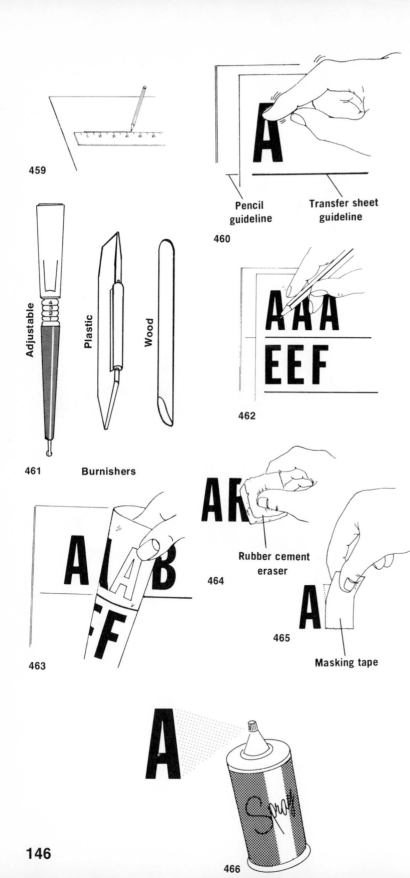

459

460
Pencil guideline   Transfer sheet guideline

462

461   Burnishers
Adjustable   Plastic   Wood

463

464
Rubber cement eraser

465
Masking tape

466

place under the acetate as a guide (459).

2   Line up the guideline on the transfer sheet, and move the letter to the desired position. Rub a finger over the letter to form contact between the carrier sheet and the surface (460).

3   Rub the first letter to be transferred with burnisher (461), a dull-point pencil, ball-point pen, or similar blunt instrument until the burnished letter changes color. Do not "scrub" or grind the point of the burnishing instrument into the carrier sheet. Burnish all thin lines and edges, if any (462).

4   Carefully peel or lift the carrier sheet away from the artwork (463). Transfer occurs because the adherence of the letter to the artwork is stronger than the adherence to the carrier sheet. Repeat the process for the remaining letters. To ensure permanence and secure placement, place the backing sheet over the transferred letters and burnish the entire area with the burnishing instrument. To remove the guideline, place the edge of a sheet of paper over the letters and erase the guideline with a soft pencil eraser.

MAKING CORRECTIONS

Pressure-sensitive tape (such as masking or drafting tape) can be used to remove unwanted letters by lightly pressing the adhesive side of the tape to the letter and carefully peeling it off the artwork. Corrections can also be made with a dry transfer letter or rubber cement eraser (464), pressure-sensitive adhesive tape, or a razor blade (465).

ADDED PROTECTION

When additional protection is desired, spray the letters with several light coats of any clear polyester-base plastic spray (466).

RUBBER STAMP PRINTING

Rubber stamp printing provides a neat, inexpensive method for printing such things as charts, graphs, maps, flash cards, nameplates, posters, and signs. A complete printing set, such as the one illustrated, includes rubber stamp type, a guide ruler, an aligning guide, a stamp pad, and a bottle of black ink and applicator. Miscellaneous type characters like &, !, ?, $, ¢ may also be included in the set. Some typical type faces are shown in (467). Some sources carry picture and symbol stamps as illustrated (468). The rubber type (letter) is securely cemented to an indexed wooden molding made to rigid specifications.

Rubber stamp

Sample letter styles

467

468

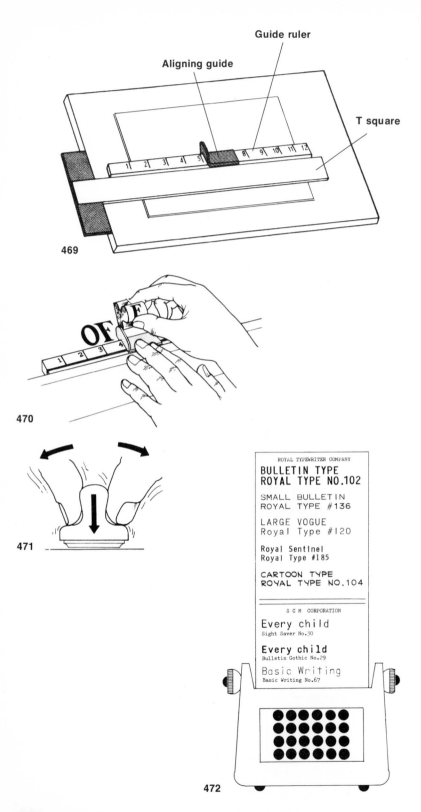

Guide ruler

Aligning guide

T square

469

470

471

ROYAL TYPEWRITER COMPANY

**BULLETIN TYPE
ROYAL TYPE NO.102**

SMALL BULLETIN
ROYAL TYPE #136

LARGE VOGUE
Royal Type #120

Royal Sentinel
Royal Type #185

CARTOON TYPE
ROYAL TYPE NO.104

S C M CORPORATION

Every child
Sight Saver No.30

Every child
Bulletin Gothic No.29

Basic Writing
Basic Writing No.67

472

Instructions

See page 115 for "Preparation of Working Surface for Lettering." See pages 111 to 113 for "Letter and Word Spacing, Alignment, and Special Effects."

1 Position the guide ruler and aligning guide against a T square or straightedge as illustrated (469).

2 Ink the first letter stamp on the stamp pad, and position the bottom portion next to the guide ruler and against the metal aligning guide; this will assure a straight letter impression. Make certain the dot on the stamp is at the lower right of the letter. Move the letter stamp and aligning guide along the ruler to the place on the surface where the impression is to be made. Make certain the stamp is tilted away from the surface to prevent the letter from making an impression before it is properly located. Hold the ruler and aligning guide in place with the left hand (470).

3 Press the stamp on the surface with a "rocking" motion. This will ensure a complete letter impression (471).

4 Print the second letter and remaining letters by moving the stamp and aligning guide to the next letter position and repeating steps 2 and 3.

BULLETIN TYPEWRITER LETTERING

The Bulletin typewriter, or Primary typewriter as it is sometimes called, is a "natural" for providing large-size type for the preparation of overhead projection transparencies, slide titles, script for public speakers, and exhibit and display captions, and can be used wherever large typewriter type can be the answer. This typewriter produces letters, in a variety of type faces, up to ¼ inch high. Carbon ribbons produce the best type impressions, especially for the preparation of originals for thermocopy or diazo reproduction. The type faces shown here (472) are available from Royal Typewriter Company and SCM Corporation.

VARAFONT INSTANT LETTERING SYSTEM (473)

An instant-producing lettering system that produces dry carbon letters in color (black, white, red, or blue) on a polyester-based tape. The tape has a matte finish on one side and is pressure-sensitive on the other. Tapes are available in translucent, opaque white, and opaque black (for reverses). Currently, numerous style letters are available in sizes ranging from 8 to 36 point (474). Uses include television, slide, filmstrip, and overhead title/captions; charts; graphs; publication art; etc. (475).

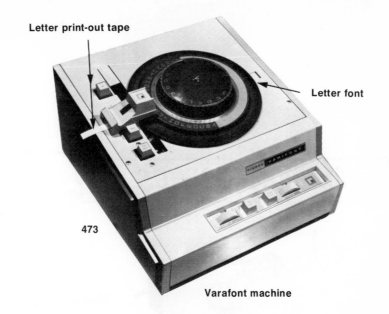

Letter print-out tape

Letter font

473

Varafont machine

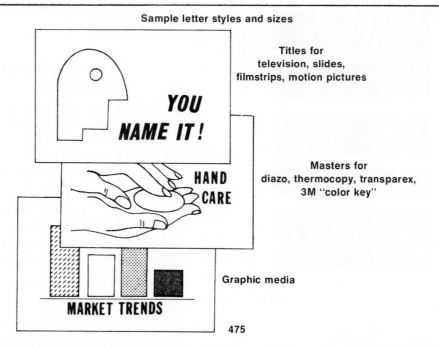

GOTHIC EXTRA COND.

GOTHIC

SCHOOLBOOK

FUTURA MEDIUM

MICROFONT

UNIVERS LIGHT COND.

HELVETICA

FLASH

MICROGRAMMA

UNIVERS MED. COND.

Sample letter styles and sizes

474

YOU NAME IT!

HAND CARE

MARKET TRENDS

Titles for television, slides, filmstrips, motion pictures

Masters for diazo, thermocopy, transparex, 3M "color key"

Graphic media

475

Here is how the system works:

1 With the desired letter font locked into the machine, letters are made at the touch of a button. Letter spacing and word alignment are automatic.
2 The printed tape is then removed from the machine, the backing peeled away, and the lettered tape adhered to most any surface (476).

See the "Lettering Selection Chart" on page 108 for Varafont applications.

← Backing

← Tape

476

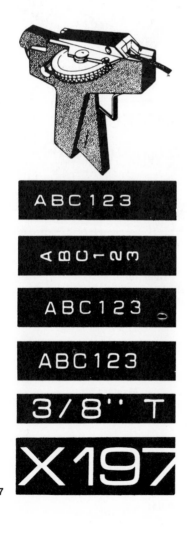

477

TAPE EMBOSSING MACHINE (477)

A letter-printing machine for producing letters, numbers, and symbols on pressure-sensitive plastic, metal, or 3M magnetic tape. Assorted letter styles, sizes, and colors are available. Tape widths range from $\frac{1}{4}$ to 1 inch. Letter heights range from $\frac{1}{8}$ to $\frac{5}{8}$ inch. Standard or optimum spacing, vertical or horizontal, reverse, and special-character embossing wheels are available for some makes and models of embossing machines. Uses include name tags, signs, equipment labeling, exhibit and display lettering, and other visual media requiring embossed-type lettering.

FLATBED PRINTING MACHINE

A fast, flexible, economical, and simple method for producing posters, signs, pennants, and the like in many sizes (up to 30 by 44 inches). Once the type is set (478), duplicate copies can be made in minutes. You can print one or more colors at the same time (479a).

In addition to letter type (479b), mounted type-high activity and symbol printing plates are available (479c). Custom-made plates are available.

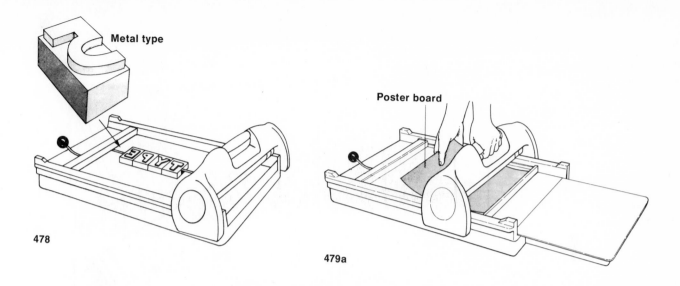

Metal type

478

Poster board

479a

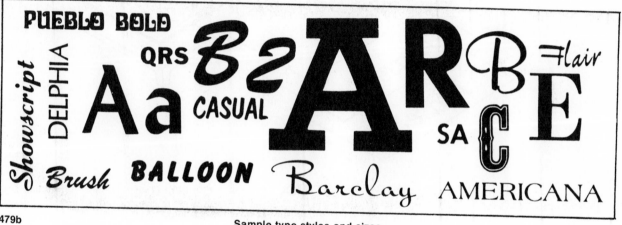

479b

Sample type styles and sizes

PUEBLO BOLD
Showscript
DELPHIA
QRS
Aa
CASUAL
B2
AR
B
C
Flair
SA
E
Brush
BALLOON
Barclay
AMERICANA

479c

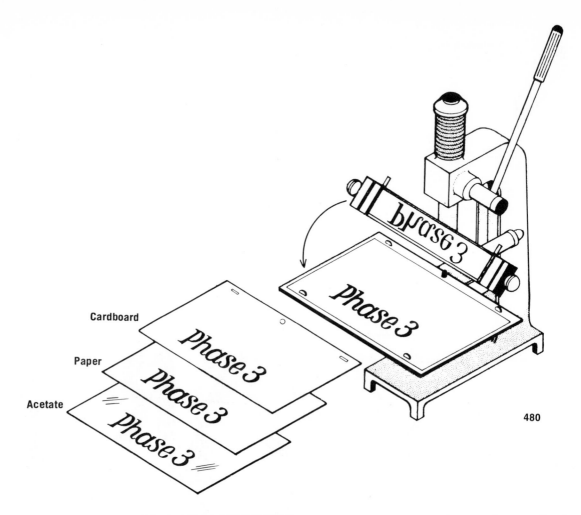

Cardboard

Paper

Acetate

480

HOT-PRESS PRINTING

A machine (480) specially designed for television and motion-picture graphics. The machine uses heated metal type (250° or slightly higher) to make letter impressions on paper, cardboard, acetate, and plastic surfaces. One advantage of hot-press printing is that the edges of the letters are sharp and clear, making it possible to use very small type successfully. Type sizes range from 6 to 120 point. In place of ink to form an impression, a roll leaf color foil is used to print letters in color.

The Veach Development Company manufactures an inexpensive heat stamping machine that is ideal for personalizing small items, such as slide mounts, greeting cards, pencils, brochures, photographs, and transparencies.

COMPOSITION ADHESIVE TYPE

Composition adhesive type (481) is another form of paste-up letter consisting of multiple alphabets printed on a thin acetate sheet with a pressure-sensitive adhesive or wax backing. The printing is usually on the adhesive side. Each letter is carefully cut with a razor blade or similar cutting tool, aligned on the artwork, and then burnished down to form the word desired. The printed lines between and underneath individual letters provide for ease of alignment and standard letter spacing of copy. Guidelines are removed when word composition is completed. For diazo or other heat-generating copying systems, the adhesive-backed rather than the wax-backed type should be used in that the wax-backed type will melt at high temperatures. A heat-resistant type is available from a number of manufacturers.

In addition to alphabets in a wide variety of sizes and styles (482), common phrases, borders, symbols, etc., are also available.

Instructions

See pages 111 to 113 for "Letter and Word Spacing, Alignment, and Special Effects." See page 115 for "Preparation of Working Surface for Lettering."

1 Draw a light-blue guideline (nonreproducing or light-blue pencil) on the lettering surface with a T square or straightedge. The guideline distance is determined by the printed guideline on the letter sheet (483). If the lettering is to be done on acetate, draw the guideline with a marking pencil directly on the acetate.

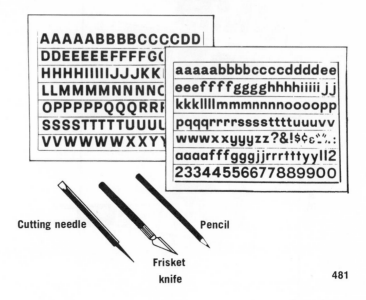

Lettering (type) sheets

Cutting needle   Pencil

Frisket
knife

481

Sample letter styles   482

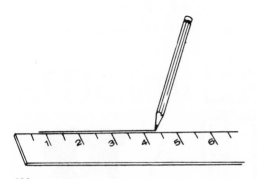

483

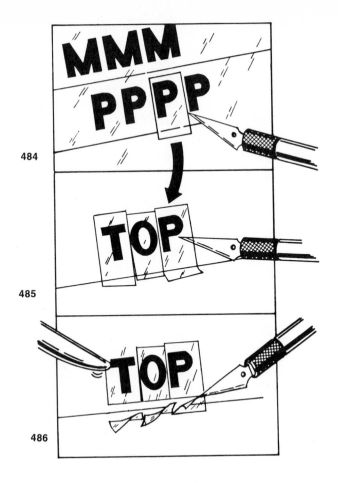

484

485

486

2 Cut lightly (not cutting through the backing sheet) around the desired letter, including the printed guideline below it, with a cutting knife, sharp stylus, or razor blade. Insert the point of the cutting tool under the letter, press the letter lightly against the point of the tool, and lift it away from the backing sheet (484).

3 Position the letter with the printed guideline in register with the guideline on the artwork, and press into place. Burnish lightly with a burnisher so that changes can be made before the final burnishing. Repeat this step for each letter until the assembly is complete. Letters or words can be carefully lifted and repositioned as desired (485).

4 When the assembly is complete and corrections have been made, burnish firmly the upper portion of the letters. Cut away the guidelines and complete burnishing. Erase the pencil guideline. The finished assembly is now ready for sharp, clear reproduction (486).

COMPOSITION PAPER TYPE

Composition paper type (487a) is a form of paste-up lettering consisting of individual, self-aligning letters printed on card-weight paper strips or tabs and assembled in a pad. Letters are assembled in a type composing stick or along a straightedge and backed with pressure-

487a

Sample letter styles

D C ER N LER GOTHIC sm LETRA R

sensitive tape to keep them in position (487b). Composition paper type is recommended where reproduction copy is needed for offset printing, zinc engravings, silk-screen printing, gravure, ozalid, verifax, diazo, blueprint, posters, television titles, visual aids, and presentations.

Some manufacturers produce reverse-color fonts. In addition, Fototype produces type printed on a transparent acetate tab which is set in a composing stick also.

Instructions

1 Assemble letters and blank spaces in the left hand as the right hand detaches characters from the pad (488).
2 Snap each letter in place if a composing stick is used. This device aligns and spaces letters automatically. The blue side of the letter should be facing up (489).
3 Apply tape to the assembled line of type. Use double-coated adhesive tape if the use of rubber cement is not desired. Lift the assembled line of type from the composing stick (490).
4 If the composing stick is not available, a straightedge can be used. Place a strip of tape on the back of the straightedge. Use double-coated adhesive tape if the use of rubber cement is not desired in the paste-up. Anchor each letter against the straightedge and next to the adhesive side of the tape. Lift the assembled line of type off the straightedge (491). See pages 87 to 89 for paste-up instructions.

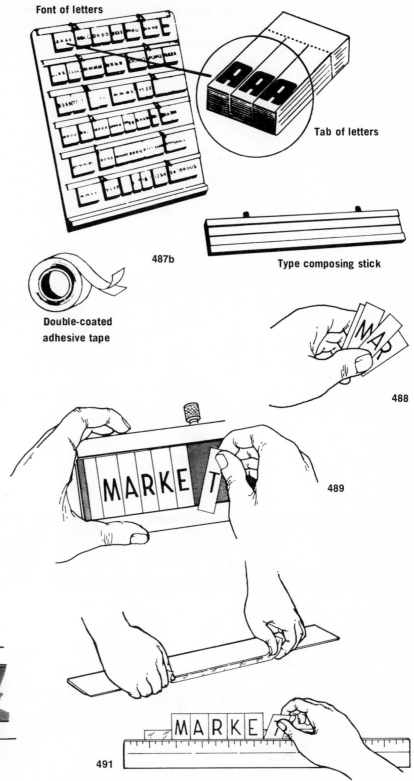

Font of letters

Tab of letters

487b

Type composing stick

Double-coated adhesive tape

488

489

490

491

5 Position the assembled line of type on the artwork. If Fototype is used, position the line of type with the black type facing up. When using double-coated adhesive tape, simply press the type into place on the artwork. Rubber cement is recommended when double-coated tape is not used (492).

Copy is now ready for photographic reproduction. Instructions that come with the composition paper type used are more comprehensive and should be consulted before the extensive use of this technique.

KINDER COMPOSITION PLASTIC TYPE

An economical process for producing photocomposition type without the use of photocomposing machines. From a single Kameratype font, an entire range of type sizes is available, limited only by the capabilities of the copy camera used; no additional fonts are necessary when another size type is needed.

Each Kameratype character is accurately formed in white on a precision-cut black plastic rectangle $\frac{1}{16}$ inch thick (493). All characters are 96 point (capitals approximately 1 inch high (494).

Kameratype is available with capitals, lowercase, numerals, and punctuation. Characters range from 3 to 9 depending upon frequency of use.

Here is how Kameratype works:

1 Kameratype is easily set by placing each character in the channel guide. A wire stop is used at either end to hold the line in position (495). Words and letters may be visually separated, or Kameratype spacers may be used. Since letters are laterally reversed like lead type, they are set from right to left. Proofreading is made easier when a mirror is used to read the

492

Rubber cement

493

KAMERATYPE

494

A 3 gh QR b L1 E F1
ef g B gh JK HI H st1 C

type. Channels for each line are placed in position on the copy board or on the floor, using a black background.

2 Composed type is photographed with a camera loaded with photographic film or paper.

3 Normal processing, following procedures recommended by the film or paper manufacturer, results in positive typography ready for use. Photostabilization machines add even greater efficiency to the use of Kameratype.

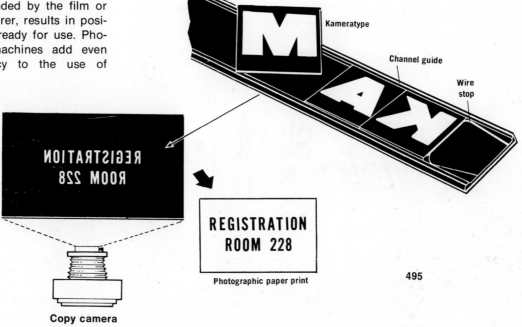

Copy camera

REGISTRATION
ROOM 228

Photographic paper print

Kameratype

Channel guide

Wire stop

495

PHOTOTYPE COMPOSING MACHINE

There are a number of machines (496) available which use the photographic process to produce display type and type matter for mechanicals, that is, paste-ups which are subsequently copied with

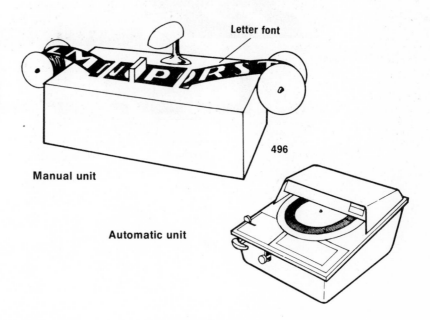

Letter font

Manual unit

496

Automatic unit

a process or copy camera to produce negatives for offset printing and visual media. Some units produce letters up to 3¾ inches high (497).

Phototype composing is considered to be one of the most sophisticated of the "cold-type" techniques (498). The phototype composing machine makes use of letter fonts, some of which are laminated in plastic or glass for greater life. These fonts are used to compose type photographically on sensitized paper or film. The sensitized paper or film is processed either in the machine, in photographic trays, or in a special processing unit. Many of the machines produce phototype on strips of 35mm film or paper which can be pasted up on artwork for copying.

Phototype composing machines vary in price depending on their flexibility. Some are manually operated, some automatic; some are contact, and some projection machines.

Sample letter styles

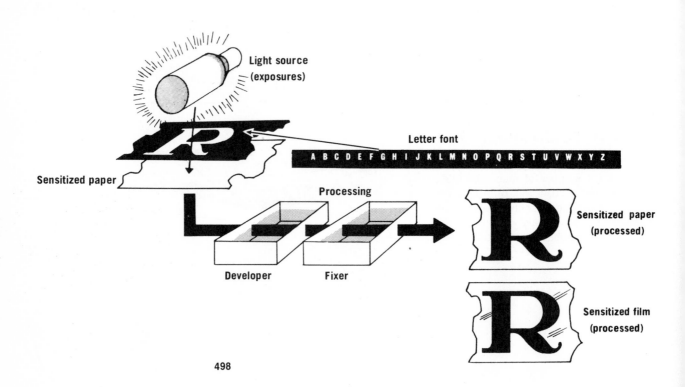

497

498

7 MOUNTING AND LAMINATING TECHNIQUES

Mounting techniques are required for attaching one surface or material to another surface or material. Mounting paper on paper, cardboard, cloth, or acetate; mounting acetate on paper or cardboard; mounting precut letters and other three-dimensional materials and objects on a variety of surfaces—these are just a few of the many situations in which a mounting or laminating technique or material or one type or another is necessary.

In almost all phases of the visual production process, some form of mounting may be required. It serves to preserve old or fragile originals and lengthens the life of heavily handled materials. It guarantees longer life of those nonreplaceable visuals collected over the years. For producers of filmstrips and 35mm art "flats," good mounting helps eliminate folds and blisters that may cause problems when the final image is to be photographed. Careful choice of mounting techniques will assure that there will be no staining or deterioration of the mounted materials.

This section on mounting techniques is divided into several parts: "Cold Mounting" includes several techniques that require no heat or expensive equipment; "Cold Laminating" covers techniques for hand and machine application of acetate to a variety of surfaces; "Mounting Aids" illustrates and discusses, in brief, useful commercial mounting aids which have not received a more detailed treatment in this section; "Heat Mounting" illustrates and discusses some unique approaches to mounting and preserving visual media with heat-mounting materials and equipment; "Heat Laminating" covers a variety of techniques and materials designed especially for preserving and protecting flat visual media with special acetates; "Picture Transfer" describes a mounting technique which results in the transfer of pictures and words from most magazines to acetate that can be projected; "Passe-Partout Mounting" is a rather comprehensive treatment of mounting materials under glass or plastic for instructional or display purposes; "Display Easels" covers the preparation of an assortment of attractive and useful display easels; and, finally, an updated coverage of techniques for mounting large or overhead projection transparencies and assorted-size projection slides is given.

COLD MOUNTING

RUBBER CEMENT MOUNTING

Rubber cement mounting is a quick, easy, and clean technique. It is ideal for mounting many flat instructional materials such as prints, photographs, drawings, and precut letters. Rubber cement is an easy-spreading adhesive for joining paper to paper, cloth, leather, glass, metal, wood, and other surfaces. Good-quality cement is nonwrinkling, noncurling, and easily removed from nonporous surfaces by rolling it off with fingers or a rubber cement eraser. To assure good adhesive quality, the cement should be stored in brown bottles and kept away from high temperatures. It should be thinned with rubber cement thinner (solvent) if the cement does not flow freely from the brush used to apply it. Special plastic or glass dispensers with a built-in brush are available.

Before starting the mounting, trim the visual to the desired size (499). The trimmed visual is then positioned on the mounting board, and a small, light pencil guideline is placed at each corner (500). A thin, even coat of rubber cement is applied (501) to the back of the visual. This should be done with smooth, even brush strokes, making sure the entire surface is covered. Going back over rubber cement which is not thoroughly dry will cause scuffing and produce a rough surface; the result will be an imperfect mounting.

Apply a coat of rubber cement to the mounting board, extending it slightly beyond the guide marks (502). Better adhesion will be assured if the brush strokes are at a 90° angle to those used on the back of the visual. Allow the rubber cement to dry. Place two sheets of household wax paper on the cemented surface of the mounting board so they slightly overlap at the center (503).

The wax surface prevents the visual from adhering to the mounting board during positioning. Place the visual on the wax paper with corners registered on the guide marks (504). Firmly hold the lower half of the picture in place as the top sheet of wax paper is withdrawn (505). This permits the two rubber-cemented surfaces to come into direct contact with each other. Next, remove the bottom wax sheet (506).

Finally, smooth down the surface of the visual, starting in the center and working in an outward direction (507). It is advisable to use a protective sheet of clean paper over the visual to prevent

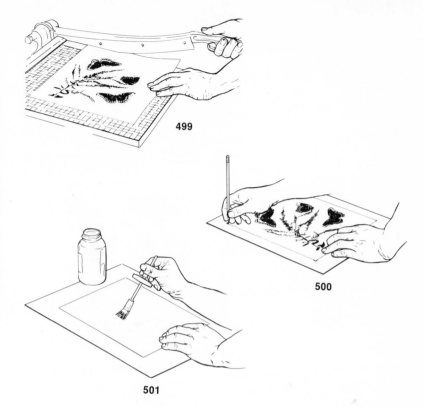

499

500

501

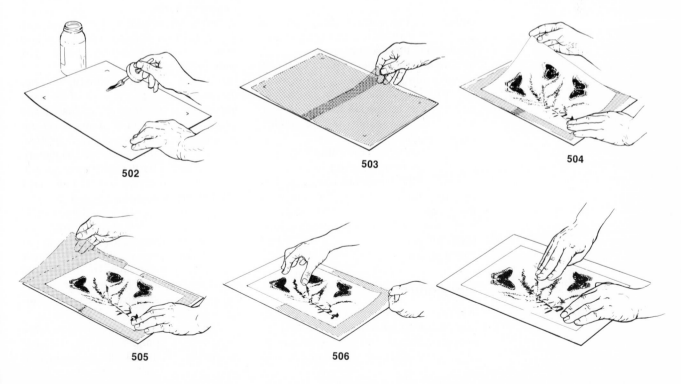

502

503

504

505

506

508

509

displays involving three-dimensional objects. This family of adhesives may be found in several forms.

For the person interested in creating displays, including both two- and three-dimensional materials, there is a wax adhesive stick often referred to as bulletin board wax. To use, take a small portion of this wax, roll it into a small ball, and place it on the contact point of the material to be mounted. Then position the material on the surface it is to be mounted on and press it firmly into place. This method can be used to suspend flat materials and lightweight three-dimensional objects. When the material is removed from the display, the small lump of wax may be scraped off and used again.

Another form in which wax adhesive material may be procured is that of wax discs. These are small plastic discs coated on both sides with adhesive wax. They may be obtained in a variety of sizes depending upon the size of material to be mounted. The disc is placed at the contact point of the material to be mounted and pressed against the mounting surface.

Spray wax adhesive in an aerosol can is excellent for coating materials with a pressure-sensitive coating of wax. It is waterproof, wrinkleproof, colorless, and fast drying. It is used primarily on two-dimensional materials. One of its most important characteristics is that it will permit repositioning of material on the mounting surface. When the final position is decided upon, burnish the material down with a hard, smooth instrument. Spray wax adhesive is easy to use. Place the material to be coated face down on a large, clean piece of paper. Spray evenly over the back of the material (510) in a smooth back-and-forth motion, being sure to coat the edges thoroughly. Allow a short time for drying. The material is then ready to press in place. For removing unwanted adhesive, follow the directions on the can.

The wax coating machine has been designed for people needing to coat quantities of material with wax adhesive.

damage to the surface (508). Often a small rubber roller is used for this purpose. When the visual is firmly mounted, remove excess rubber cement by gently rubbing with a finger along the edges of the visual. A rubber cement eraser can also be used to remove excess cement. Erase the guide marks, and the mounting is completed (509).

The technique of mounting just described is often referred to as a permanent method. It is not truly a permanent mounting, however. The quality of the rubber cement used, the mounting technique used, and the storage conditions will determine to a great extent how long the mount will last.

WAX MOUNTING

Wax adhesives have become a very popular mounting substance, especially for people involved in the process of assembling paste-up art materials or creating

It is an electrical device for heating and applying adhesive wax. These wax coaters range from small hand-held spreaders to automatic paper-fed machines capable of handling large sheets. As the material passes through the machine (511), it is coated with a layer of pressure-sensitive wax. Material coated by this method may be adhered to surfaces such as paper, plastic, foil, film, tissue, and fabrics. As with spray wax adhesive, this material may be repositioned. When the final position is set, the material is then burnished into place.

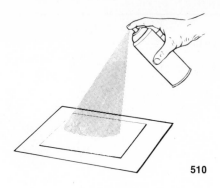

510

DOUBLE-COATED ADHESIVE ACETATE AND SHEET

A quick, easy way to mount drawings, prints, photographs, etc., without heat or liquid adhesives. Indispensable where heat or wet mounting would damage the material to be mounted. This mounting technique involves the use of an acetate or special sheet with pressure-sensitive adhesive on both sides which bonds on contact with the material to be mounted (512).

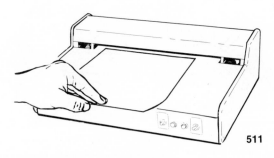

511

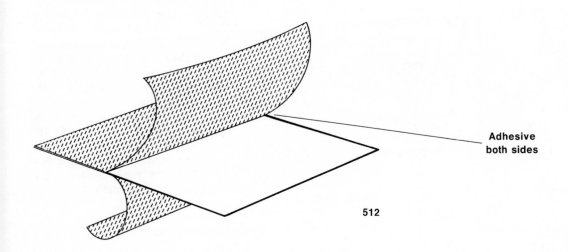

Adhesive
both sides

512

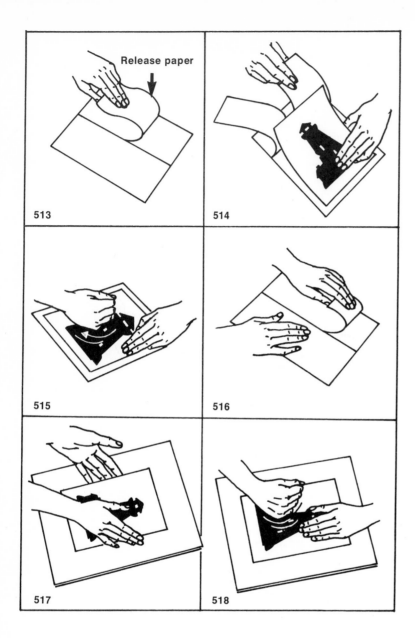

513

514

515

516

517

518

The instructions that follow are for using Falcon Perma/Mount. However, the same basic instructions can be used with other similar products.

1   Peel back the release paper from one side of the card (about halfway), and fold it against the card (513).
2   Perma/Mount cards are supplied slightly oversize to allow ease in positioning. Leaving a small margin at the top and sides, gently apply the visual to the bare adhesive (514). Then peel the remainder of the release paper from under the visual and allow the visual to smoothly come in contact with the rest of the card.
3   Press down firmly over the surface of the visual (515), applying pressure from the center out to the edges.
4   Trim the visual to final size using a paper cutter, mat knife, or scissors.
5   Turn the visual over, and remove the release paper from the reverse side of the visual (516). Try not to touch the exposed adhesive.
6   You are now ready for mounting. Gently place the print on the surface to which the visual is to be mounted in the position desired (517).
7   *Do not apply any finger pressure to the surface of the visual at this time.* First make sure the visual is accurately positioned on the mount. The position of the visual can still be shifted if necessary by just tapping against the edge of the visual to slide it to the correct position.
8   Now press down firmly over the entire surface of the visual (518). The card thickness eliminates the problem of air bubbles. Mounting is now complete, and the mounted visual can be handled normally.

WET MOUNTING

Wet mounting is a simple technique of backing paper instructional material with cloth, usually unbleached muslin. It is an age-old process and was, in fact, used centuries ago in the Far Eastern countries to protect and preserve paint-

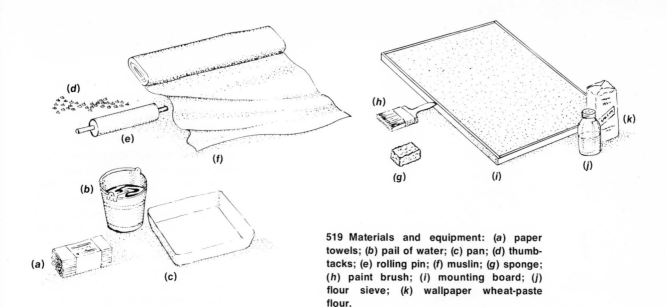

519 Materials and equipment: (*a*) paper towels; (*b*) pail of water; (*c*) pan; (*d*) thumbtacks; (*e*) rolling pin; (*f*) muslin; (*g*) sponge; (*h*) paint brush; (*i*) mounting board; (*j*) flour sieve; (*k*) wallpaper wheat-paste flour.

ings and scrolls. The preservation of these ancient works of art in museums today is evidence of the durability of this form of mounting. This mounting technique is ideal for preserving large visual materials such as charts, maps, and posters. One of the advantages of this technique of preservation is that all materials and equipment are readily available (519). The mounting surface may be any flat, waterproof surface sufficiently large to accommodate the material to be mounted, or, in cases where there is repeated demand for this method of mounting, it may be a specially prepared board.

A special mounting board (520) is relatively easy to construct. First, size must be determined by the material that will be mounted. It is always desirable to have the board 2 to 3 inches larger than the material to be mounted. Two sizes which have proved quite adequate for a great number of charts, maps, posters, etc., are 33 by 43 inches and 34 by 48 inches. The board should be as moistureproof as possible. There are a number of ways the mounting board may be constructed. However, a heavy sheet of ¾-inch plywood covered by ⅛-inch tem-

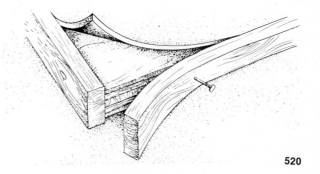

520

pered hardboard has proved to be quite successful. Glue the hardboard to the plywood, using a waterproof glue. Then nail soft pine strips ½ by 1 inch along the edges to frame the board. These strips must be of soft wood to permit the easy insertion and extraction of the thumbtacks. It is not desirable to glue these strips to the main body of the board since they will need to be replaced after long periods of use. After the board is completed, it is best to cover it with a good-quality hard-surface varnish.

521

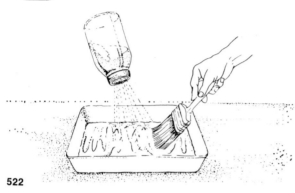

522

523

sieve. A combination sieve and storage bottle (523) may be made from a canning jar. Puncture holes in the metal lid so that the paste flour can be shaken out easily during the mixing of the paste. A circular piece of cardboard placed under the perforated lid will keep the flour clean during storage.

Stretching the cloth properly is important. A definite attempt should be made to square the thread pattern with the surface on which the cloth is being stretched. One method of stretching the cloth is shown in (524). After the cloth is thoroughly soaked in water, wring out the excess moisture and proceed with the following steps in the stretching process. (Before beginning the procedure, be sure that the mounting surface is clean and free of all foreign matter.)

1   Establish one corner, and either staple (using a staple gun) or thumbtack the corner of the cloth to the corner of the mounting board.
2   Allowing a little excess of the cloth to extend over the edge of the board, stretch the edge of the cloth to the second corner. Try to keep the thread pattern parallel to the edge of the board.
3   In a similar manner, stretch the second edge of cloth to the third corner.
4   Thumbtack these two established edges at intervals of 3 to 4 inches. Draw the final corner of cloth to the fourth corner, and tack it in place temporarily. Starting on the long remaining side AB on corner A adjacent to the already adhered edge, draw the cloth tightly and staple it at intervals of 3 to 4 inches. Do the same to the remaining side BC, always keeping in mind that the thread pattern should be parallel to edges of the board.

The stretched cloth is now ready for use, and the mounting process can be begun.

1   Before beginning the wet mounting process, make sure that the printed material is colorfast. If it is not, thor-

First, place the mounting cloth in water (521) so that it will be completely saturated by the time it is to be used. Next, mix the paste (522). Use the bristles of the brush to get an even, smooth, lump-free paste mixture. If the paste thickens after standing, add additional water. (For additional strength, add a small amount of glue size to the paste mixture.)

The mixing of the wheat paste is greatly facilitated by the use of a flour

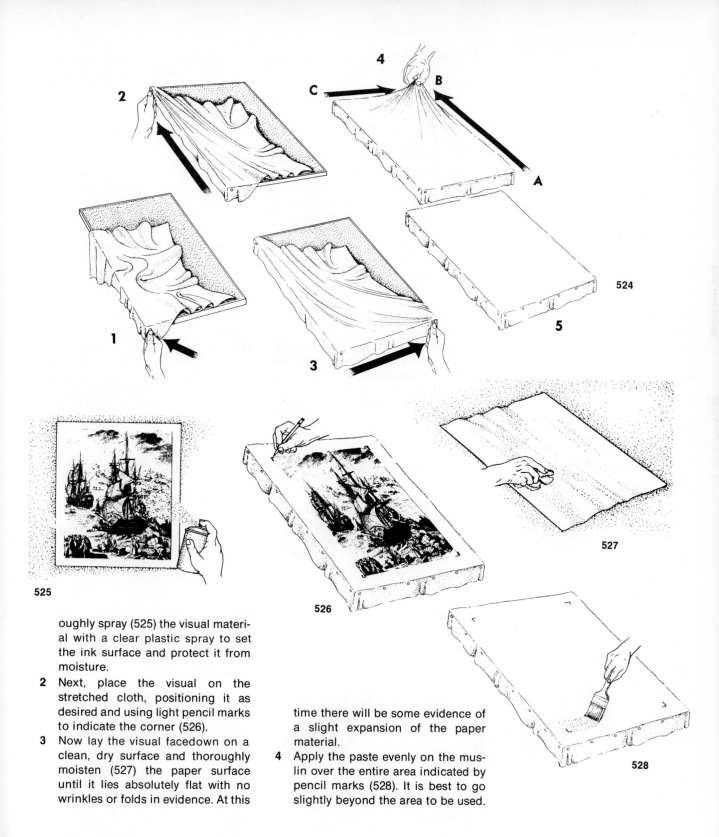

2

4

C

B

A

524

5

1

3

525

526

527

528

oughly spray (525) the visual material with a clear plastic spray to set the ink surface and protect it from moisture.

2 Next, place the visual on the stretched cloth, positioning it as desired and using light pencil marks to indicate the corner (526).

3 Now lay the visual facedown on a clean, dry surface and thoroughly moisten (527) the paper surface until it lies absolutely flat with no wrinkles or folds in evidence. At this

time there will be some evidence of a slight expansion of the paper material.

4 Apply the paste evenly on the muslin over the entire area indicated by pencil marks (528). It is best to go slightly beyond the area to be used.

5   Sponge off all excess moisture from the back of the paper material, and place it "face" up (529), positioned according to the original marks indicating the corners.

6   Working from the center of the visual, gently rub out (530) wrinkles so that the material will lie smooth and flat against the muslin surface.

7   Place the rolling pin in the center parallel to the longest dimension of the visual. With light pressure, roll from the center to the two nearest edges (531).

8   Next, roll from the center to the two remaining edges. This forms a + shape. Again, place the rolling pin in the center and roll to each corner as indicated (532). This forms an X shape.

9   To complete the mounting process, cover the edges of the visual with strips of newsprint. Start with the rolling pin in the center and roll in an outward direction (533) all along the edges. This squeezes out any excess paste onto the newsprint, which can then be discarded.

10 Next, check to see that there are no folds or wrinkles. If there is evidence of excess paste under any section of the visual, reroll that area. Finally, with a damp sponge, wipe off any excess paste from the surface of the visual (534) as well as from the marginal cloth areas. Let the material dry. When it is completely dry, remove carefully from the mounting board and finish the edges as desired.

There are many variations in the forms that wet-mounted visual materials may take. One of the most valuable characteristics of the wet mounting process is that it gives the material extra durability. Paper materials used in a scroll (535) box may be easily torn by constant use, but cloth backing will add extra durability. The extra strength of the cloth hinge

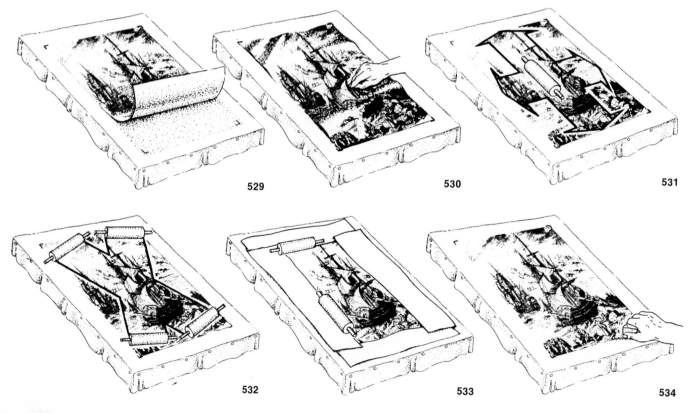

529 530 531

532 533 534

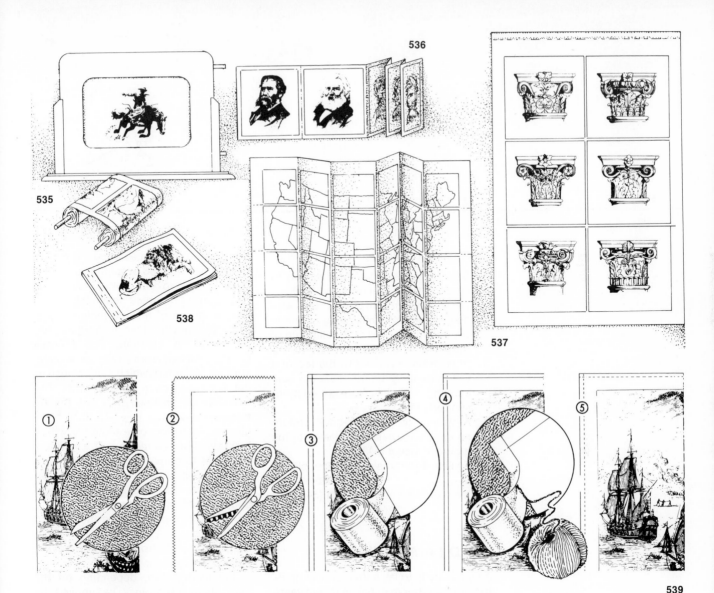

535

536

537

538

① ② ③ ④ ⑤

539

gives accordion-folded materials longer life (536 to 537) and permits constant folding. Pictures mounted on cloth and bound together in book form (538) are very durable and resist the wear from constant handling. Not only does the cloth backing add strength to the visual, but it simplifies displaying and storage, especially when a series of pictures must be kept in a certain sequence and displayed at one time.

There are a number of ways to finish the edges on a wet mounting (539). Cutting the cloth flush with the edge of the visual is the easiest method (1). However, if pinking shears (2) are used, there will be less danger of the cloth unraveling. Taping the edge (3) prevents raveling and gives added strength. In cases where the material will be handled very roughly, as would be the case with a poster or chart used outdoors in the wind, additional strength may be added by placing a string along the edge of the visual as it is taped (4). Hemming the edge (5) of the cloth material by hand or with a sewing machine makes a neat, strong edge that will be very durable.

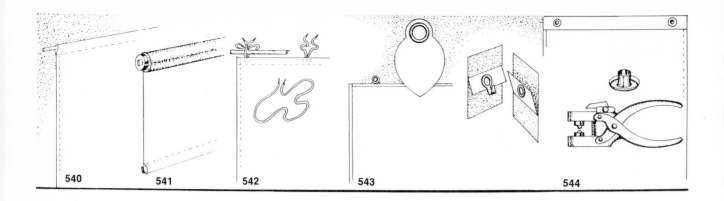

540   541   542   543   544

Methods of Displaying Wet Mountings

1 One of the most common ways is to suspend the visual on a rod (540).
2 For lightweight materials the window-shade roller makes an excellent support and permits the rolling up of the visual when it is not in use (541).
3 Shoestrings fastened to the top of a wet mounting permit ease in suspending materials from a variety of supports (542).
4 A variety of gummed-back picture hangers are available to fasten to the mounted visual (543).
5 Eyelets (grommets) may be placed directly in the mounted material with the use of an eyelet punch (544).

COLD LAMINATING

To laminate is to lay a thin layer or coating over another material. In recent years the lamination process has become extremely popular and important in the production of visual materials. The process of adhering a thin coating of transparent film as a protective surface over visual materials not only has contributed to the preservation of the visual but has also given it greater flexibility in use. As the lamination process has become more common, the number of uses for the film has increased. The creativity and imagination of the producer has developed many variations, such as creating flat and three-dimensional texture patterns, using the film as a tracing media, using it as a method of splitting a printed page in half so that both sides of the page can be mounted separately, using it as a means of making picture transfers, and many other techniques too numerous to mention. The process usually involves some type of acetate, vinyl, or Mylar film which has a transparent adhesive coating on one side. The film may be obtained in a dull (matte, frosted) finish and in a standard high-gloss surface. For some situations where low reflection is important or where it is desirable to draw on the surface of the film with pen or pencil, the frosted finish may be chosen. It is argued by some people that laminating a printed illustration gives it a glossy surface and tends to brighten the image, making it a more desirable master from which to make a photographic copy.

Laminating film, depending on the type being used, may be applied by either a cold process or a heat process. Laminating film of the cold variety may be applied by hand or in a specially designed machine having pressure rollers. Heat laminating film may be applied by using a flat iron or by using a specially designed laminating machine having a heat and roller system to ensure good adherence of the film to the base material. In some cases thermocopy machines function as laminators. The dry mounting press, because of its heat and pressure system, may also be used to laminate flat materials.

Each method of lamination has its strengths and weaknesses when cost, speed, and flexibility are considered. It is up to the producer to familiarize himself with the various laminating processes and choose the one that best fits his needs.

COLD LAMINATING ACETATE

Cold laminating acetate is a transparent film with a pressure-sensitive adhesive backing that permanently bonds on contact to most dry surfaces, without heat. Acetate can be applied to photographs, clippings, valuable documents, charts, signs, and any material requiring a permanent protective acetate covering. Nationwide Adhesive Products also carries a matte acetate that will accept pencil, ball-point pen, typewriter notations, etc.

Three techniques for laminating with cold laminating acetate will be discussed here; hand, clipboard, and machine applications.

Hand Application

1   Cut the acetate to the desired size. If the material is to be laminated on both sides and a transparent margin is desired, cut the acetate large enough to allow for such a margin. Separate the backing sheet from the acetate at one of the corners with the point of a cutting knife or by "flicking" a corner with a finger as illustrated (545).

2   Peel back the acetate sheet (546), and position the visual as desired on the backing sheet (547). *Or* completely peel off the acetate, and position the visual on the backing sheet. With the "sticky" side of the acetate down, bend the acetate in a U shape and gently lower it down onto the face of the visual (548), pressing it down in a down and outward direction.

3   Turn the visual over onto a smooth, clean surface so that the acetate side is down. Using firm pressure, rub the entire surface down with your hand

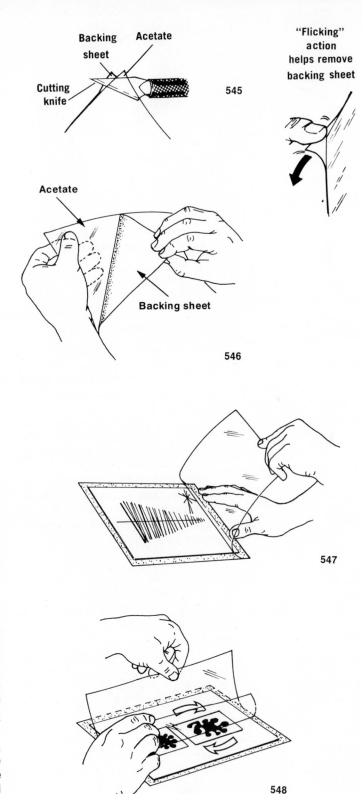

Backing sheet   Acetate

Cutting knife

545

"Flicking" action helps remove backing sheet

Acetate

Backing sheet

546

547

548

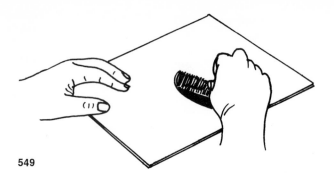

549

or a flat, smooth object—like the smooth side of a pocket comb or a ruler (549).

4 Trim the laminated visual to the desired size.

Clipboard Application

1 Insert the acetate unit (acetate and backing sheet) into the clipboard clamp. Separate the acetate sheet from the backing, and peel back to the clamp (550).
2 Lay the free end of the acetate over the top of the clamp. Position the visual or item(s) to be laminated on the backing sheet (551).
3 Roll the acetate back down. The clipboard assures accurate alignment (552). Lightly rub the finished lamination with your hand or a flat, smooth object.

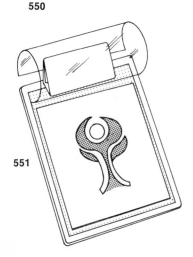

550

551

552

LAMINATING MACHINE (COLD PROCESS) APPLICATION

Equipment: film laminator (cold process)
Acetate: cold laminating acetate

Here is a technique for laminating a variety of materials. This laminating process involves a pressure-sensitive acetate and a cold-type laminating machine. Machines are available which can laminate materials up to 20 inches wide by any length and will accept materials from a few thousandths of an inch to $\frac{1}{8}$ inch thick. This process can be used to laminate valuable documents, records, photographs, signs, flash cards, illustrations, and so forth. Projection or display transparencies can also be made using this process (see pages 194 to 197).

Instructions

1 With the machine turned off, insert an edge of the acetate paper (backing sheet down) through the front opening until stopped by the machine rollers. Holding the acetate flat, push the switch to "nip" momentarily until about $\frac{1}{4}$ inch of the acetate enters the rollers (553).
2 Separate the paper backing sheet from the acetate as illustrated, and peel back to rest on the machine. Insert the material to be laminated on top of the backing paper, face side up, and slide gently into the nip at the rollers (554).
3 Hold the acetate with the left hand as nearly vertical as practical, and flip the switch to start the rollers moving. The machine will pull the acetate, material, and backing sheet through to the discharge shelf at the rear (555).
4 Trim the laminated material to size and remove the backing paper.

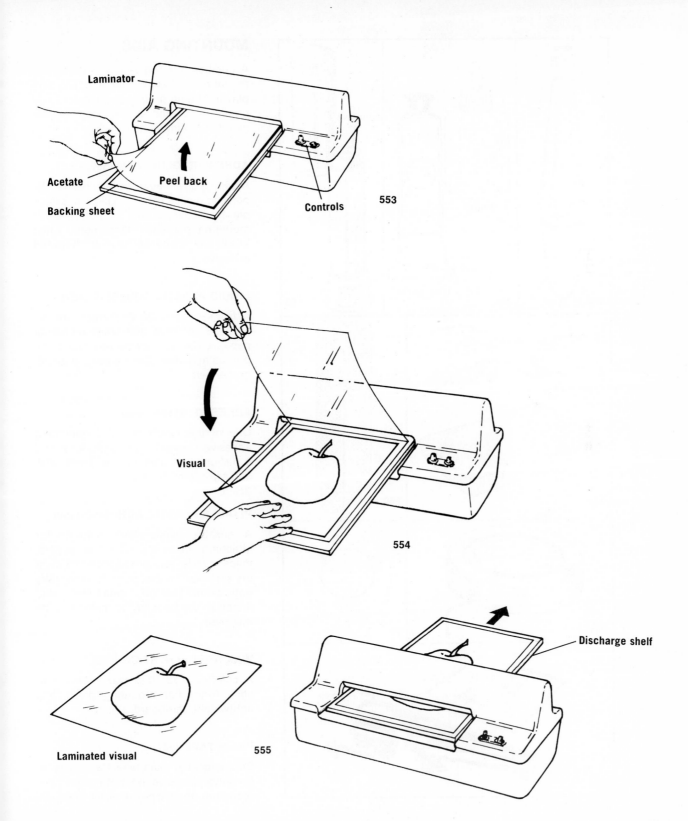

Laminator

Acetate

Peel back

Backing sheet

Controls

553

Visual

554

Laminated visual

555

Discharge shelf

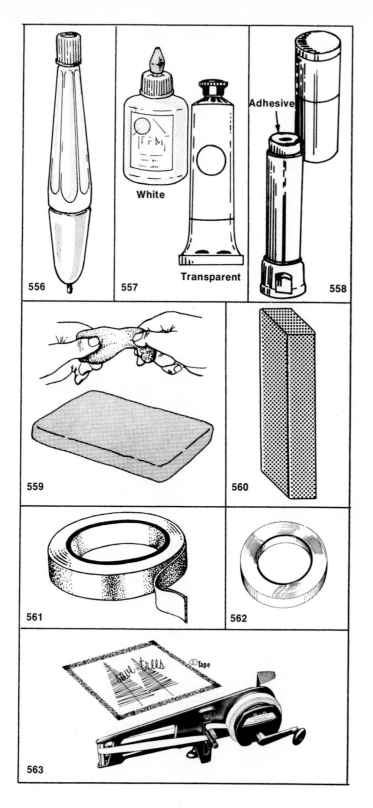

MOUNTING AIDS

A number of good-quality and unusual mounting aids are available to help simplify mounting problems. Illustrated and briefly discussed are several recommended mounting aids.

ADHESIVE (GLUE) PEN (556)

A pen-type refillable liquid-adhesive dispensing device using a ball-point principle to dispense dots of adhesive for mounting purposes. Most pens, when filled, will dispense several thousand adhesive dots.

LIQUID PLASTIC ADHESIVE (557)

A fast-setting white or transparent all-purpose adhesive that holds on wood, paper, cloth, and all porous and semiporous materials. Can be used in an adhesive pen.

ADHESIVE STICK (558)

One of the newer forms of mounting adhesive. Comes in lipsticklike form, and is designed for gluing paper, cardboard, and styrofoam materials.

PLIABLE PLASTIC ADHESIVE (559)

A reusable pliable plastic adhesive for attaching materials such as papers, maps, charts, and photographs to most dry surfaces. To use, pull like candy taffy until warm. Tear off a small piece, and attach to the back of the material to be mounted.

WAX ADHESIVE STICK (560)

A colorless, odorless wax adhesive in stick form. For mounting paper and lightweight cardboard.

FOAM TAPE (561)

Double-coated foam tape. Has pressure-sensitive adhesive on both sides. For mounting on all types of walls, tile, plaster, wood, and any surface that is clean, dry, and smooth. Not recommended for use on wallpaper. 3M brand tape is packaged as "Mounting Squares."

DOUBLE-COATED ADHESIVE TAPE (562)

A double-coated pressure-sensitive transparent tape for mounting everything from thin paper tissue to cardboard where tape mounting is desired. Some tapes have a carrier strip that must be peeled away from the adhesive tape to permit mounting.

TAPE EDGER (563)

Applies, folds, and cuts pressure-sensitive adhesive edging tape as it is needed. For mounting a tape border on papers, maps, charts, and thin cardboards.

HEAT MOUNTING

One of the most important basic areas in the production of visual materials is the mounting and preserving of flat pictorial and graphic imagery. Of all the methods of mounting and laminating, the heat processes have gained tremendous popularity in recent years. These methods of mounting involve the use of heat and pressure. The visual, backed by a dry adhesive sheet and placed on an appropriate mounting surface, is put into a specially designed mounting press. The application of heat and pressure forms a fast, clean mounting within seconds. Lamination is a process by which a special protective film is adhered to the image surface of the visual, and it may be accomplished by using the same equipment as for mounting or by using a machine so designed that heat and pressure are applied with rollers to effect excellent lamination of the picture surface. There are many variations of these processes, as well as a variety of ways in which straight mounting may be combined with lamination. A knowledge of all the possible variables expands the potential of the heat mounting methods and leads to greater flexibility in the mounting area.

The adhesives used may be of a permanent or of a removable nature. They may be purchased in dry sheets or in liquid form applied either by brush or from a pressurized can. The liquid adhesive should be dry before being used in a heat mounting machine. Some adhesives work best on rough surfaces, others on slick or highly polished finishes. It is important to know how the various adhesives adapt to the individual characteristics of printed materials and their supports, including a wide variety of paper, cardboard, cloth, and plastic, all of different weights, textures, and surfaces. Heat may damage some materials. It can affect a limited number of printed surfaces and their support through darkening, changing color, warping, or melting. Imagery produced by the thermographic process may not be exposed to the heat of this process.

Recently developed resin-coated photographic papers must be mounted with extra precaution. The manufacturers of dry mounting tissue have developed a special mounting tissue for use with these materials. Special plastic and wax surfaces on photographic prints may melt when exposed to heat. Humidity is another factor in the heat mounting process. The process may be extremely damaging, but if its characteristics are understood, it can be of great value in solving certain mounting problems.

The creative person may use heat lamination in a great variety of ways from the purely decorative to the utilitarian. Lamination film may be purchased in standard or matte surface, depending on the effect desired. It may be wrinkled and folded for special effects. Transparent watercolor, crayon, and ink applied to the adhesive side of lamination film before it is mounted can lead to a great variety of interesting and colorful effects.

The heat mounting methods lend themselves to so many variations that their extent of use is limited only by the imagination.

DRY MOUNTING TISSUE

The dry mounting technique is ideal for mounting many flat instructional materials without the use of liquid adhesives. Dry mounting tissue is a thin sheet of paper which is covered on both sides with a coating of high-grade thermoplastic or wax-type adhesive. By applying heat and pressure with a dry mounting press or hand iron, a strong bond is formed between the materials to which the dry mounting tissue has been attached. Materials can be mounted in a matter of a few seconds. When the thermoplastic type of tissue is used, a permanent bond will be made. When the wax type adhesive is used, it is possible to remove the visual at a later date. Dry mounting tissue is available in sheets of various sizes and in rolls.

To expedite the dry mounting process, precoated dry mount board is available. Mounting with this material eliminates the need for dry mounting tissue. However, material to be mounted must be the same size as the mounting board.

The effect of heat on the visual being mounted must always be taken into consideration; for example, care must be taken with materials coated with plastic sprays or varnishes, visuals made by the thermographic process, and drawings made with crayon.

Permanent Tissue

The visual (564) should be dry and free of wrinkles; if it is not, insert it in the heated press (565) with a protective sheet on top for about ten seconds. It is always important to turn the press on and set the temperature control at the proper temperature setting some time before putting it to use. Heating the press up to temperature will dry out any moisture that may have accumulated in the press because of humidity. Choose a piece of dry mounting tissue which is exactly the same size as the visual or a bit larger so that it can be trimmed with the visual after it has been "tacked" in place. Place the tissue on the back of the visual. Then tack it in two or three places near the center (566) with a heated tacking iron or the tip of a hand iron.

After the dry mounting tissue is securely tacked to the back of the visual, carefully trim (567) it to the desired size, making sure that no mounting tissue

564

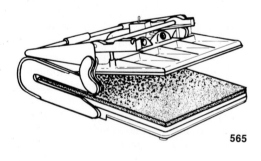

565

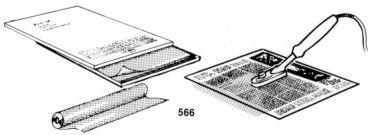

566

567

extends beyond the margins of the picture. Next, prepare to attach the visual and tissue to the mounting board. Since the tissue is not sticky, it can be positioned as desired on the board. Tack it onto the board by lifting any two opposite corners (568) and by touching the tip of the tacking iron or hand iron to the tissue. This will keep the visual in place during the actual mounting.

Check to see that the press is at the recommended temperature (225°F). Insert the visual into the press (569) with a clean sheet of paper on top to protect the surface. A special paper referred to as *release paper* may be purchased for use as a protection to the surface of the material being mounted. This paper is specially treated so that it will not adhere to surfaces. It may be used repeatedly.

Any foreign matter on the picture surface, such as grit or slivers of mounting tissue, will cause blemishes. Close the press for the recommended time (570). Thicker visuals will require additional time.

After the visual is removed from the press, it is best to allow it to cool under pressure. Metal weights are available for this purpose. Place the weight on top of the visual (571) with a sheet of paper to protect its surface. Allowing the mounted visual to cool under the weight ensures good adhesion and prevents some warping of the cardboard (572). When the picture has become cool, it is ready for use (573).

An ordinary hand (574) iron may serve as a substitute for the dry mounting press. The surface of the iron should be

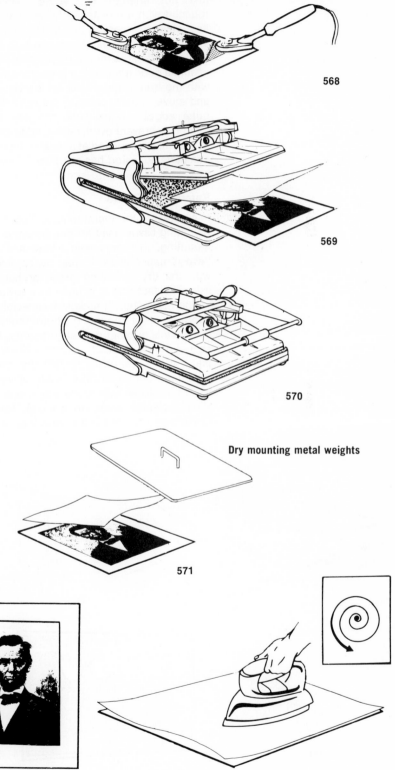

568

569

570

Dry mounting metal weights

571

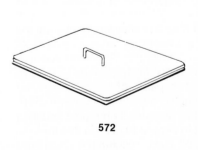

572

573

574

just hot enough to "sizzle" when touched with a moistened finger. Use a heat-absorbing paper as a protective sheet over the visual. Keep the iron in motion during the mounting process. To ensure a good adhesion, it is best to start with the iron in the center of the visual and move in an expanding spiral to the outer edges. Always keep the iron in motion to prevent overheating. Additional heat may be applied at any later time if complete adhesion has not taken place.

Removable Tissue

In contrast to the thermoplastic-type dry mounting tissue used for permanent dry mounting, the removable tissue has a "waxy" appearance. It may be applied with the dry mounting press or hand iron. The fact that it is used at a lower temperature (180°F) makes it especially appropriate for mounting photographic color prints or other delicate materials. It should not be used for mounting visuals that are to be exposed to heat for any prolonged period of time, such as visuals to be placed over heaters or in warm window-display areas. In general, this type of tissue is used in the same way the

permanent type is used. This tissue, however, does have the advantage of being removable. To remove a visual from its backing, simply place it in the heated press (200°F) for about one minute. Do not lock the press down. Quickly open the press and lift one corner (575) and gently peel the material from the base. If the material is large, it may require reheating to complete the process. This type of dry mounting adhesive will adhere to extremely slick surfaces, such as glossy photographs, metal, and plastics (576). The "waxy" adhesive will adhere to rough surfaces very well and holds well to wood or cloth surfaces. One valuable use is in the making of flannel board materials. Visuals are mounted on pieces of flannel or felt and then cut out (577). Even small flannel boards can be made by dry-mounting felt onto surfaces such as hardboard or plywood (578).

PLASTIC SPRAY (AEROSOL CAN)

The use of plastic spray adds another dimension to the dry mounting process. At times, it may be desirable to mount delicate materials that are too intricate in form to back with dry mounting tissue. Examples of such materials might be detailed cutout silhouettes, lace, or fern leaves. When care is exercised, the finest detailed image that will tolerate the heat necessary can be preserved.

In the example shown here a section of asparagus foliage (579) is mounted on cardboard. It is essential that all material be free of moisture. Place the foliage in the mounting press between several sheets of very absorbent paper, such as newsprint or blotter paper (580). In some cases it may be necessary to change the paper a couple of times because of excessive moisture. When the visual is completely dry, lay the foliage face down on a clean piece of scrap paper and spray a light coat of plastic over it (581). Allow it to dry, and then repeat spraying and again allow it to dry. Do this three or four times. Next, position the visual onto the cardboard with the sprayed side

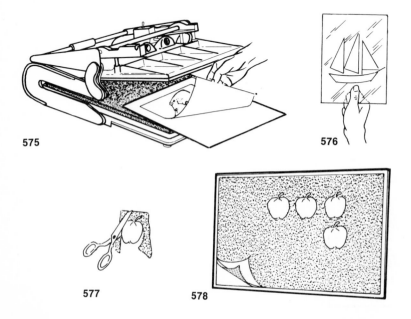

575

576

577   578

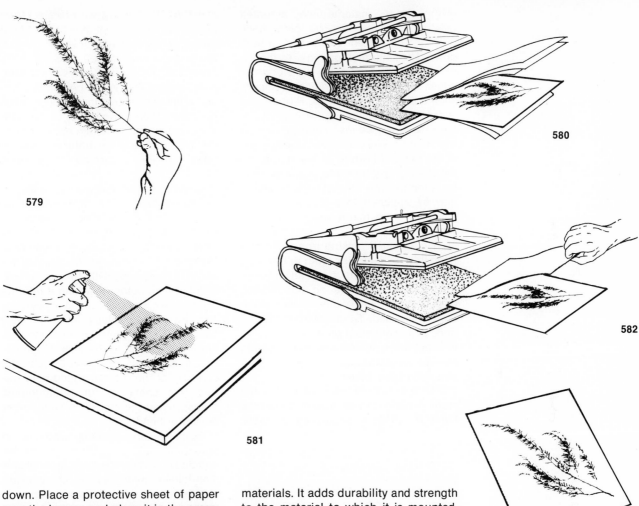

579

580

581

582

583

down. Place a protective sheet of paper over the image, and place it in the press, which should be set at about 180 to 200°F. Leave it in the press for fifteen seconds and remove (582). Quickly remove the protective sheet so that any small seepage of plastic does not stick to it. The mounting is now complete (583). For additional protection, the finished visual may be given a coating of plastic spray.

DRY BACKING CLOTH

Similar to the wet mounting technique is the use of dry backing cloth. This cloth is a high-quality cotton fabric with a thermoplastic adhesive coating on one side and is ideal for backing maps, charts, photographs, illustrations, and other flat materials. It adds durability and strength to the material to which it is mounted. Dry backing cloth is unaffected by moisture and will not shrink, buckle, or curl. When one uses this type of cloth, it is important to take into consideration the effect heat will have on the material to which the cloth is mounted. Sheets and rolls up to 42 inches wide are available; when mounting materials wider than 42 inches, the cloth may be spliced by overlapping the edges slightly.

Mounting on cloth is quite simple. Place the visual face down on a clean sheet of paper. Next, lay a sheet of dry backing cloth down over the visual with the adhesive (slick) side down. At this point a decision must be made concerning how the edges of the mounting are to be finished. The cloth may be flush (even) with the material being mounted (584), or the edges may be folded back over as illustrated (585) and ironed down. The latter method requires that an extra portion of cloth be left along the edges. Methods of hanging a mount should also be considered. Ribbon and eyelets can be sewed on (586), or grommets (587) may be inserted into the border material. When sufficient cloth is left at the top and bottom of the mount, fitted sleeves may be made to accept rods for support. The cloth-backed material may be attached to a strong window-shade roller so that it can be rolled up when not in use.

Use a heated tacking iron (588) or a hand iron to "tack" the cloth to the map. To protect the cloth from any foreign matter which may be on the tacking device, put a scrap of clean paper under the device used. The tacking should be done at a center spot on the cloth. If this is done, any wrinkles near the edge will be free to flatten out when the final mounting takes place.

There are three ways to mount the cloth. First, it can be ironed on with a hand iron (589). A clean sheet of paper over the cloth backing will protect it from any foreign matter that may come off the iron. With the iron set at low heat, keep it in constant circular motion. Start at the center of the mount and work to the outer edges. This is the best method to use when special treatment of the edges is desired. If adhesive edges of the cloth are exposed, make certain not to iron all the way to the edge until the special folds, already discussed, have been made.

A second method is the use of the dry mounting press. For flush mounting, where the backing is to be the same size as the visual, the dry mounting press works best. Set the press temperature at about 225°F, and insert the material for about five seconds (590). Be sure to cover the visual, before inserting it into the press, with a protective sheet of paper.

Third, photographic print dryers (591) can be used to produce flush mounts. Simply tack cloth to the back of the visual as instructed, and pass through the dryer set at the recommended temperature (the same as for photographic prints). Allow the mount to cool before flexing or bending it.

Because dry backing cloth is so strong, it makes excellent hinges for notebook covers, displays, and accordion-folded materials. Cloth backing may be used in combination with heat laminating films. The film laminations with their high-temperature requirements should take place first. The cloth backing should be put on last.

HEAT LAMINATING

DRY MOUNTING PRESS LAMINATING

The dry mounting press designed to mount flat pictorial material and using both heat and pressure will also serve as a laminating press. Having thermostatic controls, the press can be adjusted in temperature to satisfy the needs of the laminating film. A stiff sheet of cardboard or pressed wood used in the press will ensure better-quality lamination by not only adding pressure but also fur-

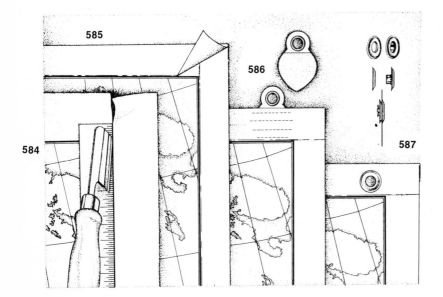

585

586

584

587

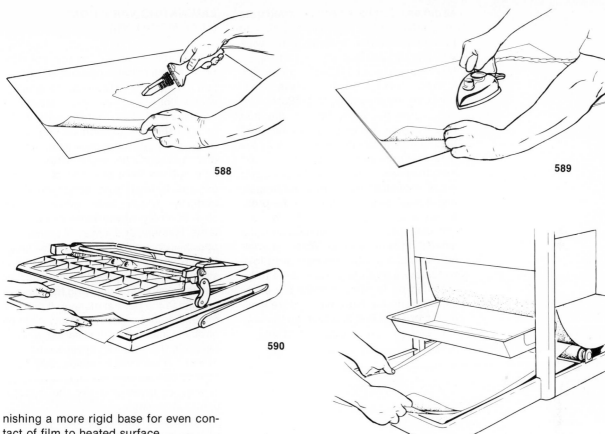

588

589

590

591

nishing a more rigid base for even contact of film to heated surface.

Both matte and glossy-surfaced laminating films are available for the mounting press. The film may be purchased in a variety of sizes in the form of rolls, sheets, and envelopes. The envelopes are designed so that both sides of a visual may be laminated at one time. The envelope is heat-sealed on three edges. The material is slipped into the appropriate-size envelope and placed in the dry mounting press. In a matter of seconds the laminating is completed. The roll and sheet film permit the laminating of one side of a visual or one side at a time. Usually visual materials mounted on cardboard will be laminated only on the face side.

It is possible to laminate materials other than paper such as wood, metal, and cloth. It must be remembered, however, that this process is limited to materials not affected by the heat. Pressure adjustments have to be made to accom-

modate the various thicknesses of these materials.

When you are dry-mounting visual materials to be laminated, it is best to use the high-temperature dry mounting tissue, because the lamination process requires a rather high temperature. Some difficulties may arise from melting or buckling if high-temperature laminating film is placed over low-temperature mounting tissue.

The process is relatively simple. Cut a piece of laminating film the size of the material to be laminated. If both sides are to be laminated, use a prepared envelope or cut the sheet two times the size of the visual and fold it over so that both sides are covered. Carefully place the material over the visual, being sure all dirt and dust have been removed from the surface (592). To hold the film in place while putting it in the press, wipe over the film surface with a soft rag so that the static electricity will hold the film in place. Place a sheet of clean newsprint over the laminating film (593) and insert it into the press for the required length of time. Always check the time and temperature instructions as given by the manufacturer. Remove the lamination from the press. The appearance of frosty areas indicates incomplete adherence, and it must be placed back in the press for an added length of time. Rough and irregular edges can be trimmed after the lamination is completed. When laminated material must be mounted with low-temperature mounting tissue or is to be mounted on low-temperature dry backing cloth, do the high-temperature laminating process first and then do the low-temperature mounting as the last step.

LAMINATING VARIATIONS (LEAF MOUNTING)

With increased use of the dry mounting press as a laminating device, the use of laminating film to protect and preserve a variety of materials has developed. Examples of only a few uses might include the preservation of iron filings formed by a magnetic field, thread designs and mathematical patterns, delicate cutouts from tear sheets, delicate designs formed from flower petals or butterfly wings and other natural objects, finely woven cloth or lace patterns, feathers, and leaves of plants. The possibilities are limited only by the imagination. In most cases the procedure is simply a matter of pressing the object as flat as possible and applying the laminating film in the normal manner. It must be remembered, however, that any material or object affected by heat cannot be laminated in this manner, because the temperature may reach nearly 300°F. In some cases, as with plants and leaves, it is wise to press and dry the material before lamination.

The preservation of leaves by the lamination method is extremely popular (594). First, carefully choose the leaf to

592

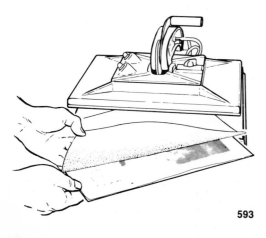

593

594

182

be mounted. Although the color of the leaf changes in the process, older leaves tend to hold their color better than younger ones. In the case of autumn colors, some leaves remain very true to their original color patterns. Stems and veins that are extremely heavy may be shaved down with a sharp knife from the back side of the leaf. This will prevent large raised areas in the final lamination. To proceed with the drying process, place the leaves between several layers of clean newsprint (595). Make sure the leaves are lying flat. Place this "sandwich" in the heated press (596). As the leaves are heated, the moisture will be absorbed by the newsprint. When working with leaves having high moisture content, it is wise to check them several times during drying to prevent their sticking to the newsprint. This can be prevented by changing their position each time they are checked. For very "lacy" (leaf) material this is extremely important. Drying the leaves at low temperatures helps preserve the color. When the leaves are dry, arrange them on the mounting surface and cover them with a sheet of laminating film (597). Rub over the film surface with a soft cloth so that the static electricity will draw the film tight to the mount. Be sure there are no serious wrinkles or folds. Cover the surface of the film with a clean sheet of newsprint, and place in the press for the specified time. Always check to see that the press temperature is up to the temperature required. After the specified time, remove the lamination from the press. If there are indications of incomplete adherence, return to the press for added time. Bridges of film formed near thick sections of the leaf such as the stem may often be tacked down using the tip of the tacking iron. If there is evidence of air trapped in these areas, a small pin prick will allow the air to escape and make adherence easier. If desired, diagrams, lettering, etc., can be added to the base mounting material prior to laminating.

Other variations in the use of laminating film made for the dry mounting press

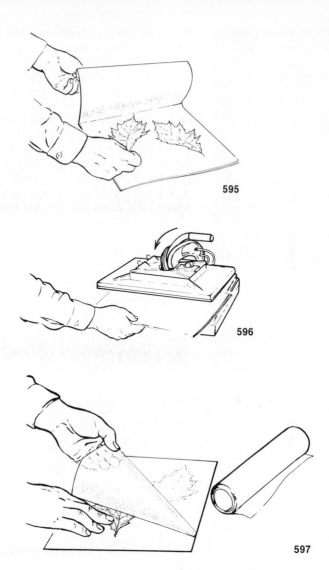

595

596

597

involve the manipulation of the film itself. The adhesive side of the film will accept ink quite well. Consequently it can serve as a tracing material. Since the tracing is made on the adhesive side of the film, the image being reproduced must be backwards. If the original is on relatively thin paper, this can be accomplished by placing it face side down on a light box. Place the film over it with adhesive side up, and proceed to trace the image. When the tracing is completed, the film may be adhered to whatever base material is desired. The drawing will appear right side up and will be pro-

598

tected by the film itself from any damage. When care is exercised, airbrushing in transparent or opaque color is possible on the adhesive surface. It must be remembered, however, that excessive amounts of ink or paint on the adhesive surface will affect its adhesive quality.

The laminating film is a tough material which will take a great amount of stress. This characteristic extends its potentials. If the film is wrinkled by crushing it into a ball and then flattened out before mounting, it will give a texture effect to the surface over which it is mounted. For instance, clear wrinkled film mounted over a snow scene gives a feeling of sparkling icing. Color wax

599

600

crayon chips may be placed beneath wrinkled or smooth film for brilliant texture patterns. As the heat of the mounting press activates the film, the crayons melt and form interesting color patterns beneath the film (598). The designs may be controlled to a limited degree by the placement of the color crayon chips.

For another example of how laminating film may be manipulated for a special effect, take a sheet and wrinkle it into a ball. Flatten it out and repeat the process. The more times this is done the finer will be the detail of the resulting texture pattern. Spread the wrinkled film out on a clean piece of scrap cardboard or newsprint with the adhesive side up. Do not flatten it completely but allow the wrinkles to form a three-dimensional pattern.

Using transparent or opaque dye or watercolor in an aerosol spray can or airbrush, spray the adhesive surface of the film at a low angle (599). The paint will strike only the surface facing the spray. Allow the color to dry. Then drymount the film onto a backing material. This may be white or tinted cardboard or paper, textured paper, wallpaper, aluminum, wood, or a variety of other materials. After mounting, the texture design created this way will still have a strong three-dimensional appearance (600).

Materials created in the aforementioned ways can contribute to the creation of displays, notebook covers, and special effects for many purposes. The effect shown in (600) may be used to represent a mountain range on a large wall map. For the creative person the possibilities are unlimited.

LAMINATING MACHINE (HEAT PROCESS)

Equipment: film laminator (heat process)
Film: heat laminating acetate

The heat laminating machine laminates film to one or both sides of paper, cardboard, film, certain flat specimens, etc. (601). The laminating film usually consists of Mylar and polyethylene inseparably welded together to form a tough, transparent protective coating. Machines will accommodate many gauges of laminating film from the thinnest, 0.0015 inch, for protecting paper, to 0.014 inch for laminating identification cards and other similar materials. The laminating film, combined with the machine that provides heat and pressure, makes up the laminating process.

Among the many types of materials that can be heat-laminated are valuable documents, printed literature, flash cards, posters, signs, illustrations, photographs, and flat specimens. Projection or display transparencies can be made with this process.

Machines are available to laminate materials from 3 to 60 inches wide, any length.

Laminating Paper or Cardboard Sheets (602)

1 Simply push a button or switch to set the heating unit of the machine in operation. A light will indicate when the machine is ready for lamination.
2 Push the control that starts the roller moving, and insert the material to be laminated. It will be discharged at the back of the machine sealed between two layers of transparent plastic film. Use the machine's cutter to cut the laminated material where desired. Material can be run through a second time if additional protection is required.

Laminating Flat Specimens or Small Sheets (603)

When laminating flat specimens or small printed sheets, thread the bottom laminating roll as illustrated. This will permit the film to serve as a conveyer. Or, if preferred, the material to be laminated can be fed directly into the machine without changing the threading of the film as suggested. Specimens such as leaves and insects should be dried out before lamination.

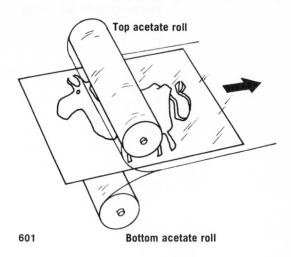

601   Top acetate roll   Bottom acetate roll

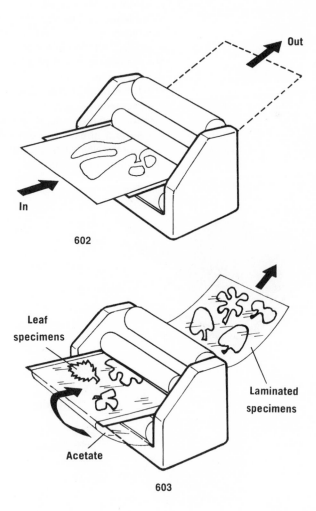

602   In   Out

603   Leaf specimens   Acetate   Laminated specimens

THERMOCOPY MACHINE LAMINATING

Many flat printed materials, such as valuable documents, photographs, and printed instructions, can have a special acetate laminated to their surfaces through use of a thermocopy machine. The acetate is designed to provide a protective covering and a surface to be written on, erased, and reused.

3M Laminating Instructions

The 3M Company manufactures a laminating film that is designed to be used in thermocopy machines as illustrated here.

1　Assemble materials as illustrated in (604). Make certain the original to be laminated is not folded, creased, or crumpled. All the necessary materials are in the box containing the film.
2　Set the speed control of the thermocopy machine at the slowest speed (darkest setting), and insert the materials into the machine. When laminating several sheets without interruption, gradually turn the dial to a slower (lighter) setting.

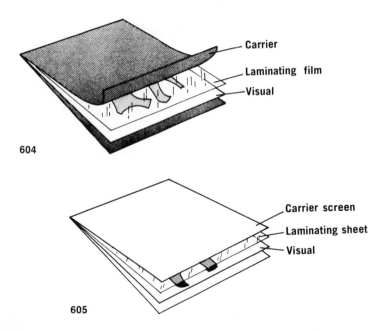

604

605

Viewlex (Viewfax) Instructions

Viewlex manufactures a laminating sheet for use in its thermocopy machines. Here are the instructions:

1　Assemble materials as illustrated, and place in a carrier screen. Insert assembled materials into the machine (605).
2　Follow step 2 of the 3M instructions.

Laminating Both Sides of Original

If lamination is required for both sides of the original, simply repeat the aforementioned steps on the reverse side of the original, using a second sheet of film.

Laminating Materials Smaller than Laminating Film (Viewlex)

If the original is smaller than the sheet of laminating film (e.g., business or membership card, photograph), the interleaf sheet must be placed underneath the original. Failure to do this will cause the film to laminate to the carrier screen.

PICTURE TRANSFER—A VARIATION OF LAMINATION

In the previous pages of this section the discussion of mounted materials was limited almost entirely to the mounting and laminating of opaque, flat pictorial images. With a little additional knowledge of both cold and hot lamination methods, it is possible to create both transparent and translucent visual materials. Although there are limitations, this process will greatly facilitate the production of large economical transparencies both in black and white and in color for use in window displays, light boxes, and many other places as well as with overhead projectors. This process has often been referred to as the "picture lift" or "picture transfer" process. It is simply a by-product of the lamination process.

The picture transfer process is a method of converting materials printed on an opaque paper surface to transparent or translucent form. Images so converted become valuable as transparencies for light-box displays, as transparent backgrounds for terrariums and aquariums, as transparent lampshades, as diazo masters, and as many other transparent objects.

The process, however, has some limitations. The visual image to be converted should be printed on clay-coated paper. With paper of this type, a white "chalky" surface is coated over the porous absorbent paper fiber (606). This coating prevents the ink image from coming in contact with the actual paper. The picture transfer process is possible because the ink image is adhering to this rather unstable water-soluble "chalk" surface. A second limitation is the fact that the size is predetermined by the original printed image. The image cannot be enlarged or reduced by this process. Thirdly, the quality and condition of the original printed image determine the final quality of the transfer. Poor printing, blemishes, or foreign matter on the surface of the printed image will be transferred.

The basic principle of the picture transfer is rather simple. A clear acetate material coated with a transparent non-water-soluble adhesive is adhered to the printed surface (607). It is then placed in water. The water dissolves the unstable clay, releasing the ink image to the adhesive acetate surface (608).

With careful washing, the remaining clay residue is removed. For better transparency the adhesive side of the picture transfer is transparentized through a variety of methods including spraying with liquid plastic laminating.

The various processes for making the picture transfer fall roughly into two categories: those using cold adhesive and those requiring heat to melt the adhesive surface. In a few instances both hot and cold methods are used in combination to create better adhesion. In all methods, pressure is an important element in guaranteeing a successful transfer. The pressure may be applied by hand, in a press, or through rollers to effect good

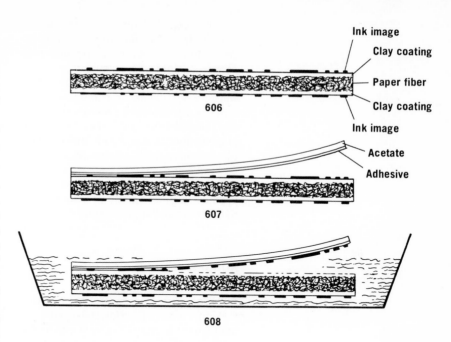

Ink image
Clay coating
Paper fiber
Clay coating
Ink image

606

Acetate
Adhesive

607

608

contact and adhesion between the clear acetate and the printed surface.

The several picture transfer processes vary, so that it is difficult to say which method is best. Some methods are inexpensive but require more time and ability on the part of the producer; some are easier to do but demand more expensive equipment and materials. The resulting transparencies from some of the methods are permanent, while others can be easily damaged.

Transparencies produced by the heat methods tend to hold more precise detail than those made by using cold adhesives. Audience surveys show, however, that transparencies made by the cold method tend to be slightly more pleasing to view. This difference in appearance is undoubtedly due to the fact that a slight spread of the halftone dot pattern of the printed picture occurs with the cold fluid adhesive, causing a slight blending of colors and tone values. Some of the picture transfer methods permit ease in lifting visual imagery from both sides of the page through the process of splitting the printed page in half. By some methods, dry transfer images and lettering can be added before the transfer process begins. Those interested in the manipulation of picture content where visual elements of one printed picture are added to another will find possibilities in some of the picture transfer processes. If it is done properly, the manipulation that has taken place cannot be detected in the resulting transparency. With a knowledge of the strengths and weaknesses of the various methods of picture transfer, one can produce a great variety of visual materials for projection and display.

RUBBER CEMENT PICTURE TRANSFER TRANSPARENCY

Although there are several methods of making a picture transfer, the use of rubber cement is one of the least expensive methods (609). This technique does, however, demand a certain amount of skill. If care is taken to choose the proper type of picture, to work under clean conditions, and to apply the rubber cement carefully, excellent results can be expected.

The success of a picture transfer depends upon whether the paper upon which the picture is printed is clay-coated or not. To check for clay coating, rub an unprinted area with a moistened finger. A white chalky residue appearing on the finger is a good indication the paper is clay-coated (610). Trim the picture larger than the area to be used (611). Apply a thin, even coat of rubber cement to the face of the printed page (612).

Care must be taken to avoid getting dirt or dust in the cement.

Cut a sheet of acetate about the size of the picture or slightly larger. Lightly etch one side of the acetate (613) with fine-grade steel wool, using smooth, even strokes. When etching is completed, remove any resulting dust. Next, apply a thin, even coat of rubber cement to the etched surface of the acetate (614). To assure better adhesion, it is advisable to brush the rubber cement onto the two surfaces at 90° angles to each other.

When both rubber cement surfaces are thoroughly dry, they are ready to adhere together. Lay the picture face up on a smooth, clean surface. Hold the coated acetate with the coated side down above the picture. Bend it into a U shape (615). Carefully lower the acetate onto the picture surface, making sure the acetate is centered over the area to be used. Let the two surfaces make contact in the center, and then firmly press down on the two edges of acetate until both surfaces are completely in contact. Next, with the finger, press the two surfaces together with a firm pressure going from the center out in all directions (616). This should help eliminate air pockets. To assure absolute contact, turn the "sandwich" over on a clean, smooth surface so that the back side of the picture is up. With a new, sharp razor blade held at an angle, draw with a firm pressure from the center outward in all directions (617). Be sure the entire surface is pressed into contact by this method.

609

188

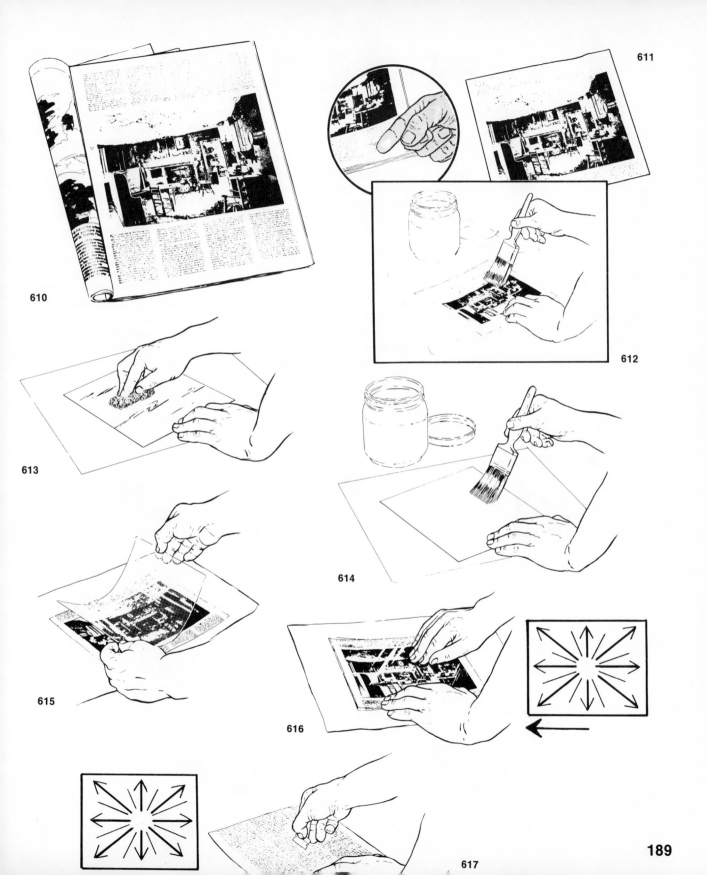

610

611

612

613

614

615

616

617

Place the "sandwich" into a pan of cool soapy water (618). The soap will speed up soaking time. Thicker paper will require longer time in the water. When the paper is completely saturated with water, gently peel the paper from the acetate (619). Care must be taken along the edges of the "sandwich" not to tear any rubber cement that might cling to the paper edge. If any paper fiber remains on the rubber cement surface, rub over it gently with the fingertip. It will generally release and wash off. When the paper has been removed, a milky chalk still remains on the picture transfer. Gently wash this off with a ball of cotton and plenty of soapy water (620). Excess water may be removed from the transparency by blotting with a paper towel.

Hang up the transparency to dry. Allow about thirty minutes for this step (621). When dry, the rubber cement side of the transparency will have a frosty appearance. The rubber cement will be very easy to damage, so handle it with care. Next, place the picture down on a smooth, dry surface with the rubber cement side up. Tape down the four corners. To make this surface more transparent and to protect the surface, spray this side with a clear plastic spray (622). Hold the spray can about 10 inches above the transparency, and spray back and forth to apply an even coating of plastic. Allow it to dry thoroughly.

Even though the rubber cement surface has been protected by plastic spray, it is still susceptible to damage. It is best to cover it with a piece of clear acetate for protection (623). Bind the transparency between two overhead transparency mounts. If the transparency is of an odd size, it is relatively easy to cut the frames from 8- or 10-ply cardboard. The open-

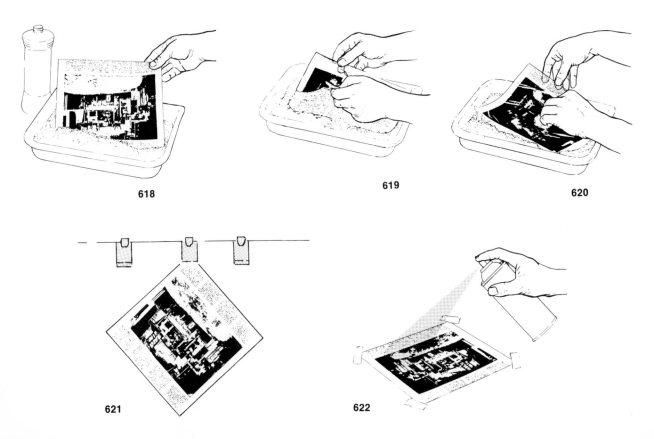

618

619

620

621

622

ing should be slightly smaller than the transparency. Tape the entire "sandwich" firmly to one frame (624). Lay the other frame over the top and tape along the edges (625). A frame constructed in this manner will be very durable. The wide borders afford a handy place to write any pertinent information or instructions concerning the transparency.

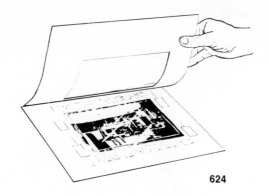

624

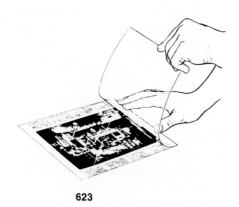

623

625

POINTS TO REMEMBER

Thin rubber cement with rubber cement thinner, so that it will run freely from the brush.

Use a wide, soft-bristle brush for ease of application.

Use commercially frosted acetate when possible to help alleviate problems of dust. Use 0.005-inch-thick acetate for best results.

Work on a clean, smooth, dry surface.

Be sure that both rubber cement surfaces are absolutely dry before placing them in contact.

Be sure to use good-quality pictures that are free of creases or surface flaws.

Always test for a clay-coated printing surface.

Avoid using transparencies smaller than the 3¼- by 4-inch size.

MATERIALS AND EQUIPMENT

COLD LAMINATING ACETATE
COMB OR RAZOR BLADE
PAN OR WATER
COTTON
LIQUID SOAP
MAGAZINE VISUAL

PAPER TOWELS
PLASTIC SPRAY
TRANSPARENCY MOUNTS
TAPE
CLEAR ACETATE

Chalky residue

626

627

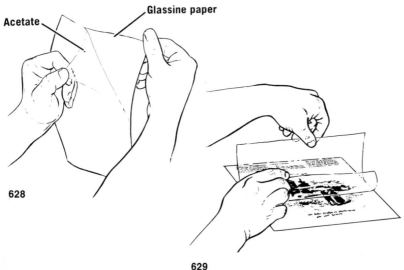

Acetate

Glassine paper

628

629

COLD LAMINATING ACETATE PICTURE TRANSFER TRANSPARENCY

Transparencies in full color or black and white can be made with cold laminating acetate used as a base material. This type of acetate is transparent and has a pressure-sensitive adhesive on one side. Printed matter on clay-coated paper, combined with pressure-sensitive acetate, can be processed to produce quality transparencies for projection or light-box display.

To assure a successful picture transfer, a test must be made to determine if the picture has been printed on clay-coated paper. This can easily be determined by gently rubbing a moist finger on an unprinted area of the page (626). A white, chalky residue appearing on the finger is a good indication that the paper is clay-coated. Be sure the picture is free of all creases, abrasions, and oily or waxy smudges and is good-quality printing. Carefully remove the picture from the magazine (627), being sure extra margin areas are left around the image area. Next, cut laminating acetate the same size as the picture to be transferred. Peel the glassine paper (628) from the acetate.

With the sticky side of the cold laminating acetate down, bend the acetate in a U shape and gently lower it down onto the face of the visual (629), pressing it in a down and outward direction. Next, gently rub acetate down (630) from the center to the outer perimeter of the picture. Do this gently so that any air that might be trapped beneath the acetate can escape.

Turn the visual over onto a smooth, clean surface so that the acetate face is down. Using a firm pressure, rub the entire surface with the flat, smooth side of a comb or razor blade held at an angle (631). It is best to systematically rub from the center in an outward direction. Avoid cutting or tearing the paper surface. Next, place the visual into a pan of cool soapy water and allow it to soak for a few minutes (632).

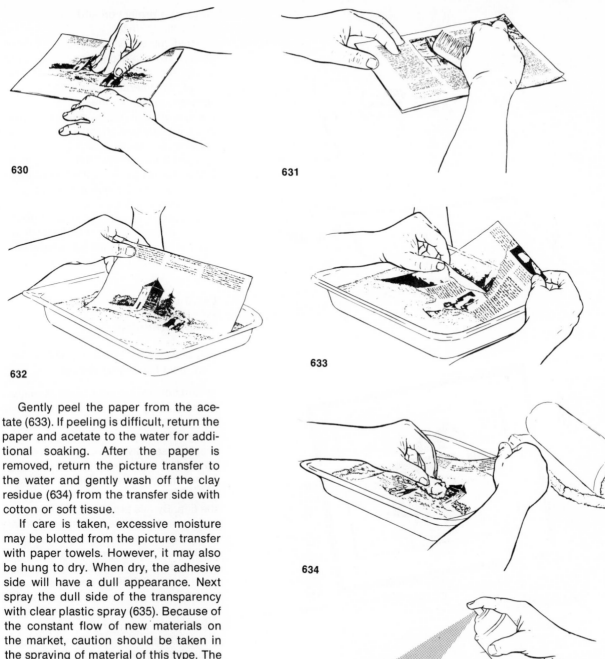

630

631

632

633

Gently peel the paper from the acetate (633). If peeling is difficult, return the paper and acetate to the water for additional soaking. After the paper is removed, return the picture transfer to the water and gently wash off the clay residue (634) from the transfer side with cotton or soft tissue.

If care is taken, excessive moisture may be blotted from the picture transfer with paper towels. However, it may also be hung to dry. When dry, the adhesive side will have a dull appearance. Next spray the dull side of the transparency with clear plastic spray (635). Because of the constant flow of new materials on the market, caution should be taken in the spraying of material of this type. The plastic spray may dissolve the adhesive and cause destruction of the ink transfer. It is wise, therefore, to run a test to see if the spraying process is safe to use. If it is not, it is often possible to use another piece of the same type of acetate to cover the tender image; the acetate will

634

635

636

637

638

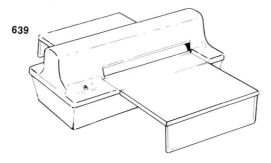

639

serve as a protection and a transparentizer of the surface.

Hold the spray can about 10 inches above the transparency, and spray across the transparency in smooth, horizontal movements from top to bottom. If sprayed properly, the surface of the transparency should have a slick appearance. Be sure to work on a smooth, level surface to avoid "runs." Allow the sprayed transparency to dry. To give the tender sprayed side of the transparency extra protection, place a piece of clear acetate over it (636).

Bind the transparency in a cardboard mount for protection and ease of use (637). The picture transfer is now completed and ready for use (638).

COLD LAMINATING MACHINE PICTURE TRANSFER TRANSPARENCY

Equipment: film laminator (cold process)
Film: cold laminating acetate

In addition to the processes of picture transfer using rubber cement and adhesive-backed acetate is the method of using a film laminator (cold process). A pressure-sensitive adhesive-coated laminating film is pressed onto the ink image by two motor-driven rollers. This assures good, even contact between the ink and the film. By this process some variations in picture transfer are possible that are not easily accomplished by some other methods. The equipment used for this process is a light, portable film laminator (cold process) (639). It contains two rollers that rotate in contact with each other at a very high, even pressure. The film used is cold laminating acetate.

As with all other picture transfer processes, the printing must be on clay-coated paper. A simple test for clay coating is to moisten a small unprinted area of the paper. If with slight rubbing a white chalky residue appears, this is a fairly reliable indication that the paper surface is clay-coated. The picture may be printed in color or black and white. Two different weights of laminating film on a special paper support are used for each picture transfer. The lighter-weight film is used first in the process.

Take a sheet of the lighter-weight film. Lay it face up on the bed of the machine. With the special switch, turn the rollers just enough to catch and hold the end of the film and its backing. Now carefully pull the film from its backing and curl it back over the top of the machine (640). Lay the picture to be transferred face up on the backing sheet (641). Be sure the picture is lying flat. Any wrinkles, dirt, or imperfections on the picture surface will prevent the final product from being perfect. Turn on the motor, and allow the picture to pass between the rollers. Hold the film firmly so that the rollers press it onto the picture surface. Always be careful to check to see that the rollers are free of dirt or other foreign matter before use.

To show an important feature of this type of picture transfer, let us assume that there are visual images on both sides of the page to convert into transparent form (642). At this point we have applied laminating acetate to only one side of the page. By following the same procedure, apply a sheet of cold laminating acetate to the reverse side (643). Both sides of the page will now be covered with a sheet of film. Trim all excess film from around the page.

The next step is to split the two pages apart. With a razor blade or other sharp instrument, make a slit in one corner

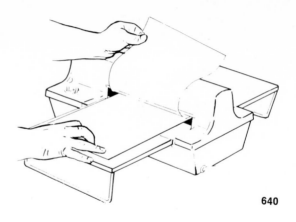

640

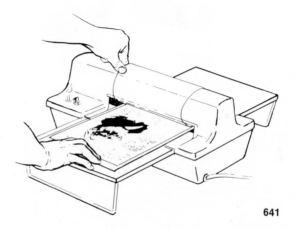

641

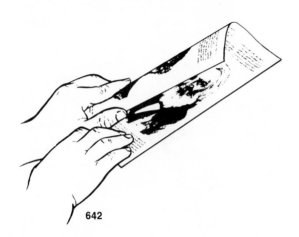

642

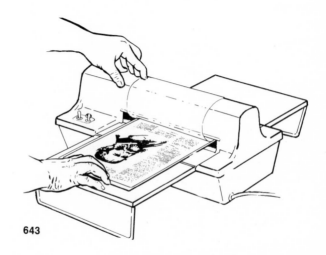

643

644

645

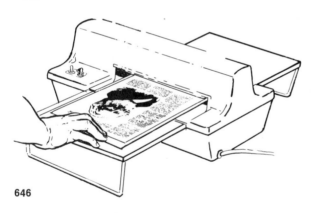

646

between the two laminated surfaces. (A small scrap of paper inserted in the corner first before the second side is laminated will simplify the problem of starting the splitting process.) Carefully take hold of each corner of the two sides and pull slowly (644), with an even force. In this manner it is possible to split the printed page in half. The two sides of the page will now be separated and can be made into two separate transparencies (645).

At this point the split pages are placed into cool soapy water. After a short period of soaking, the remaining paper fiber is peeled off. With a ball of cotton wash off the excess clay from the adhesive surface. As long as the adhesive is wet, it will not have sticky characteristics.

By placing the wet transfer back onto its backing paper as it was in its original state (adhesive side in contact with backing paper) it may again be run through the rollers to wring out the moisture (646). A couple of paper towels under the machine will absorb any excess moisture that may accumulate. After the transfer has passed through the rollers for drying, remove it from the backing paper. Place a second sheet of laminating acetate (heavier weight) in the press. With the lead edge pinched between the rollers, peel back the adhesive-coated acetate as was done previously (647).

Place the transfer, adhesive side up, on the backing sheet (648). Make sure it

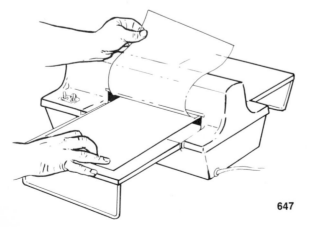

647

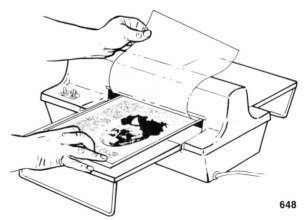

648

is lying absolutely flat. Turn on the motor. Pull gently on the adhesive sheet as the material is drawn through the rollers. This prevents the formation of folds or wrinkles. Trim the picture to the desired size, and mount (649) in the appropriate frame for projection.

HEAT LAMINATING MACHINE
PICTURE TRANSFER
TRANSPARENCY

Equipment: film laminator (heat process)
Film: heat laminating acetate

Although originally designed strictly for lamination, the heat laminating machine is one of the fastest and best methods for making transparencies from printed material. As with all picture transfer methods, the picture must be printed on clay-coated paper stock. A simple test to check whether the paper is clay-coated is to moisten the tip of your finger and gently rub an unprinted area of the paper from which you want to make the transfer. If a white, milky residue forms on your finger, you can be quite certain the paper is clay-coated and the printed image will transfer. Both black and white and color pictures can be used. Color pictures tend, however, to result in somewhat better-quality transparencies.

Since in most cases the heat laminating machine laminates both sides of a page simultaneously, it is possible to make two transparencies at one time. This can be done by placing two printed pictures of the same size back to back as they are fed into the machine (650). As they pass between the two heated rollers, a thin laminating film is applied to both outer surfaces. When the excess film is trimmed off, the two pictures will separate and have only the desired surfaces laminated. A similar situation occurs when you have a page with pictures on both sides (651) from which you want to make transparencies, and you simply pass the page through the laminator. Always make sure that the surface of the picture is free of any foreign mat-

649

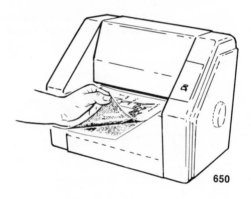

650

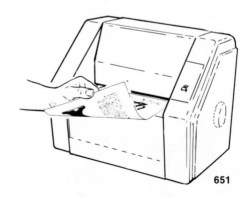

651

ter such as lint or dust before placing it in the machine. At this point it is wise to pass the material through the laminator a second time (652) to give it a double coat of lamination. (With the page doubly laminated on both sides, it is possible to split the page in half so that the printing on the two sides will be on two separate sheets. It is difficult, however, to get a start in separating the two laminated sides. If before passing the printed page through the laminator a corner or edge of the page is turned over about ¼ inch, this, when the laminated page is trimmed, will furnish a small separation of the two laminated surfaces, permitting ease in splitting the page.) As the laminated page emerges from the machine the second time, trim off the excess film flush with the page. The corner or edge turned over prior to lamination will now present a place where both surfaces of

laminating film can be grasped between the fingers.

With an even, steady pull you can separate the two film layers, thus splitting the paper page in two (653). Now both sides of the page become potential material for transparencies (654).

Place the laminated picture in warm water containing a little liquid soap. This will soften the clay between the paper and the film. When the paper is well saturated with water, strip it off (655). Allow additional soaking time for any resistant areas. When the paper has been completely removed, wash off any remaining clay from the ink and film surface with soft cotton (656). Rinse the transparency in clean water. The film may be dried by blotting with paper towels, or it may be air-dried by hanging it up.

When it is dry, pass the transparency through the machine (657), laminating it

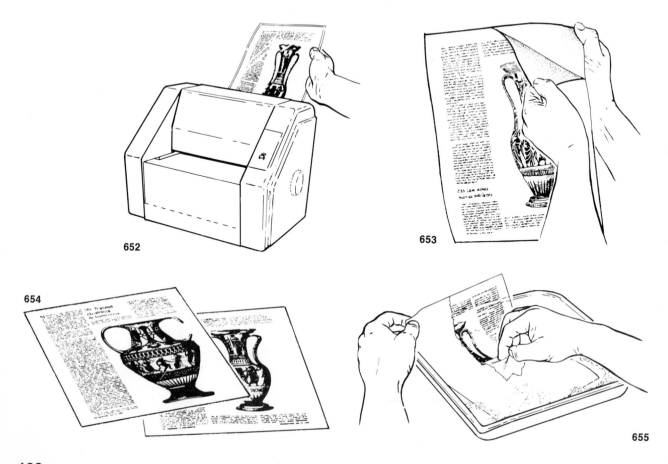

652

653

654

655

656

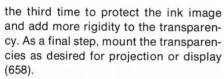

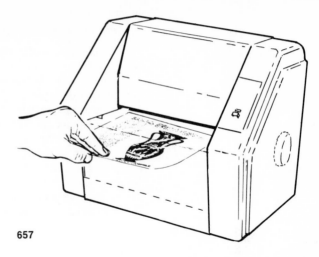

657

the third time to protect the ink image and add more rigidity to the transparency. As a final step, mount the transparencies as desired for projection or display (658).

Very closely related to the method just explained is that used in the thermocopy process. The thermocopy machine, being a heat copying machine, is ideal for use with thermocopy laminating acetate.

DRY MOUNTING PRESS PICTURE TRANSFER TRANSPARENCY (659)

Although regular laminating films can be used with the dry mounting press to create picture transfers, it may be desirable at times to create your own transfer film. Since many laminating films are of relatively thin material, it will be found that heavier-based transparencies will be more rigid and lay flatter on the projector, permitting sharper focus, especially with the more sensitive projector lens systems.

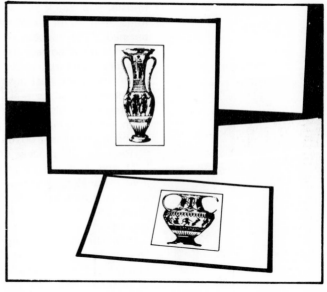

658

659

CREATING TRANSFER FILM

To create transfer film, use a transparent *stable* film of desired thickness. Stable film is supplied by art stores to artists and draftsmen working in situations where transparent overlays must remain in critical register. Usually these films are stable up to a relatively high temperature—which makes them a satisfactory base for the hot picture transfer process. Using this stable film as a base (either clear or frosted), spray one side of the film with three light coats of clear acrylic lacquer spray. Alternate the direction in which the spray is applied between coats. Permit the sprayed surface to dry between each application, and make sure the entire surface is evenly covered. The film forms a stable base upon which a relatively unstable clear plastic has been applied. When heat is applied, the former remains constant while the latter softens and functions as an adhesive, much in the same way laminating film works.

By using a dry mounting press with transfer film, black and white and color transparencies of excellent quality can be made. The success of this process depends upon correct use of heat and pressure. A picture transfer transparency produced by the heat process is one of the most durable. As in all picture transfer processes, this form of transparency is an excellent master for reproduction by the diazo process on film or paper.

Because this process depends upon heat and pressure to ensure a good image transfer, a special "sandwich" (660) must be used in the dry mounting press. This "sandwich" is made up of two smooth metal plates (a, c) such as cookie sheets or photographic ferrotype plates. They must be clean and free of any blemishes. These two plates tend to distribute the heat evenly over the entire sandwich area. A felt pad (b) serves to cushion any small blemishes, flaws, or irregularities in the printed paper image or the transfer film. The ¼-inch pressed-wood board (d) furnishes extra even pressure. It must be noted at this point that too much pressure can damage the press. Most presses have provisions for normal pressure adjustment. The press should close with an even pressure but should not require extra force. Set the temperature of the press at about 275 to 300°F. To ensure a good picture transfer, the sandwich must be preheated. Insert it into the press for a period before use so that it will be up to temperature. Do not close the press, but allow the heating element to rest loosely on the "sandwich" (661).

Choose a picture of good printing quality with no blemishes (662). As with other picture transfer processes, the printing must be on clay-coated paper. To test, rub a moist finger on an unprinted area of the page. If a chalky residue appears on the finger, you can be fairly certain that the paper is coated. After the sandwich is heated up to temperature, insert the picture and special film between the felt and metal plate (663). Have the back of the transfer film down on the metal plate and the image face down on the adhesive side of the film. Be sure the film does not extend beyond the material to be transferred. If the coated side of the film extends beyond the paper, it will adhere to the felt pad.

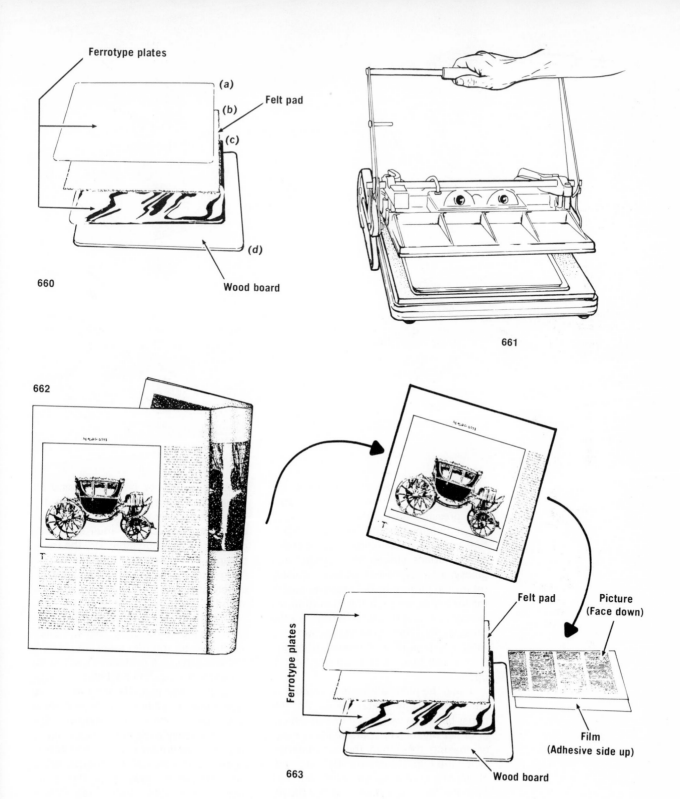

Ferrotype plates

(a)
(b)
(c)

Felt pad

Wood board

(d)

660

661

662

Ferrotype plates

Felt pad

Picture
(Face down)

Wood board

Film
(Adhesive side up)

663

201

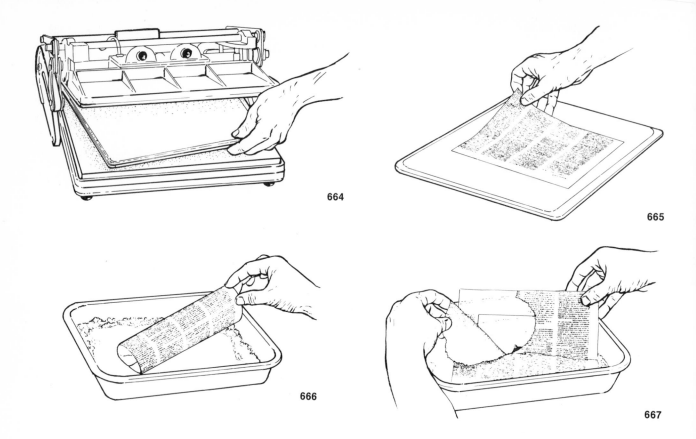

664

665

666

667

Place the sandwich carefully in the press, being sure that there is a good, firm pressure (664). After about five to seven minutes carefully remove the picture from the press (665). A quick check of the surface should find it bright and glossy. If frosty areas appear, quickly return the picture to the press as before for further heating. (If the picture transfer cools, it is difficult to return it to the press without damaging the ink surface.) After the picture is removed from the heat, it will tend to curl. Do not force it open.

Place the picture transfer into cool or lukewarm soapy water (666). As the paper becomes wet, it will uncurl. Thicker or heavily inked papers will take longer soaking time than thinner material. When the paper is completely saturated, check to see whether the paper will peel from the film (667). If peeling is difficult, allow a longer soaking period.

After the paper has been removed, return the transparency (film) to the water and gently wash off the clay residue from transfer side (dull side) with cotton or soft tissue (668). Dry the transparency by blotting with paper towels, or hang it up to dry. When the film is completely dry, the dull side will have a slightly "ashy" appearance.

Spray the dull side of the film with clear plastic spray (669). This will make the image on the film more transparent and will provide a protective coating for the transfer side. The final step of spraying in this case must be done with great care if plastic spray or acrylic lacquer is to be used. Instead of coating the film with one heavy coat, it is better to apply two or three lighter coats. Since acrylic lacquer was used as the original adhesive, excessive spraying at this point might dissolve the transferred image, causing serious damage. A safer method

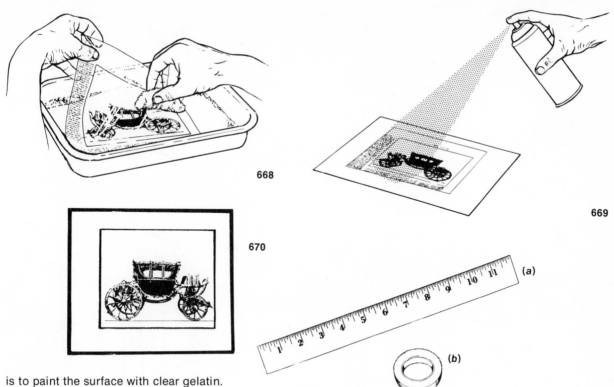

668

669

670

is to paint the surface with clear gelatin. Use a soft-bristle brush, and be sure to coat the surface with a uniformly even layer. Allow it to dry throughly. For added protection cover the image side of the film with clear acetate and bind in an overhead transparency mount (670).

PASSE-PARTOUT MOUNTING

For mounting
    Awards and certificates
    Photographs
    Tear sheets
    Specimens
    Paintings

Passe-partout mounting is a simple, inexpensive framing method for preserving flat and three-dimensional instructional materials under glass or plastic. Colored cloth, paper, or plastic-base tapes, along with a sheet of glass or plastic and a piece of thick mounting board, are all that is required to produce an attractive mounting (671).

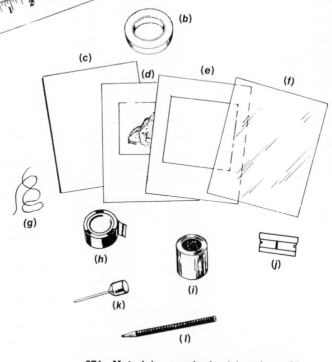

671 Materials required: (a) ruler; (b) masking tape; (c) mounting board; (d) mounted visual; (e) mat; (f) glass or plastic; (g) string or picture wire; (h) cloth or plastic tape; (i) passe-partout tape (paper); (j) razor blade; (k) awl; (l)marking pencil.

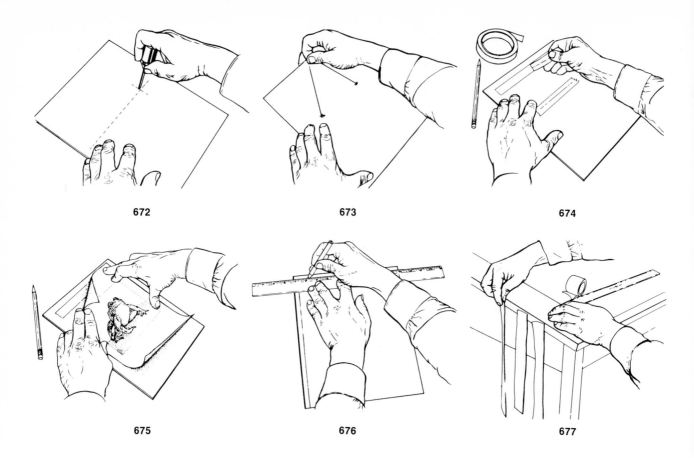

672

673

674

675

676

677

When a picture is to be suspended by a string or wire, two holes must be punched in the mounting cardboard. These holes should be on a line about two-fifths of the distance from the top of the cardboard and well in from the right and left edges. The holes may be made by using an awl (672). Through these holes thread a strong string or picture wire. Tie it so it will stretch just short of the top of the picture (673). Pull the knot to one of the holes so that it will not interfere with proper hanging. With the string drawn taut, turn the cardboard over and cover the exposed string with a piece of masking tape. This prevents the string from slipping and causing bulges. Next, place a piece of double-coated adhesive tape, mucilage, or rubber cement near the top of the mounting board to hold the visual in place (674).

Position the visual on the mounting board, and adhere it only along the top edge. This permits it to lie loosely over the slight bulge formed by the string (675). To get a uniform width of tape along the edge of the glass, use guide-lines made with a marking pencil (676). Cut four strips of framing tape. Two strips should be 2 inches longer than the vertical height of the glass, and two should be 2 inches longer than the horizontal width. If the adhesive side of the tape is sticky, suspend it from the edge of the table or desk for ease in handling (677).

Next, adhere the tape to the glass. For extra strength, place the tape on the vertical side first. In a horizontal position in front of you, place a strip of tape with adhesive side up. With marking-pencil lines facing up, slowly lower the glass down on the tape, making sure its edge coincides with the guideline (678). Do this on all four sides. When this is completed, press the tape tight against the

204

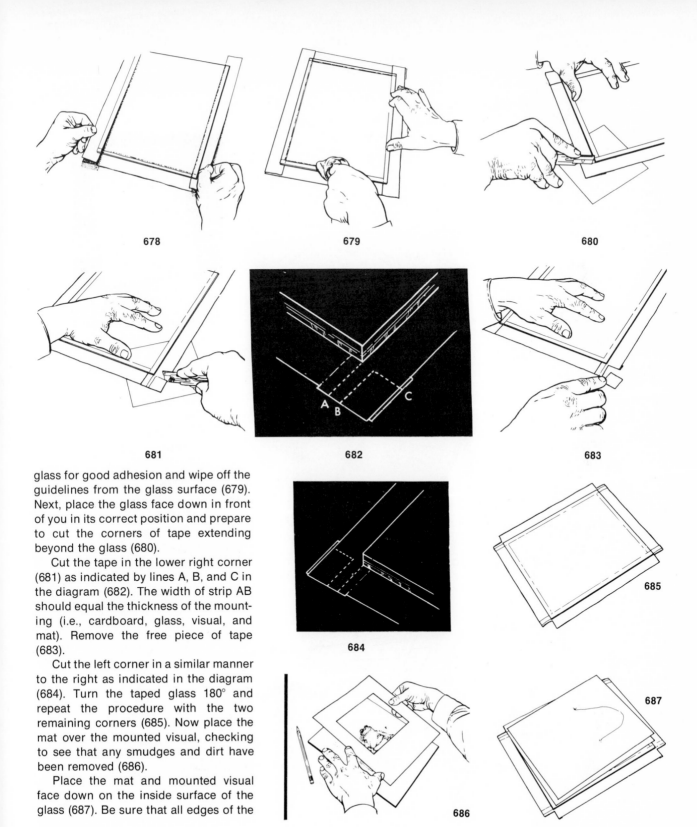

678

679

680

681

682

683

684

685

687

686

glass for good adhesion and wipe off the guidelines from the glass surface (679). Next, place the glass face down in front of you in its correct position and prepare to cut the corners of tape extending beyond the glass (680).

Cut the tape in the lower right corner (681) as indicated by lines A, B, and C in the diagram (682). The width of strip AB should equal the thickness of the mounting (i.e., cardboard, glass, visual, and mat). Remove the free piece of tape (683).

Cut the left corner in a similar manner to the right as indicated in the diagram (684). Turn the taped glass 180° and repeat the procedure with the two remaining corners (685). Now place the mat over the mounted visual, checking to see that any smudges and dirt have been removed (686).

Place the mat and mounted visual face down on the inside surface of the glass (687). Be sure that all edges of the

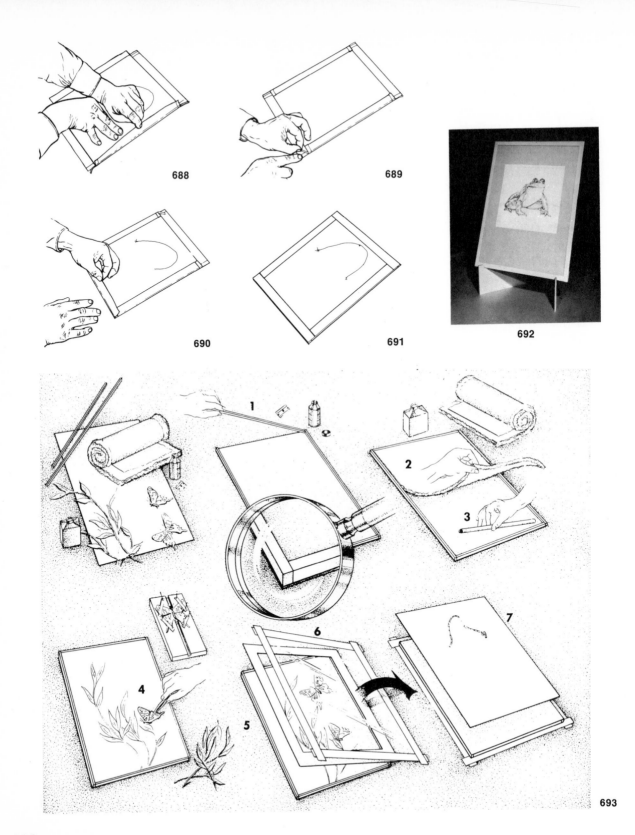

688

689

690

691

692

693

assembled mounting are flush. While holding all parts firmly in place, pull over the vertical tape edges, pressing them firmly down on the mounting board (688). Next, turn the small flaps of tape around the corners and press them in place (689).

The two remaining tape edges are pulled over the mounting cardboard (690) and pressed in place (691). The passe-partout framing of this visual is now completed (692).

The passe-partout method of framing may be adapted to the mounting of three-dimensional specimens (693). A simple balsa-wood frame is glued to a heavy cardboard. The frame is made of strips with a dimensional height slightly greater than the thickness of the specimens to be mounted (1). A sheet of cotton is placed in the frame as a soft support (2). In cases where insects might damage the specimens, moth crystals or other insecticides may be placed under the cotton layer. A small, perforated paper tube or soda straw may serve as a container for the crystals and be placed along one edge of the frame beneath the cotton blanket (3). The specimens being mounted are then positioned on the cotton (4). Small indentations can be made in the cotton blanket for objects of maximum thickness. After all specimens are in place, a cutout mat and cover glass are placed over them (5). The glass has been taped with a wide cloth, plastic, or paper tape as described in the conventional method of passe-partout mounting (6). Carefully pick up the entire assembly and turn it face down on a clean, smooth surface. If the picture is to be hung, a cardboard with string attached may be added (7). The cutting of the corners and drawing of the tape over onto the backing cardboard involve the same procedure as described in the conventional passe-partout mounting method. The visual is now ready for display (694–699).

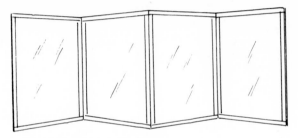

694 Passe-partout mounted pictures in an accordion fold.

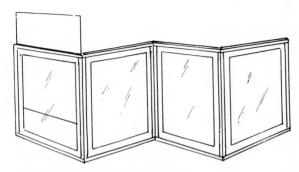

695 Passe-partout mounted pictures in an accordion fold having slits in the top to permit the changing of pictures.

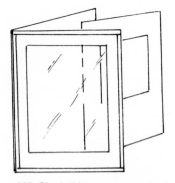

696 Single-hinge passe-partout frame permitting quick change of pictorial material.

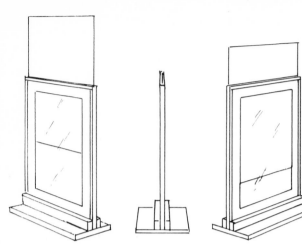

697 Two-sided passe-partout frame with slit in top to permit change of visual.

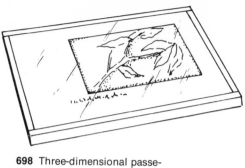

698 Three-dimensional passe-partout mounting for the display of specimen.

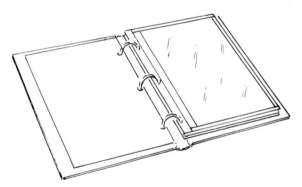

699 Passe-partout mounted pictures in a three-ring notebook.

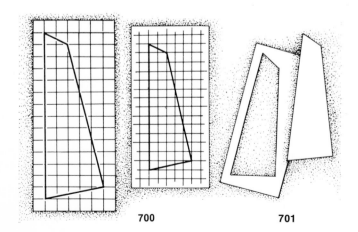

700   701

DISPLAY EASELS

ATTACHED EASEL (SIMPLE WING)

For the more permanent type of display materials—those that have repeated use and are displayed on shelves or tables— the simple wing easel may be best to use. It is simple to make and folds flat when not in use, making mailing or storage easy. This support is permanently mounted to the display. By using the grid drawing (700), you may make any size pattern to accommodate any size display. The pattern is next transferred to a sturdy cardboard sufficiently strong to support the display. An easy method to transfer a simple pattern of this type is to

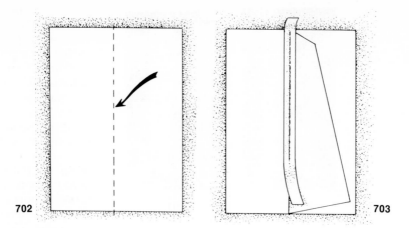

702

703

lay the pattern onto the cardboard and then with a sharp-pointed cutting needle puncture small holes through each corner of the drawn pattern. Remove the original drawing, and with pencil and ruler connect each one of the small pinholes. The pattern is now ready to cut. Because all sides of the wing support are straight, it may be cut out by using a straightedge and razor blade or a straightedge paper cutter (701). Next, a light pencil line is drawn down the middle of the back of the display (702). The wing support is laid along this pencil line, and sturdy paper or cloth tape is applied to the full length of the support (703). The wing support is folded over in the opposite direction, and a second piece of tape is applied (704). Be sure to press the tape firmly in the crease along the edge of the support. The simple wing easel is now ready to use (705).

ATTACHED EASEL (LOCK WING)

The lock wing easel is more complicated to construct than the simple wing. It is permanently mounted to the display, lies flat, and can be easily stored. The squared diagram (706) gives the basic outline of this type of easel. From this original, any size pattern can be made by enlarging or reducing through the grid drawing method. Care must be taken in making the original that the locking device is accurately drawn (707) and cut

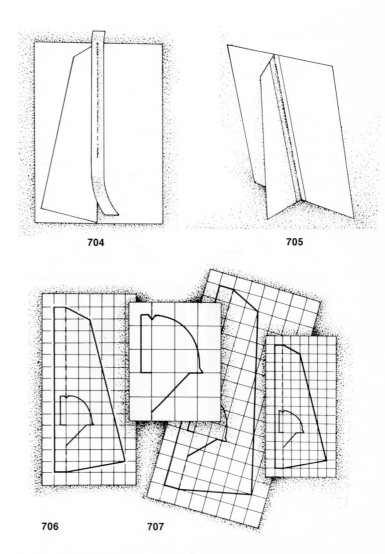

704

705

706

707

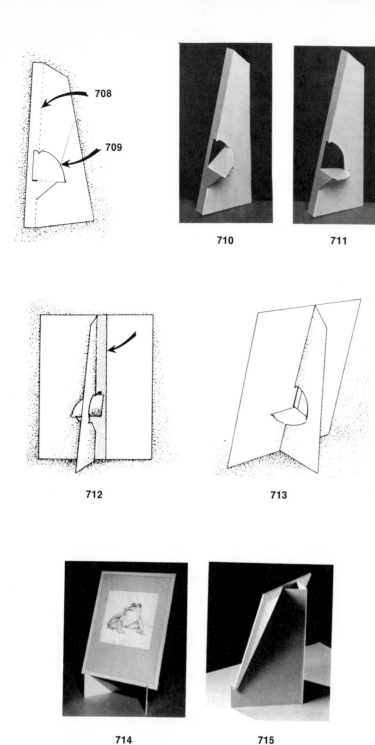

708

709

710   **711**

712   **713**

714   **715**

out. If it is inaccurately shaped, it may not lock the easel in place properly. Transfer the pattern onto a cardboard of sufficient weight to support the particular display. First, cut out the basic outline of the easel. This can be done by using a straightedge and mat knife or razor blade. Next, cut along the solid lines of the locking device (708). The dotted lines indicate where the easel must be folded (709). Next, carefully make a slight cut along the dotted lines just sufficiently deep to permit folding. If the cardboard is rather lightweight, scoring or pressing along the line with a blunt-pointed instrument may be sufficient to permit ease in folding. Check to see that the easel will fold properly along the vertical dimension (710) and that the lock will fold into place (711). Slight adjustment may have to be made by trimming the edges of the lock. The final step is to glue the vertical folded edge along a center line drawn on the back of the display (712). Place some heavy weight on the glued flap and allow it to dry. The easel is then ready for use (713).

FOLDING EASEL

A simple method for displaying mounted pictures, passe-partout mountings, flannel boards, bulletin boards, and other flat materials is through the use of the folding easel (714, 715). It is simple, sturdy in construction, and easy to store. By using the grid drawing (716) a variety of patterns can be made (717).

After a pattern of the desired size is made and traced onto a piece of cardboard, two sides are cut out (718). These pieces are laid about ¼ inch apart (719), depending upon the weight of the cardboard used.

A strong cloth tape is applied to both sides of the easel (720, 721). The excess tape is trimmed off. The hinge is then finger-pressed together to form a simple sturdy center fold (722). Check to see that the easel will fold (723). The easel is then ready for use (724). To support extra-large materials, more than one easel can be employed (725).

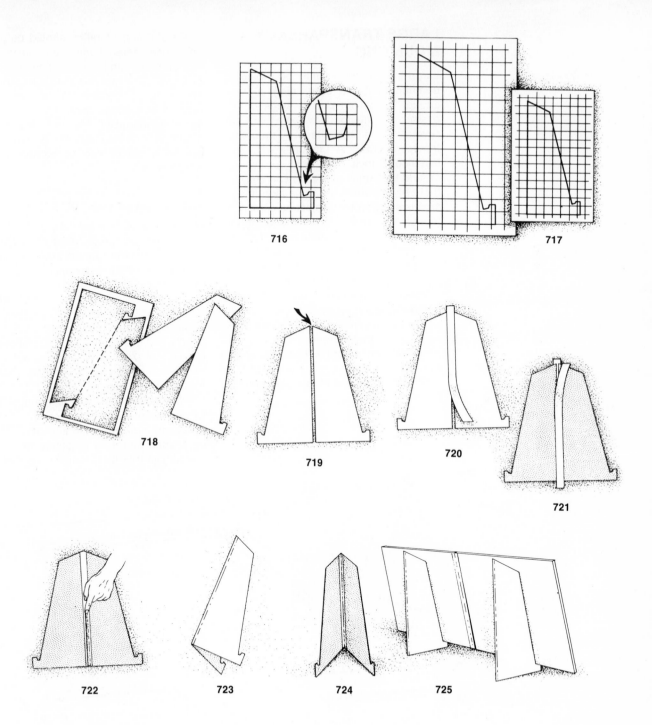

716

717

718

719

720

721

722

723

724

725

211

LARGE TRANSPARENCY MOUNTING

Large transparencies may be projected unmounted if the base (film) is thick enough to lie flat on the stage of the overhead projector. However, there are several good reasons for mounting transparencies. A mount will, for instance, block out light projecting around the edges of the transparency so that only the intended projection image area is seen on the projection screen. A mount also provides a solid base for easy handling, manipulation of overlays, and storing. Moreover, the surface of many mounts can be used to write notes related to the transparency.

Mounted transparencies can be projected horizontally or vertically. However, it is recommended that where possible the transparency should be produced and mounted horizontally so that full advantage can be taken of the most commonly used horizontal projection screens.

Careful consideration should be given to size, material, method of securing film to mount, and masking and hinging overlays when mounting large transparencies for projection. Since sizes of mounts and image areas have not yet been standardized, the recommended mount size is one that fits a standard letter-size file or can be carried in a briefcase.

TRANSPARENCY MOUNTS (726)

Mounts (frames) for overhead projection transparencies (projectuals) are available in a variety of formats and materials for reasons of economy and for various requirements.

Aperture (viewing area) sizes vary, depending upon film or projection equipment requirements, from 7½ by 9½ to 10 by 10 inches usually. This popular-size mount (727) usually has an outside dimension of 12⅜ by 13⅞ inches, and is designed to accept all 8½- by 11-inch films or acetate sheets. This mount (728) has a large writing surface on three sides and is designed to accept all 8½- by 11-inch film. It is recommended for use with all 10½- by 10½-inch films (729).

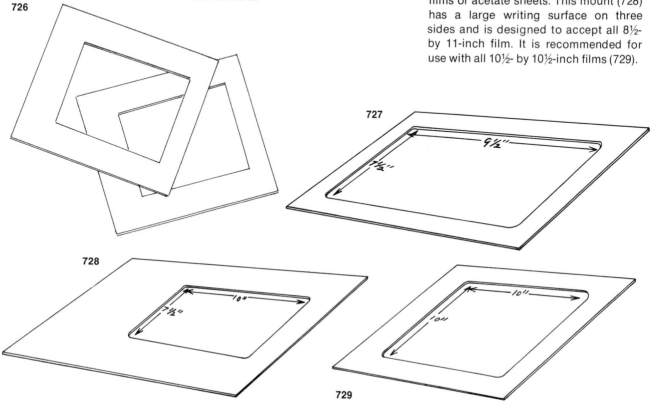

726

727

728

729

212

Cardboard Mount (Plain Back) (730)

A die-cut cardboard (pressboard) mount that is most popular because of its hard surface and durability.

Cardboard Mount (Adhesive Back) (731)

A sandwich-type cardboard mount with pressure-sensitive adhesive to permit the mounting of one or more "cells" inside. Place the mount open on a flat surface. Position the base "cell" on one side of the mount. Some mounts have registration marks to assist in the registration of "cells." Fold the opposite side of the mount over so that it locks the base "cell" in place. Rub, with firm pressure, around the top of the mount to assure good adhesion.

Solid Plastic Mount (732)

A permanent-type solid plastic mount in white or colors that resists warping caused by extreme changes in humidity. The mount is reusable and accepts mounting tape and staples.

Transparent Plastic Mount (733)

A self-contained transparent plastic mount with an opaque border. No mounting or masking is required, unless overlays are desired. Lettering, writing, coloring, etc., are done directly on the surface of the mount.

Handmade Mount (734)

Almost any opaque material with a fair degree of thickness can be used to make a mount. Regular manila file folders are ideal for mounts. Openings 7½ by 9½ inches, or the size desired, can be cut in one or both sides of the folder. Other materials such as chipboard and poster-board can be used as long as the material is stiff enough to hold the transparency.

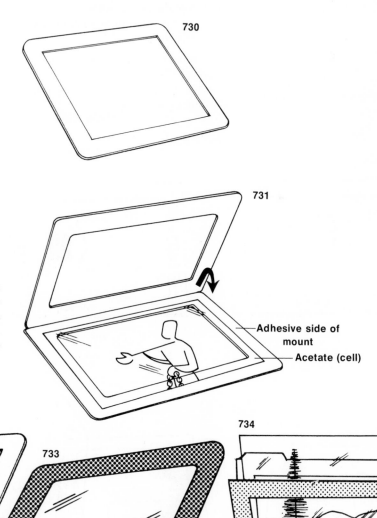

730

731

Adhesive side of mount

Acetate (cell)

732

733

734

MOUNTING BASE TRANSPARENCY AND ATTACHING OVERLAYS AND MASKS

Mounting Base Transparency

Finished transparencies can be projected unmounted (unframed). However, there are several advantages to mounting transparencies: The mount blocks light around the edge of the visual, adds rigidity for both handling and storage, and provides a convenient border for writing lecture notes. Here is a simple procedure for framing or mounting the base transparency:

1 Lay the mount upside down on a flat surface (735).
2 Center the transparency *face down* on the mount (736).
3 Tape all four sides (737).

Attaching Overlays with Tape

Overlays can help simplify complicated concepts and allow you to build your presentation step by step. Here is a simple procedure for adding overlays:

1 Lay the mounted transparency right side up on a flat surface (738).
2 Center the first overlay, and tape (or use transparency hinges) along one edge of the mount (739). If all the overlays follow the same sequence, you can attach all the overlays on the same edge.
3 Center the second overlay over the first, and tape along the other edge (740).

It is generally recommended to limit the number of overlays to four.

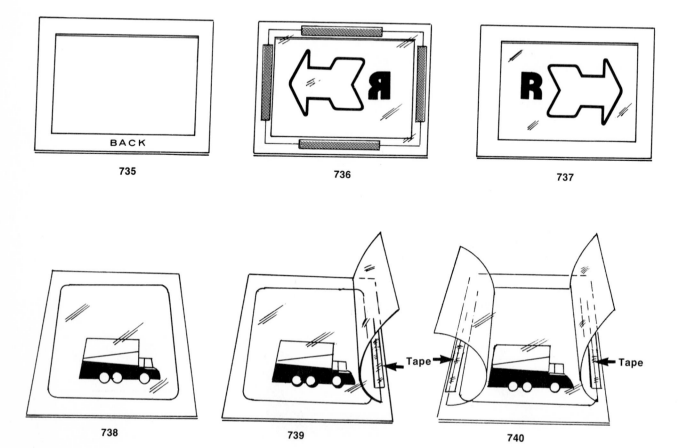

735

736

737

738

739

740

Attaching Overlays With Transparency Hinges (741)

To hinge overlays with overhead transparency hinges, remove the paper backing from the first hinge and follow these instructions:

1 Position the hinge, adhesive side up, under the film at the center position on the edge which is to be hinged (742). The bottom of the film is pressed onto the adhesive.
2 Then fold the hinge over, pressing it against the top of the film (743). The film is now sandwiched firmly between the two adhesive sides of the hinge.
3 Insert two staples through each hinge, or stack of hinges if other sequential overlays are used (744). An overhead transparency stapler is recommended since an ordinary stapler with standard staples may not penetrate the overlay and mount. Three hinges are recommended for each overlay.

SPECIAL EFFECTS OVERLAYS

Special effects can be created with the use of transparent overlays. Illustrated and discussed here are three special effects that can be created with overlays. Pivoting overlays (745) can be attached to one corner of the mount as illustrated. The corner where the grommet or thumbtack is inserted acts as a pivoting point for the overlays. To project each overlay, simply swing it into position over the opening of the base mount. When a progressive disclosure (sequential order) technique is desired, overlays can create a special effect by mounting up to four overlays to one side of the mount (746); see page 214 for mounting instructions. A build-up or take-apart effect can be created (747) by hinging overlays to opposite sides of the mount; see page 214 for mounting instructions.

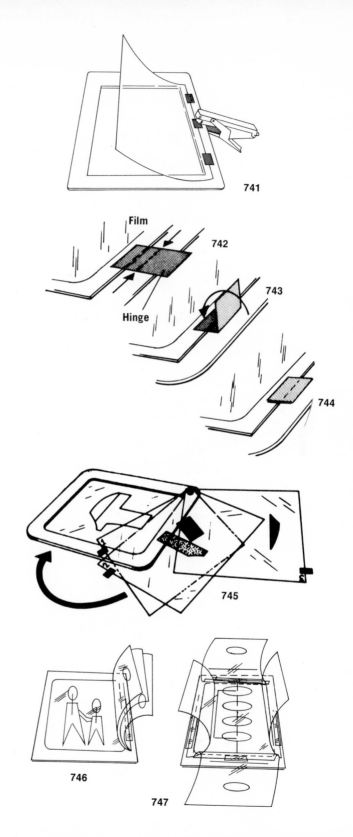

741

Film

742

Hinge

743

744

745

746

747

215

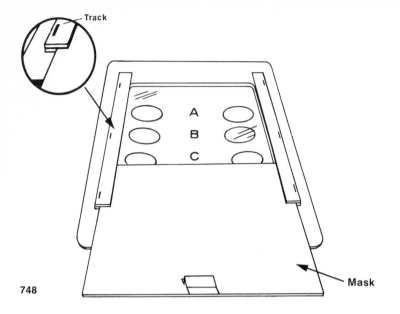

748

ATTACHING MASKS

Sliding Masks (748)

Sliding masks, made of cardboard, overhead transparency plastic mask, or other opaque material, can be used to achieve a controlled-pace presentation. The projection screen at the beginning of the presentation is dark; then, as the mask slides off the mount, the image is revealed to the viewers. The track for the mask can be made from two pieces of cardboard and stapled to the mount as illustrated, or commercial overhead transparency plastic tracks can be purchased. An overhead transparency stapler is recommended for attaching tracks to the mount, since an ordinary stapler with standard staples may not penetrate the track and mount.

Spot Masks (749)

Spot masks (or *barn door* masks) are designed to reveal a selected portion of a transparency. Masks can be cut into any shape desired and attached in much the same way as any of the other masks included in this section. Among the materials that can be used for spot masks are cardboard, file folder, and overhead transparency plastic mask.

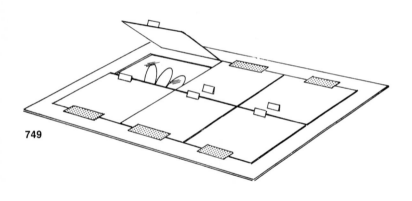

749

Folding Masks (750)

Folding masks, also known as accordion-pleat masks, are excellent for progressive disclosure of projected material. Strips of cardboard, cut the correct size, can be hinged together with pressure-sensitive tape and hinged to the edge of the mount; or simply fold an opaque sheet of heavy paper in strips the correct width and hinge to the mount. To use the folding mask, lift each fold or section as required to disclose another part of the image area. Notes and cues can be made on each fold.

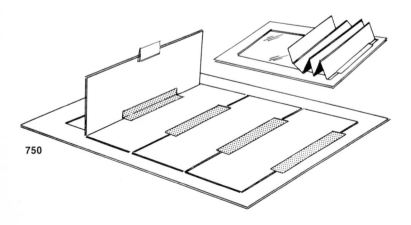

750

Hinged Masks (751)

A progressive disclosure can be achieved by masking all or a portion of the transparency with an opaque sheet, such as cardboard or an overhead transparency plastic mask. Instructions for hinging masks and attaching overlays are the same and can be found on page 214.

Circular Masks (752)

Circular masks are dramatic and effective when information that can fit into a circular design is used. A mask, cut out of cardboard, opaque plastic sheet, etc., is attached to the base transparency with a grommet or thumbtack and pencil eraser. The thumbtack is inserted from the underside of the base transparency and through the mask on top of the transparency. The eraser is attached to the point of the tack and serves as a "locking" device for the mask.

Mask Lifters (753)

Pressure-sensitive tapes or commercial overhead transparency hinges can be used to make a simple lifter (handle) for overlays and masks. To make, fold the tape or hinge, with adhesive side in, allowing enough of the adhesive side to be attached to the mask or overlay for good holding contact. Lifters serve as a handle for lifting the mask or overlay off the base transparency.

LARGE TRANSPARENCY ACCESSORIES

Transparency Stapler (754)

A heavy-duty stapler which is especially modified for attaching overlays to transparency mounts. It uses heavy, wide-faced steel staples designed for transparency mounting.

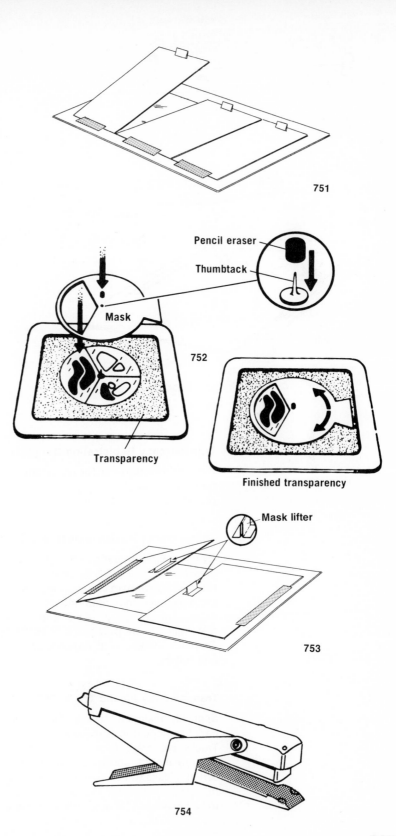

751

Pencil eraser

Thumbtack

Mask

752

Transparency

Finished transparency

Mask lifter

753

754

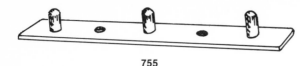

755

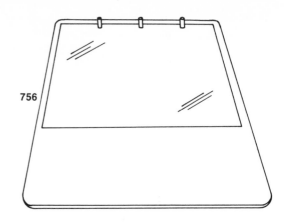

756

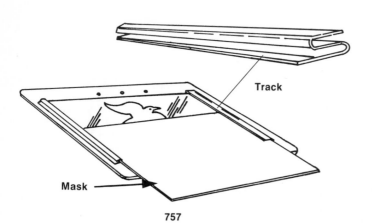

Track

Mask

757

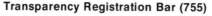

Transparency Registration Bar (755)

A pin registration bar for registration of transparencies in the production of projectuals.

Transparency Registration Board (756)

A pin registration bar inserted through a pressed-wood board. The board will not move easily when in use, thus facilitating the assembly and mounting of projectuals. Transparency films and other materials can be purchased from Scott Graphics for use with registration bars and boards.

Transparency Plastic Track (757)

Specially designed "tracks" for use with transparency cardboard or plastic mounts. Tracks are stapled or taped to transparency mount, and masks are then inserted. Masks will then slide easily along the tracks, allowing the desired areas to be blocked out at any desired moment.

Transparency Hinge (758)

Pressure-sensitized, metallized polyester film squares for hinging overlays to a base transparency. They are adhered to overlays to form small hinges and are then stapled to the transparency mount (see page 215). The hinges are extraordinarily strong and can be folded at least 12,000 times without breaking. They are packaged in a "pop-up" dispenser box.

Transparency Hinging Tape (759)

Made of the same material as transparency hinges. Designed for hinging a complete side of a transparency and for mounting a transparency on a mount and for use where a need for an indestructible tape is required. Tape is available in ½- or ¾-inch width.

Transparency Envelope (760)

A large transparent plastic or heavy-paper envelope for protecting overhead transparencies when stored. Some envelopes are hole-punched for insertion in loose-leaf notebooks (761).

Transparency Album (762)

Especially designed for storage and protection of overhead transparencies. Each pocket page holds one transparency.

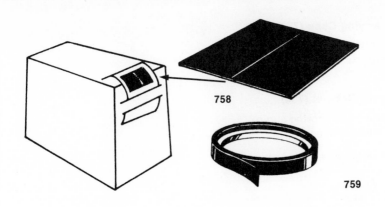

758

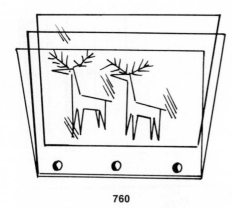

759

760

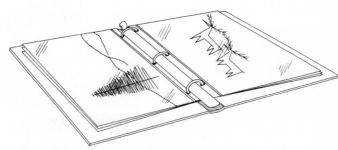

761

762

Transparency Carrying Case (763)

Vinyl case for storing or transporting overhead transparencies.

Metal Transparency Cabinet (764)

Metal cabinet designed for storing audio records or fifty transparencies.

763

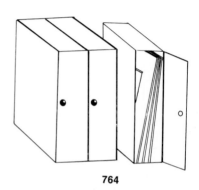

764

SLIDE MOUNTING

Usually slides are commercially processed and returned in cardboard mounts. If the slides are not subjected to rough handling or if they are stored in slide magazines or trays, cardboard mounts are satisfactory. For those making or processing their own slides, or wishing to provide a more permanent protection from dust, fingerprints, etc., a brief description of several types of mounts and accessories is included in this section.

2- BY 2-INCH SLIDE MOUNTS (765)

While 2- by 2-inch slide mounts have the same outer dimension (2 by 2 inches), the aperture (viewing area) differs to allow for the variety of film formats. Shown here are the more popular slide mounts with aperture dimensions indicated for each.

A $1\frac{1}{32}$ by $\frac{29}{32}$ inches
B $\frac{29}{32}$ by $\frac{29}{32}$ inches
C $1\frac{1}{2}$ by $1\frac{1}{2}$ inches
D $1\frac{1}{16}$ by $1\frac{1}{16}$ inches

765

On the market today are several types of 2- by 2-inch slide mounts. Illustrated and discussed here are a select group of slide mounts.

DESCRIPTION	MOUNTING INSTRUCTIONS
Cardboard mount (permanent, heat-seal) (766)	Mount with a slide heat mounting press (see page 223), electric hand iron, or dry mount tacking iron (see page 177).
Cardboard mount (permanent, adhesive-backed) (767)	Seals in film upon contact. "Kalcor" is one brand name.
Cardboard mount (reusable) (768)	Simply slip the film into the slot.
Plastic mount (permanent) (769)	Requires a special slide hand mounting press (see page 223) for sealing film in permanently.
Plastic mount (reusable) (770)	Requires no special mounting device. Mount has self-locking pins or seams that hold the film securely but is easy to open for reuse.
Metal mount (cover glass, mask, and metal frame) (771)	Insert the film, mask, and two pieces of thin slide cover glass into the open end of the mount. The mount frame's three sides hold the slide securely without the need of tape.
Handmade glass mount (cover glass, mask, and slide binding tape) (772)	An economical technique for mounting and binding all sizes of slides. Insert the film into a mask, and sandwich between two pieces of slide cover glass. Slide binding tape is used to bind the film, mask, and glass together.

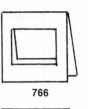

766

767

768

769

770

771

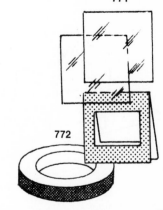

772

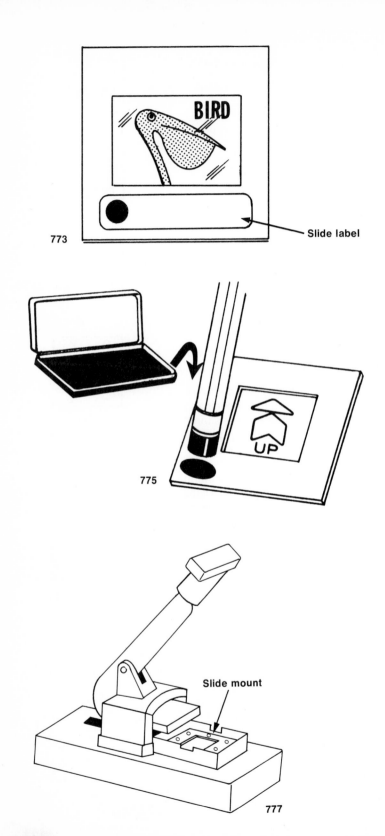

773

Slide label

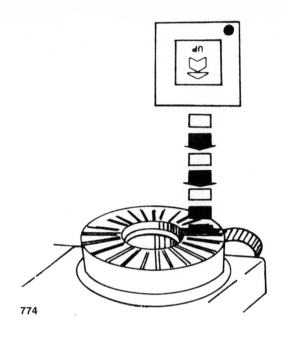

774

775

UP

Slide mount

777

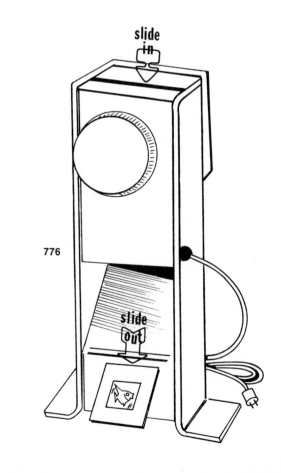

slide
in

776

slide
out

SLIDE IDENTIFICATION AND "THUMB-SPOTTING"

Photo slide labels are ideal for properly identifying slides. These labels (773), available from Visual Planning, are designed for slide identification (see "Slide Mounting Accessories" for a description).

Slide "thumb-spotting" is a guide for accurate positioning of a slide in the projector or slide tray (774). Here are directions for "thumb-spotting": After the slide has been mounted, turn so that it reads properly and place a thumb spot (commercial or hand-printed) in the lower lefthand corner of the mount (775). Commercial thumb spots (signal dots) are available for purchase. However, hand-printed spots can be made with a pencil eraser and ink stamp pad.

SLIDE MOUNTING ACCESSORIES

Slide Mounting Press (776)

A hand-operated electric press for mounting all popular sizes of slides. Models are available for mounting 2- by 2-inch, 2¼- by 2¼-inch and 3¼- by 4-inch slides in cardboard mounts designed for heat mounting.

Instructions for Seary presses

1 Place the film in a cardboard mount and fold.
2 Slip the folded mount in between heated pressure plates.
3 Squeeze the handles together like a pair of pliers. Press the locks, freeing the operator's hands for preparation of the next slide.
4 After two seconds, pull the release handle and the sealed slide drops out. Insert the next slide, and close the press while the right hand is still on the handle.

Hand Mounting Press (777)

A hand mounting press designed for mounting permanent plastic slide mounts (see page 221). The machine mounts two mount halves and film in one operation.

Slide Labels (778)

A pressure-sensitive adhesive paper label with a printed red dot (thumb spot). The red dot is for correct placement of the slide into the projector or carrier (tray) (see page 222). Blank label space is for identification information that can be typed or written with pen, pencil, or ballpoint. Labels available in white and colors.

Thumb Spots (Signal Dots) (779)

Self-sticking die-cut dots for use as thumb spots for slide mounts and other visual media requiring color-coded dot identification. Dots come in red, blue, green, gold, and silver—in a dispenser box.

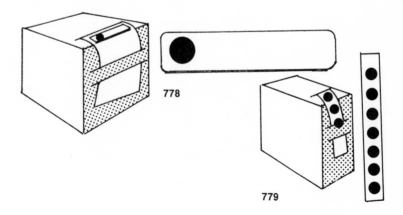

778

779

8 PHOTOGRAPHIC TECHNIQUES

High-Contrast Photography
Polaroid Land Projection Transparencies
Thermocopy Transparencies
Xerographic Transparencies
Diffusion Transfer Transparencies
Diazo Transparencies
3M Brand Color-Key Transparencies
Electronic Stencil Cutter Transparencies

A number of techniques for producing visual media can be classified as either purely photographic or related to photography. They all produce images on a sensitized or special surface by action of light or some other intense energy source. Selected photographic techniques are illustrated and discussed here, each having certain features that can be employed to produce or reproduce quality opaque, translucent, and transparent visual media.

High-contrast photography heads the list of selected photographic techniques included in this section, mainly because of the large number of visual media that can be totally or partially produced by this fine photographic technique.

In recent years the Polaroid Corporation has added a new and exciting dimension to the photographic field, a system for producing "instant" projection slides in the camera. At present, two types of slides can be produced with this system: a line (high-contrast) 3¼- by 4-inch slide and a continuous-tone 3¼- by 4-inch slide.

Perhaps the recent success of thermocopy machines in schools, business, industry, etc., as an easy-to-use copying system has greatly influenced the inclusion of thermocopy transparencies here. Agfa-Gevaert's Transparex and Arkwright's Escotherm Color-On transparency systems have been selected for this section because of their unique approach to making transparencies for projection and display.

Now overhead projection and display transparencies can be made in any Xerox copy machine. These Xerographic transparencies are of high quality and warrant inclusion in this section.

The diffusion transfer process produces line (high-contrast) overhead projection, diazo master, and display transparencies from printed or drawn originals in any color within minutes. The equipment and materials are both inexpensive compared to many of the other processes.

Because of their vivid color quality, diazo transparencies are featured here.

The process for producing color transparencies involves the use of a chemically coated film that is exposed to ultraviolet light and processed ammonia fumes.

For the creative-minded producer of transparent visual media, the 3M brand "Color-Key" system for producing color transparencies is featured here. This exciting transparency system can produce art comprehensives, packaging designs, film cels, slide and filmstrip art, and other visual media requiring color transparencies.

Finally, a system for producing a high-quality image of printed and visual material on both a stencil and a sheet of transparent film at the same time is included here—the electronic stencil cutter transparency.

HIGH-CONTRAST PHOTOGRAPHY

Photography is one area that can provide great flexibility for the production program. In most programs, however, photography must be limited to the most useful types because of the time, space, equipment, and money involved. These considerations are the reason the 35mm camera is commonly used for making continuous-tone black and white and color 2- by 2-inch slides.

LINE COPY

Another form of photography, less common but extremely valuable, is the one used to copy line originals. It is often referred to as line or high-contrast photography. Line originals (or line copy) may be defined as opaque reflection copy having only two tones, black and white, with *no* intermediate tones of gray. Some examples (780) are black and white toning or texture sheets, printed music, mechanical drawings, photosketches, scratchboard drawings, high-contrast posterizations, and silhouettes.

780

HIGH-CONTRAST FILM

Typical of the many high-contrast films manufactured for copying these types of line originals are Kodalith Ortho Type 3 (Kodak) and Ortho S Litho (DuPont). High-contrast film, extremely important to the graphic artist and printer, is available at professional graphic arts dealers. It may be obtained in varied-size sheets (cut film) and rolls, making it valuable when large transparencies are desired for overhead projection, light boxes, and transparent turnover charts. Another advantage of this relatively inexpensive film is its high-temperature tolerance when used for projection. A further advantage is that, due to the film's high contrast, undesirable imagery in the transparent areas may often be removed with negative opaque, a black or red opaque paint that is impervious to light.

Furthermore, because it is a photographic film with a gelatin emulsion, it will absorb transparent watercolor. And *since it is an orthochromatic film, it can be handled and processed under red light, permitting a person to develop the film by inspection*—an extremely important point when the facilities do not provide controlled time and temperature procedures.

CAMERA

High-contrast film is available in 100-foot rolls for the 35mm camera. Where 35mm slides are desired, a regular 35mm copy setup works very well. For those who desire larger-size negatives or transparencies, i.e., $3\frac{1}{4}$ by 4 inches, 4 by 5 inches, or 8 by 10 inches, a simple copy setup made of a view camera and tripod, copy lights, and a copy board will be quite

781

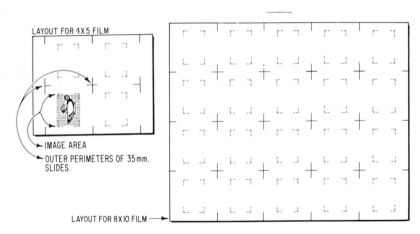

LAYOUT FOR 4X5 FILM

IMAGE AREA
OUTER PERIMETERS OF 35mm. SLIDES.

LAYOUT FOR 8X10 FILM →

782

satisfactory (781). For extensive use, a more permanent copy stand (781A) can be constructed using a flatbed view camera (781B). When a 4- by 5-inch view camera is used, a photographic enlarger will be necessary to make the larger-size transparencies. An 8- by 10-inch view camera will permit one to make overhead transparencies directly in the camera without using an enlarger. If desired, reducing backs for smaller-size cut film and 35mm roll film attachments may be purchased for use with the 8- by 10-inch camera, giving it more flexibility.

With uniform-size artwork, another approach to making inexpensive 35mm slides with either the 4- by 5-inch or 8- by 10-inch view camera is possible. Using the 4- by 5-inch camera, four 35mm slides may be photographed at one time on a single piece of 4- by 5-inch film, and, in the case of the 8- by 10-inch camera, twenty may be made at one time. The line artwork is drawn or pasted up on a special layout sheet which indicates the outer perimeter of the 35mm slide as well as the viewed image area (782). Making this layout proportionally quite large will facilitate creation of the artwork as well as the final photography. The focused image size on the ground glass of the view camera gives the exact size of the image that will appear on the photographic negative. When copying artwork laid out as indicated above, careful measurements should be made by either using a ruler or holding a 35mm slide mask against the ground glass of the view camera on which the image is focused. Each of the drawings should fit within the opening of the mask to ensure that it will project properly. Guidelines on artwork may be removed by painting over them with white paint before the artwork is copied; they may be removed from the developed negative by painting them out with negative opaque; or, if they are drawn originally with nonreproducing blue pencils, they will usually not record on this orthochromatic film.

COPYBOARD

The amount of copy work will usually determine what will be used as a copyboard. Often, where a simple setup is used with a view camera and tripod, the artwork may be adhered to any smooth, vertical wall surface or easel. However, with a more permanent setup it might be wise to create a permanent copyboard using a surface such as celotex or corkboard. Although it is not absolutely necessary, covering the surfaces with black paint or black cloth is desirable, for it will cut down undesirable glare or reflection that might result if the copyboard were white. White guidelines on the copyboard will aid in centering copy, provided the lens of the camera is centered on the board (781B). The artwork can be attached to the surface with pins, thumbtacks, or tape.

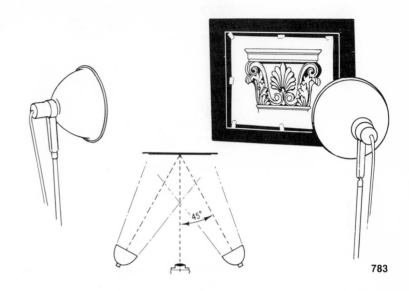

783

LIGHTING

Even lighting on the original artwork is very important, especially when the image has fine detail. Two lamps in reflectors centered on the copyboard will generally furnish adequate light for smaller copy, but a lamp on each of the four corners will ensure more even illumination when the artwork is large. Photofloods in reflectors or reflector photo lamps (3200° K) should be set at a 45° angle about 4 feet from the center of the artwork (783).

A simple method of checking light balance of the two lamps is to place a pencil in the center of the image vertical to the copyboard. If the two shadows cast by the pencil appear even in density, lighting from the two lamps is relatively equal.

COPY PROCEDURE

The following explanation assumes that a view camera mounted on a tripod is used (781B). Be sure the camera is firmly mounted in a level horizontal position on a strong, rigid tripod to minimize movement or vibrations. Check to see that the back of the camera is parallel to the surface of the copyboard so that the lens will be aimed on the center of the artwork to be copied. *Shooting at an angle will cause distortion,* which when not intended can be very disconcerting. With camera, lights, and artwork in position film must then be loaded into a film holder—a "light-tight" device which fits in the back of the camera and permits the transporting of film from the darkroom to the camera. When handling high-contrast film such as Kodalith Ortho Type 3 (Kodak) or Ortho S Litho (DuPont), one must work in a darkened room, whether it be a simple closet or a specially constructed darkroom lighted only by red light. Special red safelights may be purchased, but often a dark-red light bulb will suffice. Working in a lighted darkroom facilitates the handling of the film when loading, developing, or making contact or enlarging prints. The film is loaded with the emulsion side (light side) facing out. (At this time the silver edge of the dark slide should face out—indicating the film has not been exposed.) The holder holds two pieces of film, one on each side (784A).

1 Turn on copy lights. It is often best to eliminate or minimize room lighting to cut down on possible undesirable light reflections.

2 The ground glass on the rear of the view camera facilitates the sizing and focusing of the image. The size of the image as viewed on the ground glass will be the size of the image on the developed negative. Lock the shutter on "open" to permit maximum aperture size and to allow transmission of light through the lens (784B). (*Note:* the operation of lenses made by different manufacturers may vary slightly.)

3 Size the image by moving the tripod and camera back and forth, and then sharpen the focus (784C).

4 Close down the iris diaphragm to reduce the aperture size (784D). (f 22 may be suggested as a desirable setting.) Close the shutter.

5 Carefully place the film holder in back of the camera, making sure no movement occurs (784E).

6 Pull out the dark slide on the side facing the lens (784F).

7 With the shutter set on T, press the shutter cable release and leave open for the desired exposure time (784G); then press again to close the shutter. (Exposure may be determined by using the light meter, by using the simple exposure procedure described by the manufacturer and included in each box of film, or by

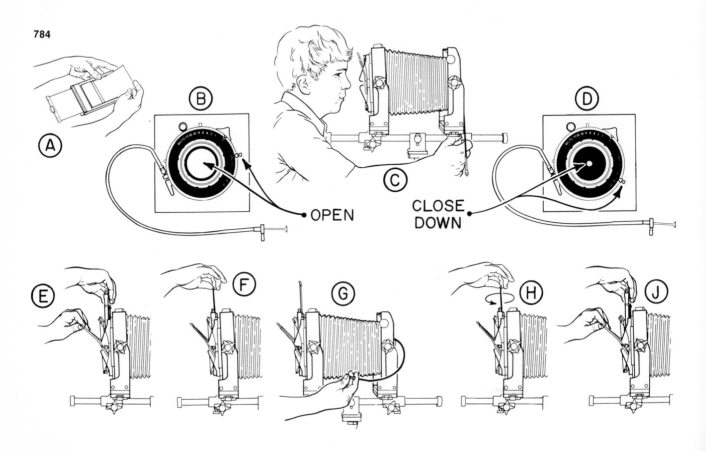

784

OPEN

CLOSE DOWN

running some test exposures. If the exposure time is acceptable, the development time will be between 2 and 3½ minutes.) The film has now been exposed.

8   Remove the dark slide from the film holder, turn it around so that the black edge of the dark slide faces out, and slide it back into the holder (784H). (The black edge of the dark slide indicates film has been exposed; the silver edge indicates it has not.)

9   Remove the film holder from the camera (784J), and take it to the darkroom.

FILM DEVELOPMENT

Now the film is ready to be developed. Be sure to work under a red safelight in a darkened room. Prepare for the developing process by setting up four trays (785). The first tray contains the developer formulated for use with this high-contrast film and made up of two parts, referred to as solution A and solution B. Equal portions of these two solutions are mixed together in a tray at the time of use. The tray life of this solution is relatively short, and consequently the solution is not saved for future use. The second tray contains the stop bath, which may be either water or an acid stop bath as recommended. The third tray contains the film fixing bath, which may be obtained from a photographic supply store. The final tray should be in or near a sink so that it is possible to have running water for washing the developed negative. Work as cleanly as possible. Handle the film by the edges with clean hands. It is best if the developer is about 68°F.

1   Place the film in the developer with the emulsion (or *light*) side down. With experience several pieces of film may be developed at one time. Be sure the entire surface of the film is immersed in the developer as fast as possible to ensure even development. To further prevent uneven development give a slight, continuous rocking of the tray to spread fresh developer over the film surface. Guard against spotty or uneven development caused when the warmth of the hand is brought into contact with the film. If exposure is correct, the film will be developed between 2 and 3½ minutes. A visual check may be made during processing to see whether good, dense black areas are developing where white areas existed on the original copy, and whether remaining image areas of the negative are staying clear and sharp. If the clear image areas begin to fill in, development may have to be stopped before full, specified development time has elapsed.

2   When development is complete, immediately rinse the film in water or (preferably) stop bath to stop any further development of the film.

3   Next, place the negative in the fixer bath to remove the light-sensitive salts that have not been acted upon by the developer. It will then be safe to turn on the room lights, for all light-sensitive areas of the film will now have been removed.

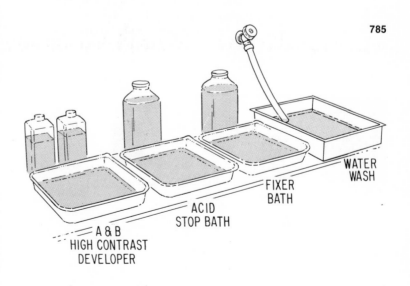

785

WATER WASH

FIXER BATH

ACID STOP BATH

A & B HIGH CONTRAST DEVELOPER

4 The final step in processing the negative requires washing in running wash water for about five to ten minutes. The negative may now be dried. Gently squeegeeing water off the surface of the negative will speed up drying. Using a clothespin or film clip, hang the negative up on a line to dry.

REVERSING AND ENLARGING THE NEGATIVE

The negative is often used for projection. At times, however, it is desirable to have a reverse or positive image to project. If the negative has been correctly sized for the projector, this reversal process can be accomplished by contact printing (786*A*).

Working in a darkened room under a red safelight, place the negative in direct contact with a piece of unexposed high-contrast film with emulsion to emulsion. To ensure good contact the film may be weighted down with a sheet of clear, clean glass. The sandwich is then exposed under light. (With the use of small pieces of film a few test exposures can be run to establish a basic exposure time. With correct exposure the development time should be between 2 and 3½ minutes.) Process the film in the same manner as described above.

If the negative must be enlarged (e.g., from a 4 by 5 to an 8 by 10 for overhead projection) to a positive, this can be accomplished by using a photographic enlarger (786*B*). The negative is placed in the enlarger. With maximum aperture opening the image may then be sized and focused on a piece of white paper corresponding to the size of film to be used. Close down the iris diaphragm to reduce the aperture size to f 11 or f 16. Under red safelight replace the white paper with unexposed film, emulsion (sensitive) side up. Determine exposure as indicated above. Process the film as described above. When the film has dried, it is ready for binding as a slide or transparency.

It is hoped that the above discussion will be regarded only as an introduction to the use of high-contrast photography. With continued study of the literature and practice in more sophisticated techniques an exciting variety of visual media can be produced using this film.

POLAROID LAND PROJECTION TRANSPARENCIES

The Polaroid Corporation, makers of the Polaroid Land camera, has developed a transparency- (slide-) making system which produces a black and white slide on the spot. No darkroom or expensive equipment is required. All that is needed is a Polaroid Land camera and Polaroid Land projection film. This system is ideally suited for displaying information to a large audience, because the transparencies give a projected image of remarkable clarity and brilliance. At present there is a choice of films to make either line-copy or continuous-tone slides. These slides can be projected as large as 20 feet square with a standard lantern slide projector. They can also be shown with overhead projectors or trimmed and mounted for use with 2¼- by 2¼-inch and 35mm projection equipment. Regardless of the projection method, there is no loss of resolution, detail, or tone.

786

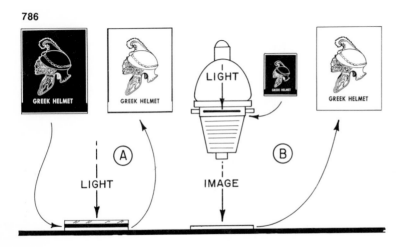

Both Polaroid Land projection films are designed to be used with Polaroid MP-4 and MP-3 (787) cameras and Polaroid roll-film cameras and backs (except the Model 80 series, J33, J66, and the "Swinger").

TYPE 146-L FILM (788)

This medium-speed, high-contrast, blue-sensitive film produces a fully developed, high-contrast transparency in thirty seconds. Eight-exposure roll. A 3¼- by 4¼-inch format sheet will produce one lantern-size slide or several 35mm-size slides. Film speed: 100 ASA, 21 DIN equivalent with tungsten lighting; 200 ASA, 24 DIN equivalent in daylight.

TYPE 46-L FILM (789)

This high-speed, medium-contrast panchromatic film produces a fully developed, continuous-tone transparency in two minutes. Eight-exposure roll. A 3¼- by 4¼-inch format sheet will produce one lantern slide or several 35mm-size slides. Film speed: 800 ASA, 30 DIN equivalent.

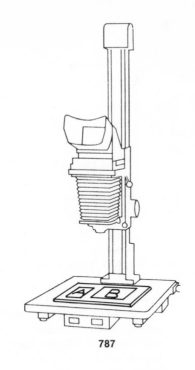

787

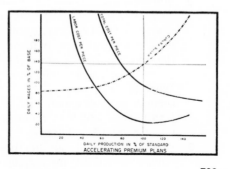

788

789

790

SNAP IT

PULL TAB 791

792

LIFT OUT

INSTRUCTIONS FOR EXPOSING AND PROCESSING FILMS

The instruction sheet included in the box of film will contain more detailed instructions than are included here.

1 *Exposure.* Snap it by exposing the film as recommended on the instruction sheet (790). Make certain the camera is held horizontal to the subject matter, because lantern slide projectors always take the slide in a horizontal position.

2 *Development.* Pull the tab slowly but steadily (791); the development will start. A fast pull can create small pinholes in the dark areas of the picture. Hesitation during a slow pull can cause streaks across the image area. Type 146-L film requires about fifteen seconds of development time at 70°F (21°C). Type 46-L film requires two minutes at 60°F and above.

3 *Development.* Lift out the positive transparency (792); the negative will remain in the camera. When the transparency is removed from the camera, the emulsion is soft and delicate, and so care must be exercised. For best results, start removal at the cutout slot in the upper right-hand corner near the cutter bar. Tear out diagonally, from the lower left. Do not allow the transparency to fall back against the negative. Do not touch the image side before hardening.

4 *Hardening.* Harden and stabilize the transparency in the Dippit (793). This should be done within one hour after removal from the camera. For best results, allow the transparency to dry in the air two or three minutes before dipping, or wave the transparency vigorously for ten to fifteen seconds. Here are instructions for using the Dippit:

a Open the hinged cover of the Dippit and carefully slide in the transparency as far as it will go. Hold the film by the tab.

b Close the cover of the Dippit. Make certain the film tab comes out through the slot in the cover. Turn the Dippit upside down and agitate for about twenty seconds (rock back and forth).

c Turn the Dippit right side up. With the cover still closed, pull the film out with a rapid motion. The lips of the Dippit will squeegee excess liquid from the film.

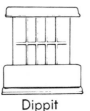

Dippit

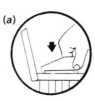
(a)

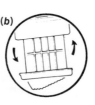
(b)

(c)

793

HARDEN

THERMOCOPY TRANSPARENCIES

The thermocopy process, also known as thermal transfer, thermal copy, dry heat, and infrared, is the only copying process in which exposure and development are simultaneous. It is one of the simplest in both construction and operation. Only one step is involved: the insertion of a specially coated film and the original together into the exposure opening of the copying machine. The image is transferred from the original to the film in about four seconds. What actually takes place during this process is this: When the original (fully opaque or translucent) is passed through the machine, the heat from the light source (infrared) penetrates through the thermocopy film to the original, which is made up of images containing some metallic substance and whose colors are visible to infrared light. The image areas absorb the heat from the infrared light; thus the "hot" image of the original forms an image on the film at the point of image contact.

HANDMADE ORIGINALS

Creating originals for the thermocopy process is both easy and fun. Discussed here are two techniques for preparing handmade originals.

Marking Devices (794)

Basic to preparing originals are marking devices that produce lines that can be

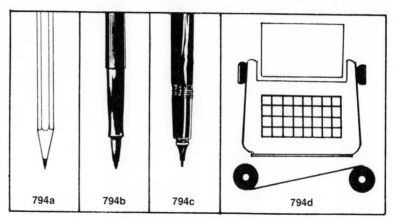

Thermocopy marking devices

reproduced by the thermocopy process. Marking devices include a #2 lead pencil (794a), 3M black marking pen (794b), India ink and pen (794c), and typewriter with a carbon ribbon (794d).

Paper Surfaces (795)

Three paper surfaces that work best for preparing handmade originals are bond paper (795a), guide sheet (795b), and graph paper (795c). The blue lines of graph paper will not reproduce when using a thermocopy machine.

Instructions: Direct Image on Paper (796)

Art and lettering can be done directly on any of the papers and with the marking devices recommended.

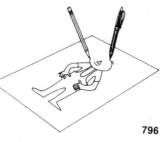

796

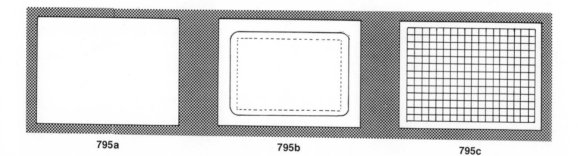

795a   795b   795c

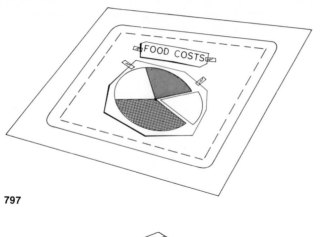

797

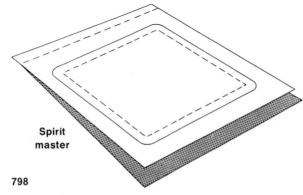

Spirit master

798

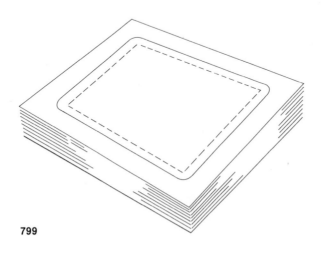

799

Instructions: Paste-up Image on Paper (797)

Art from clip-art books (see page 86), newspapers, magazines, etc., can be mounted directly on any of the papers recommended with small pieces of transparent tape.

THERMOCOPY GUIDE SHEET

Here is a valuable aid for preparing art and lettering for the thermocopy process. This guide sheet, designed by the authors, can be easily made by tracing the inside opening of the transparency mount to be used directly on a spirit master (798). Next, draw a broken line $\frac{1}{2}$ inch from the solid line (do all art and lettering within this broken line). Make white paper copies from this master with the spirit duplicator (ditto machine) (799). Guide sheets can be used to draw or trace on, or can be used for paste-up art and lettering or for typing. The guidelines will not reproduce when passed through the thermocopy machine—only the art and lettering.

Instructions for Making Transparencies

1 Place a sheet of thermocopy film, with the notch in the upper right-hand corner (away from the operator), on top of the original (printed side up) (800).
2 Set the exposure dial as indicated by the manufacturer of the film. Feed the film and original into the machine (801). *Light lines on the transparency can be darkened by running the film only through the machine a second time.*
3 Retrieve the film and original, and separate. Mount the transparency if desired.

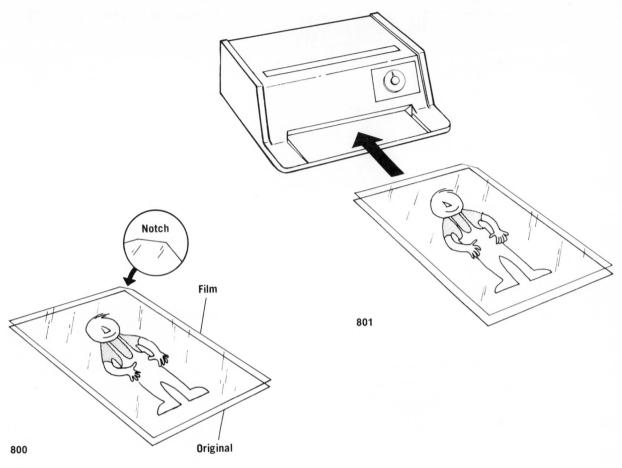

Notch

Film

801

800

Original

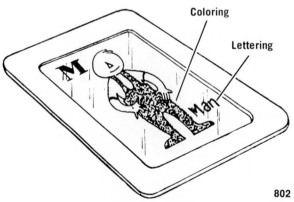

Coloring

Lettering

802

Mounted for projection

**Helpful Techniques for Enhancing
Finished Transparency (802)**

1 To add color, see page 94.
2 To add lettering, see the "Lettering
   Selection Chart," page 108.
3 To add special effects, see pages 214
   to 217.
4 To mount, see pages 212 to 214.
5 To add "motion," see page 89.

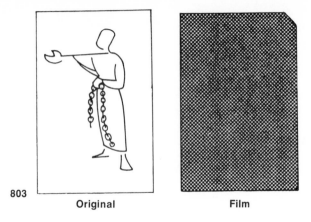

803

Original   **Film**

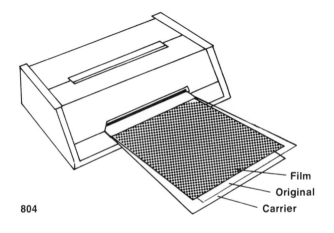

804

Film
Original
Carrier

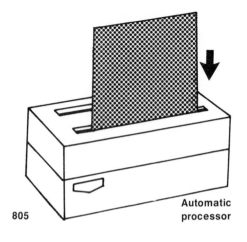

805   **Automatic processor**

TRANSPAREX TRANSPARENCIES

Agfa-Gevaert has developed a unique thermocopy overhead projection transparency system made up of three thermocopy films: Transparex film (wet process), Transparex white film (for multicolor transparencies), and Transparex dry film.

Transparex (Wet Process) Film (803)

This film is exposed in any thermocopy machine and then processed in ordinary tap water. The original (art, lettering, etc.) for Transparex transparencies must be prepared for thermocopy processing (see pages 235 to 237).

Instructions

1 Combine original art (face up) with the emulsion side of the film, and insert in the special Transparex carrier. See pages 235 to 237 for preparation of art for thermocopy. Insert assembled units into any thermocopy machine, and expose at the recommended setting (804).
2 Separate the exposed film from the original, and insert in one of the Transparex processors (805).
3 Remove the processed film from the processor (806).

Film can be processed in a Transparex hand processor (807) or hand-developed with a soft sponge and water (808).

Transparex White Film

A multicolor opaque image on clear film. Ideal for television, slide, filmstrip, and motion-picture titles; displays; package design art; etc. Transparex dyes, available in four colors, are applied to the emulsion (matte) side of the film (exposed in any thermocopy machine and processed the same as wet process film).

806

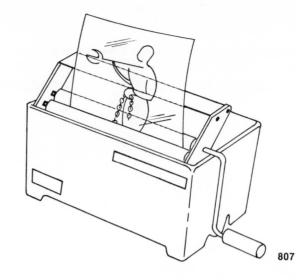

807

Transparex Dry Film

A one-step thermocopy film that can be processed in any thermocopy machine. The film comes in six transparent colors on a clear background (base). Halftone originals can be reproduced with this film.

ESCOTHERM COLOR-ON FILM TRANSPARENCY

Arkwright's Escotherm Color-On transparency is a thermocopy film that produces a frosted image on a clear acetate base. The frosted image projects as a black on white (clear) background or can be hand-colored with up to ten easy-to-use wipe-on colors.

Like other types of thermocopy film, Escotherm requires an original suitable for the thermocopy process (809). See pages 235 to 237 for instructions on preparing thermocopy originals. Also, originals to be copied may be photographs (except Polaroid) or any printed, typed, drawn, or written material, on one or both sides of the paper, halftone or line originals.

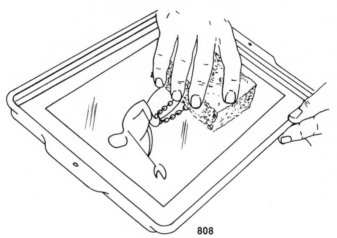

808

809

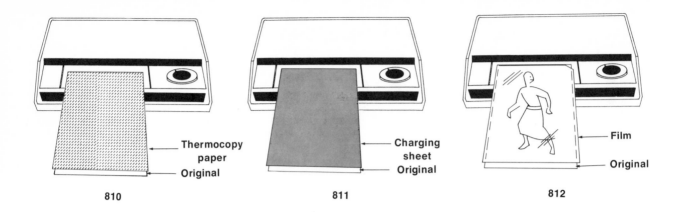

Thermocopy paper
Original

810

Charging sheet
Original

811

Film
Original

812

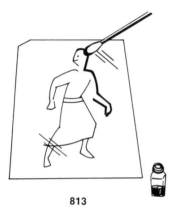

813

Instructions

1 *Testing:* As a test, place a sheet of thermocopy paper (buff side up) on top of the original and run through the thermocopy machine (810). A faint but readable copy indicates the best setting for charging the original. Test sheets eliminate unnecessary film waste.

2 *Charging the Original:* Use the speed setting determined by running the test sheet. Place the charging sheet, dark side up, on top of the original (811). Run through the copy machine once. Registration for this step is not important. For black negative film or Color-On film, charge twice using the same charging sheet. Discard the charging sheet after charging the original.

3 *Printing Film:* Place the film over the charged original with the clipped corner at the upper right, and pass through the copier (812).

4 *Applying Colors:* Apply Escotherm Applicolors to images (visuals, letters, etc.) with a Q-Tip (813). Colors wipe off nonimage areas with facial tissue moistened with water.

XEROGRAPHIC TRANSPARENCIES

Overhead projection or display transparencies can be made in any Xerox office copier (814) as easily and simply as making a regular paper copy.

There are several producers and distributors of Xerographic film. However, Arkwright's Xerographic film and process will be discussed here. Xerographic film from Arkwright comes in 8½- by 11- and 8½- by 14-inch clear, red, yellow, blue, and green sheets (815).

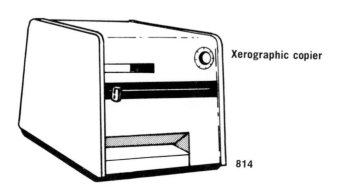

Xerographic copier

814

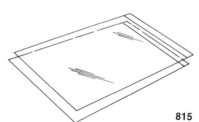

815

OPERATING INSTRUCTIONS

Xerox Models 914, 420, 720, 2400, 3100, 3600-1, 4000, and 7000:

1 Fan the film sheets to allow for easy feeding and handling.
2 Place a supply of sheets (approximately ten to fifteen) into the loading tray with the white opaque strip facing up.
3 Make prints in the normal way with the pressure lever and temperature control at the same setting as used for paper. If the print is too light, pump up the toner to the desired darkness level.
4 If fusion is not adequate, go to the next highest heat setting (use this setting when making future transparencies).

Xerox Models 813, 660, and 330:

1 Fan the film sheets to allow for easy feeding and handling.
2 Load the tray with an opaque white strip feeding into the machine, but with the strip facing down.
3 Put the dial setting on 1 after loading the tray.
4 Make prints in the normal way.

HELPFUL TIPS
Corrections

If changes are necessary after printing, delete image areas with tetrachloroethylene. New data can be added with marking pens or markers.

Removal of Oil Residue

The light oil residue on transparencies imaged in certain models will disappear eventually, but may be removed immediately by gently wiping both sides with paper tissue.

Print Quality

Always check that the copier is making clean, sharp black images on paper. The quality of the transparency will only be as good as that being produced on paper.

DIFFUSION TRANSFER TRANSPARENCIES

Diffusion transfer is a photo-reflex copying process that produces a line-copy (high-contrast) transparency from a printed or drawn original in any color within minutes (816). The original can be a single sheet or a page in a bound book or magazine. The transparency may be projected, displayed, or used as a master for diazo transparencies. The process involves photosensitized paper and film and a diffusion transfer machine. To produce a transparency, a negative photographic paper is exposed to a light source in contact with the original from which the transparency is to be made. A "reflex" exposure results (817). The exposed negative paper is passed through a liquid photographic processing solution in contact with a sheet of positive transparent film. The latent image on the negative paper develops, and then a positive image also develops and "transfers" onto the surface of the

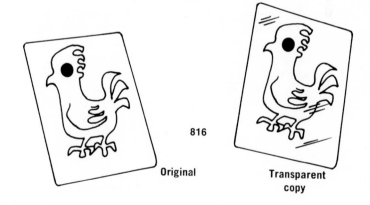

816

Original

Transparent
copy

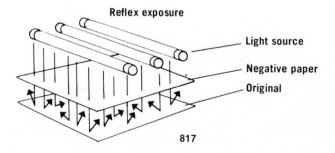

Reflex exposure

Light source

Negative paper

Original

817

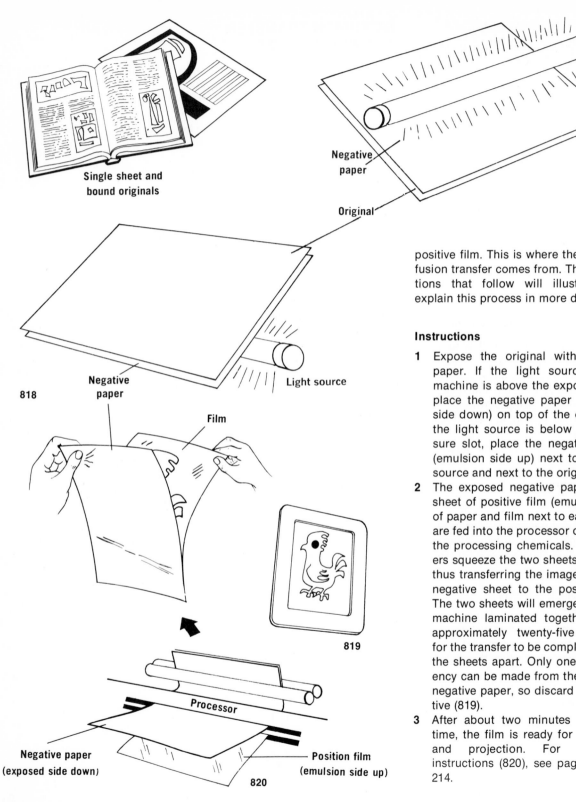

Single sheet and
bound originals

Light
source

Negative
paper

Original

818

Negative
paper

Light source

Film

819

Processor

Negative paper
(exposed side down)

Position film
(emulsion side up)

820

positive film. This is where the term diffusion transfer comes from. The instructions that follow will illustrate and explain this process in more detail.

Instructions

1   Expose the original with negative paper. If the light source of the machine is above the exposure slot, place the negative paper (emulsion side down) on top of the original. If the light source is below the exposure slot, place the negative paper (emulsion side up) next to the light source and next to the original (818).

2   The exposed negative paper and a sheet of positive film (emulsion side of paper and film next to each other) are fed into the processor containing the processing chemicals. Twin rollers squeeze the two sheets together, thus transferring the image from the negative sheet to the positive film. The two sheets will emerge from the machine laminated together. Allow approximately twenty-five seconds for the transfer to be completed. Peel the sheets apart. Only one transparency can be made from the exposed negative paper, so discard the negative (819).

3   After about two minutes of drying time, the film is ready for mounting and projection. For mounting instructions (820), see pages 212 to 214.

DIAZO TRANSPARENCIES

The diazo process is not new; it dates back to World War I when a serious shortage of photographic papers and films pointed up the need for a substitute reproduction process.

This process works on the principle of ultraviolet light passing through a translucent or transparent original (master), which destroys the chemical coating on the film (foil), except where an opaque image (line, letter, etc.) has blocked the light (821). The exposed film is developed, and the remaining chemical is converted to a visible image.

Diazo transparencies project in vivid colors far superior to those of many other techniques for producing projectables. For persons interested, additional history and information on the diazo process can be obtained from manufacturers and suppliers of diazo equipment and materials.

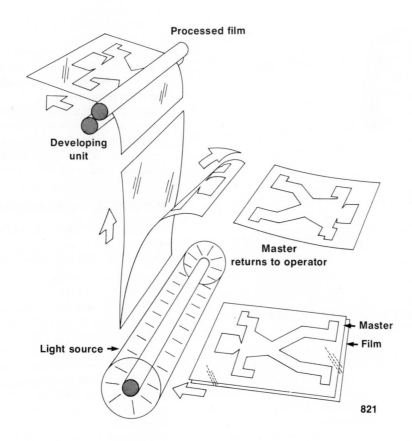

Processed film

Developing unit

Master returns to operator

Light source

Master

Film

821

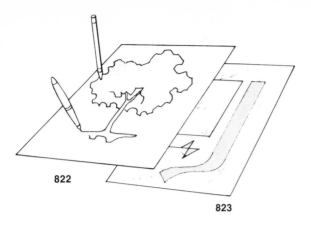

822

823

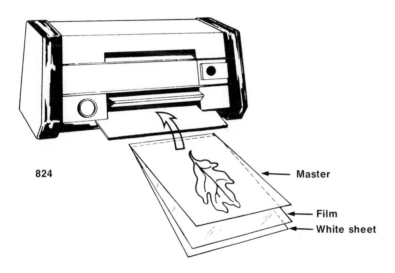

824

Master

Film

White sheet

PREPARATION OF TRANSPARENCY ORIGINALS

Diazo originals, or "masters," are usually "line" artwork. However, soft lead pencils can be used to create shading or special effects. Any well-prepared *translucent* original can be used, such as an ink or pencil drawing on tracing paper (822) or matte acetate (823), carbon-backed typewritten material, or photo-

graphic film positives. Transparency quality depends upon the relative image opacity and base translucency of the original.

TRANSFER OF ORIGINAL OPAQUE IMAGES

If the proposed transparency is printed, drawn, lettered, or typed on an opaque base (paper, cardboard, etc.), it can be transferred to a translucent or transparent base in one of the following ways:

1 It can be photographed, and a positive-transparent film can be made from the negative (enlargement or reduction of the original can be made this way).
2 A direct-positive reproducible print can be made on Kodak Auto-Positive paper or film, thereby eliminating the photographic negative.
3 Translucent or transparent-base originals can be made with thermocopy (see page 235), diffusion transfer (see page 241), or Xerographic (see page 240) copying machines.

MONOCHROME TRANSPARENCIES

Monochrome (single-color) transparencies are made by contacting the master on diazo film. Here are the instructions:

1 Place the appropriate-color diazo film in contact with the handmade or commercial master, face to face. The face side (sensitized) of the diazo film is found by locating the notch in the upper right-hand corner of the film. Use the interleaf sheet, if white or with a white side, as a backup to the master during exposure. Place the white side of the sheet behind the film (824).
2 To expose (if the light source of the diazo machine is *above* the exposure

244

stage), follow the foregoing instructions; then insert assembled materials in the machine (master on top of film), and expose the recommended time (825). To expose (if the light source of the diazo machine is *below* the exposure stage) (826), follow the foregoing instructions; then insert the assembled materials (film on top of master), and expose the recommended time.

3 After exposure, separate the film from the master and interleaf sheet. Roll the film with the sensitized (emulsion) side in, and place it in a large-mouth gallon-size jar (827) or insert it in the developing unit of the diazo machine, if it has one (828). If a large jar is used, soak a sponge or paper towel with strong ammonia water (28 percent is recommended) and place it in the jar. The ammonia can also be placed in a container as illustrated.

4 Mount, if desired, for projection. See pages 212 to 214 for tips on mounting.

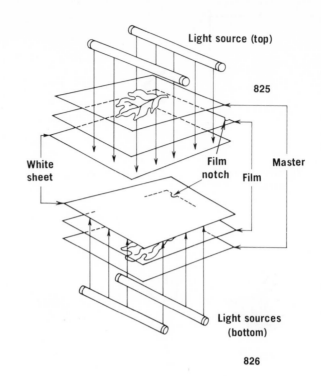

825

826

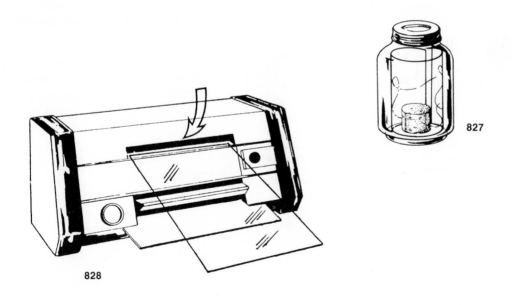

827

828

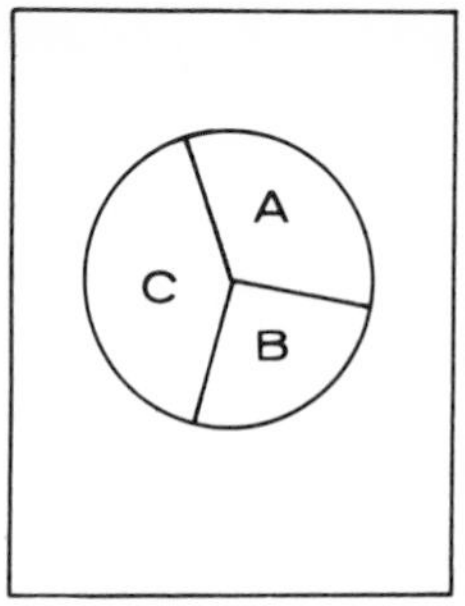

(a) Translucent base master

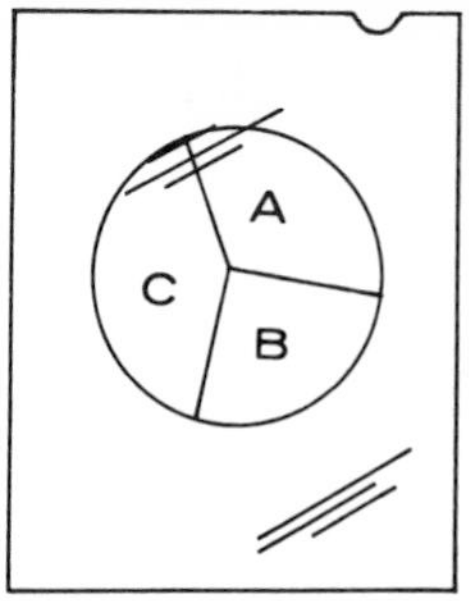

(b) Black transparent print

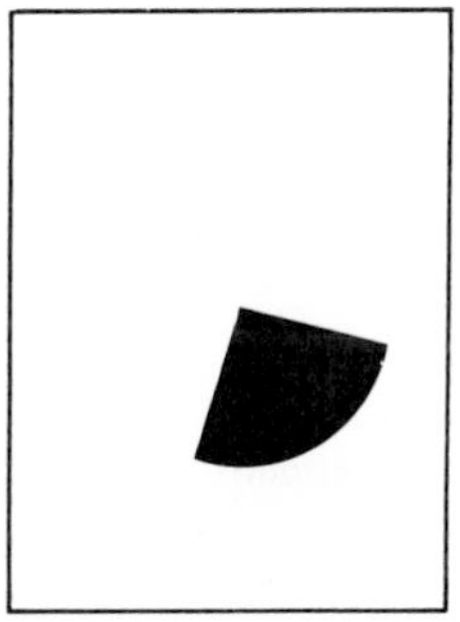

(c) Red overlay master

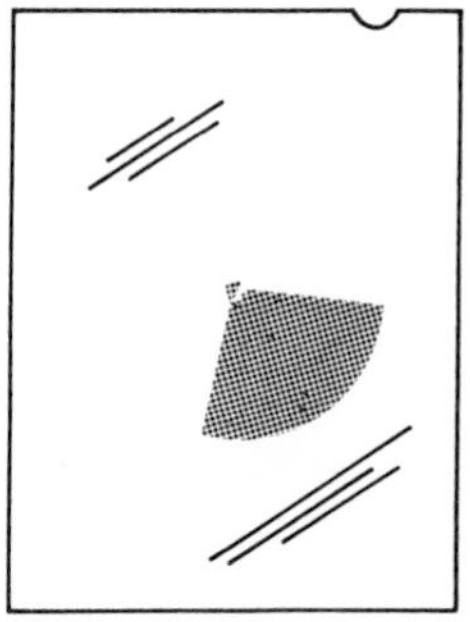

(d) Red transparent print

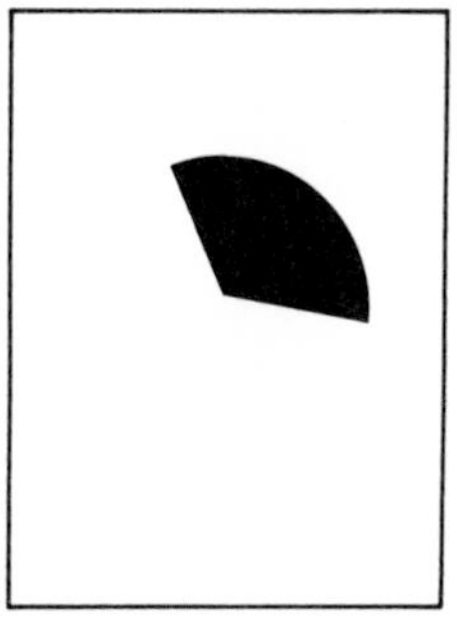

(e) Blue overlay master

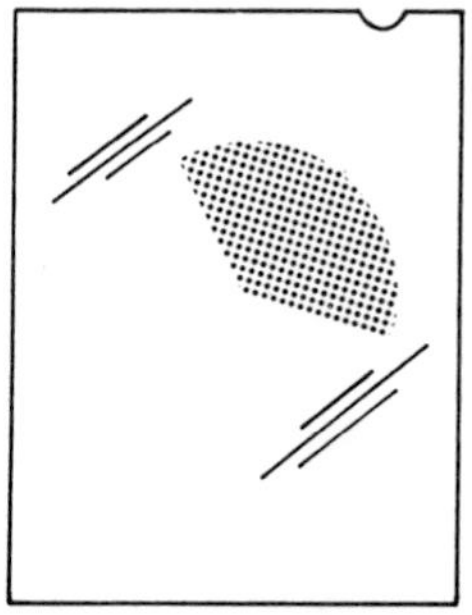

(f) Blue transparent print

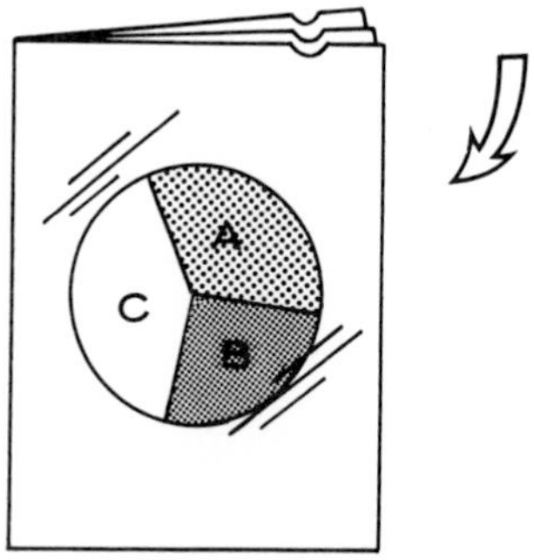

(g) Multicolor projectual

MULTICOLOR TRANSPARENCIES (829)

Multicolor and color overlay transparencies require additional masters (one for each color desired). There are several techniques for preparing masters for multicolor transparencies. Scott Graphics, upon request, will provide printed instructions on several master-making techniques. Here is a technique for producing masters for multicolor transparencies using tracing paper:

1 Prepare the base master (a) as instructed on page 244.
2 Prepare a separate master for each section to be reproduced in a color (c) and (e) on tracing paper. The tracing paper for each color master is normally held in position over the base master by tape. The use of a registration bar or board (see page 218) is recommended for precision register of color masters. Preparation of each color master is the same as for the base master.
3 Make a transparent print from each of the masters on the selected diazo color films (b,d,f). Follow the instructions for monochrome transparencies on page 244.
4 Superimpose four transparent prints to form a multicolor transparency (g). See pages 212 to 214 for mounting instructions.

Clip-art books

830

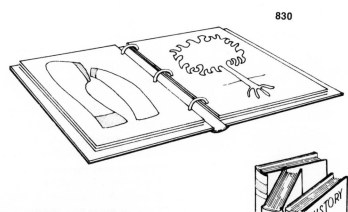

COMMERCIAL MASTERS (830)

Several manufacturers of diazo equipment and materials produce printed masters for use in the preparation of diazo transparencies. Keuffel & Esser, for example, produces masters in the areas of history, physics, chemistry, technical graphics, geometry, instructional media, and others.

831

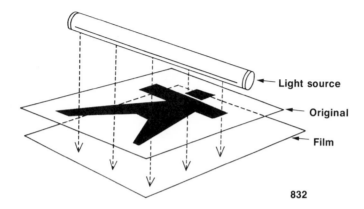

← Light source

← Original

← Film

832

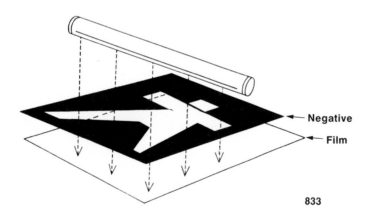

← Negative

← Film

833

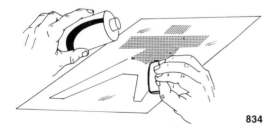

834

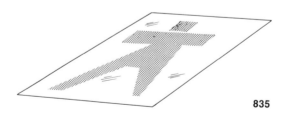

835

3M BRAND "COLOR-KEY" TRANSPARENCIES

The 3M brand "Color-Key" system produces fine-quality color transparencies for overhead projection and displays. The system involves a two-film process: a negative, and then a color positive. For the visual media designer/producer requiring quick, accurate color transparencies, "Color-Key" is one good solution.

Instructions

1   The original (831) can be a drawing, hand lettering, dry transfer lettering (see the "Lettering Selection Chart," pages 108 and 109), etc., on clear acetate, tracing paper (vellum), or other thin translucent paper.
2   Make a "Color-Key" negative by exposing to an ultraviolet light source (832). Develop with 3M brand "Color-Key" developer. From this negative you can make a positive in any of the "Color-Key" colors.
3   Expose the negative to the desired sheet of color film (833).
4   Develop the color positive with 3M brand "Color-Key" developer (834). Swab, rinse, and blot dry.
5   The results—an exact copy of the original on a clear film base in color (835).

ELECTRONIC STENCIL CUTTER TRANSPARENCY

Here is a technique for producing a high-quality image of printed and visual material on both a stencil and a sheet of transparent film at the same time. The original (836) can be anything from a page from a book to drawings, or even paste-up artwork that includes photographic halftones. The electronic stencil-cutting machine produces a stencil and a finished transparency for immediate projection.

836

Instructions

The Gestetner Corporation has prepared a booklet, *How to Make a Paste-Up Layout for Your Gestefax,* which contains instructions and illustrations for preparing artwork for the electronic stencil cutter. Refer to pages 87 to 89 for tips on paste-up techniques.

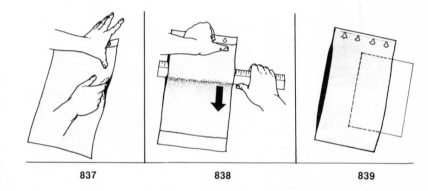

837   838   839

1. Carefully separate the stencil from the backing sheet, starting at a point approximately 3 inches from the top right side of the stencil (837). Peel just enough of the stencil to insert a ruler.
2. Insert, with care, a ruler in the opening created between the stencil and the backing sheet (838). Gently push the ruler to the opposite side of the stencil; then move the ruler downward about 11 inches. This will create a "pocket" in which the film is inserted.
3. Place a sheet of clear acetate (Gestetner Corporation's Gestefax transparency film is designed especially for this technique) in the "pocket" of the stencil (839). Thermocopy and most clear acetate film can also be used.
4. Attach the original (art, lettering, etc.) to the left-side drum of the stencil cutter (840).
5. Attach a stencil, with the film inserted, to the right-side drum (841). Use recommended machine settings for the type of original being reproduced. Start the machine.

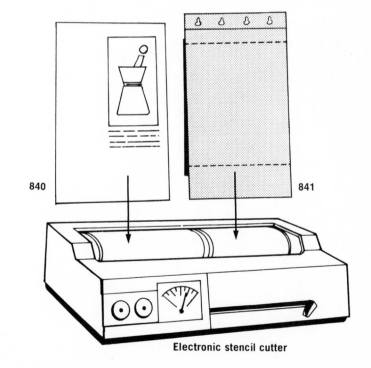

840   841

Electronic stencil cutter

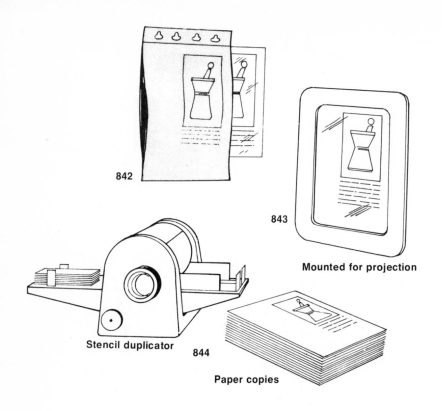

842

843

Mounted for projection

Stencil duplicator

844

Paper copies

6 After the stencil has been cut, detach from the stencil drum and remove the film (842). It is now ready for immediate use (843).

7 To add color, see pages 94 to 105. To mount or mask, see pages 212 to 217. To add lettering, see page 108 for recommended lettering techniques. To add motion, see page 89.

8 The "cut" stencil can be attached to a stencil duplicator, and hundreds of paper copies can be made (844).

9 REFERENCES

GLOSSARY

These brief definitions and descriptions of terms, materials, and equipment are provided for a better understanding of this book. Some definitions and descriptions may not completely agree with those in other publications, but they carry the meaning intended in this book.

A

Acetate Moistureproof cellulose acetate sheeting used as a base for photographic film, overlay cels, and graphic mediums requiring an acetate surface.

Acetate (Plastic) Ink Opaque or transparent color ink designed for use on acetate or plastic surfaces.

Adhesive-backed (Pressure-sensitive) Broadly, refers to any of a group of adhesives which do not have to be moistened or have heat applied for use. Such adhesives stick to a clean, dry surface on contact. Wax adhesives belong to this group.

Adhesive (Glue) Pen A pen-type refillable liquid adhesive device, using the ball-point principle to dispense dots of liquid adhesive. Most pens when filled will dispense about 5,000 adhesive dots.

Adhesive Stick A white solid adhesive in lipsticklike form for gluing paper, cardboard, styrofoam materials, etc.

Adjustable (Flexible) Curve A plastic or metal curve-drawing aid that is easily bent to any desired curve or shape.

Airbrush A precision penlike spraying device about the size of a fountain pen and connected by a hose to a controllable air supply which forces light-bodied ink, liquid colors, and paints from a small reservoir cup or bottle.

Airbrush Aerosol Pressure Tank A 16-ounce aerosol can of propellant gas with a pressure-regulating valve. Contains enough pressure for one to three hours of airbrush use depending on the size of the airbrush and type of work to be done.

Airbrush Carbonic Tank A small ready-to-use tank unit with a supply of air to last many hours of airbrush work. Can be refilled by any concern that services soda fountains.

Air Compressor A portable electric unit that produces a dependable air supply for airbrushes.

Airbrush Liquid Color Color in liquid form designed especially for airbrush work.

Align To line up, or place letters or words on the same horizontal or vertical line.

Art All original copy, whether prepared by an artist, camera, or other mechanical means. Loosely speaking, any copy to be reproduced.

Art Aid Camera A specially designed camera for enlarging or reducing original artwork. Original artwork can be opaque or transparent. Some models will accept photographic film and paper.

Art Aid Projector A wall- or floor-type projector which projects opaques, transparencies, and three-dimensionals down and upon a drawing board surface. Provides complete artwork in one operation without transferring from a tracing.

B

Ball-point Pen A special ink-controlled ball-point pen designed for smooth lettering and drawing. Ideal for use with cardboard and plastic stencil lettering guides, die-cut letters, etc. Assorted ink colors available.

Balsa Wood An exceedingly light wood used for life preservers, rafts, model building, etc. Can be cut with a small knife or razor blade.

Beam Compass A metal bar-type compass which will accept a variety of drawing and cutting attachments.

Bleed Where part of the printing area intentionally runs off one or more edges of the page. Actually most bleeds are accomplished after printing by trimming off part of the printed area.

Boldface A heavier version of a regular typeface. Indicated as BF.

Bond Paper A grade of writing and printing paper with a surface treated to take pen and ink well and have good erasure qualities. Used where strength, durability, and permanence are required.

Bourges (Pronounced "burgess.") A trade name for a thin, color-coated acetate overlay sheet keyed to standard printing inks. Used to produce color separations in art. The coating is removed either by a fluid or by scratching.

Bristol Board Also called *Bristrol*. A good grade of thin cardboard or poster board with a smooth surface. Available in a variety of finishes and colors; ideal for drawing, writing, and printing.

Brochure Strictly, any book of eight or more pages and stitched; but generally applied loosely as a term for any pretentious advertising piece, stitched or not.

Bulletin (Primary) Typewriter A manual or electric typewriter which produces approximately $\frac{1}{4}$-inch type. Letter size is ideal for overhead projection transparencies, spirit masters, mimeograph stencils, direct offset masters, and the like.

Burnisher A small bone, wood, or plastic tool for burnishing down adhesive-backed shading and color sheets, dry transfer letters, etc.

C

Camera-ready Art Copy assembled and suitable for photographing by a process or copy camera with a minimum number of steps.

Cam-lock T Square An all-steel or clear plastic-edge T square designed for use on a drawing board equipped with a Cam-lock channel.

Caption Properly, a leadline or title, especially of an illustration; but, more commonly the description accompanying the illustration.

Chalkboard Ink A white ink designed especially for the chalkboard. Will resist erasing or sponge washing with water.

Characters Individual letters, figures,

punctuation marks, etc., of the alphabet.

Circle (Compass) Cutter A metal compass device for cutting perfect circles out of paper, acetate, thin cardboard, etc.

Circle Template (Guide) A transparent plastic template for drawing circles on opaque and transparent surfaces.

Circular Proportional Slide Rule A white plastic device for obtaining proportions on reduced or enlarged photographs, artwork, etc. Gives number of times of reduction or enlargement of original size plus all new possible proportions.

Clay-coated Paper A smooth-surfaced printing or drawing paper with a clay base coating which will permit the transfer of printed or hand-drawn images to picture transfer film. Most of the popular magazines are printed on clay-coated paper.

Clear Acetate An all-purpose transparent cellulose acetate sheet. Can be used much like an ordinary sheet of paper for drawing, writing, and so forth. Surface will accept a number of marking and drawing devices.

Clear Acetate Roll (Overhead Projector) Designed for use on the overhead projector. Surface will accept a number of marking and drawing devices. Requires a roll adapter for use on the projector.

Clip Art Line and tone ready-to-use illustrations covering every practical subject classification from A to Z. Many clip-art sheets and books contain symbols, decorative borders, etc.

Coits Lettering Pen A ball-bearing lettering pen that works like a brush. Produces a clean-cut, sharp line. Available in nine widths from $1/16$ to 1 inch.

Cold Laminating Acetate A thin, transparent acetate or Mylar with a pressure-sensitive adhesive on one side. It seals itself with hand pressure or with a special applicator.

Colored Acetate An acetate sheet in vivid transparent color. Can be used to add color background for overhead projection transparencies and other visual materials. Available in a variety of colors.

Combination Plate A photoengraving in which the characteristics of a halftone and a line plate are both present. Usually obtained by double-printing a negative from line art with one from continuous-tone copy.

Composing Stick (Fototype) A precision aluminum composing device required for setting Fototype in perfect alignment and with automatic spacing.

Composition Adhesive Type (Letter) Removable opaque letters, symbols, numerals printed on the back side of a thin, transparent acetate sheet. Will adhere to most surfaces. Available in black, white, and colors.

Composition Paper Type (Letter) Opaque paste-up letters, symbols, numerals printed on paper tabs or sheets of lightweight cardboard paper. Can be used when precision hand typesetting is required. Available in many styles and sizes.

Construction Paper A wood-pulp paper of sufficient body to accept crayon, chalk, paint, charcoal, or pencil. Its many other uses include cutouts and chart making. Available in assorted colors.

Contact Print A photograph printed in direct contact with a negative and therefore the same size as the negative.

Contact Print Frame (Photographic) A frame made of sturdy wood or metal, designed for making paper or film contacts from photographic negatives or positives.

Con-Tact Transparent Pressure-sensitive Acetate A thin, transparent acetate with a pressure-sensitive adhesive on one side. It seals itself with hand pressure or with a special applicator. Ideal for making picture transfer transparencies. Most Woolworth stores carry this product.

Continuous-tone Photographic Film A photographic film which produces a negative or positive film image exhibiting a complete and continuous tonal range from black, through all the middle tones, to white.

Continuous-tone Photographic Print Specifically a photographic print, but any print not made with a halftone screen and exhibiting a complete and continuous tonal range from black, through all the middle tones, to white.

Contour Pen A ruling pen for drawing curves; will follow irregular curves with ease. Can also be used as a regular ruling pen.

Copy Reading matter as distinct from art or illustration. Any material prepared for camera. All original material for printing. The mechanical, plate, or electro sent a publication. One of an issue of a printed piece.

Copy Camera A photographic camera designed for copying flat and three-dimensional materials on photographic film, paper, and slide plates.

Corner Rounder A metal cutting device for rounding corners of cardboard, paper, acetate, etc.

Corrugated Cardboard Made up of two layers of thin cardboard glued together. The base layer is flat, while the top layer consists of a series of corrugations glued to the surface of the base layer. Available in assorted colors.

Corrugated Paper Made up of two layers of paper glued together. The base layer is flat, while the top layer consists of a series of corrugations glued to the surface of the base layer. Available in assorted colors.

Cropping Indicating by tissue overlay, drop-out mask, or pencil lines (which must not cross the photograph) the part of the artwork or photograph to be reproduced.

Crow Quill Pen A very fine pen that has a flexible point with a tubular shaft that fits a special holder. Ideal for fine-line pen and ink drawing.

Cutting Needle (Stylus or Teasing) A small cutting device for color, texture, shading, symbol, letter, and acetate sheets.

D

Diazo A copying/reproduction process (sometimes known as *whiteprint*) which employs chemicals and a machine to reproduce transparent or translucent originals.

Die-Cut Paper, plastic, or cardboard cut into shapes other than rectangular by means of die cutting.

Die Cutting The cutting of paper, plastic, or cardboard by pressure or by a blow with thin steel blades made up on a form (called a *die*).

Diffusion Transfer Film Photosensitized film designed for use with the diffusion transfer process. Produces a black positive image on a clear, transparent background.

Diffusion Transfer Process A negative-to-positive process which requires no camera or darkroom. Ideal for preparing transparencies from opaque originals.

Display Pin A steel straight pin designed for mounting display materials.

Double-coated Adhesive Acetate Clear acetate with a pressure-sensitive adhesive on both sides; useful for mounting whenever a two-sided adhesive material is required.

Double-coated Adhesive Tape Transparent or opaque mounting tape with a pressure-sensitive adhesive on both sides; useful for mounting whenever a two-sided adhesive tape is required.

Double-coated Adhesive Tape Dispenser For double-coated adhesive tape. The protective liner of the tape is removed as the tape is dispensed.

Double Shading Screen Board Bristol board on which are processed two invisible shading screens; one a light tone, the other a darker tone. Application of the appropriate liquid developer with a brush or pen makes each screen visible where desired. (See also Single Shading Screen Board.)

Dowel Rod A round wood rod used to hang maps, charts, etc.

Drafting Tape Extra-strong heavyweight paper-base tape with a pressure-sensitive adhesive side that sticks to most surfaces with slight hand pressure. Holds lightly but firmly, yet removes easily when work is completed. Leaves no adhesive residue.

Drawing Paper High-quality paper for all drawing purposes. A variety of surfaces and weights available.

Drawing Pencil A pencil with a specially compounded lead for degree uniformity and point retention.

Dry Backing Cloth A high-quality cotton fabric with a thermoplastic adhesive on one side. Ideal for mounting maps, charts, and other flat materials where a cloth backing is desired. Available in rolls and sheets.

Dry Mounting A method of adhering paper, photographs, lightweight cardboard, etc., to mounting boards by using a special thermoplastic tissue that bonds under heat and pressure.

Dry Mounting Board A thermoplastic precoated heat mounting board designed to eliminate the need for dry mounting tissue. Requires heat and pressure for mounting.

Dry Mounting Press An electrically controlled mounting device which applies the heat and pressure necessary for mounting and laminating materials treated with a thermoplastic adhesive.

Dry Mounting Release Paper A special-surfaced paper for use with dry mounting tissue. Paper is placed on top of the material being mounted to protect the surface during heat mounting. It may be used repeatedly.

Dry Mounting Tacking Iron A small electrical heating device used to "tack" dry mounting tissue and dry backing cloth to mounting surfaces. Some models are equipped with a thermostatic control, and some have a Teflon-coated base.

Dry Mounting Tissue, Permanent A thin tissue coated on both sides with a thermoplastic adhesive which fuses to both the material to be mounted and the mounting surface. It is used with a dry mounting press or an electric hand iron.

Dry Mounting Tissue, Removable Heavy-duty, low-temperature mounting tissue. Ideal for mounting delicate materials such as color prints and fabrics. Can be applied and removed with a dry mounting press, a Fotowelder, or an electric hand iron.

Dry Process Lettering Dry carbon letters printed on a polyester-based tape with a special printing machine (Varafont, Kalograph, and 3M Promat are three trade-name systems). Letters may be printed in assorted colors.

Dry Transfer Art Sheet Professionally prepared black opaque art printed on a translucent plastic carrier. Art transfers to drawing paper, acetate, cardboard, etc., with the aid of a pencil, ball-point pen, or burnisher.

Dry Transfer Letter A transparent or opaque color letter which is printed on a plastic sheet and transfers to any dry surface by rubbing the letter down with a pencil, burnisher, or ball-point pen.

Dry Transfer Letter Eraser An eraser designed for clean and quick removal of dry transfer letters, symbols, colors, etc.

Dry Transfer Shading (Texture) Sheet Black opaque shading, texture, screen, and mosaic patterns printed on a translucent plastic carrier. Patterns transfer to any dry surface by rubbing down the pattern with a pencil, ball-point pen, or burnisher.

Dummy A physically exact representation of a proposed book or publication with or without layout.

Duplicating (Mimeograph) Stencil A thin waxed paper or plastic sheet on which written or typewritten matter or drawings are made with a typewriter, stylus, or electronic stencil cutter. Stencil is attached to a stencil (mimeograph) duplicator machine when used.

E

Edging Tape Pressure-sensitive paper or transparent tape for use in a tape edger. Available in $\frac{1}{2}$- and $\frac{3}{8}$-inch width.

Electric Stylus A compact electrical device that writes like a pencil on such surfaces as acetate, plastic, glass, wood. Engraves lines, letters, visuals, etc.

Electronic Stencil Cutter An electronic stencil-cutting machine which produces stencils and transparencies directly from line or wash illustrations, photographs, etc.

Ellipse Template (Guide) A transparent plastic guide for drawing or cutting perfect forms and shapes.

Embosograf Signmaker A sign-making system that produces embossed-type letters on cardboard, plastic, and aluminum up to 14 by 48 inches in one piece. Also produces die-cut letters from Embosograf magnetic sheeting and polyethylene foam material. Letters range in height from $\frac{1}{4}$ to 4 inches.

Embossing Producing a raised image on a printed surface.

Emulsion A suspension of silver halide crystals in gelatin (or, formerly, collodion) which is coated on an opaque (paper) or transparent (film) base or support to make it light-sensitive.

Enlargement A copy, usually made by projection printing from a translucent intermediate such as a film negative, which is larger than the intermediate.

Eyelet (Grommet) Round metal or plastic reinforcement for holes punched in cloth, paper, cardboard, etc. An eyelet tool is usually required for attaching the eyelet to the desired material.

Eyelet Punch An eyelet device that punches holes and sets metal eyelets in paper, leather, plastic, cloth, and cardboard.

F

Felt-point Pen (Marker), Permanent Ink A plastic or metal fountain-type pen with one of a variety of felt points. Contains permanent color ink. Assorted points and ink colors available.

Felt-point Pen (Marker), Water-base Ink A plastic or metal fountain-type pen with one of a variety of felt points. Contains water-base color ink. Assorted points and ink colors available.

Ferrotype Plate (Chrome Tin) A flat metal sheet, usually copper, with a chrome-plated finish. Used to produce a gloss finish to photographic paper prints.

Film Laminator (Cold Process) A compact cold-process laminating machine for use with laminating film with a special pressure-sensitive adhesive backing. Also used for making picture transfer transparencies from pictures printed on clay-coated paper.

Film Laminator (Heat Process) An electrical machine which laminates clear or matte plastic film to paper or lightweight cardboard stock. Can also be used to produce picture transfer transparencies from pictures printed on clay-coated paper.

Filmstrip Projector A projection device for projecting filmstrips; also used for preparing large visuals from filmstrips.

Fixing Liquid chemical removal of unexposed silver salts from developed photographic film and paper to prevent further action of light thereon.

Flatbed Press A letterpress containing a flat metal bed on which locked-up forms of type and plates in a chase are positioned for printing.

Flocking Short fibers or pile or other particles blown onto a design printed with an adhesive ink to which they adhere.

Foam-cored Board Extremely lightweight, yet rigid and strong. Foam center with white, smooth paper facing. Ideal for displays, models, mounting, etc. Surface takes poster colors, markers, inks, etc.

Foam Tape High-density foam ($\frac{1}{16}$ inch) construction with pressure-sensitive adhesive on both sides. Flexible so that it will conform to uneven surfaces. Used for all types of mounting.

Font An assortment of metal type (or molds), all of the same type face and point size, consisting of the complete alphabet, numerals, and punctuation marks.

Format The distinctive and recurring treatment of a page or pages, usually of a publication, achieved through page size, stylized composition, and makeup. Also the preliminary concept of a proposed advertising piece.

Frisket Essentially a stencil which is cut on a photograph, acetate, or artwork to protect certain areas from airbrushing or aerosol-can spraying.

Frisket Knife A small-bladed cutting device with a plastic or wood handle especially designed for cutting frisket film, film, color and shading sheets, composition adhesive type, and the like.

Frisket Paper A slick-surfaced paper with a special rubber-base adhesive on the back, ready to use when peeled off. Will adhere to photographs, artwork, etc. Some frisket papers require a coating of rubber cement for use.

G

Gestefax Overhead Transparency Film A specially surfaced transparent film for making positive-reading overhead projection transparencies with an electronic stencil cutter.

Glassine Paper A thin, dense transparent or semitransparent paper that is highly resistant to the passage of air and grease.

Glossy As distinct from matte. A photographic paper which when ferrotyped presents a slick, shiny surface, preferred for reproduction.

Gold Ink Gold in ready-to-use ink solution for lettering, drawing, etc. For use in pen, brush, or airbrush.

Grid Paper Drawing paper with precision-printed grid lines.

Gummed-back Products Adhesive-backed articles—letters, cardboard, paper, etc.—which require the application of water to activate the adhesive.

H

Halftone May refer either to artwork which is made up of an actual graduation of tones as compared with solid black or solid colors or to the plate used to print such artwork.

Heat Laminating Acetate A transparent or matte-surfaced acetate or Mylar film for laminating with the aid of a film laminator (heat process), dry mounting press, or thermocopy machine.

Heat-resistant Capable of remaining intact and immovable when exposed to high temperatures of thermocopy, diazo, and other reproduction processes which make use of heat or high-wattage lamps.

Hectograph (Gelatin) Compound A special-formula gelatin compound for filling all types of tray or frame hectograph duplicators.

Hectograph (Gelatin) Duplicator A machine used in the spirit duplication process for making copies of writing, drawing, etc., from a prepared gelatin surface to which the original image has been transferred.

High-contrast Photographic Film An orthosensitive photographic film, specifically designed for line or half-tone reproduction in either the camera or contact printing frame. Recommended for making high-contrast photograph transparencies.

Hot-Press Printing Machine Electric-heat printing machine for printing on plastic, acetate, paper, etc. A special color foil is required.

I

Illustration Board Drawing paper mounted on cardboard backing. Generally recommended for finished artwork because it need not be mounted. Does not warp when wet. Available in several weights and finishes.

India Ink (Black Drawing Ink) A black pigment of lampblack mixed with a gelatinous substance, used in drawing, lettering, etc. Recommended for the preparation of diazo, thermocopy, and other processes requiring a dense black ink.

Ink Riser Template A spacing device for use between a drawing or lettering template and a drawing surface. Prevents ink from smearing on the surface.

Irregular (French) Curve A transparent drafting device used for making curves that cannot be made with a compass.

K

Kalvar Film A photographic film containing certain diazonium salts which can be exposed by ultraviolet light and developed by heat.

Kinder Composition Plastic Type (Letter) Laterally reversed (mirror images) letters and numbers formed in white on $1/16$-inch black plastic rectangular pieces. Characters are hand-composed in a special composing stick or channel guide and then photographed on photographic film or paper.

Kodalith Film and Paper Brand name for a high-contrast photographic paper and negative materials manufactured by Eastman Kodak for the graphic arts.

Kraft Paper A strong brown or white paper for artwork, such as murals, posters, or projects which require a strong, heavy paper.

L

Laminating Film (Cold Process) Acetate, vinyl, or Mylar laminating film for use in a cold laminating machine. Film is coated with a special pressure-sensitive adhesive.

Laminating Film (Heat Process) A transparent acetate or Mylar film for laminating with the aid of a dry mounting press, laminating machine (heat process), or thermocopy machine.

Lamination A combination of two or more dissimilar materials which function as one.

Layout The arrangement and form given to the various aspects of illustrative and reading material on any form of printed matter.

LeRoy Lettering System A mechanical tracing lettering system consisting of a scriber, template, and pen.

Letterguide Lettering System A mechanical tracing lettering system consisting of a scriber, template, and pen.

Letterpress The process of printing directly from an inked raised surface, metal plate, or master.

Line Drawing Any drawing in which there are no middle tones and in which shading (texture), if any, is obtained with black and white lines or with screen overlays.

Line Negative A photographic negative made from line copy (photograph, drawing, etc.).

Logo Abbreviation for logotype, which pertains to the design or trademark of an institution, organization, firm, or product.

Lowercase Uncapitalized type or letters.

M

Magnetic-backed Letter Precut letter for use on any surface that regular magnets hold to. Some letters are made of injection-molded magnetic rubber; others are made of plastic and backed with tiny rubber, plastic, or metal magnets.

Manila Paper A smooth, sturdy, buff-colored paper made from Manila hemp. Used for folders, envelopes, etc.

Mask Generally an opaque plastic, cardboard, or acetate overlay for covering various parts of the visual or for progressive disclosure.

Masking Tape An all-purpose crepe-finish tape. Adheres with just slight pressure. Water-repellent back.

Master Original material made for the purpose of reproducing additional copies.

Mat Board Heavyweight cardboard with or without a pebbled surface. Used for mat cutting, mounting, and presentations.

Mat Cutter Cutting device or knife designed mainly for mat board cutting.

Matrix The individual mold from which a letter is cast. Also the light metal template on which Varigraph fonts are engraved.

Matte (Frosted) Acetate A noninflammable cellulose acetate with a frosted (matte) surface on one side. Available in sheets, pads, and rolls. Surface permits drawing, lettering, coloring with pencil or pen.

Mechanical A camera-ready paste-up assembly of all type and design elements mounted on the artwork surface in the exact position and containing instructions, either in the margins or on an overlay, for the platemaker.

Mechanical Scriber A precision-engineered lettering instrument designed for use with a special-type lettering template. Scriber will accept a special India ink pen, ballpoint pens, styli, lead clutch, and cutting knives.

Mechanical Tracing Lettering System A lettering system consisting of a mechanical scriber or instrument, template (template or matrix), and pen. Letters range in height from $1/16$ to 2 inches.

Metal Brush Lettering Pen A flexible metal lettering and drawing pen that strokes like a brush. Available in widths, in some makes, from $1/16$ to 1 inch. (See also Coits Lettering Pen.)

Metal Interlocking Letter Guide Individual metal stencil letters and numerals that interlock to form a complete word. Can be separated and reassembled as needed. A complete word can be traced, sprayed with paint or ink, or applied with a stencil brush and ink.

Metal Letter A cast aluminum or bronze letter for indoor or outdoor use.

Metal Magnet A metal magnet that can be attached to letters, objects, etc. Will work on any surface regular magnets hold to. Available in a variety of shapes and sizes.

ModulArt A product of Artype, Inc., consisting of a number of specially designed illustrative figures, costumes, animals, backgrounds, vehicles, and accessories; all in modular form printed on the underside of clear, matte-surfaced, presure-sensitive adhesive acetate.

Mounted Drawing Paper Rag-content

white drawing paper mounted on muslin for added strength and durability. Paper is used for all permanent maps, important documents, etc.

Mounting Board A pressed-paper board suitable for mounting purposes. Available in several thicknesses.

N

Negative The primary photographic record of an image, in which black and white values are reversed.

Newsprint Paper An inexpensive wood pulp for making quick drawings and work not demanding permanence. Available in sheets and rolls.

Nonreproducing Pencil Produces a light shade of blue which is nonreproducing in line work. This special color pencil is also used to block in and mark key lines on sketches and line mechanicals.

Nylon-point Pen (Permanent Ink) A fountain-type pen with a specially tapered point made of nylon or fiber which produces a permanent ink line; will write on most surfaces. Available in assorted ink colors.

Nylon-point Pen (Water-base Ink) A fountain-type pen with a specially tapered point made of nylon or fiber which produces a water-base ink line; will write on most surfaces. Available in assorted ink colors.

O

Offset Duplicating A term used to denote a duplicating process in which an image is transferred first to an intermediate surface and then to a receiving sheet.

Oil Board An oil-treated board for making stencil letter templates by hand or on a stencil-cutting machine.

Opacity That quality in a sheet of paper, film, etc., that prevents the type or image printed on one side of the material from showing through to the other: the more opaque the sheet, the less show-through it will have. Also, the covering power of an ink.

Opaque Nontransparent; not allowing light to pass through. Also, to paint out unwanted areas on a film negative so that

they will not reproduce during processing.

Opaque Projector An electrical device for the projection of opaque materials and flat objects. Can also be used to produce large illustrations (visuals) from small opaque originals.

Opaquing The process of eliminating any portion of a film negative by painting over the unwanted areas with an opaque solution.

Original The piece of illustrative or printed matter to be reproduced or laminated.

Overexposure Exposure to light or heat at too great an intensity or for too long a time.

Overhead Projector An electrical device which throws a highly illuminated image on a projection surface by reflection from a mirror; it is placed in front of the viewers and may be used in a semidarkened or completely lighted room. Models available for accepting transparencies from $3\frac{1}{4}$ by 4 inches to 10 by 10 inches.

Overlay Refers mainly to one or more transparent sheets containing color, text, opaque masks, etc., attached to a base overhead projection transparency.

P

Pantograph A precision-made drawing instrument consisting of a metal or wood frame with adjustable joints. Used to make enlargements or reductions of original art by movement of the tracing point actuating a pencil point held in contact with a drawing surface for the reproduction.

Parchment Paper Genuine parchment paper is made of sheepskin or goatskin. Other parchment papers are made of Japanese vellum or fine paper having a texture resembling parchment.

Passe-Partout A picture mounting in which glass, picture, backing, and often a mat are bound together, as by strips of gummed paper or cloth-base tape along the edges.

Paste-up Layout, copy, lettering, etc., mounted into position on a mounting board or drawing paper ready for the camera.

Paste-up Letters Letters printed on paper, cardboard, or thin plastic which

may be put together to form words and headings for use on a paste-up. (See also Composition Adhesive Type and Composition Paper Type.)

Pen Humidifier A revolving reservoir pen storage container and humidifier. Humidified interior prevents ink in the pen points from drying out.

Perforating (Pounce or Tracing) Wheel A small metal cutting device with teeth for perforating patterns, signs, letters, etc., for transfer to a desired surface.

Perspective Grid Paper Drawing paper with precision-printed perspective grid lines. (See also Grid Paper.)

Photographic Enlarger An optical device used for making photographic prints and transparencies which are larger than the intermediate from which they are made; can also be used to prepare large visuals from small transparent originals.

Photographic Masking Tape A black and fully opaque tape for making masks and blocking out negatives and for other photographic uses.

Photographic Opaque Red, black, or gray liquid medium for retouching and opaquing photographic film. Soluble in water and can easily be washed off for corrections. Can be applied with brush, pen, or ruling pen.

Photographic Print Dryer Photographic device used to dry photographic prints. Drum-type dryers can be used to mount dry backing cloth to the back of charts, maps, prints, etc.

Photosketching A technique for changing an actual photograph (black and white print) into a line or high-contrast visual by drawing directly on the photograph with waterproof India ink or lead pencil and processing with an iodine solution, water, and photo fixer.

Photostabilization Process A rapid photographic process which uses photosensitized papers and films containing part of the developing and fixing agents required for processing. A special processing machine is required. No darkroom is needed for use.

Phototype Composing Machine A photographic machine which composes and photographs display type and lettering on photosensitized paper and film. Assortment of type faces and sizes available.

Picture Rubber Stamp Assorted pictures on rubber stamps mounted on easy-to-hold wood blocks. Ideal for elementary school use and pictorial chart and graph making.

Plastic Shading Plate A textured plastic plate for adding shading, depth, tone, and texture to illustrations, letters, etc., on duplicating stencils and spirit masters. Assorted patterns available.

Plastic Spray (Aerosol Can) A transparent acrylic fixative in spray-can form that gives photos, drawings, artwork, etc., the protection of glass without its disadvantages.

Pliable Plastic Adhesive A white pliable mounting adhesive that will stick to any clean, dry surface.

Ply One of several layers of paper pasted together to make bristol board or similar stock: thus, 1-ply, 4-ply, 8-ply, etc.

Polarizing Materials Specialized materials for creating simulated realistic motion in overhead projection transparencies, slides, and other visual aids. Motion is achieved through the control of variably oriented polarized light.

Polarizing Spinner A hand-operated or motor-driven rotating device containing a polarizing filter which is positioned in front of or below the projection lens.

Polaroid Land Camera A photographic camera designed for use in the Polaroid Land system. Films available for producing black and white and color photographic prints and black and white line or continuous-tone transparencies.

Positive An image of the original copy corresponding to the same in lights and shades.

Poster Usually a large printed card, often illustrated, posted to advertise or publicize something.

Poster Board A smooth pressed-paper board for posters, signs, and showcards. Takes pen and ink, poster colors, tempera, watercolors, airbrush, and silk-screen process. Assorted colors available.

Pounce Paper Granular-surfaced paper designed for pounce pattern work. Surface holds paper in place while pouncing.

Prepared (Specially Surfaced) Acetate A crystal acetate (plastic) with a special coating on both sides that will accept poster paints, watercolors, inks, and dyes without crawling. Available in both sheets and pads.

Pressure-sensitive Adhesive Broadly, any group of adhesives which do not have to be moistened or have heat applied for use; sticks to a clean, dry surface on contact. Wax adhesives belong to this group.

Pressure-sensitive Adhesive (Aerosol Can) Liquid adhesive in spray-can form, having characteristics similar to wax and rubber cement adhesives. For permanent and removable mounting. Will bind paper to most smooth surfaces.

Printed Paste-up Letter (See Composition Adhesive Type and Composition Paper Type.)

Proportion The relationship existing between the different dimensions of artwork, or the relationship existing between a dimension in enlarged or reduced size.

Pushpin A plastic or metal head pin with a ground steel point. Plastic head pins available in assorted colors.

R

Reducing Glass The opposite of a magnifying glass. Used to judge how artwork and other copy will look when reduced to printing size.

Register Exact matching in position of successive overlays of color, lettering, etc.

Register Mark Combinations of printed circles and cross lines placed on artwork, generally outside the image or copy area. When register marks exactly coincide, the multiple overlays are in perfect register.

Reservoir Pen A fountain-type pen designed for India ink drawing, lettering, and so forth. Available in eight line widths. Keuffel & Esser and Letterguide pens can be used in mechanical lettering scribers.

Reversal Artwork or copy reversed to form white or clear on a black or opaque background.

Rough A sketch or thumbnail, usually done on tracing paper, giving a general idea of the size and position of the various elements of the design.

Rubber Cement Dispenser An airtight

glass or plastic container for rubber cement. Most containers have adjustable-length sliding brush. Available in $\frac{1}{2}$-pint to 1-quart sizes.

Rubber Cement Eraser An eraser, usually made of pure crepe rubber, used to remove excess dry rubber cement from the mounting surface.

Rubber Cement, Pressure-sensitive A clear transparent cement made from pure rubber. A single coat mounts one material to another. Material coated with rubber cement may be removed and remounted without applying additional cement.

Rubber Cement, Regular A transparent liquid adhesive made from specially treated rubber, blended to a formula best suited for joining various types of materials together.

Rubber Cement Thinner (Solvent) A liquid used for thinning or reducing rubber cement. Also used as a thinner for frisket work. Can be used for cleaning metal type, rollers, stencils, and electros.

Rubber Magnet An adhesive-backed magnetized rubber sheet or strip that can be cut with scissors. Magnets can be attached to cutout letters, cardboard, objects, etc., for use on a magnetic board or any steel surface.

Rubber Stamp Printing Set Die-cut rubber letters, numbers, symbols, etc., mounted on easy-to-hold wood blocks. Most sets come complete with aligning guide, guide ruler, and stamp pad. Assorted styles and sizes available.

Ruling Pen A drafting instrument designed for drawing precision ink lines on opaque and transparent surfaces.

S

Scaling The process of calculating the percentage of enlargement or reduction of artwork to be enlarged or reduced for reproduction.

Scratchboard A high-quality white-coated paper board for scratchboard work. Surface is coated with India ink and scratched off with a scratchboard tool to complete the drawing. A brilliantly contrasting black and white drawing results. A precoated black scratchboard is also available.

Shading (Texture) Sheet Shading, texture, screen, and mosaic patterns printed on the underside of a transparent pressure-sensitive sheet that can be transferred to most surfaces. Available in white and colors.

Shelf Life The period of time during which sensitized material may be kept without loss of speed, contrast, or quality.

Sign Cloth Durable coated or treated cloth especially designed for outdoor signs, banners, charts, etc.

Silk-screen Process A reproduction process in which heavy-bodied inks are squeezed through a stencil mounted on a fabric (formerly silk) or sometimes metal screen. Best suited for display work and short runs, the photographic stencil has made the process popular also for decals, printed circuits, etc.

Silver Ink Silver in ready-to-use ink solution for lettering, drawing, etc. For use in pen, brush, or airbrush.

Single Shading Screen Board High-quality drawing paper with one invisible shading (texture) pattern brought out with the application of a chemical developer. A variety of shading patterns are available. (See also Double Shading Screen Board.)

Slide Binding Tape Paper-, cloth-, or plastic-base tape for slide binding. Some tapes are gummed-back; others have a pressure-sensitive adhesive back. Assorted colors available.

Slide Projector A projection instrument designed to accept transparent slides. Slide projectors most commonly used today are 3¼- by 4-inch, 2¼- by 2¼-inch, and 2- by 2-inch models.

Spirit Duplicator A manually operated or completely automatic duplicating machine which prints on paper materials from tissue to card stock. A special spirit master, prepared by hand or produced on a thermocopy machine, is required. Recognized as one of the most inexpensive reproduction methods, with paper copies costing as little as ½ cent each.

Spirit Duplicator Paper Master A paper and carbon sheet unit required for spirit and hectograph duplicating.

Spirit Duplicator Pencil Designed for use on spirit duplicator and hectograph masters.

Stencil A sheet of material in which an image is cut by perforating or other means and through which ink can be forced to create an image on a receiving sheet.

Stencil Brush A round bristle brush for all stenciling work.

Stencil Duplicator Art Easy-to-use drawings created by professional artists. Designed primarily for preparing visuals for stencil (mimeograph) duplication. Can also be used for preparing overhead projection transparencies and slides.

Stencil Duplicator (Mimeograph) A machine for making copies of written or typewritten matter or drawings by means of a stencil cut on a typewriter, or an electronic stencil cutter, or with a stylus.

Stencil Ink Opaque ink for use with metal interlocking-letter and oil board stencils. Applied with a stencil brush, airbrush, or spray can.

Stencil Ink (Aerosol Can) Opaque ink in an aerosol spray can for use with metal interlocking-letter and oil board stencils.

Stencil Letter-cutting Machine A hand-operated letter-cutting machine for cutting stencil letters out of stencil oil board.

Stencil Paper A semitransparent, oiled paper which retains sharp lines and is easy to cut. Used as a stencil on all surfaces.

Stencil-tracing Lettering System A lettering system consisting of a transparent template (guide), guide holder (some systems), and either a pen or pencil for tracing each character. Assorted letter styles and sizes available.

Straightedge A piece or strip of wood, metal, etc., having a perfectly straight edge used in drawing lines, testing plane surfaces, etc.

Symbol Template (Guide) A transparent plastic outline symbol template for general use, or for use on mimeograph stencils and spirit masters. Symbol can be traced with pen, pencil, stylus, or ball-point pen. Templates covering almost every major subject area are available.

T

Tape Edger A manually operated device for reinforcing and protecting edges of papers, documents, overhead transparencies, maps, etc., by applying a tape edge.

Edges materials up to ¹⁄₁₆ inch thick. Uses tape up to 1 inch wide. (See also Edging Tape.)

Tape Embossing Machine A compact embossing lettering machine which produces permanent raised letters and numerals on plastic, metal, or magnetic tape with a plain or pressure-sensitive back.

Technical Fountain Pen A nonclogging fountain-type pen which uses India inks. Some models will accept acetate inks.

Thermocopy A generic term applied to a copying process using infrared light and the heat emitted by an infrared lamp. The original copy should be prepared in black ink or lead pencil or printed with a carbon-base ink.

Thermocopy Machine A heat copying machine which exposes and develops specially coated films and papers, with a printed original, simultaneously.

Thermocopy Stencil A heat-imaging stencil for the stencil (mimeograph) duplicator. Copy to be duplicated is placed inside the stencil set and run through any thermocopy machine. The burned stencil is mounted on the stencil duplicator for duplication.

Thermocopy Transparency Film Specially surfaced film for use in the thermocopy process. Film is not sensitive to light, but reacts to heat radiated by the image area of the original when exposed to infrared light. Exposure and developing are simultaneous in a thermocopy machine.

Thermoplastic Adhesive A specially formulated adhesive that becomes activated when subjected to heat. Heat laminating films, dry backing cloth, and dry mounting board are treated with this type of adhesive.

Tracing Cloth Fine-quality cloth for tracing purposes. For use where original drawings must be made on a material that can withstand much handling and will last indefinitely. Pencil or pen can be used on the surface. Available in rolls and sheets.

Tracing Paper Fine-quality translucent paper for all tracing purposes. Available in several weights, in rolls and sheets.

Tracing Unit A translucent working surface, with incandescent bulbs or fluorescent tubes as a light source. Used in drafting, color overlay work, photographic opaquing and retouching, etc. Some units are designed especially for mimeograph stencils.

Transfer Carbon Paper A quality artists' transfer carbon paper that produces sharp greasefree color lines. These lines can be easily erased. Available in several colors.

Translucent Materials Materials that are partly transparent, permitting only a portion of complete light to pass through. Frosted glass and matte acetate are examples.

Transparency Acetate or film with a positive or negative image designed for use with a transparency projection or display device. Also used to refer to overhead projection transparencies.

Transparent Materials which transmit light and are capable of being seen through. Clear glass and acetate are examples.

Transparent Color Adhesive-backed Sheet Vivid transparent color printed on the underside of a thin acetate film with a pressure-sensitive adhesive back. Used in the preparation of transparencies, color separations, posters, charts, graphs, etc. Assorted colors available.

Transparent Color Marking Pencil A pencil that has been especially created for use with overhead projection equipment. Leads are smooth and strong and appear in deep transparent color when projected. Markings can be removed with a damp cloth.

Transparent Liquid Color (Aerosol Can) Transparent color in aerosol spray cans. Color adheres to most surfaces, including glass and plastic. Dries instantly on contact.

Transparent Watercolor Water-base transparent color for use where removable or water-base color is required. Can be applied with brush or airbrush.

Transparentizer A plastic-impregnating solution which increases the translucency of matte and semitranslucent papers, films, and acetates. Some solutions are available in aerosol spray cans.

T Square T-shaped metal, plastic, or wood ruler for drawing parallel lines; also used as a support for lettering equipment. (See also Cam-lock T Square).

U

Ultrasonic Pen Cleaner An electric device specifically designed to clean Technical and Reservoir pens. Utilizes millions of energized microscopic bubbles generated by ultrasonic action.

Uppercase Capital letters.

V

Varigraph Lettering System A mechanical tracing lettering system consisting of a head writer (mechanical scriber), matrix (template), and lettering pen. Hundreds of different type sizes in condensed, normal, and extended faces can be obtained from one matrix.

Velcro-backed Letter A molded plastic letter with Velcro ''hook'' tape attached to the back for use on Velcro (Hook-n-Loop) presentation boards.

Velcro Board A unique presentation board with unbelievable holding power. Surface of board is nylon loop fabric. Flat and three-dimensional materials attached to the board must be backed with a special nylon ''hook'' tape.

Vellum A type of translucent layout or drawing paper with a toothy finish for good ink penetration.

Velour Paper Medium-weight paper with a surface of velvetlike textile fabric. Ideal for preparing display materials and for use on the flannel board. Assorted colors available.

Velox A term, derived from the trade name Velox Print, for a high-quality screened photographic print used in the preparation of mechanicals.

Vinyl Letter A die-cut vinyl plastic letter with a pressure-sensitive adhesive back that will stick to most surfaces.

Vinyl Plastic A thin vinyl plastic-surfaced material with a pressure-sensitive back. Ideal for large cutout visuals, letters, designs, etc., that require mounting on walls, glass, metal, etc.

W

Watercolor Pencil Watercolor pigment

processed and set in pencil form. May be used to simulate a painting by applying a water-saturated brush to areas where pencil has been applied. Recommended color medium for matte acetate.

Watercolor Stamp Book Water-soluble leaves (pages) of transparent colors. Color is obtained by touching a wet brush or cotton swab to a color page, or by dissolving a page in water.

Wax Adhesive A colorless, odorless, and stainless wax adhesive used for mounting three-dimensional objects (lightweight) as well as flat materials on almost any dry surface.

Wax Coating Machine An electrical device for heating and applying adhesive wax. Wax coaters range from small hand-held spreaders to automatic paper-fed machines capable of handling large sheets.

Wheat-Paste Flour A special-formula dry flour designed for preparing the paste used for wallpaper hanging. Ideal for wet mounting.

White Ink Dense white ink for drawing, lettering, marking, etc. Many brands are water-soluble.

White Opaque A liquid white opaquing medium for use on most surfaces where corrections are to be made. Won't chip, crack, or peel. Can write, type, or draw over areas where the liquid has been applied.

Wood Letter A precision-made plywood or birchwood letter for indoor or outdoor use. Assorted styles, sizes, and colors available.

Wrico Brush Pen A metal brush pen designed for use with Wrico Sign-Maker guides. Ideal for producing $1/16$- to $1/4$-inch lines which are clean-cut, full, and solid without excess ink. Recommended for use only with black India ink.

Wrico Signmaker Lettering System A stencil-tracing lettering system consisting of a brush pen, green transparent plastic lettering guide, and guide holder. Designed for sign and poster making.

X

Xerographic Transparency Film A clear

nonsensitized film for making positive-reading overhead projection transparencies with any model Xerox copier.

Xerography A positive-to-positive process developed by the Xerox Corporation and utilizing a light-sensitive, selenium-coated plate which carries a positive electrostatic charge. Where exposed to light, the charge is dissipated, leaving a latent image to which negatively charged black powder will adhere. The powder image can afterward be transferred and fused to other positively charged surfaces such as both unsensitized paper and metal offset plates. It is a dry process.

Y

Yardstick Beam Compass Consists of two metal parts that fit a standard-size yardstick. Adjusts easily and makes accurate circles up to 66 inches in diameter.

RECOMMENDED READING

The publications annotated here have been included in this book to help supplement its contents. It should be pointed out that the extent to which a publication treats a technique may range from partial to extensive coverage. Sections of the book which a publication supplements are indicated at the end of the appropriate entry by boldface numbers in parentheses. Publications which have no section reference indicated are included for their value in contributing to a better understanding of the design, preparation, and utilization of visual media. Following the title or author(s) of each entry are the publisher, or distributor, and the date of publication. The names and addresses of publishers and distributors can be found in the Address Directory.

AMATEUR FILMSTRIP PRODUCTION, Ohio State University, 1958.
Pamphlet 7 deals with a simple approach to producing instructional filmstrips with a 35mm camera. **(8)**

AUDIOVISUAL LITERATURE PACKET (No. U-915), Eastman Kodak.
About thirty pamphlets—materials, equipment, and techniques for filmstrip, slide, and motion-picture planning, production, and presentations. **(1,2,4,6,8)**

Auval, Kenneth L.: SERIGRAPH: SILK SCREEN TECHNIQUES FOR THE ARTIST, Prentice-Hall, 1965.
A book written for the professional artist, art student, or amateur who wishes to exploit the unique characteristics of the silk-screen medium as an expressive pictorial tool. All operations of fine-art screen printing are covered.

BASIC PHOTOGRAPHY FOR THE GRAPHIC ARTS (No. Q-1), Eastman Kodak, 1974.
How to make line and halftone negatives, contacts and duplicates, screened paper prints, and offset lithographic plates for photomechanical reproduction. **(8)**

BASIC TITLING AND ANIMATION (No. S-21), Eastman Kodak, 1962.
A pamphlet covering planning, equipment, artwork preparation, titling, and techniques of animation basic to the production of an animated film. **(4,5,6)**

Belland, John C., and Sidney Rothenberg: DEVELOPING INSTRUCTIONAL MATERIALS FOR THE HANDICAPPED, National Center on Educational Media for the Handicapped, 1973.
Guideline for preparing instructional media for the physically handicapped. **(1,4)**

BETTER BULLETIN BOARD DISPLAYS, University of Texas at Austin, 1961.
Arranged so that a teacher may use its pages for bulletin board ideas, this handbook is designed specifically to acquaint the teacher with resources available for use and construction of the bulletin board. **(4,5,6)**

Bockus, H. William: ADVERTISING GRAPHICS, Macmillan, 1974.
A workbook and reference for the advertising artist. It shows the tools, design elements, and production processes that concern an advertising designer. **(2,3,4,5,6,7,8)**

Boughner, Howard: POSTERS, Pitman, 1962.
A booklet for the amateur poster maker. Covers planning, lettering, color, etc. Several pages are devoted to commercial posters. **(4,5,6)**

Bowkes, Melvin K.: EASY BULLETIN BOARDS: NO. 2, Scarecrow Press, 1974.
Design suggestions in how-to-do-it form, using common materials. **(2,4,5,6,7)**

Bowman, William J.: GRAPHIC COMMUNICATION, Wiley, 1967.
A text which integrates every existing field of graphic practice under a common visual philosophy by identifying the range of ideas which can be visually presented. Offering a design methodology to translate ideas into visual statements, the author illustrates each text element with design models which can serve as a basic graphic guide for reference use in industrial or classroom situations. **(4)**

Bretz, Rudy: TECHNIQUES OF TELEVISION PRODUCTION, 2d ed., McGraw-Hill, 1962.
A comprehensive description of the tools and techniques of television pro-

duction. A reference rather than a text, presented in nontechnical, comprehensive language. As valuable to the commercial broadcaster as it is to the educational broadcaster. **(4,5,6,7)**

Brown, James W., R. B. Lewis, and Fred F. Harcleroad: AV INSTRUCTION: TECHNOLOGY, MEDIA, AND METHODS, 4th ed., McGraw-Hill, 1973.
A revised and rewritten text emphasizing educational media and systematic procedures recommended for their use. Examples are drawn from all subject fields and from all levels of instruction. Chapters 3 to 15 discuss selecting, using, producing, and evaluating educational media. **(2,4,5,6,7,8)**

Brown, Robert M.: EDUCATIONAL MEDIA: A COMPETENCY-BASED APPROACH, Charles E. Merrill, 1973.
Treats mainly the competency-based approach to learning and instruction. Contains ten modules, two of which deal with basic production techniques to assist readers to produce their own materials to fit into their instructional design. **(1,4,7)**

Brunner, Felix: A HANDBOOK OF GRAPHIC REPRODUCTION PROCESSES, Hastings House, 1964.
A book devoted to a comprehensive coverage of major graphic reproduction processes; included are gravure and lithography. Over 400 illustrations. **(4,5,6)**

Bullard, John R., and Calvin E. Mether: AUDIOVISUAL FUNDAMENTALS, William C. Brown, 1974.
Equipment operation manual with "hands-on" instructions for producing simple visual media. **(6,7,8)**

Bullough, Robert V.: CREATING INSTRUCTIONAL MATERIALS, Merrill, 1974.

A text covering the fundamentals of producing slides, films, and audiotapes. (2,4,5,6,7,8)

Calder, Clarence R.: TECHNIQUES AND ACTIVITIES TO STIMULATE VERBAL LEARNING, Macmillan, 1970.
Part II of this book gives techniques for creating instructional materials. (1,4,6,7,8)

Callahan, Genevieve, and Lou Richardson: HOME ECONOMICS SHOW-HOW AND SHOWMANSHIP: WITH ACCENT ON VISUALS, Iowa State University Press, 1966.
An idea-packed book which presents fresh, unusual, and practical ways of bringing homemaking information to life. Written especially for teachers, extension workers, and professional people who use visual aids in presenting home economics information. (4)

Cardamone, Tom: ADVERTISING AGENCY & STUDIO SKILLS: A GUIDE TO THE PREPARATION OF ART AND MECHANICALS FOR REPRODUCTION, Watson-Guptill, 1970.
A revised book by a leading commercial artist. Explains the basic technical procedure of art studios and advertising art departments: paste-ups, mechanicals, printing processes, and specifications. (4,5,6,7)

Carlis, John: HOW TO MAKE YOUR OWN GREETING CARDS, Watson-Guptill, 1968.
Scores of simple ways to use inexpensive materials to make delightfully unique cards for every occasion. (2,6,8)

Cataldo, John W.: LETTERING: A GUIDE FOR TEACHERS, Davis Publications, 1974.
Contains a fresh approach to the evolution of letter forms and symbols with basic strokes clearly explained and illustrated. (6)

Chappel, Jack, and Alice Liechti: MAKING AND USING CHARTS, Fearon, 1960.
A booklet with instructions for the preparation and use of classroom charts. More than sixty charts are included. Shows a variety of subjects, uses, and ideas for chart making for all grade levels. (4,5,6)

Chisholm, Margaret E., and Donald P. Ely: MEDIA PERSONNEL IN EDUCATION, Prentice-Hall, 1976.
Identifies and analyzes over sixty competencies in ten functional areas.

Shows how skills can be evaluated for achievement. Contains a chapter on production functions. (1,4,6,8)

Clarke, Beverly: GRAPHIC DESIGN IN EDUCATIONAL TELEVISION, Watson-Guptill, 1974.
Covers the dos and don'ts of TV graphics for educational television. (1,4,5,6,)

Coffman, Joe W.: TECHNOLOGY OF THE DIAZOTYPE PROCESSES, Scott Graphics, 1957.
A detailed booklet dealing with the diazo process. (4,5,8)

Coplan, Kate, and Constance Rosenthal: GUIDE TO BETTER BULLETIN BOARDS, Oceana Publications, 1970.
Suggestions for the design and preparation of exciting bulletin boards. (4,5,6,7)

Craig, James: PRODUCTION FOR THE GRAPHIC DESIGNER, Watson-Guptill, 1974.
A book that fully and clearly explains the production of printed matter. Written for everyone in the world of commercial art. (2,3,4,5,6,7,8)

——— and Susan E. Meyer (eds.): DESIGNING WITH TYPE: A BASIC COURSE IN TYPOGRAPHY, Watson-Guptill, 1971.
An introduction to fundamentals of typography providing the basics needed for a career in graphic design. (3,6)

Croy, Peter: GRAPHIC DESIGN AND REPRODUCTION TECHNIQUES, Hastings House, 1972.
A comprehensive text and reference source on all stages of the transformation of design to printed page, along with a range of graphic materials and mediums and nearly all the printing methods currently in use. (4,5,8)

Cutler, Merritt D.: HOW TO CUT DRAWINGS ON SCRATCHBOARD, Watson-Guptill, 1960.
A thorough exploration of the scratchboard technique. An ideal guide for the professional interested in commercial possibilities and the amateur seeking an interesting and vital approach to the technique. (4)

DAILY BULLETIN BOARDS FOR ALL OCCASIONS, Hayes School Publishing.
Actual miniature bulletin boards are laid out and pictures are included to guide the reader in creating fresh and distinctive bulletin boards. Shows how scraps and other readily available materials can be used. (4,6)

Dale, Edgar: AUDIO-VISUAL MATERIALS IN TEACHING, 3d ed., Holt, 1969.
Recognized as one of the leading books in the area of instructional technology. Deals with the selection, utilization, preparation, and administration of audiovisual materials. (4,7,8)

D'Amelio, Joseph: PERSPECTIVE DRAWING HANDBOOK, Tudor, 1964.
A complete instruction manual and reference guide on the fundamentals of perspective for students, artists, illustrators, architects, and designers. Hundreds of clearly labeled drawings and diagrams illustrate basic concepts such as "picture plane," "vanishing line," and "cone of vision," and all basic and special techniques of determining perspective heights, widths, and depths; correcting distortions; working with shade and shadow; etc. (4)

DeKieffer, Robert, and Lew W. Cochran: MANUAL OF AUDIO-VISUAL TECHNIQUES, 2d ed., Prentice-Hall, 1962.
A revised basic text for short courses in audiovisual education. Includes information related to preparation and utilization of basic instructional materials. (4,7,8)

Denstman, Harold, and Morton J. Schultz: PHOTOGRAPHIC REPRODUCTION: METHODS, TECHNIQUES AND APPLICATIONS FOR ENGINEERING AND THE GRAPHIC ARTS, McGraw-Hill, 1963.
Covers the entire field of photographic reproduction. A complete, up-to-date, and authoritative guide, it is designed to guide the technician in the efficient performance of his task. Every reproduction task is explained in simple, step-by-step fashion, and each technique is discussed in relation to other techniques. (4,5,6)

DeReyna, Rudy: CREATIVE PAINTING FROM PHOTOGRAPHS, Watson-Guptill, 1975.
Techniques and devices, such as opaque projector and pantograph, for creating original painting from black and white and color photographs. (4)

DESIGNING INSTRUCTIONAL VISUALS, University of Texas at Austin, 1968.
Gives the concerned educator a better understanding of the design requirements which must be met in producing efficient instructional visuals. (1,2,4)

Dinaburg, M. S.: PHOTOSENSITIVE DIAZO COMPOUNDS, Pitman, 1967.

Information on production and formulation of diazo compounds and couplers. (8)

DRAWING REPRODUCTION (No. U-916), Eastman Kodak.

About thirty technical pamphlets on techniques and materials for drawing reproduction. (4,8)

East, Marjorie, and Edgar Dale: DISPLAY FOR LEARNING: MAKING AND USING VISUAL MATERIALS, Holt, 1952.

Aimed at showing the classroom teacher as specifically and clearly as possible how to prepare visual instructional materials and how to use them in and out of the classroom. (4,5,6,7,8)

EASY TO MAKE BULLETIN BOARDS, Hayes School Publishing.

A collection of creative bulletin boards for classroom or halls. Bulletin boards for holidays, special days, and special occasions. All subjects including health, citizenship, science, and current events are included. (4)

Eboch, Sidney C.: OPERATING AUDIO-VISUAL EQUIPMENT, 2d ed., Chandler Publishing, 1968.

A revised manual that explains and illustrates, step by step, the operation of all types of audiovisual equipment. Instructions are also included for mounting materials for opaque projection and for preparation of handmade slides and overhead projection transparencies. (4,5,7,8)

EDUCATIONAL DISPLAYS & EXHIBITS, University of Texas at Austin, 1965.

A handbook that discusses purposes, advantages, and guidelines for exhibits. Provides a rich source of ideas for both display and bulletin board. Information about dioramas is also included. (4,5,6)

Erickson, Carlton W. H.: ADMINISTERING INSTRUCTIONAL MEDIA PROGRAMS, Macmillan, 1968.

An outstanding handbook for instructional-media program directors and a useful reference for graduate students in communication. Contains fifteen chapters dealing with acquiring, organizing, distributing, implementing, and evaluating various media. One chapter deals with the implementation of media-preparation services. (1)

——— and David H. Curl: FUNDAMENTALS OF TEACHING WITH AUDIOVISUAL TECHNOLOGY, 2d ed., Macmillan, 1972.

A complete book on the creative use of instructional media. One chapter deals with producing audiovisual media. (4,6,8)

Erickson, Jane D., and Adelaide Sproul: PRINTMAKING WITHOUT A PRESS, Van Nostrand Reinhold, 1974.

Demonstrates how to adapt printing techniques for use without a press. Over 125 illustrations. (4,6)

Espinosa, Leonard, and John Morland: EASY-TO-MAKE DEVICES FOR LEARNING CENTERS, Personalized Learning Associates, 1974.

A booklet with directions for producing a variety of display and manipulative devices for small-group and individualized learning. (2,4,7)

FELT BOARDS FOR TEACHING, University of Texas at Austin, 1957.

Contains a wealth of ideas for use of the felt board as a teaching device, explains basic materials used in construction of the felt board, and describes how it may be utilized for effective presentation. (4)

Freedman, Edward H.: HOW TO DRAW, Bantam, 1965.

Teaches how to make fine, recognizable drawings of buildings, furniture, cars, people, animals, and countless other things as easily as one can sign one's name. (4)

Frye, Roy A.: GRAPHIC TOOLS FOR TEACHERS, 4th ed., Graphic Tools for Teachers, 1975.

How-to-do-it details for teacher production of lettering, mounting, laminating, layout, etc. (4,5,6,7,8)

Garvey, Mona: TEACHING DISPLAYS: THEIR PURPOSE, CONSTRUCTION AND USE, Shoe String, 1972.

A handbook to help teachers develop display ideas and techniques which can be applied to any subject at any level. (4,5,6,7)

Gates, David: LETTERING FOR REPRODUCTION, Watson-Guptill, 1969.

A detailed study of lettering history, tools, materials, equipment. Step-by-step techniques. (6,8)

Gilmore, Frederick T.: A GUIDE TO MAKING A DISPLAY, 1974.

A booklet on materials, tools, and techniques for producing visual displays. (2,6,7)

Goudket, Michael: AN AUDIOVISUAL PRIMER, Teachers College, 1973.

A beginner's guide to production of use-

ful classroom audiovisual materials. (2,4,6,7,8)

Halas, John: FILM AND TV GRAPHICS, Hastings House, 1967.

Design and preparation of graphics for motion-picture and television production. (2,4,5,6,8)

Hamilton, Edward A.: GRAPHIC DESIGN FOR THE COMPUTER AGE, Van Nostrand Reinhold, 1970.

An exciting treatment on graphic design and preparation for the computer age. (4,5,6,8)

Haney, John B.: EDUCATIONAL COMMUNICATIONS AND TECHNOLOGY, C. Brown, 1975.

A book written for preservice or in-service teachers seeking an introduction to education communications, media, and technology. Offers several good suggestions for teacher-made media. (1,8)

Hatton, Richard G.: THE HANDBOOK OF PLANT AND FLORAL ORNAMENT, Dover, 1960.

A collection of 1,200 line drawings of plant and floral ornaments that will reproduce excellently. Selected from woodcuts and copperplate engravings. (4)

Hawken, William R.: COPYING METHODS MANUAL, American Library Association, 1966.

A modern, comprehensive book of copying methods dealing with the processes, methods, techniques, and types of equipment which can be used for reproducing printed sheets and documents. (4,5,6,8)

Heitner, Louis: INTRODUCTION TO OFFSET, Sentinel Books, 1964.

A book written mainly for the commercial artist beginner interested in the preparation of artwork for offset reproduction. Well written and illustrated. (4,5,6,7)

Heward, William, and Jill Dardig: OVERHEAD TRANSPARENCIES: A GUIDE, Chartpak, 1974.

A booklet that contains information and suggestions on the design and preparation of overhead projection transparencies using, for the most part, Chartpak materials. (2,4,5,6,7)

Horn, George F.: CARTOONING, Davis Publications.

Treats the technique of cartooning in the classroom. Covers drawing basic cartoon shapes; composition; drawing hands, heads, feet, children; etc. **(4)**

————: POSTERS: DESIGNING, MAKING, REPRODUCTION, Davis Publications, 1966.

A book that brings together in a single volume all the elements for successful poster making. Designed to help one design and execute posters that catch and hold attention. **(4,5,6)**

————: VISUAL COMMUNICATION: BULLETIN BOARDS, EXHIBITS, VISUAL AIDS, Davis Publications, 1973.

Covers planning, designing, and making a broad range of visual materials for use in the classroom, school, and community. **(2,4,6,7)**

Hornung, C. P.: A HANDBOOK OF EARLY ADVERTISING ART, Dover, 1956.

One of the largest collections of copyright-free early advertising art ever compiled. Volume I contains some 2,000 illustrations of agricultural devices, animals, old automobiles, birds, buildings, Christmas decorations, etc. Volume II, devoted to typography, has over 4,000 specimens. **(4,6)**

HOW TO DEVELOP AND PRINT BLACK AND WHITE FILMS (No. AJ-3), Eastman Kodak, 1974.

A booklet on a simple approach to developing and printing black and white photographic films. **(8)**

"HOW-TO" GUIDE FOR DESIGN GRAPHICS (3M Color-Key), 3M Company.

A booklet on instructions and applications of the 3M Color-Key system. **(8)**

HOW TO KEEP YOUR BULLETIN BOARD ALIVE, Ohio State University.

Pamphlet No. 6 deals with preparation of materials for the classroom bulletin board. **(4)**

HOW TO MAKE AND USE THE FELT BOARD, Ohio State University.

Pamphlet No. 3 deals with the preparation and use of the felt board in teaching. **(4,7)**

HOW TO MAKE A PASTE-UP LAYOUT FOR YOUR GESTEFAX, Gestetner Corp.

A booklet of instructions for preparing artwork for an electronic stencil cutter. **(4,7,8)**

HOW TO USE KODAK AUTOPOSITIVE MATERIALS (No. Q-23), Eastman Kodak, 1955.

A booklet giving specific handling recommendations for the use of Kodak, Autopositive film. Includes instructions for making transparent positives from photographic negatives. **(8)**

Hurlburt, Allen F.: PUBLICATION DESIGN: A GUIDE TO PAGE LAYOUT, TYPOGRAPHY, FORMAT, AND STYLE, Van Nostrand Reinhold, 1971.

Graphic fundamentals of publication design and production. A fresh, creative approach to graphic design. **(2,3,4,5,6,7 8)**

Hurrell, Ron: MANUAL OF TELEVISION GRAPHICS, Van Nostrand Reinhold, 1974.

Examples and suggestions for creative graphics for television. **(2,4,6,8)**

INSTRUCTIONAL DISPLAY BOARDS, University of Texas at Austin, 1968.

Explains the use of felt, hook and loop, magnetic, peg, and marking boards. **(4,7)**

Jacobson, C. I., and L. A. Mannheim: ENLARGING: THE TECHNIQUE OF THE POSITIVE, Hastings House, 1972.

A book on visual enlarging that emphasizes color enlarging and a wide range of applications from photography to graphic design. **(8)**

Jensen, Mary, and Andrew Jensen: AUDIOVISUAL IDEAS FOR CHURCHES, Augsburg Publishing House, 1974.

A publication written mainly for the producer of audiovisual media for churches. **(2,4,6,7,8)**

Kelley, Marjorie: CLASSROOM-TESTED BULLETIN BOARDS, Fearon Publishers, 1961.

A booklet containing photographs of bulletin boards in classroom use, showing how many creative teachers have solved their bulletin board problems. **(4)**

Kemp, Jerrold E.: PLANNING AND PRODUCING AUDIOVISUAL MATERIALS, 3d ed., Thomas Y. Crowell, 1975.

An updated edition of a highly successful book on audiovisual media planning and production. Contains step-by-step instructions from concept to presentation of audovisual media. **(1,2,3,4,5,6,7, 8)**

KINDERGARTEN AND PRIMARY BULLETIN BOARDS, Hayes School Publishing.

Seasonal subjects for every month of the school year are included in this bulletin board publication designed for use on the kindergarten and primary grade levels. **(4)**

Kinder, James S.: USING INSTRUCTIONAL MEDIA, Van Nostrand Reinhold, 1973.

A basic text dealing with the selection, preparation, and utilization of audiovisual materials. **(4,7)**

KODAK PHOTOGRAPHIC MATERIALS FOR THE GRAPHIC ARTS (No. Q-2), Eastman Kodak, 1973.

A booklet containing detailed data and information on using sensitized photographic materials in the preparation of visual media. **(8)**

Koskey, Thomas: BAITED BULLETIN BOARDS, Fearon, 1954.

All aspects of bulletin board planning and arrangement; recommended by art and audiovisual educators. **(4)**

————: BULLETIN BOARD IDEA SOURCES, Fearon, 1963.

Explains where to get bulletin board ideas and how to adapt them for use in the classroom or school. **(4)**

————: BULLETIN BOARDS FOR HOLIDAYS AND SEASONS, Fearon, 1958.

An "idea" booklet covering all school holidays and months of the school year. **(4)**

————: BULLETIN BOARDS FOR SUBJECT AREAS, Fearon, 1962.

A booklet containing ideas and sources for bulletin boards in such subject areas as English, social studies, mathematics, fine arts, business, industrial arts, science, and language. **(4)**

————: CREATIVE CORRUGATED CARDBOARD, Fearon, 1957.

A how-to-do-it booklet providing many examples of the uses of corrugated cardboard in making picture frames, decorative borders for displays, three-dimensional exhibits, seasonal and holiday decorations, and other classroom creations. **(4)**

————: HOW TO MAKE AND USE FLANNEL BOARDS, Fearon, 1961.

A booklet for classroom teachers showing the application of a variety of shapes, sizes, and types of flannel boards. **(4)**

Krulik, Stephen, and Irwin Kaufman: HOW TO USE THE OVERHEAD PROJECTOR IN MATHEMATICS EDUCATION, National Council of Teachers of Mathematics, 1966.

Both general and detailed suggestions for effective use at a minimum of cost. Includes directions for making and storing projectables and a listing of materials needed. **(4,8)**

Langford, Michael J.: VISUAL AIDS AND PHOTOGRAPHY IN EDUCATION, Hastings House, 1973.

A practical manual on the production of educationally sound visual aids. Contains step-by-step procedures on making the most of available equipment in preparing instructional media. **(1,4,7,8)**

Latimer, H. C.: ADVERTISING PRODUCTION, PLANNING AND COPY PREPARATION FOR OFFSET PRINTING, Art Directions Book, 1974.

A detailed treatment of the graphic preparation of materials for offset printing. **(3,4,5,6,8)**

Laughton, Roy: TV GRAPHICS, Van Nostrand Reinhold, 1966.

A comprehensive survey of world television graphics. Profusely illustrated. **(4)**

Laybourne, Kit (ed): DOING THE MEDIA, Center for Understanding Media, 1974.

Pragmatic advice on still photography, super-8 and 16mm movie photography, and other media. **(8)**

Leach, Mortimer: LETTERING FOR ADVERTISING, Van Nostrand Reinhold, 1975.

A modern treatment of lettering techniques and aids for advertising. **(4,6)**

LEGIBILITY: ARTWORK TO SCREEN (No. S-24), Eastman Kodak, 1974.

Legibility guidelines for the preparation of artwork for projection. **(4,6,8)**

LETTERING TECHNIQUE, University of Texas at Austin, 1965.

A booklet covering such lettering techniques and aids as hand lettering, stencil lettering, precut letters, and mechanical lettering devices. **(6)**

Lidstone, John: DESIGN ACTIVITIES FOR THE ELEMENTARY CLASSROOM, Davis Publications, 1966.

An elementary art teaching guide which includes twenty-two creative things to do in the classroom. Activities include mural making, classroom sculpture, potato printing, monoprinting. **(4)**

Linse, Barbara B.: WELL-SEASONED HOLIDAY ART, Fearon, 1956.

A booklet containing more than seventy ideas and examples (illustrated) for classroom decorations and creative activities built around major school holidays. Includes basic instructions for many projects. **(4)**

LOCAL PRODUCTION TECHNIQUES, University of Texas at Austin, 1967.

A useful handbook to assist classroom teachers in the design and preparation of simple instructional materials. Topics include dry mounting, laminating, spray lettering, lettering guides, and projection for production. A suggested list of supplies and equipment required for local production is included. **(4,5,6,7,8)**

Lockwood, Arthur: DIAGRAMS, Watson-Guptill, 1969.

A survey of the range and usefulness of diagramming. **(1,2,4,5,6)**

Longyear, William: TYPE AND LETTERING, Watson-Guptill (4th ed.), 1966.

A revised and expanded textbook which shows hundreds of full alphabets and one-line type specimens, many in a variety of sizes and weights. Recommended for type specifiers and designers since it covers the mechanics of typography, printing terms and measures, and proofreading and copy-editing marks and presents examples of good type arrangement. **(6)**

Lord, John, and Robert Larson: HANDBOOK FOR PRODUCTION OF FILMSTRIPS AND RECORDS, DuKane, 1971.

Contains the technical data necessary to produce filmstrips and sound slide films according to standards now widely accepted by the industry. **(1,4,6,8)**

Luzadder, Warren J.: BASIC GRAPHICS FOR DESIGN ANALYSIS, COMMUNICATION AND COMPUTER, 2d ed., Prentice-Hall, 1968.

Written for the computer age. One will find helpful information related to computer-aided design and automated drafting of engineering components and systems. An introduction to design, sketching, and creative thinking is included. Over 1,000 illustrations. **(4)**

MacDonald, Byron J.: THE ART OF LETTERING: THE BROAD PEN, Pentalic, 1966.

A how-to-do-it book which presents its subject in such a simplified way that it can be used by anyone, amateur or professional, who wants to learn the art of lettering with the broad pen. Includes numerous examples of the commercial use of the alphabets in advertisements, posters, book jackets, testimonials, and awards—all done by the author. **(6)**

MacLinker, Jerry: DESIGNING INSTRUCTIONAL VISUALS: THEORY, COMPOSITION, AND IMPLEMENTATION, University of Texas at Austin, 1968.

An excellent treatment of visual media design. Well-prepared illustrations and discussion of all stages of media design. **(1,2,4,5)**

MAKING AND MOUNTING BIG BLACK AND WHITE ENLARGEMENTS AND PHOTOMURALS (No. G-12), Eastman Kodak, 1974.

Illustrated instructions for preparing and mounting photographic enlargements. **(7,8)**

MAKING BLACK AND WHITE OR COLORED TRANSPARENCIES FOR OVERHEAD PROJECTION (No. S-7), Eastman Kodak, 1972.

Useful information on preparing overhead projectuals with Kodak films. **(8)**

Mambert, William A.: PRESENTING TECHNICAL IDEAS: A GUIDE TO AUDIENCE COMMUNICATION, Wiley, 1968.

Deals with communication problems in business and industry. Written mainly for managers, scientists and engineers, marketing and sales personnel, teachers, writers, and anyone who wants to be a better communicator of technical information. **(4)**

Mann, William: LETTERING AND LETTERING DISPLAY, Van Nostrand Reinhold, 1974.

Graphic treatment of lettering as applied to displays. **(4,5,6)**

Maurello, S. Ralph: THE COMPLETE AIRBRUSH BOOK, Leon Amiel, 1954.

A comprehensive manual on airbrush techniques. Over 400 illustrations, diagrams, and photographs accompany step-by-step instructions on equipment, operation of the brush, rendering, retouching, and working methods. Contains examples of outstanding work by such famous artists and illustrators as Bomar, Varga, and Teague. **(4,5)**

———: HOW TO DO PASTE-UPS AND MECHANICALS, Leon Amiel, 1960.

An instructional book on the preparation of art for reproduction. Chapters of step-by-step text and pictures cover materials and tools, cutting and trimming, paste-up procedures, cropping and scaling, use of "cold type" and photo-lettering, and the technique of color separation. Over 300 drawings and photo-illustrations are included. **(4,5,6,7)**

Meyer, Franz S.: HANDBOOK OF ORNAMENTS, Dover, 1957.

One of the largest collections of copyright-free traditional art in print. Contains over 3,000 line cuts from Greek, Roman, medieval, Islamic, Renaissance, and other sources. **(4)**

Minor, Ed: SIMPLIFIED TECHNIQUES

FOR PREPARING VISUAL INSTRUCTIONAL MATERIALS, McGraw-Hill, 1962.
A manual that fills the need for a single publication covering all basic techniques necessary for the preparation of visual instructional materials. (3,4,5,6,7,8)

Morland, John E.: PREPARATION OF INEXPENSIVE TEACHING MATERIALS, Intex, 1973.
Contains instructions for preparing modern teaching materials. Topics include mounting, lettering, illustrating, etc. (4,5,6,7,8)

Nelms, Henning: THINKING WITH A PENCIL, Barnes & Noble, 1964.
A self-instruction book dealing with fundamentals of drawing with a pencil. The book was designed for (1) those who wish to use drawing as a tool for thought and communications but lack knowledge of how to make drawings and (2) those who are accustomed to drawing but want to enlarge their graphic vocabularies and extend the range of fields in which they can apply the abilities that they already possess. (4)

Nelson, Leslie W.: INSTRUCTIONAL AIDS: HOW TO MAKE AND USE THEM, 4th ed., Wm. C. Brown, 1970.
Includes a variety of instructional materials which can be prepared and used by the classroom teacher to make teaching easier and more effective. (4,5,6,7,8)

Nesbitt, Alexander (ed.): DECORATIVE ALPHABETS AND INITIALS, Dover, 1959.
No payment and no permission needed to reproduce any one of 3,924 different letters, covering 1,000 years. (6)

OPAQUE PROJECTOR, THE, University of Texas at Austin.
A booklet prepared in response to specific suggestions concerning application of the opaque projector in various areas of education. Shows how the projector can be utilized in professional and industrial training programs also. (4)

OVERHEAD SYSTEM: PRODUCTION, IMPLEMENTATION AND UTILIZATION, The University of Texas at Austin, 1967.
A practical handbook to help school administrators, supervisors, and teachers design and prepare overhead projection transparencies. Major transparency-making techniques are included. Suggestions for the implementation of a local overhead projection program are discussed. (4,5,6,8)

PREPARING LARGE TRANSPARENCIES ON KODAK EKTACOLOR PRINT FILM (No. E-58), Eastman Kodak, 1973.
A booklet dealing with the use of Kodak Ektacolor film for the preparation of large transparencies for display or projection. (8)

Price, Matlack: FOOT-HIGH LETTERS: A GUIDE TO LETTERING, Dover, 1961.
Complete alphabet of foot-high classic Roman letters, each on a separate plate. Each plate contains nine 2-inch forms of the letter in various typefaces such as Caslon, Empire, etc. (6)

Pringle, B.: CHALK ILLUSTRATION, Pergamon, New York, 1966.
Presents in work-study form the role of graphic illustration in teaching and gives practical information on the making of illustrations for the classroom. Topics covered, among others, are use of the blackboard, the strip diagram, shading and coloring, blackboard instrument work. (4,5)

PRODUCTION OF 2- BY 2-INCH SLIDES, University of Texas at Austin, 1958.
A booklet which describes physical properties of 2- by 2-inch slides and the advantage of producing them locally; discusses production techniques of black and white and color slides and describes equipment needed. A list of sources is also included. (4,8)

Raines, Gar (ed.): HOW TO DESIGN, PRODUCE AND USE BUSINESS FORMS, North American Publishing, 1971.
A comprehensive publication dealing with establishing a cost-effective forms program, design and production of business forms, selections of supplies, cost justification, etc. (1,2,4)

Randall, Reino, and Edward C. Haines: BULLETIN BOARDS AND DISPLAY, Davis Publications, 1961.
A book that combines basic design with imaginative use of materials that offer a fresh new source for making bulletin boards and displays that sparkle with originality. (4)

Ring, Arthur E., and William J. Shelley: CREATIVE TEACHING WITH THE OVERHEAD PROJECTOR, Chandler, 1969.
Design and preparation of overhead projectuals for teaching. (1,4,8)

Ross, George F.: SPEEDBALL TEXTBOOK FOR PEN AND BRUSH LETTERING, 20th ed., Howard Hunt, 1973.
A practical manual on all lettering forms. Written mainly for use with Speedball lettering pens. (6)

Rothschild, Norman: MAKING SLIDE DUPLICATES, TITLES AND FILMSTRIPS, 3d ed., American Photographic Book, 1973.
Illustrations and instructions for producing slides, filmstrips, and titles. (1,4,5,6,8)

Rott, Andre, and Edith Weyde: PHOTOGRAPHIC SILVER HALIDE DIFFUSION PROCESSES, American Photographic Book.
The definitive work on diffusion transfer process. (8)

Roukes, Nicholas: CLASSROOM CRAFT MANUAL, Fearon, 1960.
A booklet containing photographs and/or drawings illustrating easy step-by-step techniques for presenting craft activities in the elementary school. (4)

Rowe, Mack R., et al.: THE MESSAGE IS YOU: GUIDELINE FOR PREPARING PRESENTATIONS, AECT, NEA, 1971.
A well-developed set of guidelines for the design and preparation of visual media by leading visual media designers. (1,2,4,6)

Ruby, Doris: BULLETIN BOARDS FOR THE MIDDLE GRADES, Fearon, 1960.
A booklet containing over thirty bulletin boards keyed to subject areas for grades 4 through 6. Easy-to-use patterns, many of them three-dimensional. (4)

———: 4-D BULLETIN BOARDS THAT TEACH, Fearon, 1960.
A booklet for kindergarten and primary grade teachers. Contains dual-purpose, direct, dimensional, and diversified bulletin boards for instructing children. (4)

Ruder, Emil: TYPOGRAPHY: A MANUAL OF DESIGN, Hastings House.
A fundamental treatise by a distinguished Swiss typographer and teacher. Every conceivable typographic problem in relation to texture, weight, color, legibility, pacing, and leading is explained. Over 500 illustrations. (6)

Scuorzo, Herbert E.: PRACTICAL AUDIO-VISUAL HANDBOOK FOR TEACHERS, Prentice-Hall, 1967.
Filled with many new how-to-do-it ideas, plans, examples, and extensive audiovisual projects for classroom instruction at every grade level and for every scholastic subject. Special attention is given to slides and filmstrips, overhead projec-

tion, chalkboards and display boards, flat graphics, mounting, and lettering. **(4,5,7)**

SEAL INSTRUCTION BOOKLET, Seal, Inc. Illustrated instructions on dry mounting and heat laminating. **(7)**

Shaw, Robert: PRACTICAL LETTERING, Leon Amiel, 1955.
A complete self-instruction course in drawing and designing the basic letter forms, including the new script and brush styles, with scores of complete hand-lettered and type alphabets for study and reproduction. **(6)**

Sides, Dorothy S.: DECORATIVE ART OF THE SOUTHWESTERN INDIANS, Peter Smith, 1961.
An album of authentic designs (both preconquest and postconquest) from the pottery, textiles, and basketry of the Navaho, Hopi, Mohave, Santo Domingo, and over twenty other Southwestern groups. Designs include birds, clouds, butterflies, etc. Material can be used without permission or payment. **(4)**

SIMPLE COPYING TECHNIQUES WITH A KODAK EKTAGRAPHIC VISUALMAKER (No. S-40), Eastman Kodak, 1973.
Complete illustrated instructions for making photographic slides with the Kodak Visualmaker slide system. **(8)**

SIMPLE WAYS TO MAKE TITLE SLIDES AND FILMSTRIPS (No. T-44), Eastman Kodak, 1959.
A pamphlet dealing with equipment, materials, and techniques for making slides and filmstrips. **(4,5,6,8)**

Snyder, John: COMMERCIAL ARTIST HANDBOOK, Watson-Guptill, 1973.
Complete, authoritative reference book of materials and how to use them. Written for anyone who must prepare artwork for reproduction for a printer. **(3,4,5,6,8)**

Spears, James: CREATING VISUALS FOR TV: A GUIDE FOR EDUCATORS, AECT, NEA, 1962.
A well-illustrated booklet dealing with the preparation of visuals for educational television. Includes a variety of production techniques. **(4,6)**

Stankowski, Anton: VISUAL PRESENTATION OF INVISIBLE PROCESSES, Hastings House, 1966.
How to present in a visual, easily understood form the latest developments of science and technology. Among the topics discussed are functional symbols, fields of vision, transmitting of information, and advertising suggestions. Examples are included. **(4)**

Stasheff, Edward, and Rudy Bretz: THE TELEVISION PROGRAM: ITS DIRECTION AND PRODUCTION, Hill & Wang, 1968.
A comprehensive treatment of the nature of the television medium with specific, simple explanations of the duties, artwork, and science which become the craft of the television producer and director. A well-written how-to book. **(4,6)**

Stevenson, George A.: GRAPHIC ARTS ENCYCLOPEDIA, McGraw-Hill, 1968.
An encyclopedia for every phase of the graphic arts industry. Over 3,000 illustrations. Can be used to find immediate answers to graphic arts questions.

Stone, Bernard, and Arthur Eckstein: PREPARING ART FOR PRINTING, Van Nostrand Reinhold, 1965.
A book that contains all the essential information that graphic artists and students must know to do an effective job. Based on the authors' course at New York University. Over 250 black and white illustrations. **(4,5,6,7)**

Taubes, Frederic: BETTER FRAMES FOR YOUR PICTURES, Viking, 1968.
A complete how-to-do-it book, updated with information about new timesaving preparations. **(7)**

————: THE QUICKEST WAY TO DRAW WELL, Viking, 1958.
The fundamentals of drawing, with complete instructions for using pencil, pen, brush, or crayon. **(4)**

Taylor, E. A.: A MANUAL OF VISUAL PRESENTATION IN EDUCATION AND TRAINING, Pergamon, 1966.
A comprehensive manual for the preparation and use of projected and nonprojected instructional materials. Well-written and illustrated chapters cover chalkboards and charts; magnetic materials; flannelgraph, plastigraph, and cellograph; pegboard techniques; models; still projection; moving projection; overhead projection; copying and duplicating processes; and more. A detailed list of materials and equipment sources is also included. **(4,5,6,7,8)**

TELEVISION GRAPHICS PRODUCTION TEMPLATE (No. H-42), Eastman Kodak, 1973.
Contains a clear plastic template for preparing graphics for television use. Instruction sheet included. **(1,3,4)**

TV IMAGE TEMPLATE FOR USE WITH KODAK EKTAGRAPHIC VISUALMAKER (No. S-50), Eastman Kodak, 1971.
A special plastic template for use when preparing visuals for the Kodak Visualmaker system. **(1,3,4)**

Tierney, Joan D.: AN AUTO-TUTORIAL COURSE IN BASIC GRAPHICS, Joan D. Tierney Enterprises, 1975.
A thirty-lesson autotutorial course in basic graphics covering color and design, organization of space, selection of ideas, etc. A multimedia kit with texts. **(1,2,3,4,5,6,7,8)**

Turner, Ethel M.: TEACHING AIDS FOR ELEMENTARY MATHEMATICS, Holt, 1966.
Specific instructions for constructing and using seventy-nine elementary mathematics teaching aids. Each aid is illustrated in full color. **(4,6)**

USING TEAR SHEETS FOR TEACHING, University of Texas at Austin, 1956.
A booklet which explores expanded uses of tear sheets through better layout and mounting techniques. The format of this handbook is such that ideas from almost every page may be used for bulletin board layouts. **(4,7)**

VARIGRAPH OPERATING MANUAL, Varigraph.
A comprehensive manual on the operation of Varigraph lettering equipment. Written in simple terms so that the beginning user can follow instructions without difficulty. Included are instructions on layout, letter spacing, retouching, etc. **(6)**

Vessel, Matthew F., and Herbert H. Wong: SCIENCE BULLETIN BOARDS, Fearon, 1962.
An all-science bulletin board booklet written mainly for elementary classroom teachers. Includes ideas for most of the scientific problems taught in school at the elementary level. **(4)**

Wainwright, Charles A.: THE TELEVISION COPYWRITER, Hastings House.
Written by a veteran TV commercial maker. Deals mainly with creating successful television commercials. Takes one behind the scenes and examines the creative process in detail, from idea to finished film. Book includes contributions by more than twenty top creative people. Illustrated with storyboards. **(4)**

Warren, Jefferson T.: EXHIBIT METHODS, Sterling, 1972.

Photographic examples of successful exhibits with instructions for the design and construction of exhibits. **(1,2)**

WHAT TO DO FOR BULLETIN BOARDS, Hayes School Publishing.

Contains many fully illustrated, completely worked-out bulletin boards covering every school holiday. Explains how to construct bulletin boards with inexpensive materials. **(4)**

WHAT TO DO FOR KINDERGARTEN AND PRIMARY ART, Hayes School Publishing.

An activity book for primary and kindergarten teachers. It has everyday ideas with simple and easy work to develop hand control and coordination. Gift ideas with paper sculpture, crayons, clay, and paint; all to be made from easy, available, and inexpensive materials. Includes detailed instructions for teachers. **(4)**

WHAT TO DO IN ELEMENTARY ART, Hayes School Publishing.

A book especially created to help the busy teacher. Detailed and complete with graphic instructions and simplified easy-to-follow illustrations and text. Includes decorative handcraft, complete program for all holidays, special days, and in-between days. **(4)**

White, Gwen: PERSPECTIVE: A GUIDE FOR ARTISTS, ARCHITECTS, AND DESIGNERS, Watson-Guptill, 1968.

Exercises of increasing complexity leading the reader from fundamentals to mastery of perspective. **(4)**

Wiley, J. Barron: COMMUNICATION FOR MODERN MANAGEMENT, Taplinger, 1966.

Treats the entire range of industrial communication techniques. Written mainly for modern management. Included are sections dealing with the preparation of opaque and transparent visual aids. **(4,5,6,7,8)**

Wittich, Walter A., and Charles F. Schuller: INSTRUCTIONAL TECHNOLOGY: ITS NATURE AND USE, 5th ed., Harper & Row, 1973.

A complete instructional technology text for the classroom teacher and professional user of instructional media. Several chapters include instructions for preparing instructional media. **(4,5,6,7,8)**

Wolchonok, Louis: DESIGN FOR ARTISTS AND CRAFTSMEN, Dover, 1953.

Contains step-by-step instructions for the creation of more than 1,000 designs and shows how to create design that is fresh, well-founded, and original. Included are detailed exercises, with instruction hints, diagrams, and details. **(4,6)**

RECOMMENDED AUDIOVISUAL MEDIA

The audiovisual media annotated here have been included in this book to help supplement its contents. Included in the listings are 16mm motion-picture films (16mm film), 8mm (standard and super-8), cartridge-load single-concept (single idea) motion-picture films (8mm SC film), 35mm filmstrips, 2- by 2-inch slides, overhead projection transparencies, and diazo masters. The availability of an item in color or black and white (b and w) is also indicated. Sections which each item supplements are indicated by boldface numbers in parentheses following most entries. Audiovisual media which have no section reference indicated are included for their value to a better understanding of the design, preparation, and utilization of visual media. While a number of the items listed here are somewhat dated, they are still obtainable from many film-rental libraries. The names and addresses of producers and distributors can be found in the Address Directory.

ADVANCED PRODUCTION TECHNIQUES, *35mm filmstrip, 51 frames, sound, color, Educational Media, 1968.*
Various color-producing processes; diazo production techniques; "color-lifting," special color-yielding systems. **(5,8)**

AIRBRUSH MANIPULATION, *8mm SC film, three minutes, silent, color, Grafcom.*
Demonstrates, through motion picture, the movement of hand, arm, and fingers during a demonstration by a professional artist. **(5)**

AN INTRODUCTION TO THE AIRBRUSH, *35mm filmstrip, sound, color, Grafcom.*
Presents an overview of the operation and utilization of the airbrush. An explanation of both alcohol- and water-base paints is included. **(5)**

BASIC COPYING TECHNIQUES, *2- by 2-inch slides (78), sound (tape), color, Eastman Kodak Audio-Visual Library, 1972.*
A sound-slide set on basic photographic copying techniques designed mainly for the novice photographer. **(8)**

BASIC EDUCATIONAL GRAPHICS, *Multimedia package, Scott Graphics, 1967.*
A multimedia package dealing with the application of basic graphic techniques in preparing overhead projectuals. Package is made up of overhead transparencies, filmstrips, sound disks, thermocopy masters, and manuals for instructor and participants. **(2,4,5,6,7,8)**

BETTER BULLETIN BOARDS, *16mm film, thirteen minutes, sound, b and w or color, Indiana University, 1956.*
The creation and use of bulletin boards for various purposes; values of pupil participation in planning and use. Catching and holding the viewer's eye through placement, size, and design. Choices of materials; mounting and lettering devices for integrating materials into effective design patterns. **(4,5,6,7)**

BULLETIN BOARDS AND DISPLAY, *35mm filmstrips (2), 36 frames each, color, BFA, 1966.*
Amusing drawings and examples of good bulletin board design which show how the bulletin board can be made to function as an effective educational tool. Examples of various types of background materials and fastening devices along with illustrations of layouts and principles of good design and organization will encourage the design and construction of simple, powerful bulletin board displays. **(4,5,6,7)**

BULLETIN BOARDS: AN EFFECTIVE TEACHING DEVICE, *16mm film, eleven minutes, sound, color, BFA, 1956.*
Gives suggestions for the planning and organization of creatively designed bulletin boards and presents twelve displays arranged by a class. Shows a class discussing, planning, and arranging a bulletin board. **(4,5,6)**

BULLETIN BOARDS AT WORK, *35mm filmstrip, 42 frames, b and w, Wayne State University, 1950.*
Outlines the use of the bulletin board as a teaching aid. Contains many actual bulletin boards to illustrate various uses. Rules for good layout of different types of bulletin boards are presented. **(4,5,6)**

BULLETIN BOARDS FOR EFFECTIVE TEACHING, *16mm film, eleven minutes, sound, color, University of Iowa, 1953.*
Describes the elements of effective classroom bulletin board display in detail. Deals with selecting a specific topic, selecting materials, planning the arrangement, using color, using appropriate lettering, creating the proper atmosphere, making the arrangement tell a story, using eye catchers, and assembling the display. **(4,5,6,7)**

CARDBOARD PRINTING, *35mm filmstrip, 43 frames, color, Society for Visual Education, 1965.*
Making posters, book covers, programs, greeting cards, and design duplication. **(4,5,6)**

CHALK AND CHALKBOARDS, *16mm film, seventeen minutes, sound, color, BFA, 1959.*
A comprehensive film that introduces the physical properties of chalk and chalkboards, showing what they are made of and how they should be cared for. It treats at length many techniques which can be used on all grade levels to improve everyday teaching. **(4)**

CHALKBOARD APPROACH TO TEACHING TYPEWRITING, THE, *16mm film, twenty-three minutes, sound, b and w, University of Iowa, 1962.*
Shows an effective way to present the keyboard using psychological principles of skill development. Shows in detail how to utilize the chalkboard, and how and when to demonstrate. **(4)**

CHALKBOARDS AND FLANNEL BOARDS, *35mm filmstrips (4), 30 frames each, color, BFA, 1967.*

A set of four color filmstrips following the format of the highly successful set *Bulletin Boards and Display* and the motion pictures *Chalk and Chalkboards* and *Flannel Boards and How to Use Them.* The care, use, and construction of these often overlooked, yet powerful, classroom tools are covered in depth. Examples of various types of boards and materials are shown, as well as many types of presentations on the boards. **(4,5,6,7)**

CHALKBOARD UTILIZATION, *16mm film, fifteen minutes, sound, b and w, McGraw-Hill Films, 1954.*
Demonstrates the many ways a chalkboard can be used more effectively in teaching. Explains the various methods of transferring drawings to the chalkboard. **(4)**

CHARTS FOR CREATIVE LEARNING, *16mm film, ten minutes, sound, color, BFA, 1962.*
Actual school situations dramatizing the many uses that can be made of charts in primary, elementary, and secondary classrooms. **(4,6)**

CLOTH MOUNTING (Fold) Parts 1 and 2, *8mm SC films, four minutes each, silent, b and w, McGraw-Hill Films, 1965.*
Dry mounting a large map, separated into sections, on Chartex cloth for folding during storage. **(7)**

CLOTH MOUNTING (Roll), *8mm SC film, four minutes, silent, b and w, McGraw-Hill Films, 1965.*
Dry mounting a large map in one piece on Chartex cloth for rolling during storage. **(7)**

COMPOSITION, *35mm filmstrip, color, Educational Filmstrips, 1972.*
Presents a study of composition through drawings and diagrams.

COMPOSITION, *35mm filmstrip, 43 frames, sound, color, Educational Media, 1967.*
Composition discussed from an instructional point of view rather than an artistic point of view. Layout, use of color, proper letter, style standards, and the use of various mattes and background materials are discussed. **(4)**

COMPOSITION, *35mm filmstrip, sound (tape), Arizona State University.*
Illustrates guidelines for good composition, including the principles of perspective, camera angle, and optical perspective. **(2,4)**

COMPOSITION FOR INSTRUCTION, *8mm SC film, two minutes, color, Hester.*
Shows how the eye sees instructional materials and indicates ways to best plan effective displays. **(4)**

CREATING INSTRUCTIONAL MATERIALS, *16mm film, fifteen minutes, sound, b and w or color, McGraw-Hill Films, 1963.*
Stresses, through a series of classroom scenes, the importance and impact of instructional materials. From the audio-visual series.

DARKROOM TECHNIQUES, *16mm film, thirty minutes, sound, b and w, University of Minnesota, 1961.*
Shows processes and equipment used in developing film, making contact prints, and enlarging pictures. **(8)**

DEVELOPING THE NEGATIVE, *16mm film, sixteen minutes, sound, b and w, National AV Center, 1950.*
Shows procedures in developing still camera film and explains the composition of the developing solution. From the fundamentals of photography series. **(8)**

DIAZO TRANSPARENCY PRODUCTION, *16mm film, eleven minutes, sound, color, University of Iowa, 1964.*
Demonstrates the elementary concepts of exposing and developing diazo film. Shows techniques of applying letters, shading, inks, and cutouts to the master sheet. **(4,5,6,8)**

DISCOVERING FORM IN ART, *16mm film, twenty-one minutes, sound, color, BFA, 1967.*
Shows the five basic forms in art: the sphere, cube, cone, cylinder, and pyramid. Each form is a structure of planes or surfaces which join to create a distinctive volume. The artist creates with these forms, combining them and varying the proportions endlessly. The illusion of volume may be suggested, as in drawing and painting, or actual forms may be created from a variety of materials. **(4,5)**

DISCOVERING PERSPECTIVE, *16mm film, fourteen minutes, sound, color, BFA, 1967.*
We live in a world of depth, of distance. Some things are close to us, some far away. We can create the appearance of distance on a flat surface by using perspective. Overlapping, vertical position, graying colors, varying detail, varying size, and converging lines are techniques used to create perspective. Any

one or more of these methods helps create the appearance of depth. **(4)**

DISPLAY AND PRESENTATION BOARDS, *16mm film, fifteen minutes, sound, color, International Film Bureau, 1971.*
Provides a compact, practical, and up-to-date look at display and presentation boards. Explores the nature and potential of six different boards—felt, Hook-n-Loop, magnetic, peg, electric, and combination. **(2,4,6,7)**

DRY MOUNTING, *35mm filmstrip, 51 frames, sound, color, Educational Media, 1967.*
Use of the dry mount press and various types of tissue. Treatment of tear sheets and other materials prior to dry mounting, cover-sheet use, tacking iron, cutter, and matting and framing are discussed and explored. Numerous examples are illustrated. **(7)**

DRY MOUNTING (Hand Iron), *8mm SC film, three minutes, silent, b and w, McGraw-Hill Films, 1965.*
Using a hand iron and dry mounting tissue to mount a magazine picture on cardboard. **(7)**

DRY MOUNTING (Press), *8mm SC film, three minutes, silent, b and w, McGraw-Hill Films, 1965.*
Using a dry mount press and dry mounting tissue to mount a magazine picture on cardboard. **(7)**

DRY MOUNTING AND LAMINATING PICTURES, *16mm film, ten minutes, sound, color, BFA.*
Illustrates dry mounting and plastic lamination methods using a dry mounting press, tacking iron, and household iron. Techniques for applying captions and punching permanent pinholes to create professional-looking study guides are demonstrated. **(7)**

DRY MOUNTING INSTRUCTIONAL MATERIALS: BASIC TECHNIQUES, *16mm film, five minutes, sound, color, also available in 8mm optical or magnetic sound. University of Iowa, 1965.*
Presents the basic dry mounting techniques that involve dry mounting tissue and Fotoflat, shows how these materials are used and the purpose for which each is appropriate, and outlines the techniques of operating dry mounting presses. **(7)**

DRY MOUNTING INSTRUCTIONAL MATERIALS: CLOTH BACKING, *16mm film, five minutes, sound, color, also* available in 8mm optical or magnetic sound, University of Iowa, 1965.

Shows what Chartex backing cloth is, how it is applied with a dry mounting press, and some of the ways it can be used in preparing, presenting, and preserving instructional materials. Stresses step-by-step procedures and techniques which will yield good results and long service. (7)

DRY MOUNTING INSTRUCTIONAL MATERIALS: CREATIVE APPLICATIONS, 16mm film, seven minutes, sound, color, also available in 8mm optical or magnetic sound, University of Iowa, 1969.

Demonstrates some possibilities for use of the dry mounting press as a creative tool. Useful for basic design courses. (4,7)

DRY MOUNTING INSTRUCTIONAL MATERIALS: DISPLAY AND USE, 16mm film, five minutes, sound, color, also available in 8mm optical or magnetic sound, University of Iowa, 1965.

Illustrates various classroom uses of instructional materials prepared with the dry mounting press. (7)

DRY MOUNTING INSTRUCTIONAL MATERIALS: LAMINATING AND LIFTING, 16mm film, six minutes, sound, color, also available in 8mm optical or magnetic sound, University of Iowa, 1965.

Presents the concept of laminating flat instructional materials with a clear plastic sheet, thereby preserving materials destined for hard use or much handling. A further extension of this technique known as "lifting" (a process whereby full-size transparencies for the overhead projector are made from printed pages) is also demonstrated. Both techniques are illustrated in step-by-step detail. (7,8)

DRY MOUNTING INSTRUCTIONAL MATERIALS: SPECIAL TECHNIQUES, 16mm film, five minutes, sound, color, also available in 8mm optical or magnetic sound, University of Iowa, 1965.

Illustrates special applications and processes utilizing a variety of dry mounting materials and techniques. (7)

DRY MOUNTING INSTRUCTIONAL MATERIALS: USING IDEAS, 16mm film, eight minutes, sound, color, also available in 8mm optical or magnetic sound, University of Iowa, 1969.

Shows ways in which the dry mounting process can be put to use in the classroom, once you have mastered the tech-

niques illustrated in the previous films of the series. Suggests the potential of dry-mounted materials as an instructional aid. (7)

DRY MOUNTING LARGE MATERIALS, 8mm SC film, four minutes, silent, color, Hester.

Techniques for dry mounting materials as large as an open newspaper using a standard dry mounting press. (7)

DRY MOUNT YOUR TEACHING PICTURES, 16mm film, ten minutes, sound, b and w, McGraw-Hill Films, 1958.

Shows the step-by-step procedure for using dry mounting tissues and an ordinary iron in mounting pictures. (7)

DUPLICATING BY THE SPIRIT METHOD, 16mm film, fourteen minutes, sound, color, BFA, 1961.

A demonstration of spirit duplicating (also known as liquid or fluid duplicating) showing carbon master sets and illustrating the dye transfer process. Typing the master set, making corrections by various methods, and using hand lettering and colored carbons are shown in detail. Close attention is given to each step in operating the machine. Proper care of equipment is stressed. (4,5,6,8)

EDUCATIONAL MEDIA KIT, McGraw-Hill Films, 1968.

A carefully developed and integrated series of audiovisual materials (films, slides, transparencies, and recordings) designed for use in presenting developments in education which involve many types of instructional resources. This media kit is the culmination of many years of work by outstanding media specialists around the nation and was originally developed under contract by San Jose State College with the United States Office of Education (NDEA Title VIIB). (4,5,6,8)

ELECTRIC BOARDS FOR LEARNING, 16mm film, six minutes, sound, b and w, University of Iowa, 1965.

Introduces various types of electric boards, shows their construction, and suggests a variety of uses for these simple but effective teaching devices.

EXCITING BULLETIN BOARDS, 35mm filmstrips (2), 40 frames each, sound, color, McGraw-Hill Films, 1963.

Shows color, lettering, and three-dimensional bulletin board materials. (4,5,6)

FELTBOARD IN TEACHING, THE, 16mm

film, nine minutes, sound, color, Wayne State University, 1951.

Suggests uses which the classroom teacher may make of the feltboard. The feltboard is also known as the visual board, feltogram, or flannelgraph. (4)

FELT PEN SKETCHING, 16mm film, eleven minutes, sound, b and w, McGraw-Hill Films, 1957.

Demonstrates how the common felt-point marking pen can be used in a variety of ways for sketching. (4)

FLANNEL BOARDS AND HOW TO USE THEM, 16mm film, fifteen minutes, sound, color, BFA, 1958.

Explains what flannel boards are, how they are made, and how they may be used. (4,6,7)

FLAT PICTURES, 16mm film, eighteen minutes, sound, b and w, Pennsylvania State University, 1959.

Discusses the potentialities and limitations of using flat pictures. Shows the principles of these aids. (4)

GRAPHICS, 16mm film, twenty-nine minutes, sound, b and w, Great Plains ITV Library.

Demonstrates the main steps in the production of word, photo, and simple animated captions and other graphics in general use. (4,6,8)

GRAPHICS: ADVERTISING, 16mm films (4), seven minutes, sound, b and w, Scope, 1965.

A series of films which covers brochures, mailouts, posters, and source file. There are four 1- to 2-minute films. (1,2,4,6)

GRAPHICS: PHOTOGRAPHY, 16mm films (4), eight minutes, sound, b and w, Scope, 1965.

Four 2-minute films dealing with flip card and single-frame animation, storyboard, and gallery. (1,4,8)

GRAPHICS: PHOTOMECHANICAL, 16mm films (9), twenty-five minutes, sound, b and w, Scope, 1965.

Lighting, comprehensives, lettering, line negative, paste-ups, copy camera, etc. This film package is made up of nine 2- to 4-minute films covering the subjects listed above. (3,4,5,6,8)

HANDMADE LANTERN SLIDES, 35mm filmstrip, 46 frames, color, Ohio State University, 1954.

Shows simple techniques for preparing 3¼- by 4-inch slides. Includes supplementary information on making and using glass and cellophane slides. (4,5,6,8)

HANDMADE MATERIALS FOR PROJECTION, *16mm film, twenty minutes, sound, b and w or color, Indiana University, 1956.*
The principles of transparency, translucency, and opacity applied to materials for overhead, slide, and opaque projectors. A variety of techniques and materials for inexpensive projected materials: carbon film; dot-dusted stencils; coated acetate; adhesive shading and coloring materials; transfer of magazine pictures to acetate (lifting). (4,5,6,8)

HANDY-DANDY DO-IT-YOURSELF ANIMATION FILM, THE, *16mm film, eleven minutes, sound, color, Learning Corporation, 1974.*
Three young students cooperate in making animated super-8 movies, using pen and ink, cutouts, etc. (4,8)

HIGH CONTRAST PHOTOGRAPHY FOR INSTRUCTION, *16mm film, fourteen minutes, sound, b and w or color, Indiana University, 1956.*
Making negatives and prints on high-contrast film; the preparation and duplication of materials for making slides, large transparencies, and paper prints; making a photogram; copying a line drawing from a book; making photocopies of material assembled on a flannel board, menu board, and a paste-up; coloring; combining two negatives; and making multiple copies. (4,5,6,8)

HOW A COMMERCIAL ARTIST WORKS, *16mm film, fifteen minutes, sound, b and w, Modern Talking Pictures.*
Shows a commercial artist working on an advertisement from rough layout through finished artwork. (4,5,6,7)

HOW KODALITH FILM IS MADE, *16mm film, twenty minutes, sound, color, Eastman Kodak Audio-Visual Library.*
Acquaints the graphic arts trade, or those interested in the trade, with the highly sophisticated technology required in the manufacture of Kodalith films. (8)

HOW TO ANIMATE A GINGERBREAD BOY, *16mm film, fourteen minutes, sound, color, Churchill Films, 1973.*
Illustrates various techniques of animation, including cutout, three-dimensional, time lapse, etc. Shows how these techniques are used in producing films to be used in the classroom by telling a story about the adventures of a gingerbread boy. (4,8)

HOW TO DO CARTOONS, *16mm film, twenty minutes, sound, b and w, Schulman, 1957.*
Artist Russell Patterson demonstrating a simple and direct approach to cartooning. (4)

HOW TO KEEP YOUR BULLETIN BOARD ALIVE, *35mm filmstrip, 32 frames, color, Ohio State University, 1951.*
Attempts to diagnose the present faults of most bulletin boards. Some general rules about captions, illustrations, and text. (4,5,6)

HOW TO MAKE A MOVIE WITHOUT A CAMERA, *16mm film, five minutes, sound, color, Churchill Films, 1971.*
Shows the limitless possibilities of film-making without photographic processing. (4,8)

HOW TO MAKE AND USE A DIORAMA, *16mm film, twenty minutes, sound, color, McGraw-Hill Films, 1956.*
Demonstrates the construction of the diorama framework and the preparation of its realistic miniature scenes. (4)

HOW TO MAKE A STENCIL PRINT, *16mm film, twelve minutes, sound, color, BFA, 1961.*
Introduces simple ways to cut and print original stencils as an approach to creative design. Demonstrates the use of tempera paint on different textured paper and printing on cloth with permanent textile paints. (4,5)

HOW TO MAKE BIOLOGICAL DRAWINGS, *16mm film, fifteen minutes, sound, b and w or color, McGraw-Hill Films, 1964.*
Describes the technique for translating a gross specimen into an accurate drawing. (4)

HOW TO MAKE HANDMADE LANTERN SLIDES, *16mm film, twenty-one minutes, sound, b and w or color, Indiana University, 1947.*
The production of seven basic types of 3¼- by 4-inch slides: clear and etched glass, plastic, translucent paper, cellophane, gelatin, and silhouette. The variety of materials for coloring and shading; sources of materials; special production techniques; binding methods. Examples of handmade slides for a variety of learning situations. (4,5,6,8)

IMPROVING THE USE OF THE CHALKBOARD, *35mm filmstrip, 44 frames, silent, color, Ohio State University, 1956.*
Shows techniques for teachers to improve the use of the chalkboard with artwork and photographs. (4)

INSTRUCTIONAL MEDIA, *diazo master book (Stanley A. Huffman, Jr., author), Keuffel & Esser Co., 1969.*
The most extensive visual instructional media diazo master book available today. Contains masters created mainly to assist professional personnel to teach potential and experienced teachers functions of and techniques for using various types of media. The masters are designed for quick, easy reproduction with diazo color projection films. Included are masters related to the production of visual instructional media. (2,4,5,6,7,8)

INSTRUCTIONAL USE OF PREPARED MATERIALS, *35mm filmstrip, 27 frames, sound, color, Educational Media, 1967.*
This filmstrip combines, in models and examples, the various skills covered by the skill filmstrips in the Basic Educational Graphics series. Proper use of chalkboard areas, walls, and bulletin boards, as well as stand-up teaching charts, student-prepared materials, etc. (4)

INTRODUCTION TO CONTOUR DRAWING, *16mm film, twelve minutes, sound, color, BFA, 1967.*
Most of us only half see the objects at which we look. This film shows how we can use the technique of contour drawing to develop our powers of observation. Through contour drawing we learn to see details we might otherwise overlook. Contour drawing is also an aid in developing hand and eye coordination. A perfect likeness of the subject being drawn is not the objective. Practice in contour drawing is valuable training in drawing technique. (4)

INTRODUCTION TO DRAWING MATERIALS, *16mm film, nineteen minutes, sound, color, Film Associates, 1966.*
Introduces various drawing materials, such as chalk, crayons, pencils, tempera, watercolor, felt-tip pens, and oil pastels. Stresses the special qualities of each material and the value of experimentation. (4,5)

INTRODUCTION TO GESTURE DRAWING, *16mm film, twelve minutes, sound, color, BFA, 1968.*
Shows and explains that gesture drawing is an exercise that describes motion. Expresses the direction and rhythm of

an action. Practice in this rapid technique will add vigor and life to your other types of artwork. It will also make you aware of the different kinds of motion while helping you to develop skill and spontaneity in expressing those motions. **(4)**

INTRODUCTION TO GRAPHIC DESIGN, *35mm filmstrips (2), 50 frames each, sound, color, BFA, 1967.*
A basic introduction to the materials and techniques of the graphic artist, covering the materials and tools used in all phases of work from layout to lettering and the basic techniques from ruling to rubber-cementing. **(4,5,6,7)**

LAMINATING, *35mm filmstrip, 49 frames, sound, color, Educational Media, 1967.*
Laminating is accomplished with the flat-type dry mount press. This filmstrip covers step-by-step laminating of conventional items and then explains processes for laminating very large items, section by section, and cutting and rehinging. **(7)**

LAMINATING LARGE MATERIALS, *8mm SC film, four minutes, silent, color, Hester.*
Procedures for using Seal-Lamin film in preserving instructional materials. This process makes such materials waterproof and wear-resistant. **(7)**

LAMINATING LEAVES, *8mm SC film, two minutes, silent, color, Hester.*
Many teachers require permanent leaf collections; here are shown techniques for permanently preserving such collections. **(7)**

LEARNING TO DRAW, *16mm film, eleven minutes, sound, b and w, University of Iowa, 1954.*
Demonstrates the advantages of using the overhead projector and a complete set of transparencies with overlays and other transparent aids in teaching beginning drafting (mechanical drawing). By using these materials, one can present information and procedures quickly and effectively to pupils with high aptitude and ability, or they can be used to drill the slower or younger pupils. **(4)**

LEARNING TO DRAW, *16mm film, nine minutes, sound, b and w or color, Beseler, 1954.*
A presentation of the fundamentals of perspective as treated in the *Drawing Textbook* by Bruce McIntyre. Illustrates

one use of the overhead projector. **(7)**

LET'S DRAW WITH CRAYONS, *16mm film, eleven minutes, sound, color, Coronet, 1952.*
How to use, how to care for, and how to store crayons. Shows many interesting effects one can achieve through different crayon techniques. Includes information on creative drawing, poster making, and numerous other crayon crafts. **(4,5)**

LET'S MAKE AN ENLARGEMENT, *2- by 2-inch slides (49), sound (tape), color, Eastman Kodak Audio-Visual Library, 1971.*
About the basics of making black and white enlargements. Shows how to mix developer, stop bath, and fixer. Includes instructions for using test strips for determining exposure. **(8)**

LETTERING, *8mm SC film, four minutes, silent, color, Hester.*
Presents a simple but effective means of teaching lettering principles. Several basic letters are analyzed. **(6)**

LETTERING, *35mm filmstrip, sound, color, Doubleday Multimedia, 1970.*
Discusses the various types of lettering and describes some of the common errors of the beginning mechanical artist. Depicts the correct size, shape, and proportion of lettering. **(6)**

LETTERING: THE FELT PEN (Applications), *8mm SC film, four minutes, silent, color, McGraw-Hill Films, 1965.*
Results of using felt pens for preparing lettering styles, flash cards, displays, charts, and bulletin boards. **(6)**

LETTERING: THE FELT PEN (Basic Skills), *8mm SC film, four minutes, silent, color, McGraw-Hill Films, 1965.*
Characteristics of commonly used felt pens; proper finger, wrist, and arm position as pen is used; methods of forming letters; and proper pen speed during use. **(6)**

LETTERING FOR PROJECTION, *8mm SC film, four minutes, silent, color, Hester.*
Shows proper size standards for lettering projectables, as well as the use of lettering guides and pens. **(6,8)**

LETTERING INSTRUCTIONAL MATERIALS, *16mm film, twenty minutes, sound, b and w or color, Indiana University, 1955.*
Easy-to-use lettering equipment for lettering on signs, posters, bulletin boards, displays, and materials for projection.

Lettering techniques using rubber stamp letters; cutout letters; stencils; pens and lettering guides; mechanical lettering systems; projection and photographic reproduction. **(6)**

LETTERING: LEROY 500 AND SMALLER, *8mm SC film, three minutes, silent, b and w, McGraw-Hill Films, 1965.*
Using LeRoy template, scriber, and pen for lettering ½ inch and smaller. **(6)**

LETTERING: LEROY 700 AND LARGER, *8mm SC film, three minutes, silent, b and w, McGraw-Hill Films, 1965.*
Using LeRoy template, scriber, and pen for lettering ¾ inch and larger. **(6)**

LETTERING: PREPARED LETTERS, *8mm SC film, four minutes, silent, b and w, McGraw-Hill Films, 1965.*
Shows use of construction-paper cutouts, gummed-backed letters, and dry transfer letters. **(6)**

LETTERING: SKILL DEVELOPMENT, *35mm filmstrip, 52 frames, sound, color, Educational Media, 1967.*
Explains simple lettering techniques. Explores the use of stencils, spray paints and lettering fonts, lettering standards, and other lettering devices. **(6)**

LETTERING: WIRE BRUSH LETTERING EQUIPMENT, *35mm filmstrip, 38 frames, sound, color, Educational Media, 1967.*
Exhibits applications for and use of pen and guide lettering sets. Simple sets of this type require little time and effort in in-service education and have multiple uses in the classroom. Details such as pen and guide sizes and styles, felt-pen sets, and step-by-step processes of use are explained. **(6)**

LETTERING WITH FELT PENS, *8mm SC film, three minutes, silent, color, Hester.*
Proper methods for professional-quality lettering in color with felt pens. **(6)**

LETTERING WITH GUIDES, *8mm SC film, four minutes, silent, color, Hester.*
Shows the procedures for obtaining professional-quality lettering through the use of the Wrico lettering set. **(6)**

LETTERING: WRICOPRINT, *8mm SC film, two minutes, silent, b and w, McGraw-Hill Films, 1965.*
Using Wricoprint stencil lettering guide and pen for lettering ½ inch and smaller **(6)**

LETTERING: WRICO SIGNMAKER, *8mm SC film, four minutes, silent, b and w, McGraw-Hill Films, 1956.*
Using Wrico Signmaker stencil lettering

guide with brush pen and felt pen for lettering ½ inch and larger. **(6)**

LINE PHOTOGRAPHY, *35mm slides (79), color, Eastman Kodak Audio-Visual Library, 1968.*

Unit includes seventy-nine color slides and typewritten script. The general procedures in line photography, a process important to industry, are discussed in this special program for graphic arts education. Other topics covered include preparation of copy for line photography, and exposure, processing, and preparation of the line negative for lithographic plate making and printing. **(4,8)**

MAGAZINES TO TRANSPARENCIES, *16 mm film, twelve minutes, sound, color, International Film Bureau, 1958.*

Demonstrates the making of transparencies from magazine photographs with common materials—scissors, rubber cement, and sheets of frosted acetate. **(4,8)**

MAGIC OF THE FLANNEL BOARD, THE, *16mm film, nineteen minutes, sound, color, Instructo Products, 1964.*

Shows ways creative visual cutouts may be used to stimulate student curiosity and motivation, to drill students in mathematics and reading, and to introduce abstract ideas and difficult concepts. **(4)**

MAKING MAPS AND CHARTS, *8mm SC film, three minutes, silent, color, Hester, 1966.*

Covers advantages of using movable instructional materials rather than static posters and bulletin boards. **(4,6)**

MANIPULATIVE DEVICES, *8mm SC film, four minutes, silent, color, Hester, 1966.*

Covers advantages of using movable instructional materials rather than static posters and bulletin boards.

MIMEOGRAPH, THE, *35mm filmstrip, twenty-four minutes, sound, color, A. B. Dick.*

Shows choosing the right ink, inking the machine, and operating the mimeograph as well as shortcuts to color work. **(4,5)**

MIMEOGRAPHING TECHNIQUES, *16mm film, sixteen minutes, sound, color, BFA, 1958.*

Demonstrates the complete process of typing a mimeograph stencil, making corrections, using the mimeoscope for hand lettering, and operating a modern electric mimeograph machine. Supplies,

equipment, and specialized tools are shown. Handy tips are offered to improve mimeographed copies in both black and white and color. The film also discusses different types of duplicating processes, their purposes and advantages. **(4,5,6)**

MOUNTING: A CUT-OUT PICTURE, *8mm SC film, three minutes, silent, b and w, McGraw-Hill Films, 1965.*

Dry mounting a picture that requires removal of advertising or other material from the page around the picture. **(7)**

MOUNTING AND MASKING PROJECTUALS, *35mm filmstrip, 41 frames, sound, color, Educational Media, 1968.*

Identification of various terms associated with special mounting techniques, effective use of single- and multiple-overlay projectables, and examples of basic masking techniques. **(7)**

MOUNTING: A TWO-PAGE PICTURE, *8mm SC film, four minutes, silent, color, McGraw-Hill Films, 1965.*

Dry mounting a picture that extends across two separate pages in a magazine. **(7)**

MOUNTING: OVERCOMING DRY MOUNTING PROBLEMS, *8mm SC film, three minutes, silent, b and w, McGraw-Hill Films, 1965.*

Preventing the formation of bubbles when dry mounting, and what to do if they appear after mounting. **(7)**

MOUNTING PICTURES, *35mm filmstrip, 58 frames, color, University of Texas at Austin, 1957.*

Presents methods of mounting pictures for a variety of purposes. Describes materials used, steps in mounting, and ways of protecting pictures. Shows basic steps in mounting with rubber cement and dry mounting tissue. **(7)**

MOUNTING: SETTING GROMMETS, *8mm SC film, two minutes, silent, b and w, McGraw-Hill Films, 1965.*

Setting metal grommets (rings) in a clothbacked map for ease in displaying. **(7)**

MOUNTING: USING LAMINATING FILM, *8mm SC film, four minutes, silent, b and w, McGraw-Hill Films, 1965.*

Dry mounting a Mylar film, for protection, over the surface of a mounted picture. Shows other uses for laminating film. **(7)**

MURAL MAKING, *16mm film, six minutes,*

sound, color, International Film Bureau, 1956.

Explains that the urge to draw and paint can be encouraged along constructive lines in the classroom. Shows the making of a mural as a class project with everyone participating. **(4)**

OPAQUE PROJECTOR, THE, *35mm filmstrip, 46 frames, color, Ohio State University, 1957.*

Presents a pictorial analysis of the instructional use of the opaque projector together with suggestions on operation and the preparation of materials to be projected. **(4)**

OPAQUE PROJECTOR: ITS PURPOSE AND USE, THE, *16mm film, 6 minutes, sound, b and w, University of Iowa, 1958.*

Shows how to adjust the projector for screen size, how to clean the lenses, how to focus, and how to handle other details of preparation of the projector for use in the classroom. **(4)**

OVERHEAD PROJECTOR, *16mm film, seventeen minutes, sound, b and w, University of Iowa, 1953.*

Shows a variety of materials that can be used and different techniques for preparing transparencies, including drawing and writing on transparent materials and using carbon-backed film and cutouts. Demonstrates the preparation of diazo transparencies (diazo process) and the use of autopositive paper. **(4,6,8)**

OVERHEAD PROJECTOR, THE, *16mm film, twenty-seven minutes, sound, b and w, 3M Company, 1967.*

Details and demonstrates effective classroom use and reinforcement techniques as related to the overhead projector. **(4,5,8)**

OVERHEAD PROJECTOR, *35mm filmstrips (4), silent, color, Education Filmstrips, 1969.*

A series of four filmstrips treating the elements of overhead projection use and transparency design and production. Evaluates commercially produced transparencies. **(2,4,5,6,7,8)**

OVERHEAD TRANSPARENCIES, *8mm (super-8 also) SC films (13), silent, b and w, McGraw-Hill Films.*

A series of films covering the production of overhead projection transparencies. Subjects include features of transparencies, making overlays, coloring transparencies, felt pens on acetate, diazo process, heat process, picture transfer, and high-contrast film process, etc. **(2,3,4,5,6,7,8)**

PAPER IN ART, *16mm film, seventeen minutes, sound, color, Churchill Films, 1967.*
Demonstrates the processes of chalking, painting, crayoning, decorating with objects, folding, cutting, stenciling, weaving, collage, paper sculpture, puppet making, and papier-mâche. **(4,5)**

PAPER MACHE, *16mm film, fifteen minutes, sound, color, ACI Productions, 1967.*
Presents the basic processes involved in making three-dimensional forms of papier-mâche. **(4)**

PASSE PARTOUT FRAMING, *16mm film, ten minutes, sound, b and w or color, Indiana University, 1957.*
Framing flat and object materials using a transparent cover, a picture, a cardboard backing, and a tape binding; framing three-dimensional materials; the uses of passe-partout materials and the means of displaying and filing them. **(7)**

Pett, Dennis W.: COPYING AND DUPLICATING PROCESSES, *35mm filmstrips (6), sound, color, Indiana University Audio-Visual Center, 1973.*
Six sound (audio cassette) filmstrips which include these topics on copy and duplicating processes: carbon transfer, diazo copy, electrostatic copy, photocopy, screen stencil, and thermal copy. **(4,8)**

PHOTOGRAPHIC SLIDES FOR INSTRUCTION, *16mm film, eleven minutes, sound, b and w or color, Indiana University, 1957.*
The preparation and use of slides made by the photographic process. The range of materials that can be copied from books and magazines; the use of color and black and white film in indoor and outdoor situations; flash photography, copying, and the use of Polaroid transparency film for making slides in a variety of subject areas. **(4,5,6,8)**

PHOTOGRAPHY, *8mm SC films, silent, b and w, McGraw-Hill Films, 1968.*
A series of films covering the topics of camera setting, close-up and copywork, composition, determining exposure, film characteristics, lighting scenes, making titles, processing black and white film, etc. **(1,3,4,6,8)**

PHOTO GREETING CARDS ARE FOR KEEPS *(No. 0015), 2- by 2-inch slides*

(62), sound (tape), color, Eastman Kodak Audio-Visual Library, 1975.
Easy-to-follow details on the making of photographic greeting cards.

PLANNING THE PROJECTUAL, *35mm filmstrip, 47 frames, sound, color, Educational Media, 1968.*
Setting objectives and storyboarding; projectual composition; using color and overlays. **(4,5,6,8)**

POSTER, *16mm film, sixteen minutes, sound, color, BFA, 1969.*
Explores the art of poster design in the works of Martin Jacobs, Ken Whitmore, and Gordon Wagner. Points out that modern commercials are posters in motion. **(2,4,5,6)**

POSTER MAKING, *8mm SC film, three minutes, silent, color, Hester.*
Various ways of creating posters which are clean-cut, easily read, and effectively designed. Also, consideration is given to the spacing of letters. **(4,5,6)**

POSTERS, *16mm film, fifteen minutes, sound, color, ACI Productions, 1968.*
Explains the basic concepts and methods of poster design. **(2,4)**

POSTERS FOR TEACHING, *35mm filmstrip, 40 frames, silent, b and w, McGraw-Hill Films, 1963.*
Presents arrangement, lettering, and color as they apply to poster making. **(4,5,6)**

PREPARING MATERIALS, *16mm film, twenty-seven minutes, sound, b and w, 3M Company, 1967.*
Explains different functions and use of various transparency-making materials and gives best sources of acquiring visual originals. **(4,5,8)**

PREPARING PROJECTED MATERIALS, *16mm film, fifteen minutes, sound, color, BFA, 1965.*
Illustrates the growth of the audiovisual field by contrasting the old magic lantern with the modern projection materials. Discusses the use of projectors, 35mm cameras, Polaroid copying stand, and Thermofax copier. **(4,8)**

PRINTING THE POSITIVE, *16mm film, nineteen minutes, sound, b and w, National AV Center, 1950.*
Shows hand and machine methods of making photographic prints. Emphasizes cleanliness, timing, temperature, testing of solutions, and drying. **(8)**

PROCESSING BLACK-AND-WHITE FILM, *2- by 2-inch slides (60), sound (tape),*

color, Eastman Kodak, Audio-Visual Library, 1971.
A fundamental approach to processing photographic film. Designed to make it easy for beginning photographers to learn film processing without the need for prior darkroom experience. **(8)**

PROJECTING IDEAS, II: DIAZO TRANSPARENCY PRODUCTION, *16mm film, eleven minutes, sound, color, University of Iowa, 1964.*
Provides a source of visualized information concerning the basic aspects of diazo transparency production. Demonstrates elementary concepts of exposing and developing diazo film and the step-by-step procedure for preparing a transparency. Stresses procedures that can be used by persons unfamiliar with diazo materials. **(4,5,6,8)**

PROJECTING IDEAS, III: DIRECT TRANSPARENCY PRODUCTION, *16mm film, five minutes, sound, color, University of Iowa, 1964.*
Introduces production of hand-drawn and -lettered transparencies, primarily on acetate, and illustrates use of various types of pencils, felt-tipped pens, and lettering devices. Discusses types of sheet material available, and use of printers' ink, watercolors, and colored transparent tapes. **(4,5,6,8)**

PROJECTING IDEAS ON THE OVERHEAD PROJECTOR, *16mm film, seventeen minutes, sound, color, University of Iowa, 1960.*
Outlines the advantage of the overhead projector as a visual aid to learning in classrooms and in business and industry. Shows the great variety of uses of the equipment with opaque, translucent, and transparent materials, and combinations of these, both in contrasting colors and in monochrome. Stresses the ease with which effective presentations can be improvised through the use of movable graphic components, overlays, Polaroid filters, transparent working models, and even chemical reactions in a test tube. **(4,5,8)**

PUT YOUR BEST HAND FORWARD IN LETTERING, *35mm filmstrip, 60 frames, color, Howard Hunt Pen, 1960.*
Shows techniques of hand lettering with Speedball pens taught in junior and senior high schools. Illustrates the need of lettering as it fits into the classroom situ-

ation and how it can improve your work in school. **(6)**

RUBBER CEMENT MOUNTING, *8mm SC film, four minutes, silent, b and w, McGraw-Hill Films, 1965.*

Using rubber cement on the back of a picture and on cardboard to mount permanently a magazine picture. **(7)**

SCREEN PRINTING, *16mm film, fourteen minutes, sound, b and w, University of Iowa, 1958.*

Shows examples of amateur and professional screen printing and gives suggestions for design and materials. A demonstration makes a screen, transfers a design, and prints a fabric. **(4,5)**

SIGNS, SYMBOLS, AND SIGNALS, *16mm film, sixteen minutes, color, AIMS, 1969.*

Shows a kaleidoscope of basic visual communication depicting the signs, symbols, and signals that individuals and the community rely on. **(2,4)**

SILK SCREEN PRINTING, *16mm film, ten minutes, sound, color, AV-ED, 1957.*

Demonstrates the technique whereby hand screen printing has been brought up to date. Shows preparation, washing, dyeing, printing, and completion. **(4)**

SIMPLE LETTERING TECHNIQUE, *8mm SC film, four minutes, silent, color, Hester, 1966.*

Simple procedures for using precut letters, spray paint, and stencils for the rapid production of classroom bulletin boards and posters. **(6)**

SIMPLE PROJECTUAL PRODUCTION, *35mm filmstrip, 40 frames, sound, color, Educational Media, 1968.*

Part A: techniques of preparing handmade projectuals which will have professional appearance and effectiveness. Part B: procedure for making heat transfer masters and production of heat transfer projectuals. **(4,5)**

STENCIL, THE, *35mm filmstrip, twenty-two minutes, sound, color, A. B. Dick.*

Shows how to type stencils; make corrections; select the right stencil; and draw, letter, and shade stencils; gives principles of electronic stencil imaging. **(4,5,6)**

TAPES, HINGING AND STORING, *35mm filmstrip, 39 frames, sound, color, Educational Media, 1967.*

Concerned with the multitude of adhesive materials which are now available, and very useful, for classroom use. Covered are edging and binding tapes, plus special polyesters used in hinging. Educational storage problems are discussed. **(7)**

TEACHER EVALUATION, *35mm filmstrip, 26 frames, sound, color, Educational Media, 1967.*

Techniques which can be used by teachers in evaluating their own materials and that of others in the basic graphics area. This filmstrip is designed to be used after lab exercises in skill areas and should be of considerable assistance in the development of critical and analytical thinking where visual materials are concerned.

TEACHER ORIENTATION, *35mm filmstrip, 56 frames, sound, color, Educational Media, 1967.*

Designed to familiarize classroom teachers with the meaning of such terms as basic educational graphics and local production. Also includes an overview of basic classroom skills, the equipment and materials required, and rationale for use.

TECHNIQUES OF MODERN OFFSET, *35mm filmstrips (7), sound, color, A. B. Dick.*

This series provides teachers and students with a complete course in how to use the offset duplicating process, including preparation of artwork, master and plate imaging, selection and use of inks and papers, and machine operation. **(4,5,6)**

TRAINING AIDS: SLIDES, LARGE DRAWING AND TRANSPARENCIES, *16mm film, eighteen minutes, sound, color, National AV Center, 1952.*

Urges instructors to make their own 3¼- by 4-inch lantern slides and large transparencies for use with the overhead projector. Explains the nature of the equipment and materials which are needed and the opportunity for preparing and using such aids. **(4,6,8)**

TRANSPARENCIES: ADDING COLOR, *8mm SC film, three minutes, silent, color, McGraw-Hill Films, 1965.*

Using felt pens, diazo films, and transparent color adhesives for coloring areas on transparencies. **(5,8)**

TRANSPARENCIES: DIAZO PROCESS, *8mm SC film, three minutes, silent, color, McGraw-Hill Films, 1965.*

Exposing a translucent paper master drawing and a diazo film in a Beseler Vugraph ultraviolet printer and developing the film in a jar containing ammonia vapor. **(5,8)**

TRANSPARENCIES: HANDMADE METHOD, *8mm SC film, three minutes, silent, color, McGraw-Hill Films, 1965.*

Using felt pens and transparent marking pencils on clear acetate. **(4,5,8)**

TRANSPARENCIES: HEAT PROCESS, *8mm SC film, two minutes, silent, color, McGraw-Hill Films, 1965.*

Using thermocopy (infrared) projection film to prepare a transparency from an original diagram in the "secretary" model copying machine. **(4,8)**

TRANSPARENCIES: MAKING OVERLAYS, *8mm SC film, three minutes, silent, color, McGraw-Hill Films, 1965.*

Preparing translucent paper master drawings as a series of overlays from an original sketch with emphasis on use of corner registration marks to ensure alignment of final transparencies. **(4,5,8)**

TRANSPARENCIES: MOUNTING AND MASKING, *8mm SC film, three minutes, silent, color, McGraw-Hill Films, 1965.*

Using tape to mount a single-sheet transparency and one with overlays to a cardboard frame. Shows results of masking and disclosing information on transparencies with a sliding mask and hinged masks. **(7)**

TRANSPARENCIES: PICTURE TRANSFER 1 and 2, *8mm SC films, three minutes each, silent, color, McGraw-Hill Films, 1965.*

Shows how to use a dry mount press to seal a clay-coated picture to Seal Transpara film; then how to separate, in water, the paper from the picture and film. Shows the resulting transparency after drying and spraying. **(4,7)**

TRANSPARENCIES: PRINCIPLE OF DIAZO PROCESS, *8mm SC film, four minutes, silent, color, McGraw-Hill Films, 1965.*

Results of four experiments to illustrate the principle of the diazo process: (1) developing diazo film without exposure; (2) exposing diazo film to sunlight and developing; (3) partially covering diazo film with paper, exposing, and developing; (4) covering diazo film with a diagram on tracing paper, exposing, and developing. **(8)**

TRANSPARENCIES: SPIRIT DUPLICATOR, *8mm SC film, three minutes, silent, color, McGraw-Hill Films, 1965.*

Using a spirit duplicator machine to prepare a transparency on frosted acetate from a spirit master in three colors. **(4)**

USING THE OVERHEAD PROJECTOR, *35mm filmstrip, 43 frames, sound, color, Educational Media, 1968.*

The development of overhead projection as a classroom technique; comparison of the overhead projector with the opaque projector; flexibility of the overhead projector; some basic rules for use; and some applications. **(4)**

WET MOUNTING PICTORIAL MATERIALS, *16mm films, twelve minutes, sound, b and w or color, Indiana University, 1952.*

Selecting a map to be mounted, mixing the paste, preparing the map, tacking the cloth backing to the working surface and applying the paste, rooling to spread the paste evenly, and finishing the edges. Methods of displaying and using the mounted materials including film or turnover charts, opaque projection strips, and wall charts. **(7)**

ADDRESS DIRECTORY

This coded directory is made up of addresses of suppliers, manufacturers, and producers of purchasable items listed in the INDEX/SOURCES. Names and addresses were correct as of the publication date of this book. Should an item in the INDEX/SOURCES be impossible to locate for purchase, please feel free to contact the authors for assistance.

A

A1 ACADEMIC DIMENSION SYSTEMS, INC., 502 S. Hamilton, Saginaw, MI 48602

A2 ACI PRODUCTIONS, 35 W. 45th St., 11th Floor, New York, NY 10036

A3 ADDRESSOGRAPH MULTIGRAPH CORP., 1200 Babbit Rd., Cleveland, OH 44117

A4 ADHESIVE LABEL CO., 2450 Louisiana Ave. N., Golden Valley, NM 55427

A5 THE ADVANCE PRODUCTS CO., INC., Central at Wabash, Wichita, KS 67214

A6 AECT, NEA, 1201 16th St., NW, Washington, DC 20036

A7 AGFA-GEVAERT, INC., 275 North St., Teterboro, NJ 07608

A8 AIMS INSTRUCTIONAL MEDIA SERVICES, INC., P.O. Box 1010, Hollywood, CA 90028

A9 S. B. ALBERTIS, 5 Tudor City Place, New York, NY 10017

A10 ALVIN & CO., P.O. Box 188, Windsor, CT 06095

A11 AMERICAN JET SPRAY INDUSTRIES, INC., P.O. Box 14006, Denver, CO 80214

A12 AMERICAN LIBRARY ASSOCIATION, 50 E. Huron St., Chicago, IL 60611

A13 AMERICAN OPTICAL CORP., Scientific Instrument Div., Eggert & Sugar Roads, Kenmore, NY 14215

A14 AMERICAN PHOTOGRAPHIC BOOK PUBLISHING CO., INC., 750 Zeckendorf Blvd., Garden City, NY 11530

A15 AMERICAN POLARIZERS, INC., 141 S. 7th St., Reading, PA 19603

A16 AMERICAN PRINTING EQUIPMENT & SUPPLY CO., 45-25 Ninth St., Long Island City, NY 11101

A17 LEON AMIEL, PUBLISHER, 225 Secaucus Rd., Secaucus, NJ 07094

A18 A. A. ARCHBOLD, PUBLISHERS, P.O. Box 57985, Los Angeles, CA 90057

A19 ARIZONA STATE UNIVERSITY, Tempe, AZ 85281

A20 ARKWRIGHT, Main St., Fiskeville, RI 02823

A21 ART DIRECTIONS BOOK CO., Advertising Trade Publishers, Inc., 19 W. 44th St., New York, NY 10036

A22 ARTOGRAPH, INC., 529 S. 7th St., Minneapolis, MN 55415

A23 ARTYPE, INC., 345 E. Terra Cotta Ave., Crystal Lake, IL 60014

A24 ATLAS ENTERPRISES, P.O. Box 22106, San Francisco, CA 94122

A25 AUDIO VISUAL SUPPLY CO., 2 Rome St., Farmingdale, NY 11735

A26 AUGSBURG PUBLISHING HOUSE, 426 S. Fifth St., Minneapolis, MN 55415

A27 AV-ED FILMS, 7934 Santa Monica Blvd., Hollywood, CA 90046

B

B1 BANTAM BOOKS, INC., 414 E. Golf Rd., Des Plaines, IL 60016

B2 BARNES & NOBLE, INC., Keystone Industrial Park, Scranton, PA 18512

B3 BECKLEY-CARDY CO., 1900 N. Narragansett, Chicago, IL 60639

B4 BELL & HOWELL CO., 1000 Driving Park Ave., Rochester, NY 14613

B5 BEMISS-JASON CORP., 3250 Ash St., Palo Alto, CA 94306

B6 CHARLES BESELER CO., 8 Fernwood Rd., Florham Park, NJ 07932

B7 BFA EDUCATIONAL MEDIA, 2211 Michigan Ave., Santa Monica, CA 90404

B8 BIENFANG PAPER CO., INC., Amboy Ave. & Linsley Pl., Metuchen, NJ 08840

B9 DICK BLICK, P.O. Box 1267, Galesburg, IL 61401

B10 BLU-RAY, INC., P.O. Box 337, Essex, CT 06426

B11 BOGEN PHOTO CORP., P.O. Box 448, Englewood, NJ 07631

B12 BOOK AND LEARNING SYSTEMS DIV., 401 N. Broad St., Philadelphia, PA 19109

B13 ROBERT J. BRADY CO., INC., Routes 197-450, Bowie, MD 20715

B14 W. H. BRADY CO., P.O. Box 571, Milwaukee, WI 53201

B15 BRO-DART, 1609 Memorial Ave., Williamsport, PA 17701

B16 BROOKS MFG. CO., Box 41195B, Cincinnati, OH 45241

B17 ARTHUR BROWN & BROTHER, INC., 2 West 46th St., New York, NY 10036

B18 WILLIAM C. BROWN BOOK CO., 135 S. Locust St., Dubuque, IA 52001

B19 CHARLES BRUNING CO., 1834 Walden Office Square, Schaumburg, IL 60172

B20 BUHL PROJECTOR CO., INC. 60 Spruce St., Patterson, NJ 07501

B21 BURKE & JAMES, 690 Portland Ave., Rochester, NY 14621

B22 BURLEIGH BROOK, INC., 44 Burlews Court, Hackensack, NJ 07601

C

C1 UNIVERSITY OF CALIFORNIA, Extension Media Center, 2223 Fulton St., Berkeley, CA 94720

C2 CALUMET PHOTOGRAPHIC, INC., 1590 Touhy, Elk Grove Village, IL 60007

C3 CANON USA, INC., 10 Nevada Dr., Lake Success, NY 11040

C4 CARTER INK CO., 239 First St., Cambridge, MA 02142

C5 CENTER FOR UNDERSTANDING MEDIA, INC., 75 Horatio St., New York, NY 10014

C6 CENTRAL PLASTICS DISTRIBUTORS CO., 2701 N. Pulaski Rd., Chicago, IL 60639

C7 CHANDLER PUBLISHING CO., 257 Park Ave. S., New York, NY 10010

C8 CHARTPAK, One River Rd., Leeds, MA 01053

C9 CHILDCRAFT EDUCATION CORP., 964 Third Ave., New York, NY 10022

C10 CHURCHILL FILMS, 662 N. Robertson Blvd., Los Angeles, CA 90069

C11 CLARIDGE PRODUCTS AND EQUIPMENT, INC., Harrison, AR 72601

C12 COLOR-STIK CO., 8 Fernwood Rd., Florham Park, NJ 07932

C13 COLUMBIA RIBBON-CARBON MFG. CO., Herbhill Rd., Glen Cove, NY 11542

C14 CORONET INSTRUCTIONAL FILMS, 65 E. South Water St., Chicago, IL 60601

C15 THE CRAFTINT MFG. CO., 18501 Euclid Ave., Cleveland, OH 44112

C16 CREATIVE PLAYTHINGS, INC., Princeton, NJ 08540

C17 CREATIVE VISUALS, INC., P.O. Box 1911, Big Springs, TX 79720

C18 THOMAS Y. CROWELL CO., College Division, Dept. JG, 666 Fifth Ave., New York, NY 10019

C19 C-THRU GRAPHICS, 6 Britton Dr., Bloomfield, CT 06002

D

D1 THE D. E. SUPPLIER, P.O. Box 214, Morrisville, PA 19067

D2 DAVIS PUBLICATIONS, INC., 50 Portland St., Worcester, MA 01608

D3 L. F. DEARDORFF & SONS, INC., 11 S. Des Plaines St., Chicago, IL 60606

D4 DEMCO EDUCATIONAL CORP., Box 1488, Madison, WI 53701

D5 DENNISON MFG. CO., 300 Howard St., Framingham, MA 01701

D6 DIAZO SPECIALTY CO., 11325 Maryland Ave., Beltsville, MD 20705

D7 A. B. DICK CO., 5700 West Touhy Ave., Chicago, IL 60648

D8 DISPLAY MEDIA, INC., 120 Laura Dr., Addison, IL 60101

D9 DITTO, INC., 6800 McCormick Rd., Chicago, IL 60645

D10 DOUBLEDAY MULTIMEDIA, P.O. Box C-19518, Santa Ana, CA 92705

D11 DOVER PUBLICATIONS, INC., 180 Varick St., New York NY 10014

D12 DUKANE CORP., 2900 Dukane Dr., St. Charles, IL 60174

D13 E. I. DUPONT, DE NEMOURS & CO., 1007 Market St., Wilmington, DE 19898

D14 D. VAN NOSTRAND CO., 450 W. 33rd St., New York, NY 10001

E

E1 EASTMAN KODAK CO., 343 State St., Rochester, NY 14650

E2 EASTMAN KODAK CO., Audio-Visual Library Distribution, 343 State St., Rochester, NY 14650

E3 EBERHARD FABER, Crestwood Rd. 3, Wilkes-Barre, PA 18703

E4 EDMUND SCIENTIFIC CO., Edscorp Building, Barrington, NJ 08007

E5 ED-TECH SERVICE CO., 295 Main St., Chatham, NJ 07928

E6 EDUCATIONAL FILMSTRIPS, Box 1401, Huntsville, TX 77340

E7 EDUCATIONAL MEDIA LABS, 4101 S. Congress Ave., Austin, TX 78745

E8 EHRENREICH PHOTO-OPTICAL INDUSTRIES, INC., 623 Stewart Ave., Garden City, NY 11530

E9 EMBOSOGRAF CORP. OF AMERICA, 38 W. 21st St., New York, NY 10010

E10 E-Z LETTER-QUIK STIK CO., P.O. Box 829, Westminister, MD 21157

F

F1 A. W. FABER-CASTELL CORP., P.O. Box 330, Lewisburg, TN 37091

F2 FALCON SAFETY PRODUCTS, INC., Mountainside, NJ 07092

F3 FEARON PUBLISHERS, INC., 6 Davis Dr., Belmont, CA 94002

F4 SAM FLAX, 25 E. 28th St., New York, NY 10016

F5 FLAX'S, 250 Sutter St., San Francisco, CA 94108

F6 FOTOTYPE, INC., 1414 Roscoe St., Chicago, IL 60657

F7 A. I. FRIEDMAN, INC., 25 W. 45th St., New York, NY 10036

G

G1 GAF CORPORATION, 140 W. 51st St., New York, NY 10020

G2 GANS INK CO., 1441 Boyd St., Los Angeles, CA 90033

G3 GAYLORD BROS., INC., Box 8489, Stockton, CA 95208

G4 GENERAL BINDING CORP., Northbrook, IL 60062

G5 GENERAL PHOTO PRODUCTS, P.O. Box 230-C, Morristown, NJ 07961

G6 GESTETNER CORP., Gestetner Park, Yonkers, NY 10703

G7 M. P. GOODKIN CO., 140-146 Coit St., Irvington, NJ 07111

G8 GRAFCOM, P.O. Box 202, Pittsburg, KS 66762

G9 GRAPHIC LAMINATING, INC., 5122 St. Clair Ave., Cleveland, OH 44103

G10 GRAPHIC PRODUCTS CORP., 3601 Edison Pl., Rolling Meadows, IL 60008

G11 GRAPHIC TOOLS FOR TEACHERS, Mapleville, RI 02839

G12 GREAT PLAINS INSTRUCTIONAL TV LIBRARY, P.O. Box 80669, Lincoln, NE 68501

G13 M. GRUMBACHER, INC., 460 W. 34th St., New York, NY 10001

H

H1 HARPER & ROW PUBLISHERS, INC., 10 E. 53rd St., New York, NY 10022

H2 HASTINGS HOUSE PUBLISHERS, INC., 151 E. 50th St., New York, NY 10022

H3 HAYES SCHOOL PUBLISHING CO., INC., 312 Pennwood Ave., Wilkinsburg, PA 15221

H4 D. C. HEATH & CO., 125 Spring St., Lexington, MA 02173

H5 H. T. HERBERT CO., INC., 21-21 41st Ave., Long Island City, NY 11101

H6 HERNARD MFG. CO., INC., 374 Executive Blvd., Elmsford, NY 10523

H7 HESTER & ASSOCIATES, 11422 Harry Hines Blvd., Suite 212, Dallas, TX 75229

H8 HEYER, INC., 1850 S. Kostner Ave., Chicago, IL 60623

H9 THE HIGHSMITH CO., INC., Box 25, Fort Atkinson, WI 53538

H10 HILL & WANG, 19 Union Square, New York, NY 10003

H11 THE HOLES-WEBWAY CO., Webway Park, St. Cloud, MN 56301

H12 HOLT, RINEHART & WINSTON, INC., 383 Madison Ave., New York, NY 10017

H13 HORDER'S STATIONERY STORES, INC., 231 S. Jefferson St., Chicago, IL 60606

H14 HOWARD HUNT PEN CO., Advertising Dept., 7th and State St., Camden, NJ 08101

H15 HUDSON PHOTOGRAPHIC INDUSTRIES, 2 S. Buchhout St., Irvington-on-Hudson, NY 10533

I

I1 ILFORD, INC., Box 288, Paramus, NJ 07652

I2 INDEX, INC., P.O. Box 239, Charlotte, NC 28230

I3 INDIANA UNIVERSITY, Audio-Visual Center, Bloomington, IN 47401

I4 THE INSTRUCTO CORP., 1635 N. 55th St., Paoli, PA 19301

I5 INTERNATIONAL FILM BUREAU, INC., 332 S. Michigan Ave., Chicago, IL 60604

I6 UNIVERSITY OF IOWA, AV Center, C-5 East Hall, Iowa City, IA 52240

I7 IOWA STATE UNIVERSITY PRESS, South State Ave., Ames, IA 50010

J

J1 JOHNSON PLASTICS, INC., Box 523, Hazelton, PA 18201

J2 CHARLES A. JONES PUBLISHING CO., 10 Davis Dr., Belmont, CA 94002

K

K1 KAISER PRODUCTS CORP., 3555 N. Prospect St., Colorado Springs, CO 80907

K2 KALART VICTOR CORP., Hultenius St., Plainville, CT 06062

K3 F. D. KEES MFG. CO., 700-800 Park St., Beatrice, NE 68301

K4 KENRO CORP., Horse Hill Rd., Cedar Knolls, NJ 07927

K5 KENWORTHY EDUCATIONAL SERVICES, INC., P.O. Box 3031, Buffalo, NY 14205

K6 KERSTING MFG. CO., 504 S. Date St., Alhambra, CA 91803

K7 KEUFFEL & ESSER CO., Educational/Audiovisual Div., 20 Whippany Rd., Morristown, NJ 07960

K8 KEYSTONE VIEW CO., Hallet Square, Boston, MA 02124

K9 KIEFER INTERNATIONAL PRODUCTS, INC., 219 Michigan St., NE, Grand Rapids, MI 59403

K10 THE KIMAC COMPANY, Wilmington, VT 05363

K11 KINDER PRODUCTS, INC., 1105 Jefferson St., Wilmington, DE 19801

K12 KOH-I-NOOR, INC., 100 North St., Bloomsbury, NJ 08804

K13 ROBERT E. KRIEGER PUBLISHING CO., P.O. Box 542, Huntington, NY 11743

K14 KROY INDUSTRIES, INC., Graphic Systems Div., P.O. Box 269, Stillwater, MN 55082

L

L1 LABELON CORP., 10 Chapin St., Canadaiqua, NY 14424

L2 LACEY-LUCI PRODUCTS, INC., 2679 Route 70, Manasquan, NY 08736

L3 LAMINEX, INC., P.O. Box 577, Matthews, NC 28105

L4 LANDAU BOOK CO., INC., 272 W. Park Ave., Long Beach, NY 11561

L5 LANSFORD PUBLISHING CO., P.O. Box 8711, San Jose, CA 95155

L6 LASSCO PRODUCTS, INC., 485 Hague St., Rochester, NY 14606

L7 LEA A-V SERVICE, 240 Audley Dr., Sun Prairie, WI 53590

L8 LEARNING CORP. OF AMERICA, 711 Fifth Ave., New York, NY 10022

L9 LECTRO-STIK CORP., 3721 Broadway, Chicago, IL 60613

L10 E. LEITZ, INC., Link Drive, Rockleigh, NJ 07647

L11 LETRASET USA, INC., 33 New Bridge Rd., Bergenfield, NJ 07621

L12 LETTERGUIDE CO., INC., P.O. Box 30203, Lincoln, NE 68503

L13 LEWIS ARTIST SUPPLY CO., 6408 Woodward Ave., Detroit, MI 48202

M

M1 MACMILLAN COMPANY, 866 Third Ave., New York, NY 10022

M2 MAGNA VISUAL, INC., 1200 North Rock Hill Rd., St. Louis, MO 63124

M3 MAIER-HANCOCK SALES, INC., 13212 Raymer St., North Hollywood, CA 91605

M4 MARSH STENCIL, 707 E. B St., Belleville, IL 62222

M5 MASK 'N' MOUNTS, 200 Saint Paul St., Rochester, NY 14604

M6 CHARLES MAYER STUDIOS, INC., 140 E. Market St., Akron, OH 44308

M7 McGRAW-HILL BOOK CO., 1221 Avenue of the Americas, New York, NY 10020

M8 McGRAW-HILL FILMS, 1221 Avenue of the Americas, New York, NY 10020

M9 MEDIA SYSTEMS, INC., 3637 E. 7800 South, Salt Lake City, UT 84121

M10 CHARLES E. MERRILL PUBLISHING CO., 1300 Alum Creek Rd., Columbus, OH 43216

M11 METRO/KALVAR, INC., 745 Post Rd., Darien, CT 06820

M12 METRO SUPPLY CO., 1420 47th Ave., Sacramento, CA 95822

M13 MICHAEL BUSINESS MACHINES, 145 W. 45th St., New York, NY 10036

M14 UNIVERSITY OF MINNESOTA, Audio Visual Library Service, 2037 University Ave., SE, Minneapolis, MN 55455

M15 UNIVERSITY OF MISSISSIPPI, Dept. of Educational Film Production, University, MS 38677

M16 MITA COPYSTAR AMERICA, INC., 158 River Rd., Clifton, NJ 07014

M17 MITTEN DESIGNER LETTERS, Mitten Bldg., Redlands, CA 92373

M18 MODERN TALKING PICTURE SERVICE, 2323 New Hyde Park Rd., New Hyde Park, NY 11040

M19 THE MORGAN SIGN MACHINE CO., 4510 N. Ravenswood Ave., Chicago, IL 60640

M20 MULTIGRAPH DIVISION, Addressograph-Multigraph Corp., 1800 West Central Rd., Mt. Prospect, IL 60056

M21 MUTUAL EDUCATION AIDS, 1924 Hillhurst Ave., Los Angeles, CA 90027

N

N1 NASCO, 901 Janesville Ave., Fort Atkinson, WI 53538

N2 NATIONAL AUDIOVISUAL CENTER (GSA), Washington, DC 20409

N3 NATIONAL CENTER ON EDUCATIONAL MEDIA AND MATERIALS FOR THE HANDICAPPED, 220 W. 12th Ave., Columbus, OH 43210

N4 NATIONAL COUNCIL OF TEACHERS OF MATHEMATICS, 1906 Association Dr., Reston, VA 22091

N5 NATIONWIDE ADHESIVE PRODUCTS, INC., 19600 St. Clair, Cleveland, OH 44117

N6 NORTH AMERICA PUBLISHING CO., 134 N. 13th St., Philadelphia, PA 19107

N7 nuARC COMPANY, INC., 4110 W. Grand Ave., Chicago, IL 60651

O

O1 OCEANA PUBLICATIONS, 733 Plymouth Rd., Claremont, CA 91711

O2 OHIO FLOCK-COTE CO., INC., 13229 Shaw Ave., East Cleveland, OH 44112

O3 OLIVETTI CORP OF AMERICA, 500 Park Ave., New York, NY 10022

O4 OLYMPIC MEDIA INFORMATION, 161 W. 22nd St., New York, NY 10011

O5 ORAVISUAL CO., INC., 321 15th Ave., S., St. Petersburg, FL 33701

O6 OXBERRY, 516 Timpson Pl., Bronx, NY 10455

P

P1 PARA-TONE, INC., 150 Fencl Lane, Hillside, IL 60162

P2 PARKER PUBLISHING CO., Prentice-Hall, Inc., Englewood Cliffs, NJ 07632

P3 PEERLESS COLOR LABORATORIES, 11 Diamond Pl., Rochester, NY 14609

P4 PENNSYLVANIA STATE UNIVERSITY, Audio Visual Aids Library, University Park, PA 16802

P5 PENTALIC CORP., 132 W. 22nd St., New York, NY 10011

P6 PERGAMON PRESS, INC., Maxwell House, Fairview Park, Elmsford, NY 10523

P7 PERSONALIZED LEARNING ASSOCIATES, Box 886, San Jose, CA 95106

P8 PETER SMITH PUBLISHERS, INC., 6 Lexington Ave., Gloucester, MA 01930

P9 PIERCE DIVISION, 6238 Oasis Ave., North, Stillwater, MN 55082

P10 PITMAN PUBLISHING CORP., 6 East 43rd St., New York, NY 10017

P11 POBLOCKI & SONS CO., 620 S. First St., Milwaukee, WI 53204

P12 POLAROID CORP., 549 Technology Square, Cambridge, MA 02139

P13 FREDERICK POST CO., Box 803, Chicago, IL 60690

P14 PRENTICE-HALL, INC., Englewood Cliffs, NJ 07632

P15 PROFESSIONAL TAPE CO., INC., 144 Tower Dr., Hinsdale, IL 60162

R

R1 THE REDIKUT LETTER CO., 12617 South Prairie Ave., Hawthorne, CA 90250

R2 HENRY REGNERY CO., 180 N. Michigan Ave., Chicago, IL 60601

R3 REYNOLDS/LETERON CO., 9830 San Fernando Rd., Pacoima, CA 91331

R4 RICHARD MFG. CO., P.O. Box 2910, Van Nuys, CA 91404

R5 RISE, Williamsport Area School District, Williamsport, PA 17701

R6 RONEO VICKERS, INC., One Alsan Way, Little Ferry, NJ 07643

R7 ROYAL TYPEWRITER CO., INC., 850 Third Ave., New York, NY 10022

S

S1 SALT LAKE STAMP CO., 380 West 2nd South, Salt Lake City, UT 84101

S2 SCARECROW PRESS, INC., Box 656, Metuchen, NJ 08840

S3 SCHOLASTIC MAGAZINES, INC., 50 West 44th St., New York, NY 10036

S4 SCHULMAN PRODUCTIONS, P.O. Box 1794, Trenton, NJ 08607

S5 SCM CORP., 299 Park Ave., New York, NY 10017

S6 SCOPE, Dowling College, Oakdale, NY 11769

S7 SCOTT GRAPHICS, INC., 195 Appleton St., Holyoke, MA 01040

S8 SCOTT MACHINE DEVELOPMENT CORP., P.O. Box 217, Walton, NY 13856

S9 SCOTT PLASTICS CO., P.O. Box 2958, Sarasota, FL 33578

S10 SEAL-IN-PLASTIC CO., INC., 20727 Dearborn St., Chatsworth, CA 91311

S11 SEAL, INC., 251 Roosevelt Dr., Derby, CT 06418

S12 SEARY MFG. CO., 19 Nebraska Ave., Endicott, NY 13760

S13 SENTINEL BOOKS PUBLISHERS, INC., 219 Park Ave. S., New York, NY 10003

S14 SETON NAME PLATE CORP., 592 Blvd., New Haven, CT 06505

S15 SHOE STRING PRESS, INC., 995 Sherman Ave., Hamden, CT 06514

S16 SHOWCARD MACHINE CO., 320 West Ohio St., Chicago, IL 60610

S17 THE SIGNPRESS CO., P.O. Box 1267, Galesburg, IL 61401

S18 SOCIETY FOR VISUAL EDUCATION, INC., 1345 Diversey Parkway, Chicago, IL 60614

S19 SOS PHOTO-CINE-OPTICS, INC., 315 W. 43rd St., New York, NY 10036

S20 SOUTHPORT GRADING STAMPS, P.O. Box 512, Southport, CT 06490

S21 SOUTHWEST PLASTIC BINDING CO., 123 Weldon Pkwy., Maryland Heights, MO 63043

S22 SPRAYWAY, INC., 484 Visto Ave., Addison, IL 60101

S23 SQUIBB-TAYLOR, INC., P.O. Box 20158, Dallas, TX 75220

S24 J. S. STAEDTLER, INC., P.O. Box 68, Montville, NJ 07045

S25 STANDARD PROJECTOR & EQUIPMENT CO., INC., 3070 Lake Terrace, Glenview, IL 60025

S26 STAREX, INC., 655 Schuyler Ave., Kearny, NJ 07032

S27 STERLING PUBLISHING CO., INC., 419 Park Ave., New York, NY 10016

S28 STIK-A-LETTER CO., 1787 S. Iris Lane, Escondido, CA 92026

S29 STRATHMORE PAPER CO., Front St., West Springfield, MA 01089

S30 STRIPPRINTER, Box 18-895, Oklahoma City, OK 73118

T

T1 TABLET & TICKET CO., 1021 W. Adams St., Chicago, IL 60607

T2 TAPLINGER PUBLISHING CO., 200 Park Ave. S., New York, NY 10003

T3 TEACHERS COLLEGE PRESS, Columbia University, 1234 Amsterdam Ave., New York, NY 10027

T4 TERSCH PRODUCTS, INC., Industrial Blvd., Rogers, MN 55374

T5 THE UNIVERSITY OF TEXAS at Austin, Instructional Media Center, Drawer W, University Station, Austin, TX 78712

T6 3M CO., Promat Project, 3M Center, St. Paul, MI 55101

T7 3M CO., Visual Products Div., 3M Center, St. Paul, MI 55101

T8 JOAN DE TIERNEY ENTERPRISES, 26 Melbourne Ave., Westmount, Que., H3Z 1H7 Canada

T9 TIME SAVING SPECIALTIES, 2922 Bryant Ave., South Minneapolis, MN 55408

T10 TIMESAVER TEMPLATES, INC., P.O. Box 34286, Dallas, TX 75234

T11 TRANSFERITE, P.O. Box 11949, Phoenix, AZ 85017

T12 TRANSILWRAP WEST CORP., 274 Harbor Way, South San Francisco, CA 94008

T13 TREND ENTERPRISES, INC., P.O. Box 3073, St. Paul, MN 55165

T14 TUDOR PUBLISHING CO., 221 Park Ave., South New York, NY 10003

V

V1 VALDES ASSOCIATES, INC., Box 362, Westbury, Long Island, NY 11590

V2 VALIANT INSTRUCTIONAL MATERIALS CORP., 237 Washington Ave., Hackensack, NJ 07601

V3 VARIGRAPH, INC., P.O. Box 690, Madison, WI 53701

V4 VEACH DEVELOPMENT CO., 14535 Arminta St., Van Nuys, CA 91402

V5 VIEWLEX AUDIO VISUAL, Holdbrook, NY 11741

V6 VISUAL PLANNING DIVISION, MPC, North Main St., Champlain, NY 12919

V7 VISUALCRAFT, INC., 12842 S. Western Ave., Blue Island, IL 60406

V8 HARRY C. VOLK, JR., ART STUDIO, Box 72C, Pleasantville, NJ 08232

W

W1 WALLACH & ASSOCIATES, INC., 5701 Euclid Ave., Cleveland, OH 44103

W2 WATSON-GUPTILL PUBLICATIONS, 1 Astor Plaza, New York, NY 10036

W3 WAYNE STATE UNIVERSITY, Instructional Services Dept., 2978 W. Grand Blvd., Detroit, MI 48202

W4 F. WEBER CO., Wayne & Windrim Avenues, Philadelphia, PA 19144

W5 JOHN WILEY & SONS, INC., 605 Third Ave., New York, NY 10016

W6 H. WILSON CORP., 555 W. Taft Dr., South Holland, IL 60473

W7 WINSOR & NEWTON, INC., 555 Winsor Dr., Secaucus, NJ 07094

W8 WOLD AIR BRUSH MFG. CO., 2171 N. California Ave., Chicago, IL 60647

W9 WOOD-REGAN INSTRUMENT CO., INC., 184 Franklin Ave., Nutley, NJ 07110

X

X1 XEROX CORP., Xerox Square, Rochester, NY 14644

Z

Z1 ZIPATONE, INC., 150 Fencl Lane, Hillside, IL 60162

INDEX/SOURCES

INDEX/SOURCES

This Index/Sources serves two purposes: (1) To assist the reader in locating, within the book, information, instructions, etc., related to the items listed; (2) to recommend reliable purchase sources for the items. Descriptions and definitions for many of the items can be found in the Glossary, pages 252–261. Here is a sample entry to suggest how best to use the Index/Sources:

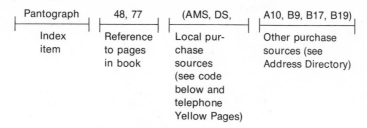

Pantograph	48, 77	(AMS, DS,	A10, B9, B17, B19)
Index item	Reference to pages in book	Local purchase sources (see code below and telephone Yellow Pages)	Other purchase sources (see Address Directory)

Code for Local Purchase Sources

AMS—Artists' Materials and Supply Stores
AVS —Audiovisual Equipment and Supply Stores
BHS—Building and Hardware Supply Stores
DMS—Duplicating Machines and Supply Stores
DS —Drafting Equipment and Supply Stores
PS —Photographic Equipment and Supply Stores
SS —Stationers' Stores

Acetate:
　clear, 27, 67, 74 (AMS, AVS, DS, B9, C12, I4, S7, V6)
　cold laminating, 171, 172, 192, 194 (AMS, DMS, D4, F4, N5)
　colored, 28 (AMS, AVS, C12, I4, V6)
　double-coated adhesive, 163 (AMS, DS, F4, G3, W7)
　heat laminating, 181, 184, 186 (AMS, AVS, DMS, G4, G9, L3, S11)
　matte (frosted), 28, 68 (AMS, AVS, DS, B8, B9, B17, C8, C15, H5)
　prepared, 28, 67 (AMS, AVS, DS, B9, B17, E5, L13)
Acetate ink, 43, 68 (AMS, DS, B9, C12, I4, S7, V6)
Adhesive-backed letters (see Cardborad letters)
Adhesive-backed paper, 24 (AMS, DMS, SS, D5)
Adhesive-backed paper tab, 119 (DMS, SS, D5)
Adhesive (glue) pen, 174 (AMS, SS, B17, N1)
Adhesive stick, 118, 174 (AMS, SS, B9, D4, D5, N1)
Adhesives:
　adhesive (glue) pen, 174 (AMS, SS, B17, N1)
　adhesive stick, 118, 174 (AMS, SS, B9, D4, D5, N1)
　epoxy cement, 118 (AMS, BHS)
　glue size, 166 (AMS, BHS)

Adhesives:
　liquid plastic adhesive, 118, 174 (AMS, BHS, SS, B17)
　pliable plastic adhesive, 174 (AMS, SS, B16, G3)
　pressure-sensitive adhesive (aerosol can), 118, 162 (AMS, SS, B9, B17, F17, L13, V6)
　rubber cement, 88, 118, 160, 188 (AMS, SS, B9, B17, F5, L13)
　spray wax, 162
　　(See also Pressure-sensitive adhesive-aerosol can)
　wax adhesive stick, 118, 174 (AMS, SS, B3, D4, L7, L9)
　wheat paste flour, 165 (BHS)
Adjustable curve, 46, 113 (AMS, DS, A10, B9, B19, S24)
Aerosol can:
　paint, 123 (AMS, BHS)
　plastic spray, 56, 69, 100, 167, 178, 191, 193, 200, 203 (AMS, BHS, DS, SS)
　pressure-sensitive adhesive, 118, 162 (AMS, SS, B9, B17, F17, L13, V6)
　propellant gas (airbrush), 101 (AMS, DS, B9, V6)
　stencil ink, 134 (AMS, BHS, B9, H11, M4, S1, S22)
　transparent liquid colors, 99, 184 (AMS, DS, B9, B17, L13)

Airbrush:
　air compressor, 101 (AMS, DS, B9, F4, F5, F7, V6)
　airbrush, 100 (AMS, DS, B9, F4, F5, F7, V6)
　carbonic tank, 101 (AMS, DS, B9, F4, F5, F7, V6)
　liquid colors, 101 (AMS, DS, B9, F4, F5, F7, V6)
　propellant gas, 101 (AMS, DS, B9, B17)
Alcohol colors, 101 (AMS, DS, B9, B17)
Arkwright Xerographic film, 240 (A20)
Art aid projector, 123 (AMS, DS, A22, B9, B17, E4, G7, K3, L2, W4)
Art Brown freehand lettering pen, 38 (AMS, B17)
Art paste-up techniques, 87
Artwork preparation:
　art paste-up techniques, 87
　diazo master (original), 244
　diffusion transfer, 241
　electronic stencil, 249
　Escotherm Color-On, 239
　high-contrast photography, 79, 86–88, 228
　polarized transparencies, 89
　spirit duplication, 60
　stencil duplication, 60
　thermocopy, 87, 235
　3M "Color-Key", 248